D0422734

THE SELF-DEFEATING ORGANIZATION

THE
SELF-DEFEATING
ORGANIZATION

A Critique of Bureaucracy

Alexander J. Matejko

PRAEGER SPECIAL STUDIES • PRAEGER SCIENTIFIC

New York • Philadelphia • Eastbourne, UK
Toronto • Hong Kong • Tokyo • Sydney

Library of Congress Cataloging in Publication Data

Matejko, Alexander J.
    The self-defeating organization.

    Bibliography: p.
    Includes indexes.
    1. Organizational effectiveness.
2. Bureaucracy.   I. Title.
HD58.9.M38   1985   302.3'5   85-9524
ISBN 0-03-005488-5 (alk. paper)

Published and Distributed by the
Praeger Publishers Division
(ISBN Prefix 0-275)
of Greenwood Press, Inc.,
Westport, Connecticut

Published in 1986 by Praeger Publishers
CBS Educational and Professional Publishing, a Division of CBS Inc.
521 Fifth Avenue, New York, NY 10175 USA

6789 052 987654321

Printed in the United States of America on acid-free paper

INTERNATIONAL OFFICES

Orders from outside the United States should be sent to the appropriate address listed below. Orders from areas not listed below should be placed through CBS International Publishing, 383 Madison Ave., New York, NY 10175 USA

Australia, New Zealand
Holt Saunders, Pty, Ltd., 9 Waltham St., Artarmon, N.S.W. 2064, Sydney, Australia

Canada
Holt, Rinehart & Winston of Canada, 55 Horner Ave., Toronto, Ontario, Canada M8Z 4X6

Europe, the Middle East, & Africa
Holt Saunders, Ltd., 1 St. Anne's Road, Eastbourne, East Sussex, England BN21 3UN

Japan
Holt Saunders, Ltd., Ichibancho Central Building, 22-1 Ichibancho, 3rd Floor, Chiyodaku, Tokyo, Japan

Hong Kong, Southeast Asia
Holt Saunders Asia, Ltd., 10 Fl, Intercontinental Plaza, 94 Granville Road, Tsim Sha Tsui East, Kowloon, Hong Kong

Manuscript submissions should be sent to the Editorial Director, Praeger Publishers, 521 Fifth Avenue, New York, NY 10175 USA

ACKNOWLEDGMENTS

This book is based on the material elaborated by the author in relation to his studies and teaching academic courses in social organization, sociology of complex organizations, work and leisure, and comparative societies. Parts of Chapter 1 have appeared in *The Guru Nanak Journal of Sociology*, 1. Chapters 2 and 7 appeared before in *Beyond Bureaucracy? Materials on Sociotechnics,* vol. 1, edited by A. B. Cherns, A. J. Matejko, and A. Podgorecki. A small part of Chapter 3 appeared in the Newsletter of Research Committee 26 on Sociotechnics (International Sociological Association. No. 4, August 1984, pp. 32–36).

Chapter 4, in a previous form, appeared in the article "The Sociotechnics of Autonomous Work Groups as Social Systems" in the *Guru Nanak Journal of Sociology* (1981) 2, 2: pp. 13–55. The text on pp. 135–43 appeared in the article "Dilemmas of Hierarchical Organizations and of Industrial Democracy," in *Proceedings of the Workshop Conference on Blue-Collar Workers and Their Communities,* edited by A. H. Turritin, Toronto: York University, 1976, pp. 1–36.

Part of Chapter 5 has appeared in the article by A. J. Matejko and S. Rubenowitz, "The Sociotechnics of Working Life: Experiences from Sweden," *Europa* (1980) 3, 2: pp. 155–84. Also in the article by these authors, "The Optimalization of Sociotechnical Conditions," Newsletter of the Research Committee 26 on Sociotechnics (International Sociological Association (1980) 5: pp. 14–39).

In Chapter 6, the sections dealing with East European sociologists appeared in their previous form in an article by the author, "Sociologists in-Between," *Studies in Comparative Communism* (1972) 5, 1–2: pp. 277–304.

Some parts of Chapter 7 on bureaucracy have appeared in "From the Crisis of Bureaucracy to the Challenge of Participation," an article of the author included in *Management and Complex Organizations in Comparative Perspective,* edited by Raj P. Mohan (Westport, CN: Greenwood Press, 1979), pp. 9–50, and also in the article by the author "The Obsolescence of Bureaucracy," *Relations Industrielles/Industrial Relations* (1980) 35, 3: pp. 95–106.

Chapter 8 incorporates material, part of which has appeared in the an article by the author, "The Manipulated Freedom in Mass Societies (West and East)," *International Journal of Sociology* (1980) 16, 2–3: pp. 238–76.

Material in Chapter 9 in its previous form appeared in the article, "Dialectics of Systems," *Guru Nanak Journal of Sociology* (1983) 4, 2: pp. 15–71. Some fragments have appeared also in "The Structural Criteria of Social System Maturity," in *Soziale Beziehungsgeflechte,* edited by H. Niemeyer (Berlin: Duncker and Humblot, 1980), pp. 59–76; "The Structural Criteria of Social System Maturity," in *Current Topics in Cybernetics and Systems,* edited by J. Rose (Berlin: Springer Verlag, 1978), pp. 271–72; "The Dialectical Approach to Social Reality," *Sociologia Internationalis* (1975), 13, 1–2: pp. 5–27; and "Can Social Systems Mature?" *Sociologia Internationalis* (1973) 11, 1–2: pp. 37–82.

CONTENTS

INTRODUCTION

This book manifests a concern of the author with the too low level of innovativeness in the field of modern social organization, not only in the state socialist societies, where doctrinal and practical circumstances keep structures rigid,[1] but also in industrial democracies. We should be "change masters"[2] in flexibly adapting forms to the changing social and economic content. There is a strong element of intellectual and moral laziness in leaving organizational matters to experts, who themselves are exposed to "trained incapacity," and allowing our imagination to be diverted to other priorities.

It is obvious to me that bureaucracy currently represents only one of the possibilities and becomes more and more obsolescent in facing realities of modern people, technologies, power relations, and world tensions.[3]

In the Dictionary of the French Academy published in 1789, bureaucracy was identified with the power and influence of government bureaus. The bureaucratic power obviously may endanger the public interest. On the other hand, Max Weber identified bureaucracy with the rational organization. It is a reasonable question whether or not specific institutions act rationally.

The tendency to rationalize the world around us quite often means the projection of our own wishes upon others. What looks rational from one perspective may appear irrational from another. A government may appear as fussy and meddlesome from the perspective of people who pay heavy taxes but do not receive much in return. The rule of the minority which pretends to represent the interests of the majority may be much biased in favor of particular interests.

Bureaucrats are just people like others, and the bureaucratic institutions do not necessarily show lower effectiveness than other organizations.[4] However, does it really mean that all criticism of bureaucracy does not have any validity whatsoever? We may be misled by the vagueness of the concept "bureaucracy."

Charles T. Goodsell (1983) summarized various accusations of inefficiency, corruption, and other wrongdoing by bureaucracy, in order to test the actual state of affairs, based upon performance records, surveys, and so forth. He comes to the conclusion that the U.S. bureaucracy especially is actually not so bad. Indicators of client satisfaction and efficiency are quite often favorable. It is true that bureaucracies suffer from contradictory goals; being responsive to one audience they are not able and willing to satisfy other audiences. "Bureaucracy cannot win. It responds not to market demand but to political process, which means it must always be judged by multiple and inconsistent standards. Hence it must inevitably dissatisfy at least somebody" (Ibid., p. 67).

Goodsell shows that quite often the clients are satisfied with what bureaucracy offers them; many bureaucratic functionaries are democratically oriented; most of the bureaucratic offices are quite small; it is not true that the bureaucracies are mostly big, by no means do larger bureaucracies perform more poorly; aging institutions do not necessarily produce rigidity. "Available evidence does not support concepts of constantly expanding government bureaus or inevitable bureaucratic decay" (Ibid., p. 125).

It is true that quite often the expectations of the public imposed upon bureaucracy are unrealistic, especially when agencies practice the "administration by proxy" and have only a limited control of events. However, why assume that bureaucracy is the only available organizational form? The alternative forms are already available and should not be ignored. The public sector does not necessarily have to depend only upon the bureaucratic tradition as presented by Weber. For example, in Israel the kibbutz movement plays a quite effective, major public role and almost certainly is more efficient than the agencies run directly by the government.

The state's practice of farming out various projects to the self-governmental teams of people who show a collective initiative, or to private business, has several advantages. For example, what is the purpose of government offering postal services that are expensive, inefficient, full of conflict, and in general dissatisfactory? Even if several social scientists exaggerate the negative role of bureaucracy, there are still genuine problems related to the dehumanization of organization, too much dependence of subordinates on the supervisors, decision making oriented more to specific vested interests than to public issues, external pressures distorting the functioning of organization, and so forth.[5]

We should not ignore the historical character of bureaucracy. With the changing sociohistorical and economic conditions of society there is an obvious need to modernize adequately organizational forms and principles. Throughout the Western world the role of the state has grown considerably. In the period 1961–81 the U.S. government's share of the gross national product, including social insurance, has grown from 29 percent to 35 percent; in West Germany from 34 percent to 49 percent, with similar developments in France, the United Kingdom, and Italy. Even in Japan, the share of government in the gross national product has grown in the same period of time from 17 percent to 34 percent. In the period 1970–83 the average cost of the German labor hour has doubled, due to rising social costs. Several other industrial democracies have experienced similar developments.

The market economy remains in conflict with the welfare economy; there is no effective way to eliminate the misuse of various welfare activities by people who actually do not deserve them; politicians, in order to remain popular, defend various privileges or even extend them; in order to defend their living standard, many taxpayers engage in activities not accepted by the state (moonlighting, tax evasion, and so on); there is not enough economic incentive to make welfare services cheaper and more efficient.

Experts who bother about innovation and entrepreneurship, among others Rosabeth Moss Kanter (see her *The Change Masters,* 1984 Simon and Schuster) expose the failure of a highly segmented and formalized social organization which is unable to meet present-day challenges and leads to the waste of potential human resources. In my recent book *Beyond Bureaucracy?* (Cologne: Verlag für Gesellschaftsarchitektur 1984), I am proposing a model of social organization based on management participation, autonomous work groups (so far most effective in Sweden), and the reinforcement of mutual trust between people who work together.

One of the major problems of developing countries is too much bureaucracy imported from the West and remaining in conflict with the local traditions of mutual aid. Even in the Communist world there are evident signs of awareness that the bureaucratic version of socialism is actually obsolete. The new Soviet leadership is widely expected to bring some reforms; the more or less successful organizational changes in People's China make it necessary for the U.S.S.R. to enter a new road. In the democratic West the depersonalized model of *mass society* is also obsolete.

In the United States there is a growing dependence on imports (in the period 1950–1984 imports have grown from 1 percent to 9 percent of GNP), the trade deficit is 4.4 times higher in 1984 than in 1980, the productivity growth is much slower than in other advanced countries (real GNP per employed person has grown in the period 1960–83 in the U.S. only by 1 percent in comparison with around 6 percent in Japan and South Korea), and there is a high federal budget deficit—all of these factors do not promise a rosy future. The capital flows from abroad to the U.S. but two fifths of it is located in government securities and only one fifth in equities. The accumulation of physical capital in the U.S. lags behind not only Japan but also France and West Germany. At present the improvement in the U.S. happens too much at the expense of the rest of the world, and particularly the developing countries which remain heavily in debt and unable to place all their products on the world markets.

The democratic West with all its weaknesses and difficulties remains the major hope of mankind because poverty coupled with authoritarian rule does not offer much chance of positive alternatives. Civil virtues need to be encouraged by a new type of social organization based not on cheap manipulation and the reinforcement of narcissism but on the strengthened sense of duty. In this respect much has to be done by the responsible leadership.

There is much evidence of a structural crisis, deeply rooted in the development of civilization, which makes many modern institutions to a large extent outdated. Trade unions in several Western countries definitely lose their power and influence because some categories of workers refuse to join them, or to maintain their membership; leadership loses its chances, in unions there is not enough internal democracy. Public education has opened the opportunities of advancement to a majority of society, but at the same time the promises of quality training are largely lost due to the lack of a learning discipline, displaced vested interests of teachers, and the sacrifice of effectiveness for the sake of organizational efficiency. The military squeezes out of public funds major subsidies, but their utility in several cases remains questionable. Other vital public expenditures are neglected; the weaponry soon becomes outdated; in several cases the military might creates a challenge to the political status quo. Political parties lose much of their socializing potential when the general public gains sophistication but at the same time loses its trust in public institutions. Religions do not fare well in the competition with leisure institutions, and the spread of a democratic spirit in societies. There has always been a gap between the religious message and the actual behavior of people, but only now does it become significant.

There are several reasons for this widespread crisis. First of all, the fast pace of change does not allow many institutions to adapt and prepare themselves fast enough. This is particularly evident in the challenge between mass media and the educational institutions which remain retarded in growth (only partly their own fault). Secondly, on behalf of existing institutions, the vested interest groups develop which look for their own benefits to the detriment of public interest. Even in the educational institutions it is clearly evident that teachers are not necessarily the best defenders of professional standards; easy marks and entertainment instead of quality-learning defeat the noble purpose of public funding of education. Thirdly, so far many institutions lack the ability to be sensitive to the changing environment and initiate adequate transformations well in advance. The short-term perspective kills many projects promoted by people mainly concerned with immediate rewards.

Increasing size of social groups leads to the multiplication and reinforcement of regulatory mechanisms. Work processes and work groups are increasingly fragmented (specialization). Mutual relations between working people are standardized. People differ in the nature of work tasks, prerequisites for entry into the workforce, the work situation, and the type of social organization for the task. Education, income and prestige, combine to place people on the social hierarchy. There is a gap between aspirations and occupational realities that is much reinforced by mass advertisement, consumer orientation, easy entrance to educational channels and general permissiveness. Especially among the young people in the West there is much confusion about the values of the society they live in; they receive conflicting messages from the "significant others." For example, "The confusion in American society—the constant stress on sex at all levels at the same time as many organized groups oppose realistic sex education—causes a similar confusion in most of the students who are both obsessed with sex and strangely ignorant about how to cope."[6] High unemployment among the young contributes to confusion and the feeling of insecurity. Many people do not know what to do with themselves. Several categories of the public even in rich countries remain disadvantaged; there is a definite gender inequality, for instance. In the multicultural societies certain groups remain privileged and others remain under-privileged.

In dealing with *work organizations* there is so far too much emphasis on structured identities but no insight into the mission these organizations have. In the modern world

the awareness of this leading factor seems to be definitely
too weak in the West, and this lowers the competitive power
of its complex organizations. There is also the issue of
weak socialization potential of basic institutions. For example, one of the problems of the Western industrial democracies is their reluctance to tax their citizens more heavily
when offering more social benefits. The extension of these
benefits has grown at the expense of national debt; in the
period 1974–84 the debt load in percent of GNP has grown
from 58 percent to 85 percent in Italy (10%),[7] from 20
percent to 40 percent in West Germany (3%), from 44 percent to 58 percent in Canada (8%), from 28 percent to 37
percent in France (3%), from 41 percent to 46 percent in
the United States (5%), from 18 percent to 68 percent in
Japan (5%); in the United Kingdom it has declined from 70
percent to 55 percent (5%).[8]

Living beyond our means appears to be the main problem of the present-day organizational society and this
definitively affects all issues of work. A sustainable development strategy includes stabilizing population, reducing
dependence on oil, developing renewable energy resources,
conserving soil, protecting the earth's biological systems,
and recycling materials.[9] A different reasoning is badly
needed. For example, oil use has almost doubled in the
period 1950–1973 making many weak economies particularly
vulnerable to the rising price of oil. Not only car production has suffered but even more the food production—its
annual growth has declined from 3 percent in the period
1950–73 to 1 percent in the period 1979–83. The cost of oil
in wheat production has grown eleven times in the period
1973–82. The topsoil depletion is a very serious problem;
forests are devastated; there is a steady decline in the
world's beef consumption; the increase of world fish caught
fell from 6 percent in the period 1950–70 to less than 1
percent. The world is engaging in wholesale biological and
agronomic deficit financing. The debt overhang is a problem in several countries; for example, the U.S. debt per
person has grown in the period 1960–84 from $1,616 to
$6,827. The world exports have declined by 12 percent in
the period 1980–83, and gross world product per person has
declined in annual growth from 1.7 percent in the period
1973–79 to 0 in the period 1979–83. The depletion of resource basis needs a heightened awareness about the urgency of our world problems. The value of arms imports
into the Third World has now climbed above that of grain
imports but the impoverished population needs food and not
guns.[10]

The changing nature of the consumer market has consequences on the way the enterprises are run. The mass production of standardized products gives way to much more entrepreneurial and diversified activities in which medium-sized and even small enterprises show more success than big bureaucracies; in bureaucracies innovation is frequently not adequately appreciated.[11] Data show that particularly medium-sized enterprises have better profits in this respect than do big enterprises. There is more job security, the satisfaction from work is higher. The great advantage here is a much shorter and less cumbersome decision process.

People in new jobs appearing now in the new technical fields in which medium-sized and small enterprises thrive are particularly likely to achieve success. For example, in the U.S. during 1974–82 data processing jobs grew almost three times faster than other office jobs. The success of the U.S. in the creation of jobs[12] is due mainly to the new technology and services, and in both these fields big bureaucratized enterprises do not have much to offer. The example of West Germany illustrates well the impact of technological and market changes on employment. In order to defend their market position, several enterprises substituted machines for people, lowering the labor cost in the period 1975–83 from 25 percent to 20 percent. This was particularly true for coal mining, construction, shipyards, and textile where the decline of jobs was high. On the other hand, machine construction, electronics, car production, and chemistry together have grown in the total industry during the period 1960–83 from one-third to one-half.[13]

These are very important and difficult problems for the modern welfare state; even more dramatic are the difficulties of the omnipotent socialist state bureaucracy in the Soviet-bloc countries and in China.[14] The Western public administration is not necessarily so malfunctioning and sinister as its critics claim. However, the public administration faces challenges that require organizational innovation. It is not enough to defend public administration; one must also show new developmental potential hidden in the alternatives to bureaucracy.

It is an obvious error to identify organization with bureaucracy; this is common not only among specialists in business administration but even among some sociologists. The coordination of activities and the stimulation of motivations of those who are supposed to make their contribution is the essence of any organization. There are many difficulties regarding priorities (what should be done first), competence of those who lead and those who are expected to follow, programming of action, execution of decisions, and so forth.

There are various ways of approaching complex organizations and understanding their problems. A historical perspective on organizations helps to understand how they have developed and have met challenges of various kinds.[15]

Organizational intelligence is of growing importance with the progress of modernization. Without this intelligence it would be impossible to deal with many problems that are becoming more and more complicated. It is up to present-day managers of the public sector to appreciate the importance of adequate and reliable information. Organizational intelligence is an institutionalized mechanism of collecting such information and supplying it to the managers. Sociology of complex organizations and social technology are active concerns in the field of applied social sciences.[16] It is up to practically oriented experts in the field to utilize the praxiological perspective[17] in order to construct organizational models that can reconcile the principle of rationality and effectiveness with the principle of participatory management and humanitarianism.[18]

In any modern organization both *integration* and *conflict* are needed. The disintegrative forces have to be kept under control and it would be catastrophic to allow the organization to disintegrate.

There is a great need to integrate the actions of individuals and groups within an organization, as well as promote a team spirit. On the other hand, to keep peace and order at any cost would be ineffective in the long run. Therefore, there is a growing tendency in many excellent organizations to institutionalize conflict within their own frameworks and use it for the benefit of the organization.[19]

So far there has been too much concern among the managers to keep organization under their full control. They should show more courage to delegate power and rely on *trust* relationships (Table I-1). The anxiety to keep all decisions and responsibility to themselves prevents higher-up managers from concentrating on their main duties.[20]

Some people support the idea of participatory management with the understanding that it is a substitute for unions. For me this is difficult to accept, especially in face of more and more evidence that unions play a crucial and beneficial role in improving workplaces, increasing productivity, reducing inequality, offering nonwage benefits, protecting vulnerable employees, and promoting employment stability.[21] Being a collective voice of the members, unions are able to challenge management but at the same time contribute to a better mutual communication between bargaining partners. "Unionism on net probably

TABLE I-1. Trust Relationships in Organizations

---

1. Organization is an artificial <u>mechanism</u> to reduce uncertainty <u>inside</u>
    and <u>outside</u> by: coordination of parts, division of labor, stimulation
    of organizational actors, integration of them into cohesive units,
    elimination of redundancy, and mobilization of collective conscious-
    ness.

2. Trust relationships are the <u>grease</u> of this mechanism. Cooperation
    between organizational actors can be controlled from outside only to a
    limited extent. With the mass computerization, actors actually gain
    more power to act. The question is how much <u>reliable</u> are their
    actions, and this is a matter of mutual trust.

3. Trust is a matter of ability, goodwill, skill, job discretion, style
    of supervision, and other <u>soft</u> items. However, the <u>hard</u> items also
    play a major role. People in organizations function under a set of
    <u>constraints</u> dictated by the technology of work, legal status, com-
    munication network, etc. The nature of <u>convention</u> in which people are
    located makes much difference regarding the chance of mutual trust.
    By changing material conditions of work as well as the nature of
    <u>convention</u> it is possible to augment or diminish the trust.

4. Delegation of power and extension of job discretion both usually offer
    more trust. However, the cultural and organizational context plays
    here a major rule. To have more power is not a right but a privilege;
    people have to deserve it. Organizational order has to gain out of it
    instead of becoming weaker.

5. Any experimentation of new work conventions based on delegation and
    discretion makes sense only when it is based on clear goals and
    reliable criteria of performance. The growth of <u>entitlements</u> has to
    be kept under control in order not to spoil the nature of what is
    actually done. Teams based on trust can function well only in re-
    lation to <u>tasks</u>.

6. Any organizational change influences <u>games</u> played by organizational
    actors and is itself also influenced by them. It is not easy to
    understand these games and even it is more difficult to shape them.
    However, there is no trust as long as the awareness of games actually
    played remains inadequate. Privacy of individuals has to be rec-
    ognized but their games are not purely private affairs. It is a
    matter of organizational policy to shape career patterns of the
    personnel and in this manner to promote games favorable for the
    employer.

7. Superiors influence the behavior and values of subordinates by their
    actions and personal example. Games played by superiors are carefully
    watched and what they do counts much more than what they say. Often

TABLE I-1. Continued

___

we have a perception of ourselves much different from how we are seen by others. We should pay attention to the accuracy of the reflected self.

8. Mobilization of organizational commitment is one of the most important conditions of team success. It is much more an art than a science but something may be learned in this field. There are several basic questions in this respect: who cares about what? who gains what? how much do people differ regarding their perceptions? which are the psycho-social triggers? which are the factors of self-fulfillment? do we have the adequate conflict resolution mechanisms? More important is to look for what makes people to work better than how to keep them happy. Workplace is not necessarily the center of happiness.

9. The gap between various ranks in organization may create many prob- lems. There is much room here for imagination on how to improve communication, create joint tasks, open room for promotion, eliminate boredom and sense of futility. Joint target teams may be very helpful in order to promote close cooperation between people representing various ranks and professions.

10. There is always a danger of mediocrization. In order to "keep safe" actions are taken by mediocre elements against innovators. Mutual trust within organization is crucial for keeping proper balance between stability and change. Both of them are needed and therefore both orientations deserve to have their protagonists. The team spirit allows the adversaries to recognize each other and not to indulge in "trained incapacity."

11. Organizational consulting may be helpful in the following: locating the hidden resources of a given workplace, encouraging policies to take advantage of these resources, and influencing indirectly the events. The potential of a given team may be seen more from outside than from inside. There is a great variety of possible ways to reinforce this potential.

___

raises social efficiency, and if it lowers it, it does so by minuscule amounts except in rare circumstances . . . Unions, for the most part, provide political voice to all labor and they are more effective in pushing general social legislation than in bringing about special interest legislation in the Congress."[22]

The pressure exercised by unions helps to balance various vested interests and prevents some of them from dominating over others.[23] The voice/response face of unionism needs to be strengthened and the monopoly face needs to be weakened. Any economic protectionism seems to be wrong but at the same time there is an obvious need to protect workers dislocated by competition.

A continued decline of unionization is harmful to the economy as well as to society, and management, unfortunately, is not adequately aware of this fact. "In a well-functioning labor market, there should be a sufficient number of union and of nonunion firms to offer alternative work environments to workers, innovation in workplace rules and conditions, and competition in the market. Such competition will, on the one hand, limit union monopoly power and on the other, limit management's power over workers."[24]

It is significant that the social cost of the monopoly wage gains of unionism in the United States remains at the modest level of 0.3 percent of the GNP or less. The union wage effect is greater for less-educated than more-educated workers, for younger than for prime-age workers, and for junior than for senior workers, and it is greater in heavily organized industries and in regulated industries than in others. It increased in the 1970s.

In addition to raising wages, unions alter the entire package of compensation; this particularly benefits older workers. Wages of organized blue-collar workers have been raised relative to the wages of the unorganized. At the same time these improvements have reduced income inequality between the blue-collar and white-collar workers. "Quantitatively, the inequality-reducing effects of unionism outweigh the inequality-increasing effects, so that on balance unions are a force for equality in the distribution of wages among individual workers."[25]

The existence of well-functioning unions (voice in determining rules and conditions of work, grievance and arbitration procedures, seniority clauses, and so forth) helps to diminish labor mobility in the United States. The swings in the economy are faced by unionized companies with more concern for the vital interest of workers: temporary layoffs rather than constant hiring and firing. There is less subjectivity in dealing with employees and much greater job protection. The protection devices sponsored by unions benefit both unionized and nonunionized workers. Greater joblessness as a result of higher union wages is not a major phenomenon.

Unions galvanize worker discontent in order to make a stronger case in negotiations with management. This factor, as well as the relative stability of unionized workers, who have an interest in keeping their jobs, leads to lower satisfaction with their jobs among unionized workers in comparison with nonunionized workers. An important question for management is how to improve work satisfaction by giving employees more chance and more voice.

Unions are *not* a major deterrent to productivity and in many cases the opposite is true: unions contribute to lower turnover rate, push management to perform better, and offer cooperation in facing new challenges. It is in the interest of unionized employers to improve the rate of return per dollar of capital by creating conditions favoring higher productivity. The positive Japanese example is very important in this respect. Most of the U.S. unions are highly democratic, with members having access to union decision-making machinery, especially at the local level.[26]

Peaceful cooperation between management and trade unions in the promotion of more flexible and innovative structures of work is obviously much needed. It is practically impossible for management to gain the full trust of employees when their collective representation is excluded. Trade unions acting from the position of weakness are unavoidably defensive and extremely cautious not to appear to their members as "selling out" to the employer. The Scandinavian practice of close cooperation between management and unions from the position of union strength, and not weakness, is quite illuminating. Unfortunately, trade unions take quite often a conservative position against any job reform being afraid of undermining their control of membership. On the other hand, only a spirit of cooperation between unions and management may secure in the long run a climate of human relations conducive to a genuine business success.[27]

The main purpose of this book is to justify the need of a genuine organizational innovativeness in the democratic West by a sociological diagnosis of present-day trends and social necessities originating from them. The first chapter deals with the challenges faced by the West and the inadequate organizational responses. The second chapter focuses on the limits of organizational structuralization. The simplistic notion that any problem may be solved by an "adequate" manipulation is questioned. Spontaneous human actions have great advantages, which should be recognized in the business of structuralization. The third chapter deals with problems arising in complex organizations when dealing with modern technology. In this field there is the latent psychosocial impact of innovations difficult now to predict, especially regarding computerization.

The fourth chapter deals with the phenomenon of bureaucracy as it is understood (or misunderstood) by various authors and the extent of its historical nature. The obsolescence of bureaucracy is treated as almost unavoidable because of the dysfunctions, which are enumerated and analyzed.

The fifth chapter deals with the new forms of group autonomy and participation at work, some of which may have a much more promising future than the formalized representation of employees in the company (share in the board of directors, workers' council). Autonomous work groups are particularly popular in Swedish industry and their experience is analyzed in the sixth chapter.

The seventh chapter deals with the contradictions of professional ethics with bureaucratic concerns. Sociologists as professionals practicing in the framework of universities and research institutes are here under scrutiny. With the growing role of professionals in modern society, the institutional framework has much to do with their productivity as well as with ethics.

Chapter 8 is devoted to the mass society and its difficulties in a pluralist political system, and the pressure of consumers looking for advantages and avoiding the duties of a "public man." Problems appear here because of the preoccupation of people with leisure and the hedonistic attitudes stimulated by mass media. Several organizational strains originate just from the fact that the hierarchy of values is changing as people feel that they deserve this or that in contrast to previous generations that were more preoccupied with survival. Complex organizations have to be sensitive to the value orientation not only of their clients and public controllers but also of their own employees.

The last chapter provides a broad theoretical perspective on complex organizations as social systems, which may be evaluated in terms of their relative "maturity." Systems face external and internal challenges, lose and gain, compete with other systems, look for a suitable "niche," have a more or less suitable steering mechanism, solve problems or aggravate them. Conflict resolution is one of the most important evidences of "maturity." The dialectical process of organizational growth[28] is herein presented as the set of problem-solving experiences of complex organizations in their search for excellence.[29]

This book is based on several years of teaching and research promoted by the author, first in the cooperative movement in Poland (workers' cooperatives),[30] later at the University of Warsaw (1959–68), University of Zambia (1968–69) and since 1970 at the University of Alberta.[31]

Most fruitful was the study of research teams in various disciplines, promoted by the author and several collaborators in the 1960s.[32] The author owes his gratitude to the Department of Sociology, University of Alberta, for the generous allocation of time to prepare this book. The author would like to thank word processing operators Valerie Irwin and Shirley Stawnychy at the same department for their good work and kindness.

NOTES

1. See Jozef Wilczynski, *Comparative Industrial Relations. Ideologies, Institutions, Practices and Problems under Different Social Systems with Special Reference to Socialist Planned Economies* (London: Macmillan, 1983); and Alexander J. Matejko, *Comparative Work Systems: Ideologies and Reality in Eastern Europe* (New York: Praeger 1986).

2. See *Change Masters,* by Rosabeth Moss Kanter (New York: Simon and Schuster, 1984).

3. I presented this view in *Beyond Bureaucracy? A sociotechnical Approach to the Dialectics of Complex Organizations* (Cologne: Verlag für Gesellschaftsarchitektur, 1984).

4. Charles T. Goodsell, *The Case for Bureaucracy. A Public Administration Polemic* (Chatham, NJ: Chatham House, 1983)

5. Goodsell seems to ignore these issues. It is relatively easy for him to do it because he deals with bureaucracy in a very rich country where the waste of resources is relatively less painful than in the countries which are worse off. Also, he ignores the fields in the United States sensitive to the negative aspects of bureaucratization, particularly public education. The mediocre educational results of the U.S. high schools are quite obviously related to the security orientation at the expense of efficiency orientation. The school administration does not want to rock the boat; school discipline is too much relaxed; students are not expected to learn much; teachers bother about their own interests and do not have courage to promote the professional values; the internal weakness of the schools is covered by the administration in order to keep good public image at any cost; schools become unemployment shelters rather than the institutions of learning. Of course, this is an open question whether or not schools organized on the nonbureaucratic principles would be much better. However, without providing suitable organizational conditions it is almost impossible to upgrade the U.S. high school educa-

tion.

6. W. J. Weatherby, The Future New York Offers the World, *Manchester Guardian Weekly,* 1984, 132, 14:8.

7. Debt service in 1984 as percent of GNP.

8. *Die Zeit,* 1985, 9:13.

9. Lester R. Brown et al. *State of the World 1984.* A Worldwatch Institute Report on Progress Toward a Sustainable Society. (New York: W. W. Norton, 1984).

10. Ibid.

11. See Karl Aiginger and Günther Tichy, *Die Grösse der Kleinen — Die überraschenden Erfolge kleiner und mittleren Unternehmen in der achtizer Jahren,* Vienna: Signum Verlag, 1984.

12. In the period 1970–83 employment in the U.S. has improved by 27 percent in comparison with 5 percent decline in West Germany.

13. *Die Zeit,* 1985, 11:10.

14. Privileges for the few, favor-trading, gluttonous, and lazy part of leadership, enormous distances between various ranks of society, hard work for low pay, a far-reaching centralization of power, dependence of people on the omnipotent bureaucracy, lack of inspiration—this is the image of the life in China. See Jay and Linda Mathews, *One Billion: A China Chronicle* (New York: Random House, 1983). Nevertheless, the Chinese enjoy small satisfactions. This is much related to the traditional social culture and the pride of being a big nation. There is the old distrust and avoidance of government. The waste of time for empty meetings is an agony for many people. The informal connections often rescue people from many critical situations, for example, from the separation of husband and wife due to their allocation to different places of work. "The Chinese enjoy the web of human relationships. The old ties make their days more comfortable and their futures more secure. But they dislike devices like the pay-raise meetings that force them to compare themselves to other members of the group" (Ibid., p. 325). The government controls the life of people effectively but at the same time the government itself is deeply penetrated by the network of private connections and the exchange of favors that undermine the official model.

Freedom has among Chinese a very selfish connotation and it is not possible to expect much "democratization" in a Western sense as long as at the informal level there is a complicated play between citizens and government. Bureaucrats avoid responsibility but the same is valid for average citizens. There is an unquenchable thirst for petty influence; working people enjoy a relaxed approach to their duties; people informally accommodate each other in bending the formal rules; there is a widespread emotional need to do everything possible by the back door; the cruel methods of ruling are justified by the authorities as a necessity for a poor and overcrowded country endangered by its internal and external enemies.

The internal changes of China as well as the external exigencies make necessary modernization but at the same time the whole formal system, as well as the tradition, make very difficult any genuine transformation. "It is a daily struggle between a popular yearning to grasp material incentives and democracy, and stubborn resistance from an office-holding class stiffened by centuries of experience in holding on to power" (Ibid., p. 343).

Will the commitment to the system evaporate among the young generation? There are already many signs that the political loyalty is mainly a matter of convenience and that any weakening of the central power opens more room to a mass behavior quite different from what is officially expected. Chinese are skillful in sliding through the barriers of their system but any modernization almost unavoidably has to lead to the tension between human aspirations and the official recipe.

15. See N. P. Mouselis, *Organization and Bureaucracy* (London: Routledge and Kegan Paul, 1975).

16. See Adam Podgorecki, *Practical Social Sciences* (London: Routledge and Kegan Paul, 1975), and Albert Cherns, *Using the Social Sciences* (London: Routledge and Kegan Paul, 1979). See also Alexander J. Matejko, *The Social Technology of Applied Research* (Meerut, India: Sadhna Prakashan, 1975).

17. See Tadeusz Kotarbinski, *Praxiology* (London: Pergamon Press, 1965).

18. I deal with this complicated issue in my book, *Beyond Bureaucracy?*, Chapters 8, 9, and 10.

19. See T. J. Peters and R. H. Waterman, *In Search of Excellence* (New York: Harper & Row, 1982).

20. A much more enlightened and progressive approach should be expected from the managers of public enterprises. They badly need adequate training in how to promote integration, as well as resolve conflict, without depending on the traditionalistic authoritarianism, which becomes obsolete in the modern times.

21. See Richard B. Freeman and James L. Medoff, *What Do Unions Do?* (New York: Basic Books, 1984).

22. Ibid., p. 247.

23. On the other hand, a thriving, profitable company loses upon being unionized and this is the paradox of the

U.S. unionism: a plus on the overall social balance sheet and a minus on the corporate balance sheet.

24. Ibid., pp. 250–51.

25. Ibid., p. 20.

26. There is a danger of the definitely negative orientation of many present-day U.S. employers vis-à-vis the unions. In the period 1956–80 the percentage of unionized U.S. private nonagricultural workers declined from 34 to 24. In the same period in the NLRB elections to new union representation voters in union victories as percentage of those eligible to vote have declined from 73 to 37. There is a definite decline in unionization, even in traditional areas of union strength. Unions have lost much interest in organizing activity and take mostly a defensive position. Management beats unions by offering unorganized workers most of the benefits of unionism, conducting tough legal campaigns against unionization, and even breaking the law by firing prounion workers. One in 20 workers who favors the union gets fired. All this leads to the potential major deterioration of industrial relations in the United States. The U.S. trend differs much from the rest of free developed countries, where unionism is growing instead of diminishing.

27. See Peters and Waterman.

28. See Alexander J. Matejko, "A Paradigm of Managerial Dilemmas. Its application to the problem of employees' activism," in *Arbeitsperspectiven angewandter Socialwissenschaft*, edited by Helmut Klages, Westdeutscher Verlag 1985, pp. 188–244.

29. Peters and Waterman.

30. See Alexander J. Matejko, "Marxists Against a Polish Anarcho-Syndicalist: The case of Jan Wolski," in *A Critique of Marxist and Non-Marxist Thought,* edited by A. Jain and A. Matejko (New York: Praeger 1986).

31. A detailed bibliography dealing with the published work of the author may be found in *Beyond Bureaucracy?*, pp. 435–59.

32. See Alexander J. Matejko, Institutional Conditions of Scientific Inquiry. Survey of Research Teams in Poland, *Small Group Behavior,* 1973, 4, 1:89–126; and, by the same author, *Uslovia Tworczeskogo Truda* (Moscow: Izdatelstvo Mir, 1970).

SUGGESTED READINGS

Theodore Caplow. 1983. *Managing an Organization,* New York: Holt, Rinehart & Winston.

Alan Fox. 1974. *Beyond Contract,* London: Faber.

Alexander J. Matejko. 1984. *Beyond Bureaucracy?* Cologne: Verlag für Gesellschaftsarchitektur (P.O. Box 130152, 5000 Cologne 1, West Germany).

Henry Mintzberg. 1983. *Power in and Around Organizations,* Englewood Cliffs: Prentice Hall.

Walter S. Neff. 1985. *Work and Human Behavior,* New York: Aldine Publishing Company.

Colin Crouch. 1982. *Trade Unions,* Glasgow: Fontana Paperbacks.

J. B. Cunningham and T. H. White, eds. 1984. *Quality of Working Life: Contemporary Cases,* Ottawa: Minister of Supply and Services.

THE SELF-DEFEATING ORGANIZATION

1

A SOCIO-ORGANIZATIONAL CHALLENGE FOR THE WEST

HOW CRITICAL IS THE SITUATION?

According to some social critics, Western civilization is moving toward the brink of collapse. There is a growing challenge to its dominance, coming not only from communism of the Soviet, Chinese, Cuban, or Vietnamese style, but also from those developing countries which are producing cheaper products, and are better able to keep their households in order, and have the population willing and able to work harder than in the West for much less money. Within Western civilization, the revolt from inside is also very evident: millions of young unemployed people have good reasons to question the wisdom and skills of the current establishment; the critics of the market economy have gained the upper hand at many universities and other cultural centers; sensationalism in the mass media distorts the knowledge of citizens about their own societies; the spread of narcissism[1] undermines the process of socialization; fun-seeking activities divert the attention of people from public duties; the struggle of various pressure groups to promote their own vested interests constantly endangers the public welfare.

Despite these facts, the awareness of how grave the situation is remains low for all Western countries. According to public opinion polls, covering West Germany, France, the United Kingdom, United States, and Japan from 1982 to 1984, the concern about the danger of war has declined (at least in the United States, West Germany, and Japan). The U.S. armament seems to many people, no less dangerous than the Soviet armament. Half to two-thirds of the people are ready to sacrifice industrial modernization for the benefit of keeping more people at work. Only a small minority (except in the United States) expect their own economic situation to improve. Only one-fifth of the people worry about the extension of the Soviet influence. The same is valid about social injustice.[2]

The people of the West seem to be so involved in their own affairs that they miss the realities of growing competition and major inequities. The gap between the more developed and the less developed countries is growing instead of diminishing: a difference in the per capita GNP[3] (1983 data) US$9,380 and US$700 ($880 if China excluded), the great gap in the fertility rate (2.0 versus 4.2), population "doubling time" (118 years versus 34 years); and infant mortality (18 versus 90). The average per capita GNP in western Europe is 18 times higher than in western Africa, 36 times higher than in eastern Africa, 46 times higher than in middle south Asia, and so forth. At least these developing countries, in which pragmatism and patience dominate, are creating a new potential. For example 1983 was the sixth consecutive year in People's China that growth of the GNP exceeded 5 percent.

In the increasingly interdependent world, there is a growing difficulty in accommodating the divergent interests peacefully. "If the industrial countries fail to regain the growth rates they managed in the 1950s and 1960s, many countries in the developing world will have great difficulty making progress in the years ahead."[4] This is particularly true for sub-Saharan Africa. Industrial countries provide a market for two-thirds of the developing world's exports. If this market should deteriorate there would be great suffering, especially in the countries showing a particularly high population growth (for example, Brazil, India, Indonesia, Nigeria, and so on). Since 1950, real income per person has increased in the world sixfold, life expectancy has risen dramatically, and education has become widespread. In the period 1900–80, the developing countries grew from 66 percent to 75 percent of the world population, but remained at the level of one-fifth of the world production. In comparison with the period 1960–73, the 1983 GDP growth declined in industrial-market economies from 5 percent to 2 percent, and in developing countries it declined even more dramatically from 6 percent to 1 percent. The growing consumer demands in developed countries, and also in developing countries, contribute to inflation.

The developing countries are becoming more and more dependent on the developed countries. The ratio of debt to GNP has grown in the period 1970–83 from 13 percent to 27 percent and the ratio of debt to exports has grown from 99 percent to 121 percent; the ratio of interest payments plus amortization to exports has grown from 13 percent to 21 percent. The developing countries are forced to cut their imports very considerably; the growth of import has declined by one-half in the first half of the 1980s, in comparison with the 1960s. The population growth of 2 percent per year makes the situation even worse because the ailing economies are not able to absorb the new arrivals in the labor force. More often than not, current fertility and mortality rates are inversely related to income, but the relation between income and life expectancy and between income and fertility, has shifted over time. The burden of the "surplus" population does not have a place to move to. In Europe, during the period 1881–1910, one-fifth of the population increase emigrated (only 4 percent in the 1970s); but the current emigration from the developing countries remains minimal. The investment per potential new worker remains negligible in developing countries ($2 to $40) in comparison with developed countries (from $200,000 to more than $500,000). Food growth in the 1960s and the 1970s remained at the level of 0.4 percent per year, in comparison with more than 1 percent in the industrial-market economies. Human skills remain at a very low level, especially in low-income countries in which the labor force is rapidly growing.

Is the reduction of population growth a reliable vehicle to diminish poverty and social inequalities? So far only in the People's Republic of China family planning does work effectively (in the period 1970–81 the proportion of first births grew from 21 to 47 percent). Female infanticide is practiced. Without sustained improvements in living conditions, there is not much hope of slowing down population growth. There is a mismatch between population and income-producing ability. The vicious circle of poverty and high fertility goes closely together with the economic ineffectiveness of socio-organizational structures dominating in the developing countries. The dramatic decision of China in the fall of 1984 to relax the rigid central planning is evidence of the search for new alternatives. "Population growth would not be a problem if economic and social adjustments could be made fast enough, if technical change could be guaranteed, or if rapid population growth itself inspired technical change."[5]

The developed countries produce labor-saving devices,

not labor-using innovation; the latter would provide new opportunities for their own unemployed, and even more for the developing countries. As long as society is unable, or unwilling, to offer "old age security," there is a dependency on larger families. Poor people do not have the resources to spend more on the health and schooling of their children. The positive answer to all these dilemmas is better cooperation between the developed countries and the developing countries. They need each other in order to achieve a satisfactory equilibrium.

The current employment crisis in the West has highly negative consequences for the developing countries also. The problem of public debts is valid throughout the world. In the period 1970–82, external public debt has grown from 21 percent of GNP to 29 percent in low-income economies (except India and China) and from 12 percent to 25 percent in middle-income economies. Debt service as a percentage of exports of goods and services has grown, respectively, from 6 percent to 10 percent and from 10 percent to 17 percent. In the low-income economies (except India and China), in the period 1960–82, the labor force grew twice as fast as in the industrial-market economies, but without much opportunity for jobs. Government revenue and its importance in the industrial-market economies has grown, in the period 1972–81, from 25 percent to 30 percent of the GNP; but this does not necessarily mean that governments have been able to deal successfully with vital problems.

The crisis of the modern world lies mainly in its faulty social organization: ineffectiveness of international institutions, division into hostile blocs, diverse vested interests preventing the promotion of common good, major discrepancies in the living standard and life perspectives, and the heavy load of military expenditure.[6]

THE BUREAUCRATIC BURDEN

The growth of government[7] is a common fact in industrial democracies, particularly at the middle and lower level.[8] The number of governmental programs is constantly multiplying; it is an important issue to determine how effective they really are.[9] "Goals are vague to accommodate multiple points of view, and translating that vagueness into specific concrete implementation actions renews the potential for conflict and compromise."[10]

The great importance of the service sector in industrial democracies diminishes the chance of achieving a higher GNP growth. Organized labor has enough power to obtain higher wages (or at least to keep them at certain level) but people who do not have enough bargaining power suffer unemployment. The real rate of return on corporate capital has considerably diminished in the 1960s and the 1970s. Protection against cheap imports harms the international trade and lowers the domestic productivity. The net savings in seven major industrial democracies declined in the period 1973–81 from 14 percent of the GDP to 9 percent.

The crisis of the state under capitalism as well as under socialism inspires the revival of interest in the critique of governments.[11] This critique comes from various positions: moral concern (such as, social gospel), individualism,[12] class conflict,[13] and so forth.

In society quite often conformity is the standard and the individual is nothing. People consciously sacrifice their own interests in the name of speculative abstractions. By making a fetish out of an imagined objectivity, the manipulatory rulers deprive common people of all value and sacrifice them to the "great design," in reality, to the vested interests of the ruling elite. The realization of Marx's ideas has led to the omnipotent state, in which only lip service is paid to the common welfare. On the other hand, in the democratic West, the perfection of manipulatory devices has led to the illusions of freedom and choice.

There is a good reason to regard any organization as a threat to individual autonomy. "The alternate social forms must be created by the participants and not by administrative fiat."[14] The fate of state socialism is the best proof in this respect. The lack of civil rights in the communist countries has a highly negative effect on the economies as well as on the spirit of a genuine citizenship.

One of the unexpected trends from the Marxist perspective has been the "service class" phenomenon modifying the class structure and introducing a substantial correction to our understanding of society.

The growing organizational density of modern societies has contributed—according to Goldthorpe[15]—to the growth of managers, administrators, and professionals, who together constitute 20 to 25 percent of the labor force in comparison with 5 to 10 percent earlier. This "service class" takes its title from the sense of duty and dedication; however, this is not necessarily the way the "service class" always works. The vested interests of professional and administrative groups may gain priority over the code of professional ethics and loyalty to the employer. In such cases, unavoidable "tough" bargaining occurs between the state, or other corporate employers, and the more or less powerful collectivities of those who deliver sophisticated services.

As long as the state has enough resources, generous gratifications are possible. However, with the slow down of economic progress and much expenditure on social services, as well as on armament, there is less and less room for a peaceful settlement. Under such circumstances, the process of radicalization within the "service class," as well as the deterioration of their professional morale is almost unavoidable. The interests of the top organizational leadership and the interests of the middle stratum of the hierarchy diverge. Accompanying this is a loss of mutual trust and cooperation; strikes and slow-downs appear not only among the blue collar workers and clerks, but also among people higher in the organizational hierarchy (nurses, teachers, medical doctors, lower administrators).

The message, which arises from the "service class" phenomenon, focuses on the role of the sense of duty and its importance to the well-being of the society. The concept of honor, so basic for the socialization of people, has deep historical roots. Social virtues, courtliness, courage, and generosity, loyalty to the plighted word, independent spirit—all these characteristics are very much needed in any society which trains its members in citizenship. In Europe, between the eleventh and the sixteenth centuries, chivalry played a major educational role.[16] "Chivalry taught the gentleman of a succeeding age to place honour at the centre of his mental and social world, as the treasure dearer to him than life . . . The strong streak of individualism in chivalrous culture, which found such emotive expression in its ideal of the knight errant, also left a powerful mark on European attitudes of later times."[17]

Under circumstances unfavorable to the concepts of honor and duty, there is not much hope to keep people together. Any social structure needs reinforcement in moral beliefs, as well as in collective mutual dependencies and even pressures. As long as the subordination of individual good to the common good remains seen as an external, inevitable, and impersonal condition, people remain loyal. The disruption of social structure happens due to the split of loyalties, as well as the growing conviction that the spirit of discipline and commitment are objects of external manipulation harmful to people. This is exactly what is happening now in the modern manipulatory mass society.[18]

The positive example of Austria and Sweden encourages the neo-corporatist approach based on a welfare state in which the social welfare system is seen closely related to the economic, industrial and public sectors. Obviously, the current financial crisis of Western welfare states makes necessary some basic rethinking. A full return to free market or a socialist revolution both seem impractical. A measure of working consensus over the system of mixed economy and state-protected minimum standards of welfare may be treated as an appropriate answer. The matter of public welfare is supposed to be understood not much as a right or as a guaranty of equality (anyway, there is not much of it) but as a consensus among all major partners to care about the public good. It is necessary to harmonize group relationships and prevent the particularistic interests (for instance, the interests of professionalists and bureaucrats) to dominate the public scene.

The New Right criticizes the welfare state but in most cases is neither able nor willing to eliminate welfare programes, cut substantially taxes, and diminish the public debt. The prospect of a balanced budget remains as remote as ever in the U.S. as well as in the U.K. "There is obvious failure to recognize the problem of social integration in a market society, namely how to counter the socially disruptive effects of the market economy and maintain a cohesion of the national community."[19] The conservative rhetoric does not address the practical issue of social organization providing a support to community feeling and community practice, a backbone of economic progress. Conservative complaints of government failure and policy failure miss the point that actually this is more the failure of an apolitical, consensual and scientistic model of policy. "The neo-conservative argument is premised on the values of individualism, liberty and property rights, and on inequality as the natural outcome of the workings of the market. Focused on atomized individuals it has no conception of the nation-wide state as a community nor any idea of the *social* (as distinct from *individual*) consequences of the market order that may need political intervention . . . The absence of any conception of nation-state as a community, the denial of the social, the attempt to constitute a rather spurious 'spontaneously' evolving market order to endow it with a sense of sacred fatality, the absence of any historical appraciation of capitalist development makes neo-conservatism highly inadequate both intellectually and as a viable practical doctrine for advanced industrial democracies."[20]

The Marxist alternative is not better. "A fundamental weakness of the Marxist position in the West seems to be that it has not come to terms (perhaps it cannot) with the entire historical experience of 'actually' existing socialism."[21] So far there is not a genuine socialist alternative to liberal capitalism and to the welfare state. The class interpretation of the state does not illuminate much the mechanism of modern nation-states and the socialist correction remains unclear. The Soviet and Chinese models remain not attractive as long as they are based on coercion and lead to much waste of resources.

Mishra offers the model of the corporatist welfare state based on the regulation of the economy from both demand and supplyside, consensus-building, trade-offs between the economic and the social policy making, centralized pluralism (bargain between the representants of major economic, social and political interests), and liberal market society. A voluntary co-operation among major economic groupings and the limited institutional coordiantion of policies in the context of a free society is an ideal type suggested by the author. Austria, Sweden, West Germany and the Netherlands are offered as suitable patterns to follow.

There is an obvious need to build a broad consensus among the major power-holders but this is definitely not an easy task. The economically privileged strata of the population have enough power to defend their position or even to extend it; for example, in Canada the upper 20 percent of the population control 42 percent of income when the lowest 20 percent of the population control only 4 percent of income. Several segments of the population, mainly the unemployed, do not have a chance to articulate their demands and transform them into a political power. Due to political passivity and inadequate channels a very considerable part of the population remain outside the political process.

The corporate welfare state needs some non-conventional organizational roots of social energy mobilization which would allow to articulate the *common will* of the population. Israeli kibbutzes are a good example of the self-governmental units in which common people are active participants in the decision making process at the grass-root level. Of course, there are many other channels of self-government not so intensive as kibbutzes: local community committees, co-ops, and so on. The organizational penetration of society is a difficult task but how to imagine a well-functioning state without an *organized* civil society behind it? As long as the state remains *outside* the society there is not much chance to make it actually the executor of common will. On the other hand, the state penetration of society may endanger the civil character of the latter (totalitarianism). The answer is in the reconciliation of "civil" and "state" at the local level, and kibbutzes are a very positive example in this respect.

Owing to political pressure, favoritism, red tape, financial security, and avoidance of risk, bureaucracies often do not perform at an efficient level. It is paradoxical that the growth of state bureaucracy is mostly due to the growing complexity of the society, while at the same time, bureaucracies remain at the low efficiency level. Much of the bureaucratic income is fixed; in the United States, federal grants-in-aid to states and localities have grown, in the period 1950–80, from 9 percent to 21 percent of domestic federal outlays; and from 10 percent to 25 percent of the state-local expenditures.

The flow of public money from the center to the local agencies and private contractors (including consultants) is not adequately controlled according to effectiveness. How much of the assistance offered by the government (subsidies) really has a long lasting effect? How justified is the priority given to some deliverers over others (for example, discrimination against foreign deliverers)? How much protection of the public really leads to positive results? How justified is the transfer of benefit from one group of the population to another group? The growing load of welfare programs, which already have become an entitlement, makes the situation of the government versus the taxpayers very difficult.[22]

Both the organizational set of bureaucratic processes and the politicized set of interactions and interrelationships influence policy implementation. For example, the tough anti-inflation policies applied by some governments have several negative side-effects: among others, the decline of technological investment and the dependence of business on the labor power and older technologies.[23]

The welfare benefits in the West make labor quite costly. According to 1982 data (OECD), the nonwage element constitutes from 40 to 50 percent in Italy, France, West Germany, Belgium, and Sweden, but only 16 percent in Japan (28 percent in the United States). This nonwage element has grown perceptibly in the industrial democracies during the 1970s.[24]

In Canada, in 1983 productivity rose only by 2 percent but employment rose by 4 percent.[25] The output per hour in manufacturing remains 25 percent lower than in the United States. In the period 1978–82 Japan improved manufacturing productivity by 42 percent in contrast to only 2 percent in Canada and 6 percent in the United States.[26] During the same period of time in Japan, consumer prices rose only by 25 percent, compared with 63 percent in Canada and 59 percent in the United States. The basic difference lies in management techniques, relationships between management and workers, and specialization.[27] More capital investment is an important element in rekindling productivity growth, as well as a fuller utilization of the existing capacity in manufacturing (only 70 percent in Canada in 1983).

Shortage of well-trained personnel is one of the weak spots in Canada and there is the question of how to improve the quality of education in order to establish the background for an economic growth.[28] There is too much leniency in the evaluation of performance of students,[29] neglect of teaching for the benefit of other duties and professional ambitions, lack of a single national system of education, inadequate professionalization of the teaching personnel, and the unmotivated management staff.

Bureaucracies are omnipresent but not omnipotent. "They bargain for influence just like other actors although they have a head start in some cases because of numbers and prior development of information. They also have legal authority—but even that is subject to constant legal challenge."[30] Various levels of government differ in their perspectives and vested interests. Various pressure groups exercise their influence in order to shape the policy decisions according to their interests. Administrative routines are challenged by changing pressures and circumstances. Bargaining, coalition building, and flux characterize all policy implementation in the democratic countries, but some similar elements may also be traced in the authoritarian regimes. "The best bargainers with the most political support get more of what they want during implementation than other actors. The bureaucrats are themselves bargainers much of the time in this process."[31]

When examining four basic types of policies (distributive, competitive regulatory, protective regulatory, and redistributive) it is found that they differ a considerable amount in the likelihood of generally accepted stable implementation routines; in the degree of stability of identity of principal actors and the nature of their relationships; in the degree of conflict and controversy over implementation; in the degree of opposition to bureaucratic decisions; in the degree of ideology in debate over implementation; and the degree of pressure for less government activity. Various organizational bodies react to policies according to their vulnerability, competence, and vested interests.

Governmental policies badly need effective controls, not only of a formal nature (auditing), but also from the general perspective of effectiveness. Social science has much to offer in this respect, and social technology has a distinct future.[32]

THE JAPANESE CHALLENGE

Among the industrial democracies there is a growing gap between Japan and the West. According to the 1985 OECD predictions, Japan's annual growth of GNP will be 3.75 percent (3.0 in 1983), in comparison with 2.5 percent in the United States and the same on average for all OECD countries. In the period 1977–83 the real GNE (gross national expenditure) growth in Japan was 4.3 percent. This was double the 2.1 percent that represented the growth in the big industrial democracies overall: Canada, United States, West Germany, France, United Kingdom, Italy, and Japan. These democracies, in the period 1977–82, spent on the average 24.9 percent of GNP on new capital formation; but in Japan this expenditure was 31 percent. Already in the period 1966–73, Japan's productivity growth of 9.3 percent was more than double the average for all seven big industrial democracies (3.9 percent, but only 1.4 percent in the period 1981–84), and since that time Japan has stayed much ahead of the others. In the period 1963–1983, Japan's share in world export grew from 3.9 percent to 8.9 percent, while the share of the most economically successful Western country, West Germany, remained at a level of 10 percent.[33]

". . . We Japanese have no principles. Some people think we hide our intentions, but we have no intentions to hide. Except for some few leftists or rightists, we have no dogma and don't ourselves know where we are going." This statement more than 10 years ago by Nakane still seems valid today.[34] The industrial system of Japan appears as a practical arrangement based on careful planning done by the government with the corporations' close cooperation.

There is a massive shift in Japan toward a highly modernized industrial structure based on the "hardware" technology (electronics, and so on), while at the same time maintaining several traditional "software" systems of management. "In what Japanese truly believe is a new industrial revolution in the form of microelectronics, the general direction of the country's evolution thus takes on the form of strategies emerging piecemeal, haphazardly, sometimes with luck, guile, and even questionable legalities."[35]

Only one-tenth of the economy depends on export, but Japan has managed to greatly improve her position in the world market. In-house training in administration and in science has been practiced very successfully for many years. The governmental structure is designed so that it orients the national economy toward international trends.

There is considerable room for internal pluralism, competitiveness, and innovation; but the facade of cooperation and consensus is well maintained. "The Japanese have developed work systems which combine human intellectual effort with machine precision and computational facility in a way unrivaled by Western societies. It is not hardware alone, nor is it software alone—it is both."[36] The business-government relationship is very close and this contributes very much to the growth. "Japan's industrial policy is one of orchestrating national levers—taxation, banking, monetary and fiscal measures, administrative guidance, science policy, and the like—into a coherent framework of investment decisions, for both big and small firms, public and private enterprises."[37]

The Japanese are particularly successful in emerging sunrise sectors or declining sunset sectors. It is up to government to promote competition by assuring several entrants in each sector. Japan traditionally imports foreign technology in order to learn or even resell. The highly developed managerial skills in Japan allow absorption largely on a selective basis. Continuous training within companies helps to achieve excellence and the very demanding educational system helps to keep standards high.

The long-term perspective of the companies, and their unique focus on achieving an internal harmony, help to keep business competitive. According to one author:

> Japanese management combines many structural features of the American corporation, but incorporates a management philosophy nurturing individual commitment and corporate integration. . . . Beneath the veneer of individual participation and involvement is a highly formalized system of financial controls and an excellent information system. . . . Human resource policies are integrated with other functions as marketing, production, and finance.[38]

The fact that wages are a fixed cost in big Japanese companies, makes it necessary to follow policies of innovation and productivity improvements. There is a growing tendency to depend on highly sophisticated industrial engineering. Many Japanese managers are using progress cost curves, time-investing management, and robotics. "Shop floor work in Japan, as well as operations management, reflect many of the philosophical concerns expounded by Taylorism, including scientific decision-making and management-labor cooperation."[39] The local weaknesses of marketing become gradually eliminated. On the international markets Japan gains more and more learning experience, and there is a growing emphasis on building its own banking basis. Among the world powers the place of Japan has changed very considerably: from one-quarter Britain's per-capita income in the early 1950s, to double that now.

It seems necessary here, to warn against the overestimation of the virtues of the cooperation policy followed by the big Japanese companies. There is another side of patronage widely practiced in Japan, which is less and less eagerly accepted by the young generation. With the spread of education it becomes more difficult for graduates to find good careers in big corporations. In Japanese manufacturing, almost three-fifths of all workers are employed by the establishments of 100 or fewer workers; the average number of employees per manufacturing establishment is 15, in contrast to 53 in Canada and the United States, and 80 in West Germany. These small companies are much more dependent on the giants and have few resources to accommodate their employees. Therefore, any generalizations based on big companies are not necessarily valid for most of the Japanese workers. Except for the relatively privileged portion of labor, advantages are not extended to the rest, especially when the official social welfare program remains modest.

It is very likely that with economic and educational progress, the individualistically articulated demands and aspirations of the Japanese will grow; patronization and an inferior position of trade unions may become more and more questioned, especially with the intensification of international competition and the deepening dependence of Japan on foreign raw materials. Of course, there are still many sociopsychological and structural predispositions making the Japanese work hard, save, avoid confrontation with bosses, and accept the business creed preached by the employers. However, how long will this last?

The pragmatic orientation of Japanese people and the apparent advantages of the economic "miracle" both work in favor of playing safe and not rocking the boat. On the other hand, several undeniable assets of the existing system are already taken for granted. New aspirations growing among the young people are not necessarily fitting well into the status quo. The Japanese economy is much more vulnerable to the international situation and any crisis on the world scale could have some very serious consequences for the internal balance of Japan. The fact that other nations are learning more and more from the Japanese experience makes foreign trade tougher. The resistance of

Japan to accept the foreign penetration of internal markets creates a source of tension with trade partners.

THE SHAKY WELL-BEING

The well-being of the common people in the West remains relatively high even under conditions of widespread waste and unemployment. Several Western countries have even achieved major improvements. For example, in West Germany between 1962 and 1983, the number of gadgets per 100 households has grown considerably: from 37 to 94 television sets; from 14 to 88 telephones; from 34 to 83 washing machines; from 27 to 65 personal cars; from 3 to 65 freezers; and 0 to 24 dishwashers.[40] Much has been done to initiate some large-scale employment projects, but unemployment in several Western countries (Netherlands, United Kingdom, Italy, Canada, France, West Germany) remains at the level of 12 percent or more,[41] and people treat this as one of the major concerns.[42] Well over 30 million people remain unemployed in the industrial democracies. In several of these nations unemployment has been recognized by the government as a permanent condition, impossible to cure. The situation varies among individual countries.

Why is Canada in a deeper recession than the United States? Real growth of the Canadian GNP has been quite substantial in the last 25 years (the economy more than doubled): from Can$55 billion in 1960 to Can$137 billion at the end of 1983.[43] Canada entered the recession with a greater corporate and consumer debt than the United States and has been more vulnerable to interest-rate increases. Canadians reacted to recession by cutting consumption and saving much more than Americans. Canadian interest rates continue to be higher than in the United States. The fiscal boost to the economy has also been much higher than in the United States. The larger deficits and the dependence on resource-based economies are additional factors. The federal government's net indebtedness has been growing since 1975 from the level of 5 percent of GNP to probably 35 percent in the late 1980s, and this will almost unavoidably lead to the reduction in the well-being of Canadians.[44]

A comparison of international competitiveness of industrial democracies, done by European Management Forum, shows Canada close to the average (53 percent), in comparison with Japan at the top (70 percent) and Portugal at the bottom (33.5 percent). The main weaknesses of Canada appear in industrial efficacy (productivity, labor costs, profitability), innovative forecast orientation, social political consensus and stability, as well as impact of the state and dynamics of the market.

In Canadian international transactions, during the period 1973–83, there was a constant growth of service deficit, met by the trade surplus in forest products, energy, grain, and mining products. The real GNP growth remained at the level of a few percent. Productivity ceased to grow since the second half of the 1970s. The "misery" index (unemployment and inflation) has remained during the period 1980–83 at the level of around 20 percent.

Canada depends very much on exports (24 percent of GNP in 1982, in comparison with 21 percent in the United Kingdom, also in 1982, and 31 percent in Sweden in 1983). Foreign investment[45] declined in the period 1970–83, from 30 percent of GNP to 19 percent.[46] The welfare systems cost much; benefit packages constitute one-third of the payroll. In the period 1970–82, the cost of health care grew from 7.3 percent of the GNP to 8.4 percent (in the United States from 7.5 percent to 10.5 percent). In spite of recent decline of work stoppages (in 1983, 23 percent fewer person-days not worked than in 1982), but Canada still remains a leader in labor conflict, and the power of unions is growing.[47]

There is a gradual shift of the balance of power between the U.S.-headed unions and the Canadian unions. In the period 1973–83, the membership of the latter has grown from one-third to two-fifths. In the Canadian Labor Congress, the membership of all-Canadian unions has slightly surpassed the internationals. This change is due to the decline of union membership in heavy industry, the growth of public-sector and service unions, and the autonomization of some unions that used to be steered from the United States. One of the powerful agents of change are the all-Canadian public sector and service unions, which account for 70 percent of the country's female trade-union members.

There is a growing gap between those Western people who remain relatively safe in employment or their own business, who activate themselves in the labor market,[48] push for higher wages (and higher consumption), and better working conditions,[49] and those people permanently unemployed, who gradually lose any hope to establish themselves at work. Both of these categories of the population remain under the pressure of a consumer society, even under the conditions of an economic depression. This pressure also has its impact on the work satisfaction of employed people, especially when the economic depression frustrates their expectations.[50] The consumer-oriented economy conditions people to buy, even in the case of depression. For example, in West Germany during the year 1983 the personal expenditure still grew by more than DM 35 billion at the same time that wages and salaries fell by DM 0.5 billion. This unexpected growth was due to social benefits (DM 10.5 billion) and declining savings (DM 8.5 billion) among the poorer population, as well as higher profits among the businessmen and professionals (DM 15.5 billion).

PUBLIC DEBT AND GOVERNMENTAL DEFICIT

The welfare society in the West is largely maintained through higher taxes,[51] state deficits,[52] government grants,[53] and the government debt. The welfare state costs a large amount of money (in seven major industrial democracies during 1961–81 the total public expenditure has grown from 29 percent of GDP to 41 percent) and leads to growing public debt. Taxes have risen in the period 1961–81 in the seven major industrial democracies from 29 percent of GDP to 38 percent.[54] Meanwhile, the share of government expenditure on education, health care, income maintenance, and old-age security has grown from 10 percent of GNP to 23 percent.

According to 1982 data, taxation and compulsory social security payments amount to 40 percent of GDP in EEC countries, 50 percent in Sweden, 35 percent in Canada (26 percent in 1965), 30 percent in the United States (26 percent in 1965), but only 27 percent in Japan. This growth is quite often due to the growth in government revenues from the personal income tax: in Canada, during 1965–82, this grew from 23 percent to 35 percent (the share of taxes borne by corporations declined from 15 percent to 8 percent); and in the United States personal income tax grew from 31 percent to 38 percent (the share borne by corporations declined from 16 percent to 7 percent). In Canada, from 1965 to 1982, the per capita tax load grew seven-fold, from $683 to $5,311 per person ($7,385 in Sweden and $4,908 in the United States); and during the same time period, the GDP grew from $58 billion to $375 billion, six and a half times.

There is growing public pressure to cut the universality of social programs in order to lower the tax load or at least to contain it. Inflation undermines family allowances, unemployment insurance and old-age pensions, but governments view it as politically unfeasible to raise taxes in order to keep social benefits at the present level. The personal income tax is the most important tax revenue in several Western countries (in Canada 48 percent) and neither the imposition of higher taxes nor increased corporate (13 percent of tax incomes in Canada) and sales taxes (11 percent of tax income in Canada) would be welcomed in those societies.

Public deficits impose a heavy pressure on the money market and by keeping the loans expensive the growth of business is endangered. The savings rate remains high only in Japan (more than one-fifth of disposable personal income—the highest rate from all OECD countries) and Canada (13 percent in 1983); and this leaves some room for the potential capitalization, as well as improvement of the economy.

The U.S. federal debt of $1.6 trillion drives up interest rates worldwide and makes the situation of several indebted countries, which already spend most of their export receipts on debt-service, even more difficult. Every increase in the U.S. prime rate makes the service of the debts more expensive.[55] In the period 1974–84, the U.S. federal debt grew from 34 percent to 45 percent of GNP (estimated to be nearly 50 percent in 1986) and the interest payment, as a percent of federal receipts, has grown from 11 percent to 18 percent. "Since 1979, the cumulative deficit has risen 89 percent in the U.S. and a staggering 143 percent in Canada. The per-capita debt in both countries is approaching $7,000 but rising more rapidly in Canada."[56] A similar situation has arisen in several other Western developed countries. Under the pressure of demands, the "entitlements" of Western people are growing, but they are justified neither by higher productivity nor by the growth of the GNP. The dependence on foreign workers in some countries goes together with the high level of unemployment.[57]

One of the great dangers to the West is the weakness of its financial system. For several years the Western banks have been fed with petrodollars and in order to find borrowers for the great sums deposited they must relax their loan conditions, especially to governments of *developing* countries; at the end of 1983, more than $700 billion (U.S. dollars) was due from them, a half of it from Latin America. Owing to ailing economies, many debtors are unable and unwilling to pay even current interest rates. The growth of U.S. interest rates makes the situation of the debtor countries even worse. Most of the previous loans were either improperly invested (for example, after nine years and $18 billion, the Itajpu hydroelectric project has not produced a single kilowatt of electricity for Brazil), or spent on foreign consumer goods, or consumed by corruption. The policy of the International Monetary Fund to impose restrictions on the borrowers has been met with much resistance. The Western banks, particularly in the United States, are overextended in terms of the amount loaned compared with capital assets. For example, the nine largest U.S. banks have loaned more than double their combined capital. In order to avoid the default of the debtors, additional loans are made. The potential collapse of the debt pyramid would have catastrophic consequences, especially when taking into consideration the U.S. Monetary Control Act of 1980, which provides the grounds for banks being bailed out by the government.

Western countries are more and more endangered in their competitive position, but at the same time, they do not want to cut their consumption. The U.S. share in world export has a declining tendency: from 14 percent in 1970 to 11 percent in 1982; during the same period, the share of the developing countries in the U.S. export has grown from 28 percent to 40 percent. In addition, the United States is becoming more and more dependent on foreign imports. According to the OECD data, the trade and payment deficit of the United States in 1983 ($41 billion), will grow until 1985 by 157 percent, when Japan's surplus ($20.8 billion) will grow by 73 percent![58] The share in the world export of the United Kingdom, France, Belgium, Luxembourg, the Netherlands, and Sweden has also declined.

During the 1970s, exports of the European Community more than doubled (in current prices), but in the period 1980–82, they declined by 12 percent. It is just a matter of time before the most ambitious developing countries challenge the traditional Western industrial dominance. For example, South Korea, Taiwan, and Singapore have greatly improved their modest shares in the world market.

THE WESTERN CIVILIZATIONAL CRISIS

In the West, there is a growing demand for subsidized leisure, better medical care, higher quality of social services, and more democracy at work (as well as outside of it); but the shape of the Western economies does not provide an adequate material basis for the revolution of "growing expectations." Moving into a era of high technology, the Western nations are not ready to provide such a workplace of the future which would be open to fundamental change, continuous innovation, a well-educated and strongly motivated labor force, a flexible management style, and participatory cooperation.[59] There is too much manipulation and not enough high-quality public commitment. The impact of television on political leadership is far-reaching.

> A leader need not be smart, only quick; . . . he need not be original, only aggressive, . . . he doesn't have to be truly brave under pressure, only equipped with sweat ducts that refuse to gush under TV lights. . . . A candidate need not be a leader at all, only handsome and cool enough to imitate one. . . . The TV age has imposed a frightening new tyranny of looks and style.[60]

A good television presence plays a more important role than political skill, administrative genius, and devotion to the public cause. Appearances on television and elsewhere in public take the time and effort of politicians to the detriment of their other duties. There is a new elitism of style which lowers down the quality of public life and further contributes to the "manipulatory society."[61]

Under such circumstances it is justified to ask the fundamental question: how much longer can Western civilization manage to survive in competition with other civilizations? The relative attractiveness of the non-Western civilizations seems to grow and some of them, primarily the Japanese, are very clever in taking advantage of the West.

People who are genuinely committed to the Western tradition have several reasons to be anxious. In the West, the civil rights of citizens are acknowledged and the collapse of Western civilization may mean the elimination of basic freedoms (Russia and China under communism provide good evidence in this respect). The Christian spirit may be of questionable value for people from the other religious traditions, but there are several obvious cultural and moral assets which are worth defending.[62]

The current crisis of the West, appearing as high unemployment (especially among the young), industrial-relation conflicts, government deficits beyond reasonable limits, trade deficits, and loosening control of the internal and external situation, makes us aware of how important it is to better understand the nature of our civilization.

In this respect, it is interesting to compare the advantages of this civilization as presented by Max Weber[63] with the present-day reality. Science and reason still are prevailing but they are no longer the monopoly of the West. The trained official—"the pillar both of the modern state and of the economic life of the West"[64]—appears more and more often as a soulless bureaucrat or a clever manipulator following primarily his/her personal or group vested interests at the cost of public well-being. With the saturation of the internal markets in the developed countries and the economic despair of the developing countries, the opportunities for profit making become much more selective than before. A "rational, industrial organization, attuned to regular market, rather than to political or irrationally speculative opportunities for profit"[65] is not necessarily the most characteristic form today.

The collusion of interests between private business and the government, the impact of trade unions, and the difficulty of small business to compete with large business have introduced several new elements into the situation. Free labor is not "free" as long as there is a shortage of jobs. The development of a "manipulatory" society undermines the ideal of citizenship based on the devotion to public interest. Hegel was aware of how the growth of liberalism undermines the "public man" and exposes the freedom-seeking people to the tyranny of manipulators.

The sober bourgeois capitalism—with its rational organization of free labor, rational structures of administration, ethical ideas of duty, religious support given to the economic entrepreneurship, expert officialdom, and rational law (which can be counted upon like a machine)—is to a large extent a matter of the past.

Weber was aware of the trends which are now in full force. He wrote:

> In all probability some day the bureaucratization of society will encompass capitalism too, just as it did in antiquity. We too will then enjoy the benefits of bureaucratic "order" instead of the "anarchy" of the free enterprise, and this order will be essentially the same as that which characterized the Roman Empire and—even more—the New Empire in Egypt and the Ptolomaic state.[66]

Weber did not live long enough to learn about Soviet communism; however, his studies of several non-European social systems provide insight on the obstacles to innovation. Communities united by rigid kinship bonds and despotic government were not open to reform.

> The patrimonial nature of administration and legislation created a realm of unshakeable sacred

tradition alongside a realm of arbitrariness and favoritism. These political factors impeded development of industrial capitalism, sensitive to the lack of rational and calculable administration and law enforcement, whether in China, India, Islam, or elsewhere.[67]

Probably now, Weber would also add to this list communist systems.

Western civilization was rescued from the same pattern of stasis[68] due to corporate and local political autonomy, indispensable legal institutions defending the rights of individuals and groups, and the royal prerogative being able to override common law. Only this particular combination of factors taken together contributed to the profit-making entrepreneurship.

The lack of spiritual foundations supporting rational industrial capitalism[69] made a major difference between the West and the rest of the world. In India, the devotion of people to the caste system prevented modernization. "A lasting devotion to one's calling is anchored in the Hindu promise of rebirth more firmly than in any other ethic."[70]

Capitalism is not able to develop without some basic conditions allowing rational capital accounting: disposable property of production means, freedom of the market, rational technology, calculable law, free labor, and commercialization of economic life.[71]

> The factor which produced capitalism is the rational permanent enterprise, with its rational accounting, rational technology and rational law—but again not these alone. Necessary complementary factors were the rational spirit, the rationalization of the conduct of life in general and a rationalistic economic ethic.[72]

Several of these factors are still with us in the West but some other developments undermine the traditional foundation of entrepreneurship. The developing part of the world offers demands and challenges unknown before. The growth of the nation-state and modern corporatism suppresses many initiatives of a grass-root nature. There is a growing criticism of ideological and religious practices which were taken for granted until recently. The competition coming from the bureaucratized version of socialism plays a major historical role. The revolution of growing expectations and entitlements imposes several restraints on the free capitalistic activity.

The provision of *meaning* was treated by Weber as the basic function of religion. The nature of secular society devoid of meaning but at the same time intellectualized, systematized, specialized, and utilitarian, was studied in depth by Weber as a product of the historical process of rationalization and secularization.[73] For Weber, religious orientation played a primary causal role as the strategically central part of a general evolutionary view of the development of human society.

How people order their relationship to supernatural powers has great consequences with regard to the shape of the society in which they live and work. Religion formulates "man's basic understanding, at any moment in history, of himself, of the world in which he lives, and how life should be lived."[74] Man's continuous effort to deal rationally with the irrationalities of life, is based upon his/her religion which provides him/her with an ultimate order and direction. On the other hand, rationalization promoted by religion "has implied the progressive disenchantment, de-mystification or de-magnification of the world and religion has, in a sense, acted as its own grave digger."[75]

For Weber, rationalization as an organizing, regulating, and preserving function was not identified with secularization. He fully acknowledged the role of religion not only in social change and conflict but also in social consensus and cohesion. "This tense ambivalence is, not surprisingly, expressed unambiguously in those dichotomous and dialectically opposed categories Weber generates in his attempt to grapple intellectually with the complexity and flux of religious reality."[76]

The sanctification and legitimation of the status quo by religion eliminates the potential contrast between what is and what ought to be. But religion may help man adapt to the world, as well as repudiate the world for the sake of a higher moral order.[77] The intellectual and emotional meaning is present in each of these cases. Man is engaged in a struggle to live meaningfully and this factor plays a major role in what happens in society. The activity of prophecy is of special significance among the religious routes of rationalization. The ever-increasing rationalization does not exclude—according to Weber—the return of the sacred or the rebirth of the gods as at least a remote possibility.

The relationship between Calvinism and capitalism as presented by Weber may look much different from the current simplistic interpretation when taking into consideration that the Protestant revolution weakened the "holy alliance" of the traditional establishment and created more room for the people and concerns of a new kind. These groups of interests existed before but could not express themsleves freely as long as the traditional order was strong enough to preserve control.[78] Any direct connection between a specific religious doctrine and the socioeconomic and political order may be questioned as long as other factors are excluded. Unfortunately, a vulgar version of the refined analysis done by Weber on the mutual relationship between Protestantism and capitalism is still very common.[79] This is owing to the fact that much of the German writings of Weber remain unknown to Anglo-Saxon readers.

IN THE SEARCH OF A MORAL COHESION

In order to flourish, civilization needs a cohesive socioeconomic and moral basis. With the growing atomization of modern societies there is increasing difficulty in defending various formal groups and institutions from depersonalization. The preoccupation with mass media suppresses private and highly personalized contact between people. However, people who control the media have their own vested interests which are not necessarily in the public interest. An emphasis on pleasing the public and the reinforcement of narcissistic tendencies contribute to degradation of quality; there are appeals to emotionality rather than to reason; more interest is stimulated in anything deviant rather than in anything normal.

There are several objective and subjective reasons why the moral appeal of *society* is weakening in industrial democracies. One of them is the material and organizational dependence on each other envisaged by Durkheim as an "organic solidarity," as well as the growing tolerance of cultural difference and nonconformism. There is not so much need anymore for such collective representations (symbols) which would command and receive mass obedience. The powerful "sacred" being, according to Durkheim, provides the backbone of society; it is society that originates basic categories of time, space, class, and cause. "Not only is it society which had founded them, but their contents are the different aspects of the social being."[80] However, the "organic solidarity" of a highly organized technological society replaced "God" by machines, bureaucratic procedures, and rational manipulations.

Society, as a single moral community, is now practiced only under communism or religious totalitarianism (for example, Iran). It works only by the power of oppression and its success remains highly doubtful as long as people do not have free choice to opt for, or against, such a "community." On the other hand, the industrial democracies suffer from the fact that their moral foundations remain shallow. Lip service is paid to democratic values and the public welfare remains at the level of a manipulation. Various groups in society are involved in the process of mutual denunciation and accusation for wrongdoing; not much place is left for the "sacred."[81]

The traditional rule of religion as a system of communication of ideas and sentiments and as a means of specifying and regulating social relationships is much diminished, and the secular ingredient of social life has become dominant. Under such new conditions it remains difficult to maintain the thesis of Durkheim that religious beliefs symbolize or model social forces, structures, and relationships, which condition and compel the action of people in society, as well as produce social solidarity. Even with the interpretation of religion, broad enough to include Soviet communism, the ritual loses its importance as a way to sustain the existing core of common values. The factor of organizational manipulation appears to be more powerful than the ritualistic practices; the latter play more and more the role of window-dressing. Communal wrath as a means to reaffirm the moral order—so strongly emphasized by Durkheim—practically disappears from the field of law.

Durkheim was very much concerned with the progressing moral depreciation of the modernizing societies and the deterioration of their "sacred" quality, even though he himself was a nonbeliever. He simply recognized the danger of unrestrained appetites reigning in place of cooperation, of the strong taking advantage of the weak, and of egoism being identified with individualism. According to Durkheim, "A state of order or peace among men cannot follow of itself from any entirely material causes, from any blind mechanism, however scientific it may be. It is a moral task."[82] He was against private inheritance, in order to prevent the perpetuation of wealth. He supported the reinforcement of occupational and other associations fulfilling combined economic and moral functions in order to socialize people effectively into the society.

> Durkheim believed the state could not regulate the various functions of the economy, except at a very general, coordination and planning level; regulation had to be pluralistic and decentralized, in the

hands of people actually involved in production. Furthermore, this pluralistic self regulation of producer groups was a more basic prerequisite of change than a single socialist measure as changing the ownership of the means of production.[83]

Lukes, in the introduction to his valuable book,[84] makes clear why it is not easy for contemporary readers to understand Durkheim. First, there are several concepts that look ambiguous and are not clearly defined, but at the same time these are of crucial importance: collective conscience, collective representations, social facts, and so forth. Second, Durkheim uses a number of binary oppositions which need much explanation: sociology—psychology, social—individual, moral rules—sensual appetites, concepts—sensations, sacred—profane, normal—pathological. His reasoning and argumentation remain within the frameworks of these sharp dichotomies and it is not possible to understand him without being clear on what they actually mean. Third, Durkheim's style of presentation of his ideas is often not easy to digest.

Of particular interest is the validity of Durkheim's analysis to the current crisis of industrial democracies. The realm of the "sacred" has diminished considerably and this gives individuals plenty of freedom, as long as they have adequate resources to enjoy it; but on the other hand, social organization based on utilitarian principles does not penetrate the conscience of individuals deeply enough.

The "sacred" fuses individual consciences into spiritual community, imposes respect and love, and transfers the dispersed individuals into the society. The "profane," on the other hand, remains at the level of private existence and egoistic passions.[85] In most of the present-day industrial democracies, the "profane" has become upgraded to the position of "the sacred," except in Japan, where the values of a consumer society coexist peacefully with the "sacredness"of the national cause. The present widespread criticism of society, justified or not, undermines the mass commitment to public interest. Even more damaging is the devotion to the "profane," which is exercised systematically by the advertising business and reinforces the narcissistic orientation of consumers.[86]

It is difficult to upgrade the commitment of people to the level of a "pure" citizenship as long as the "profane" prevails under the conditions of a cheap mass culture, manipulation of the public appealing to the most elementary urges and passions, and the perpetual contest between various power centers to gain popularity. However, all attempts to substitute democracy by other systems has failed in the field of socialization; instead of voluntary commitment, the survival of these systems depends on the enforcement of their rule by sheer oppression.

The advocacy of occupational associations as a medium between individual and the state looked very rational in the time of Durkheim, but now their potential egoism is becoming obvious. It is not unusual for trade unions and professional associations to promote their particularistic interest at the expense of the general public. However, was Durkheim wrong in this respect? Is there any better chance of a "just" society than by multiplying the vehicles of socialization which appeal to the most common commitments of people: jobs, workplaces, professional colleagues, work and pay conditions?

There is a need in present-day sociology to study systematically the perspectives of a genuine pluralism by reinforcing cooperation between various major agencies of society: state, corporations, trade unions, professional associations, welfare agencies, political parties, and so forth. This is exactly what Durkheim had in mind when looking for an equilibrium, the matter of "working with steady perseverance to maintain the normal state, or reestablishing it if it is threatened, and of rediscovering its conditions if they change."[87]

According to Lukes (and many others), Durkheim "tended to idealize societies to be thought of as integrated, ignoring the tensions and conflicts within them, while seeing the realities of his own society only as pathological deviations from its future, normal, ideally integrated state."[88] However, from a sociotechnical perspective the intention of Durkheim to appreciate the "healthy state" of society seems to be worthwhile.[89] In order to improve any society it is necessary to make a distinction between what is "normal" and what is "pathological." He was aware of the fact that it is almost impossible to apply this distinction to societies undergoing periods of transition and not yet stabilized in a new form.[90] However, even in this peculiar case, the reformers who strive to improve their societies obviously need certain models and evaluative criteria based on them.

PRIVATE VERSUS PUBLIC

To reconcile private and public interest is one of the basic civilizational challenges. In the present-day Western civilization, individual growth is widely identified with success in gaining power and money; both these values have a side-effect in the growing separation between people, depending how much they accumulate. It is more and more widely practiced to raise claim for entitlements based, not on actual achievement, but on the collective responsibility to take care of everybody.[91]

Loyalty, generosity, and courage are the virtues that provide societies with valuable citizens. "Chivalry's most profound influence lay in just this, in setting the seal of approbation on norms of conduct, recognized as noble when reproduced in individual act and style—and in dictating, in many respects, the mode of this approbation."[92] This was the morality and life-style of free people who accepted for themselves ideals of self-growth, subordinating other pre-occupations to a higher goal. Chivalry taught "the gentleman to place honor at the center of his mental and social world, as the treasure dearer to him than life."[93]

How to create a world in which the nobility of good manners and superior motives would always top the nobility of wealth, power, and origin? Honor and dishonor have their insignia and much depends on their application. Nobility, in order to have permanent social value, has to be related to virtue. Orders of chivalry used to be rooted in an elaborate social organization: lay confraternities, statuses, and so forth.

Another problem worth more attention is the growing organizational congestion of modern Western societies and its negative consequences for private entrepreneurship. The institutional games dominate over the individual endeavors. People act in their institutional roles and hide their own vested interests under the guise of universal interests. It is a vital question how much institutionalization and formalization civilizations are able to tolerate before they become totally ossified. The drama of the Soviet communism is its built-in inability to overcome ossification.[94] The Soviet bloc is able to mobilize science to a much greater extent than is practiced in the West; but at the same time, scientists, as obedient servants of governmental power, are very often either totally useless for the society or even dangerous. The distinction between the state and the society is of valid importance for each civilization and needs to be treated from a comparative perspective.

Historically, Western civilization has shown dynamism to a higher degree than any other civilization.[95] Now the gap between the West and the rest of the world becomes a greater danger. Western products are too expensive to compete with other products. The millions of people who are unemployed in the industrial democracies create a great burden. The growing size of government deficits (4 percent or more of the GNP) is dictated by the needs of the welfare state and the situation does not change for the better, even under conservative rule. Politicians are trapped in their own games and are unable to promote any unpopular reforms. The growth of bureaucracy happens at the expense of professional standards and public interest. The particularistic concerns of various pressure groups confuse the criteria of actual performance. There is great difficulty in applying external scrutiny to what actually happens in the institutions supported from the public pocket.[96] The selection of leaders becomes a matter of popularity, artificially managed by experts in advertising. The mass media mentality orients public actions more than the well-being of society.

One of the examples of difficulties faced by the Western welfare state is the health service. In 1984 in the United States around $1,500 ($129 in 1960) was spent per person for health care, almost four times more than in the United Kingdom ($400), and almost eight times more than in Singapore ($200). All three countries have the same life expectancy. In the United States, only 30 percent is spent on health directly by private persons; 40 percent is spent by government; and the rest is spent by private insurance, with three-quarters of the premiums paid by employers. Both the U.S. and the U.K. health systems are very expensive, but they are not necessarily better than the cheaper systems of Japan or Singapore. In the United States, the rate of surgery is more than twice as high per person as in the United Kingdom. In Great Britain patients wait a long time for hospital placements. Preventive medicine is often neglected and waste is tolerated by health-care systems, which put too much burden on the taxpayer directly or indirectly. According to N. Macrae, any reform government today should introduce politically unpopular cost-benefit analyses into inexpensive public-health programs.[97]

The challenge of the education system is another example of a problem faced by the modern Western societies. On one hand, a growing number of people want to have diplomas. On the other hand, there is an evident danger of mediocrity frustrating the best intentions and sufficiently lowering the public utility of major educational investments.[98]

In the bureaucratized universities there is not much hope to defend excellence effectively. Any elitist reorientation under such circumstances will only reinforce the position of those who already are responsible for mediocrity and who have a strong vested interest to promote the old content under the new guise. However, there is some hope that the public debate on the issue of quality education, in the long run, may mobilize the forces able and willing to push for a real reform.

MASS ESTRANGEMENT

Organizational conformism is not a good answer to the current problems of the West, and the Japanese patterns of socialization do not fit into the Western heritage. But there is an obvious necessity to design and experiment with such "action systems"[99] that may be optimal for the current stage of civilizational development.

The structural changes toward a mass society may be well observed in the case of the United States. There is growing isolation of people; the nonfamily households have grown in the period 1970–82 from 19 percent to 27 percent (rising age at first marriage, the high incidence of divorce[100] and separation, the ability of many elderly persons to maintain their own homes alone); the number of one-parent families has doubled; the proportion of singles among young people has grown dramatically and an increased number of them will probably never marry; the share of childless, ever-married women in the age group 25–29 has grown from 16 percent to 28 percent (in the age group 30–34 it has grown from 8 percent to 15 percent); two-fifths of elderly women live alone. All these data show the progressing individualization and isolation.

At the same time, the population is becoming more sophisticated. The proportion of persons 25 and over who graduated from high school, in the period 1970–82, has grown from 55 percent to 71 percent; among people in the age group 25–34 it has grown from 74 percent to 86 percent, and in the age group 65 and over it has grown from 28 percent to 44 percent. The completion of four years or more of college among persons 25 years old and over has grown from 11 percent to 18 percent (22 percent for men and 14 percent for women); in the age group 25–34 it has grown even more—from 16 percent to 24 percent. The main gains in total employment have taken place in the professions and management, among women more than among men.[101] Employment in manufacturing has grown in the period 1972–82 much slower (2.1 percent) than the total employment (22 percent), a consequence of deindustrialization. Professional and related services have the largest numerical increases.

Due to inflation, unemployment, and the pockets of poverty (below the poverty line in 1981 were 34 percent blacks and 26 percent persons of Spanish origin, but only 11 percent whites) the median family income level has actually dropped about 3 percent in the period 1971–81. There is a growing discrepancy between the relatively well-to-do families, where both husband and wife are gainfully employed, and on the other side, broken families, as well as single persons, remaining in poverty. In 1981, one-fifth of children under age 18 were poor and the same was valid for 15 percent of elderly. Also, 41 percent of households were not covered by employer-provided group health insurance.[102]

The well-to-do and established segments of the population are in general more politically active. Voting is two times more common in the higher-income categories than among poorer people; the same is true in comparing home-owners with tenants. Equally, when comparing college graduates with those that attended only elementary school, voting by college graduates is double the rate. However, overall, more than half of voters do not participate in Congressional elections and more than 40 percent of voters do not participate in Presidential elections.

In the modern industrial democracies there is a general trend toward a mass society model,[103] and the demographic trends mentioned above for the United States appear, more or less, in the other parts of the West also. Young generations become more independent of the older, but at the same time are more vulnerable to anomie. People are better off, but there is a gap between those who succeed and those who fail, not necessarily due to their own fault. The level of sophistication is growing but this does not mean that people find suitable application for their skills. Professionalization advances very substantially, but many job-seekers with lower skills or no skills at all are not able to find any opportunities; in addition, some professional or semiprofessional skills become obsolete due to the technological progress.

CONCLUSIONS

There is a contradiction between the political potential of the Western population and its actual involvement in the citizenship practice. The well-to-do people have an evident stake in practicing their citizenship but even among them only some become active; the lower ranks of the population remain passive.[104] It is in the vested interest of bureaucrats to keep the population only selectively active. However, this selectivity quite often works against the system when claims and intentions of various groups, institutions, and categories of the population become incompatible. The claims on the expense of the taxpayers multiply with the growing sophistication of the population; the public welfare becomes endangered by the vested interest groups, among which each tries to promote its particularistic claim under the guise of a general good. People make a life career out of milking the government under the pretention that they articulate a publicly justified claim. The administrators and the politicians have a growing difficulty in handling claims and complaints dictated mainly by hidden vested interests. The tax evasion, the misuse of unemployment benefits or welfare funds,[105] the promotion of private projects at the expense of public grants, the waste of governmental funds under false pretensions, the endeavor of various public agencies to justify their own existence—all these dysfunctions impose a heavy pressure on the system of modern industrial democracies in the West.

These obvious weaknesses of the modern Western civilization have deep historical roots. It is a pity that many textbooks in the field do not pay enough attention to these roots. Historical consciousness is not among the main virtues of our epoch. In North America young people learn little of the world history, and have limited interest in public affairs unless there is some relevance to their private lives. This is due, among others, to the leisure-oriented public education in the West in comparison with the definitely work- and duty-oriented education in Japan, in the Soviet Union, People's China, South Korea, Taiwan, and Singapore.

In order to survive, each civilization must be able and willing to face several internal and external challenges.[106] Moving from one situation to another, the civilization has to adapt and control, fight or make a compromise, advance or retreat. It is an interesting question how much, in this respect, the awareness of our current civilizational condition is recognized; and how much we differ in this respect from other civilizations. In history there is only a limited room for theatrical gestures. The art of salesmanship is definitely not the only necessary virtue of public leaders. It would be quite useful in this respect to compare the abilities of various civilizations to promote innovations and implement them effectively.

The quality of the complex organizations providing the backbone of modern society is of crucial importance to the future of our civilization and this is a good reason to learn from the experience of others.[107] Several traditional organizational principles lose their sense when facing the rapidly changing external and internal environment. We need to learn new organizational ways and stimulate the managerial imagination. The organizational creed has to be considered in close relationship to the civilizational creed and this simple truth is the main message of this chapter.

According to Toynbee, "Social life is impossible without some meaning of both personal liberty and social justice. Personal liberty is an indispensable condition for any human achievement, good or evil, while social justice is the sovereign rule of the game of human intercourse."[108] This moral dimension is valid also for all complex organizations; the sociotechnical solutions are needed to reconcile freedom with justice. Death is indeed a possibility confronting any civilization,[109] and therefore, there is no escape in our own Western civilization from facing the major organizational challenge of our time.

In the organizational analysis one of the basic questions—asked by Talcott Parsons and other functionalists—is whether there is enough "*integration* within the social system itself and between the social system and the cultural patterns, on the one hand, and between the social system and the personality system, on the other."[110] Are we good enough in the West to motivate our work force in accordance to the requirements of the economy? According to Parsons, social systems must avoid "commitment to cultural patterns which either fail to define a minimum of order or which place impossible demands on people and thereby generate deviance and conflict."[111] Daniel Bell in his insightful analysis of the present-day U.S. society shows how much contradiction exists among culture, policy, and community.[112]

With the growth of claims, particularly on well-being and leisure, it is more and more difficult to mobilize people within the exiting organizations. For example, according to the opinion polls, in West Germany during the period 1962–79, the percentage of people who felt really happy only when they were free from work has grown from 33 percent to 48 percent; the percent of those feeling happy during the time of work has declined from 58 to 46. In Japan the percent of people feeling satisfied with their work has grown in the period 1974–82 from 70 percent to 79 percent.[113]

There is no escape from the organizational challenge of our times, and sociotechnics[114] may be helpful in this respect. It is not justified to limit the sociotechnical approach only to the job-enrichment projects and similar practical actions to improve the quality of working life. The broader application of sociotechnics as a planned and scientifically verified transformation of social systems has to be based, among other things, on clear recognition of the major civilizational problems. In order to improve the complex organizations we need a vision of what should be done, and rational calculation of how things can be done most effectively, without too much nuisance for the people. The humanistic failure of the Soviet model comes from the confusion of values (what is good for the Soviet empire is not necessarily good for socialism and society), as well as from the waste of people and resources for grandiose projects of no benefit to anybody.[115]

The rational choice of goals has to go together with the rational implementation of them. In both these cases sociotechnics is focused on optimalization. However, the micro-scale may not be enough. Therefore, a macro-perspective is needed and this chapter presents an attempt to locate the organizational phenomena in a civilizational framework.

NOTES

1. See Lauren Langman and Leonard V. Kaplan, "Self, State and the Crises of Capitalism," in *Marx and Marxism,* eds. A. Jain and A. J. Matejko (New York: Praeger, 1984), pp. 209–40.

2. *Die Zeit,* 24, (1984), pp. 4–5. This was a relatively small sample of around 9,000 people.

3. Nominal GDP differs more or less from the real GDP, which is calculated taking into consideration the price level. According to OECD (Working Paper No. 17) in 1984 in the United Kingdom and the Netherlands the real GDP represented close to 70 percent of the U.S. level when the nominal GDP was respectively 49 percent and 55 percent. Canada was in real GDP almost at the U.S. level. Japan, Belgium, Denmark, France, and West Germany were at the 75–80 percent level. Italy was at the level of 57 percent (nominally only 41 percent), a little better than Spain (52 percent), but much better than Ireland (45 percent) or Greece (38 percent). It is worth mentioning that there were important differences in the share of investments in the national income: 32 percent in Japan, 25 percent in West Germany, 23 percent in France, 20 percent in the United States but only 15 percent in the United Kingdom. Spending on machinery and equipment was in the United Kingdom only half of the U.S., Japanese, and Canadian

levels, and two-thirds of the German and French levels (*Manchester Guardian Weekly,* 132 (1985) 1:3.

4. *World Development Report,* 1984. The World Bank (New York: Oxford University Press), p. 111.

5. Ibid., p. 184.

6. During the period 1972–82, governmental expenditure on defense in the low-income countries has grown from 11 percent to 18 percent (in the industrial-market economies it has diminished from 23 percent to 14 percent). What is the future of a world heavily armed and trying to solve its problems mainly by the use of weapons?

7. For example, in the United States, the share of government has grown from 26 percent of GNP to 38 percent in the period 1950–77.

8. In the United States during the period 1951–81 the share of the federal level in the total government civil employment has diminished from 38 percent to 18 percent.

9. It is up to the experts to judge the ultimate facilitating or nonfacilitating impact of various policy-implementation options. The matter of political convenience is not enough to judge the real impact of a given policy. There is a need of better management, delegation of power to the nongovernmental bodies whenever this is suitable, offering of block grants to the local branches of government, coordination of various programs, networking of supporters at the local level, refinement of program design and expectations. See Garry D. Brewer and Peter deLeon, *The Foundations of Policy Analysis* (Homewood, IL: Dorsey Press, 1983). Also, A. J. Matejko, *Beyond Bureaucracy?* (Cologne: Verlag für Gesellschaftsarchitektur, 1984).

10. R. B. Ripley and G. A. Franklin, p. 28.

11. For example, according to Frank Harrison, the privileged capitalist and communist ruling elites have a vested interest in each other's perpetuation. "Each uses the other to promote its own authoritarianism over its own subjects. Both claim to be democratic, but in ways in which justify the concentration of power in the hands of the few. Though contradicting each other, neither provides a satisfactory alternative. That alternative exists only in the rejection of both" (*The Modern State* [Montreal: Black Rose Books, 1983], pp. 223–24). Harrison therefore locates his hope in the social movements concerned in the maintenance of individual autonomy within the framework of nonexploitative socioeconomic relations. They remind the general public that there is an alternative to the omnipotent but inefficient state and that the freedom from deprivation and domination is possible. The Solidarity movement in Poland

is an example. See A. Jain, ed. *Solidarity* (Baton Rouge, LA: Oracle Press, 1983).

12. W. Godwin and M. Stirner both looked for a social condition where man would no longer be subject to the guardianship of a higher power and where the regulation of mutual relationships between human beings would be based on a joint consent. Stirner, on his side, was oriented mainly against the self-denying ideas and the voluntary subjection to those who control these ideas. It is not surprising that Marx definitely rejected Stirner as being indifferent to the reality. According to Harrison:

> The problem with Marx's criticism is that, by emphasizing the dependent and determined character of ideas, he relegates ideas to a position of relative unimportance. Stirner, on the other hand, by emphasizing beliefs and ideas as the essential conditioning agent of our behavior and environment, gives to ideas an overly-exclusive authority of their own" (*The Modern State,* pp. 59–60).

13. A distinctly socialist labor process meant to Marx the democratization of all areas of social life and a collective participation in decision making, and not only the class domination as such. A. Giddens criticizes M. Weber as well as H. Braverman for not taking into consideration the active role of people in shaping their destiny. In the phenomena of bureaucracy and alienation there is no determinism. "Because they are not machines, wherever they can do so human actors devise ways of avoiding being treated as such." Anthony Giddens and Gavin Mackenzie, eds. *Social Class and the Division of Labour* (Cambridge University Press, 1981), p. 45.

14. F. Harrison, p. 69.

15. A. Giddens and G. Mackenzie.

16. The Crusades kept the flame of enthusiasm alive and contributed much to the attraction of chivalry. A Christian gentleman was morally obliged to put the preoccupation with honor over all other obligations. Men inspired to magnify their names and fortunes in knighthood followed the secular code of honor in a martially oriented aristocracy. As long as the noblemen depended mainly on their own resources, and the standing armies remained relatively weak, there was room and justification for the individualistically oriented martial business. With the progress of the division of labor, many functions executed traditionally by individual knights were taken over by the government. It was too expensive for knights to equip

themselves and to meet the expense of war. "It was one thing, in accordance with ancient ways, to expect a man at arms to come to the host equipped with his own horses and armour, but no one, in the new conditions of war, expected a master of artillery to provide his own cannon" (Maurice Keen, *Chivalry* [New Haven: Yale University Press, 1984]), p. 241. Infantry became much enlarged at expense of the cavalry. Historical changes made chivalry obsolete and opened room to the widespread governmental service.

> Thus the conception of an estate of knighthood, with a general mission to uphold justice and protect the weak, was being passed down into the conception to the officer whose business it is to fight the King's enemies. Even though armies were larger, the path forward to military glory was thus made narrower—and became better controlled (Ibid., p. 243).

The nobility had to look for other sources of income than their territorial patrimonies. Royal power made headway. "Martially, the officer and gentleman of the post-medieval period felt, and was encouraged to feel, much the same sort of pride in his service of his King as the knight had taken in the service of his natural lord and of his order" (Ibid., p. 247).

17. Keen, p. 250.
18. See Alexander J. Matejko, *The Organizational Phenomenon in a Mass Society* (Edmonton: University of Alberta Bookstore, 1983)(a script for students).
19. Ramesh Mishra, *The Welfare State in Crisis. Social Thought and Social Change* (Brighton, U.K.: Whitesheave Books, 1984), p. 54.
20. Mishra, pp. 61, 63.
21. Mishra, pp. 98.
22. The growth of the welfare state is particularly evident in Sweden, where tax revenues and social security contributions add up to 70 percent of GDP (1983). In other Western countries this percentage is lower, but it has been growing. The welfare state is based mainly upon duties taken by the government versus the citizens. For example, in the Canadian federal budget, around 30 percent is immovable (interest payments, defense) and 40 percent are various social affairs difficult to move. An additional 25 percent are transfers also not very open to reduction. (See Douglas J. McCready, *The Canadian Public Sector* (Toronto: Butterworths, 1984).
23. John McCallum, "It is Not Technology That Makes

Unemployment Rise," *Financial Post,* March 3, 1984.

24. People who are permanently employed gain from additional wage increases and fringe benefits, while at the same time, unemployment increases. In 1983, in North America, 12.1 million people were unemployed, and in OECD European countries 17.8 million (in 1985 it was expected by OECD to grow to 19.5 billion).

25. In the period 1980–84 in Canada, real GNP grew by around 3 percent per year, the unemployment rate remained at around 11 percent, productivity (real GNP per employee) was below 1 percent (it was much better in the 1960s and the 1970s), the federal deficit more than doubled, and the current balance of payments remained approximately equal on both sides (goods surplus equalized the deficit of services and transfers).

26. The advantage of Japan is in a highly trained and motivated work force, high rate of personal savings, not much government regulation, export orientation, and peaceful management-union relations.

27. *Financial Post,* February 25, 1984, p. 2.

28. *Globe and Mail,* May 12, 1984, p. 6.

29. Edmonton *Journal,* February 29, 1984, p. B1.

30. R. B. Ripley and G. A. Franklin, p. 188.

31. Ibid., p. 190.

32. A. Podgorecki, *Practical Social Sciences,* London: Allen and Unwin, 1975.

33. However, West Germans constitute 1 percent of the world population, in comparison with more than 2 percent by the Japanese. On the Japanese industrial system see also Masanori Moritani, *Japanese Technology,* Tokyo: Simul Press, 1983; Ezra E. Vogel, *Modern Japanese Organization and Management,* Berkeley: University of California Press, 1975; Thomas J. Nevies, *Labor Pains and Gaijin Bon. Hiring, Managing and Firing the Japanese,* Tokyo: The Japan Times, 1984; Richard Tamer Pascale and Anthony G. Athos, *The Art of Japanese Management,* New York: Warner Books, 1981; Jon Woronoff, *Japan's Wanted Workers,* Tokyo: Lokus Press; Mikami Tatruki, *Management and Production Improvement in Japan,* Tokyo: JMA Consultants, 1982; E. S. Krauss, T. P. Rohlen, and P. G. Steinholf, *Conflict in Japan,* Honolulu: University of Hawaii Press, 1984; Satoshi Kamata, *Japan in the Passing Lane: An Insider's Account of Life in a Japanese Auto Factory,* New York: Pantheon Books, 1982.

34. *Newsweek,* October 15, 1973, p. 60.

35. Charles J. McMillan, *The Japanese Industrial System.* Berlin–New York: Walter de Gruyter, 1984, p. 15.

36. Ibid., p. 41.

37. Ibid., p. 63.

38. Ibid., pp. 168, 169.

39. Ibid., p. 226.

40. *Die Zeit,* 23, p. 11, 1984.

41. Not included are people who lost hope of finding any job and did not register as unemployed.

42. In April 1984, unemployment was a major concern for people at the following level: 78 percent in France, 60 percent in the United Kingdom, 52 percent in West Germany, 36 percent in the United States, and only 16 percent in Japan. *Die Zeit,* 24, p. 4, 1984.

43. The per-capita GNP in 1983 in Canada was US$13,000 in comparison with East Germany US$9,300 and Poland US$5,800. *The Economist* 294, 7386, p. 111, 1985.

44. Wages differ much in Canada, depending on the industry (in December 1983, Can. $287 per week in wholesale and retail trade, in comparison with Can. $637 in mining); and on the province (Can. $320 in Prince Edward Island and Can. $434 in Alberta). It is also noted that the goods-producing industries offer much better wages than service positions. There is a shift in employment to lower-paying industries and regions (see *Financial Post,* March 10, 1984, p. 10). Wage settlements calmed down in the period 1981–84.

45. In the period 1970–81, the share of foreign-owned corporations in the total Canadian sales of nonfinancial firms went down from 37 percent to 30 percent. "Foreign-owned" means in this case more than 50 percent voting equity held outside Canada (*Financial Post,* August 11, 1984, p. 12). In the period 1971–81 U.S. direct investment in Canada has grown only 123 percent in comparison with a 370-percent increase in Canadian direct investment in the United States. Travel of Americans to Canada has declined while travel of Canadians to the United States has risen sharply (around 13 million visitors). The balance of services between both countries has been unfavorable for Canada. The U.S. economy is declining in the global world economy and the fact that Canada is so much dependent on the U.S. economy has some far-reaching consequences. See Jorge Niosi, "The Decline of the American Economy: Consequences for Canada," paper to the Canadian Sociology and Anthropology annual meeting (the John Porter Memorial Lecture), Guelph, Ontario, June 1984.

46. Over 50 percent of foreign ownership is still in tobacco, rubber, transport equipment, petroleum and coal products, chemicals, electric products, nonmetalic mineral products, oil and gas, machinery and textiles. *Financial Post,* December 3, 1983:26.

47. Among the nonagricultural, paid workers, the share of union members has grown from 29 percent in 1964 to 40 percent in 1984—31 percent of the civilian labor force.

48. For example, in the period 1951–81, in Canadian families the percentage of households with two or more earners has grown from 33 to 60, while at the same time the share of no-earner families has grown from 7 to 11 percent. The family model changes very substantially when the household, based on the earnings of the husband and father only, is in decline (*Charting Canadian Incomes, 1951–1981*, Ottawa: Statistics Canada, 1984).

49. During the period 1977–82, in France, West Germany, United Kingdom, and Sweden, the average weekly hours of work have declined by 5–6 percent, in Italy by 4 percent, in the United States by 3 percent, and in Canada by 2 percent. In Japan they have grown by 1 percent.

50. For example, comparative data on work satisfaction in Canada for the period 1977–81, show the decline of those "very satisfied" from 31 percent to 21 percent, especially among employees in the age group 30–40 (the number of these workers increased by 32 percent in the period 1971–81), professionals, managers, skilled laborers, and women. Painfully felt were declining opportunities for advancement and low participation perspectives. "Top-downs management appears to be gaining strength in spite of the press given Japanese management styles, which stress greater work involvement." Tom Atkinson, "Changing Attitudes Toward Work in Canada," *Canadian Business Review*, Spring, 1983.

51. In the countries of the European Community the share of taxes and social-welfare expenditure in the whole economy has grown considerably in the period 1970–83: from 35–40 percent to around 50 percent in France, West Germany, Belgium, and Ireland; from 44 percent to 57 percent in the Netherlands; from 31 percent to 45 percent in Italy; from 36 percent to 48 percent in Luxembourg; and from 46 percent to 52 percent in Denmark. In the United Kingdom it has remained at the level of 43 percent; and in Greece it has grown from 27 percent to 37 percent. *Die Zeit,* 18, p. 10, 1984.

52. In 1983, in the United States, the deficit was equal to 5 percent of the GNP. In Canada it was over 6 percent. However, in Italy it was 12 percent (1982). See Martin Krossel, "The Competition Bulk Ahead," *Executive,* 26, 6, 1984: pp. 63–65.

53. For example, in the Canadian federal budget there is a heavy load of fiscal transfers of the federal government to the provinces (Can. $25 billion per year) in order to

shore up the weak revenue bases of the poorer provinces, and help in health care and higher education.

54. In the United States during the period 1960–84 the national debt per capita has grown from $130 to $500 (inflation excluded); the spending on social security and medicare has grown from 2.3 percent to 6.6 percent of GNP. At the same time all nonpayroll taxes have declined from 16.4 to 13.0 percent of GNP (the payroll taxes have grown from 2.1 percent of GNP to 5.7 percent of GNP). Taxpayers do not want to have a higher income tax but at the same time they want continuation or even extension of existing benefits.

55. *Financial Post,* June 30, 1984, p. 15.

56. Douglas J. Tigert, "How Debt Has Piled Up Over the Years," *Financial Post,* 78, 24, 1984, p. 9.

57. In West Germany, foreign workers constitute, since the 1970s, around one-tenth of the wage- and salary-earners (9.1 percent in 1981). This includes 540,000 Turks; 305,000 Yugoslavians; and 238,000 Italians (in June 1983). See Petra Lehnert, "Reise ohne Wiederkehr," in *Die Zeit,* 20, 1984, p. 10.

58. See *Time,* 124, 1, 1984, pp. 28–32. At the end of 1985 in billions US$ the current account balance was approximately minus 120 for the U.S. in comparison of plus 44 for Japan (*The Economist,* 297, 7916 [1985]: 118).

59. See Diane Butler, *Futurework: Where to Find Tomorrow's High-tech Jobs Today.* Toronto: Holt, Rinehart & Winston, 1984.

60. Don Braid, "Only Mediocrity survives the Tyranny of the Tube," *Edmonton Journal,* July 29, 1984, p. 47.

61. See Alexander J. Matejko, "The Manipulatory Society," *Guru Nanak Journal of Sociology,* (forthcoming).

62. See the interesting analysis of the conflict within Christianity between the organizational power and the moral values. Malachi Martin, *The Decline and Fall of the Roman Church* (New York: G. P. Putnam, 1981).

63. The world of Max Weber was obviously different from ours. Therefore there is even a greater value in his writings, in that he was able to predict at least some of the developments. See Stanislav Andreski, ed. *Max Weber on Capitalism, Bureaucracy and Religion: A Selection of Texts* (London: George Allen and Unwin, 1983).

64. Ibid., p. 23.

65. Ibid., p. 26.

66. Ibid., p. 159.

67. Ibid., p. 82.

68. The condition of a society that neither develops nor regresses.

69. See Gerhard Lenski and Jean Lenski, *Human Societies: An Introduction to Macro-sociology* (McGraw-Hill, 1982), part III, pp. 231–365. See also M. Martin.

70. Andreski, ed., p. 108.

71. Ibid., p. 110.

72. Ibid., p. 128.

73. Talcott Parsons, *The Evolution of Societies* (Englewood Cliffs, NJ: Prentice-Hall, 1977).

74. Theodore Steeman, "Max Weber's Sociology of Religion," in *Sociological Analysis,* 25, (1984): p. 56.

75. Roger O'Toole, *Religion: Classic Sociological Approaches* (Toronto: McGraw-Hill Ryerson, 1984), p. 139. The one-dimensional analogy of religion as an opiate in orthodox Marxism, and the treatment of religion as a totally dependent variable, seems to be obsolete, from the position taken by O'Toole. Religion is not a mere passive effect of social relation of production; it may play an important role in the birth and consolidation of a particular social structure; it may bring about a social revolution (Ibid., p. 192). O'Toole treats the heritage of Marx as a "rich intellectual capital to be drawn upon by scholars now and in the future" (Ibid., p. 194) as long as the vulgarized interpretation of religion taken from an evolutionist-teleological-scientific perspective widely practiced in eastern Europe is abandoned.

76. Ibid., p. 141.

77. The search of meaning and the devotion to supreme beings appear as the most promising approaches to the phenomenon of religion. We still do not know enough empirically how people actually perceive their religious meanings. Data from the surveys are unreliable because they miss the most important dimension: the depth of feelings and understanding. The recent growth of an existential sociology provides some good promise in this respect. In order to study *meanings* it is necessary to acknowledge circumstances in which this complicated phenomenon may be actually investigated. As long as the research project remains at the superficial level, there is not any good hope in this respect. Actually the sociology of religion needs badly a methodological imagination and courage going much beyond what is available now. See Alexander J. Matejko, "The Existential Anguish," in *Guru Nanak Journal of Sociology* 3, (1982):1–2.

78. See S. N. Einsenstadt, ed. *The Protestant Ethic and Modernization* (New York: Basic Books, 1968).

79. The heritage of Durkheim is even more controversial. Religious symbols treated as a reflection of underlying social-structural realities satisfy some interpreters

but not others. Symbolic reality loses its depth by being reduced to empirical propositions. As R. Bellah says, religion is true. There are multiple realities and human growth necessitates movement between them (A. Schutz). However, there is some good reason for Durkheim to take a conservative position. "It appears intellectually myopic to study social dynamics to the utter neglect of social statics" (O'Toole, p. 202). The integrative function of religion does not exclude its function as a factor of change.

80. E. Durkheim, 1965. *The Elementary Forms of the Religious Life* (New York: Free Press), p. 488.

81. According to Durkheim, "there can be no society which does not feel the need of upholding and reaffirming at regular intervals the collective sentiments and the collective ideas which make its unity and its personality" (p. 475). In the time of mass disintegration, egoistic orientation, and the dominance of particularism over universalism, much reinforced by the vested-interest groups and institutions, the preoccupation of Durkheim with social integration is again of much validity. He devoted his major studies to the mutual relationship between various layers of social organization: substratum (population, territorial allocation of people and resources, technology), institutions (formal and informal, rules and norms, moral codes, sanctions), and collective symbols (social values, public opinion, religion, ideologies). He was very sensitive to the dynamic aspect of social life. According to him,

> structure itself is encountered in *becoming,* and one cannot illustrate it except by pursuing this process of becoming. It forms and dissolves continually; it is life arrived at a certain measure of consolidation; to disconnect it from the life from which it derives or from that which determines is equivalent to dissociating things that are inseparable (Durkheim, "Sociology and its Scientific Field," in Emile Durkheim et al., *Essays on Sociology and Philosophy,* edited by Kurt H. Wolff (New York: Harper and Row, 1960), p. 362.

82. Emile Durkheim, *Professional Ethics and Civil Morals* (London: Routledge and Kegan Paul, 1957), p. 12.

83. Kenneth Thompson, *Emile Durkheim* (Chichester, England: Ellis Horwood; London: Tavistock Publ. Series: Key Sociologists, ed. by P. Hamilton, 1982), p. 179.

84. Steven Lukes, *Emile Durkheim: His Life and Work; A Historical and Critical Study* (Harmondsworth, England: Penguin Books, 1975).

85. Ibid., p. 26.

86. See Alexander J. Matejko, "Marxists Versus Christians: A Dialogue?" in *Marx and Marxism,* edited by A. Jain and A. J. Matejko (New York: Praeger, 1984), pp. 241–78.

87. Emile Durkheim, *The Rules of Sociological Method* (Glencoe, IL: Free Press, 1950), p. 75.

88. Lukes, p. 30.

89. Durkheim was not only a sociologist but also a reformer, even if he made a very clear distinction between both of these roles. His sympathy to socialism [see E. Durkheim, *Socialism* (New York: Collier Books, 1962)] came from his appreciation of those who had the courage and imagination to take into consideration the alternative version of society. At the same time, Durkheim looked for reform and not for revolution; he had distrust for schemes based on the state's taking over almost all power. Instead, he wanted to see a society being able to activate its own internal potential. People interested in the sociotechnical orientation very often share this perspective with Durkheim, and therefore, his heritage is of particular value for them.

90. Durkheim, 1960, pp. 60–61.

91. See Daniel Bell, *The Cultural Contradictions of Capitalism* (New York: Basic Books, 1976).

92. M. Keen, p. 249.

93. Ibid., p. 250.

94. The bureaucratic government run by Leonid Brezhnev was oriented against liberal or tyrannical extremes. "Being a colorless apparatchik with no strong political conviction, he became a figure of shifting compromise between different tendencies, both at the top level in the Kremlin and among the lower classes" (Vladimir Solovyov and Elena Klepikova, *Yuri Andropov* (New York: Macmillan, 1983), p. 266. Without any evident improvement in the economic situation within the country, the political program of Brezhnev later followed by his close collaborator, Konstantin Chernenko, did not have much chance against the numerous, steadfast, and aggressive neo-Stalinists of an Andropov kind. Is there any major chance that another Andropov will lead the Soviet Union to a police state depending more on power than on ideology? The campaign of Gorbachev against sloth and decay, treated as quick-acting medicine, has great appeal in Russia under the present circumstances. "Russian chauvinism is an ideology of fear. But it is a perfectly natural fear of collapse which in the final analysis becomes a national stimulus to the empire, both on the government level and on that of the people as a whole" (Ibid., p. 59).

95. See, among others, Joseph R. Strayer and Hans W. Gatzke, *The Mainstream of Civilization,* 4th ed. (1st edition in 1969) (San Diego: Harcourt, Brace Jovanovich, 1984). The authors admit that the selection of data and insights in such a book is of a critical importance. "The massing and linking of facts is not only essential, if history is to rise above the level of a catalogue; it is also inevitable, since it is the way the human mind deals with past experience" (p. ix). In the epilogue of this book, our current problems are briefly discussed: the population explosion in much of the world, the decay of the environment, poverty, women's rights, human rights, fear of nuclear war, the biological revolution, the bewilderment, the revolt of youth, and violence. It would be much more helpful and advisable, when dealing with such issues, to look closer into their civilizational meaning, as well as at some statistical material.

96. See Brewer and deLeon.

97. Norman Macrae, "Reducing Medical Costs: A Prescription for Pressing Western Problems," *World Press Review* 31, 7 (1984):29 (reprinted from *The Economist,* April 28, 1984).

98. David J. Bercuson, Robert Bothwell, and J. L. Granatstein, *The Great Brain Robbery: Canada's Universities on the Road to Ruin* (Toronto: McClelland and Stewart, 1984).

99. "Action involves actors making subjective decisions about the means to achieve goals, all of which are constrained by ideas and situational conditions," Jonathan H. Turner, *The Structure of Sociological Theory,* 3rd ed. (Homewood, IL: Dorsey Press, 1983), p. 42.

100. The ratio of currently divorced persons, per 1,000 married persons living with their spouse, has increased in the period 1970–82 from 47 to 114. The proportion of children under age 18 living with two parents dropped from 85 percent to 75 (42 percent among black children). *Population Profile of the United States: 1982* (Washington: U.S. Bureau of the Census, 1983).

101. Women account for 45 percent of employment in the professional group (39 percent in 1972), 28 percent in the managerial groups (18 percent in 1972), 45 percent in the sales groups (42 percent in 1972), and 81 percent in the clerical group (76 percent in 1972). In the period 1970–82, women accounted for 59 percent of the growth in the civilian labor force; their share in this force has grown from 38 percent to 43 percent, and their participation rate has grown from 43 percent to 53 percent; among married women with husbands present, and with children under age 6, the participation rate has grown from 30 percent to 49

percent. Families maintained by women have increased by 53 percent in the period 1971–81 (in comparison with 15 percent growth for all families) and their average income in 1981 represented only 44 percent of the income gained by the married-couple families. On the other hand, in the latter, those families where the wife was working had the income higher by 44 percent than the average. Ibid., pp. 3 and 4.

102. Ibid., pp. 22, 23.

103. See Alexander J. Matejko. *Social Organization* (Edmonton, Canada: University of Alberta Bookstore, 1983)(a script for students).

104. According to J. Habermas, this is a fundamental contradiction of any social formation. See his *Legitimation Crisis* (Boston: Beacon, 1974). On "Critical Theory" of Habermas and others, see Axel van den Berg, "Critical Theory: Is There Still Hope?" *American Journal of Sociology,* 86, 3 (1980):449–78, 488; 6:1250–70.

105. See Diane Vaughan, *Controlling Unlawful Organizational Behavior: Social Structure and Corporate Misconduct* (Chicago: University of Chicago Press, 1983).

106. According to Arnold J. Toynbee, war and militarism have been the most potent cause of the breakdown of society throughout history. The West has, so far, wrestled unsuccessfully with this disease even if it has achieved successes in other fields. There is an ominous dissension in the West between dominant minority and internal and external "proletariats." The West enters a difficult period of time when the credibility of leadership is challenged and the ability to adapt is endangered (Arnold J. Toynbee, *A Study of History,* Abridgement by D. S. Sommerwell [New York: Dell, 1978], vol. 2, pp. 344–53). It is one of the historical paradoxes that the "internal proletariat" in the West consists mainly of the intellectuals and challenges the establishment by using Marxism as a "universal religion." See A. Jain and A. Matejko, eds. *Marx and Marxism* (New York: Praeger, 1984.)

107. See, among others, William G. Ouchi, *Theory Z: How American Business Can Meet the Japanese Challenge* (New York: Avon Books, 1982); also Charles J. McMillan, *The Japanese Industrial System* (Berlin: de Gruyter, 1984); J. Wilczynski, *Comparative Industrial Relations: Ideologies, Institutions, Practices and Problems under Different Social Systems, with Special Reference to Socialist Planned Economies* (London: Macmillan, 1983).

108. Toynbee, vol. 2, p. 374.

109. Ibid., p. 389.

110. Jonathan H. Turner, p. 45.

111. Talcott Parsons, *The Social System* (New York: Free Press, 1951), pp. 27–28, quoted after Jonathan H. Turner, p. 45.

112. Daniel Bell.

113. Michael Jungblut, "Mehr Freude an der Arbeit," in *Die Zeit,* 25 (1984), p. 11.

114. See Adam Podgorecki.

115. See John Barron, *KGB Today: The Hidden Hand* (New York: Reader's Digest Press, 1983). This book shows how wasteful and morally destructive the intelligence-gathering apparatus is as a powerful weapon of the imperial policy. Its functionaries are using all possible measures in order to recruit innocent people to the service, from which there is no escape. Intelligence, going together with disinformation, terrorism, and exploitation of human beings, contributes much to international tensions. Stealing of industrial inventions corrupts the market relationships. On the criticism of CIA in this respect, see Philip Agee, *Inside the Company: CIA Diary* (Harmondsworth, England: Penguin Books, 1975).

REFERENCES

Brown, Lester R. et al. *State of the world 1984. A World Watch Institute Report on Progress Toward a Sustainable Society,* New York: W. W. Norton, 1984.

Lenski, Gerhard and J. Lenski, *Human Societies,* New York: McGraw-Hill, 1982.

Matejko, Alexander J. *Beyond Bureaucracy?* Cologne: Verlag für Gesellschaftsarchitektur, 1984. Chap. 2, pp. 49–110.

Report on the World Social Situation. New York: United Nations, 1982.

Statistical Abstract of the United States. Washington, DC: U.S. Department of Commerce (published every year).

World Development Report 1984. New York: Oxford University Press, 1984.

2

VULNERABLE STRUCTURES

HOW MUCH STRUCTURALIZATION
IS REALLY NEEDED?

Structuralization of human actions is a matter of necessity but there are several costs involved: formalization of rules, conformism, dependence of some people on others, and so forth. There is a question how much the structures are really unavoidable and to which extent they are dictated by the vested interests of these who promote them. Another important question is how much structuralization is just a product of our habitual thinking which takes for granted the highly structured alternatives and does not provide enough room for the alternative solutions. Another fascinating question is under which circumstances and why people are ready to abdicate their freedoms without a real necessity. We can ask also how to control those people who look for their own benefits on the expense of common good. Is it possible to limit structuralization and open much room for community feeling without giving too much room for the misuse of public welfare?

The development of a bureaucratic state is justified by the necessity to preserve the social order and defend the public good against all those who want to take advantage of it. According to some critics, with enough altruism the rationale for the state evaporates and by the establishment of sociomoral conditions supporting the community spirit it would be possible to limit the objective need of state services. The modern states have developed by co-opting, subordinating, or destroying the historical communities which kept social order more or less effectively by applying social controls, promoting an effective socialization based on the widespread participation, threat of retaliation, moral sanctions, institutionalized public shaming, threats of sorcery, the crosscutting ties, and so on.

The *community* has several effective measures to keep members obedient to the established social order. In the small and very stable communities the reciprocity and approval/disapproval both keep people together.

> Public goods are more likely to be provided, or provided in optimal amounts, by the members of small publics than by those of large ones. . . . The only rational cooperation is conditional cooperation whereby an individual contributes if and only if enough others contribute, and such conditional cooperation is possible only in a relatively small public in which people have contact with and can observe the behavior of many of their fellows, and which has a fairly stable membership (Taylor, p. 93).

The organizational experience of small-scale hunting, gathering, and horticultural groups may be interesting for everybody who looks for some alternatives to bureaucracy. Egalitarianism, public controlled leadership, great participation of all involved persons in decision making, and spontaneity appear very evidently in the preagrarian societies. The organization based on bands functions on decisions taken by full communal participation and consensus. Kinship, ceremony, and mythology enrich the communal life and bring people closely together. In these societies "leadership is informal and largely achieved; it may be invested in technicians such as the good hunter among the Eskimos or Northern Athabascan Indians, or in the shaman, or, as in Australia, ascribed to the older men of the community; rules are enforced through diffuse and religious sanctions and egalitarianism, at least within a given age-sex group, prevails" (Barclay, pp. 46–47). There is no place for a monopoly of force. Most social-control mechanisms function effectively preventing the ambitious individuals to gain a permanent dominance and secure leadership also for their sons.

Horticulturalists are more sedentary than hunters-gardeners: they have created decentralized, functionally generalized, segmentary types of social organization. A fine mesh of counterbalancing obligations keeps people together and prevents some of them to gain an upper hand over the rest permanently. It is rewarding to gain some popularity but it is not easy to transform this popularity into an established authority.

Among the pastoral people a segmentary tribal system functions sometimes without any stable centralized government. There may be feuds between individual segments of the society but they are regulated and mediated by ritual specialists. A cultural pattern which induces a maximal dispersal of counterbalancing social bonds goes together in this case with a highly mobile and reproductive form of wealth (Ibid., p. 81).

Even among the agricultural societies it is possible to find cases of highly decentralized confederations with the basic units governed with more or less consent of the population. The religious rural communes represent a similar pattern and some of them have managed to survive for centuries. In the modern societies there are successful examples of communes but many of them suffer due to the adverse publicity and external interference, inadequate screening of members, lack of individual responsibility, inadequate technical capability, and too much communality (Ibid., pp. 107–8).

It is impossible to maintain a genuine community when tolerating any gross assymetries in the exercise of power. Even the inequality of *prestige* has to be kept within limits. The norm of reciprocity and the right to subsistence are generally acknowledged. Under the pressure of the vested interests of a particularistic nature the communal tradition has broken down giving a way to the state organization. "The weakening of the community and the development of gross inequality are the concomitants and consequences of state formation" (Taylor, p. 133).

On one hand, the growing inequality has historically led to the concentration of power and privilege in some people at expense of others. On the other hand, the growth of the state organization has much contributed to the weakening of the communal bonds and traditions.

With the more and more threatening environment there was less and less place for the communes primarily oriented in their own internal affairs and relatively defenceless. Under the adversarial condition the communities could not multiply (the fission process) splitting off and forming the new centers. "State formation has its roots not in the growth of economic inequality but in the combination of conditions which strengthen the leadership that is found in every stateless society and conditions which make fission impossible or undesirable" (Ibid., p. 138).

The process of *mutual negotiation* is typical for communities free from a doctrinal orientation. The internal equilibrium in them may be more shaky than in the utopian communities expecting from their members a total immersion in the communal spirit but at the same time there is also much more room for personal freedom. Liberty is maximized in, or possible only in community as long as people are not expected to surround all their privacy to the collective body.
Is it possible to apply the same reasoning to much larger and more complicated societies? The anthropological evidence shows that

> large populations may be integrated by a more complex arrangement which affiliates the individual with a number of crosscutting and bisecting groups so as to extend his or her social ties over a wide area. . . . Individuals and groups constitute a multitude of interconnected loci, which produce the integration of a large social entity, but without any actual centralized co-ordination (Barclay, p. 110).

According to M. Taylor, "in a world constituted of communities, order and a rough material equality among communities can be maintained insofar as the relations between communities themselves are those characteristic of community, unless the communities themselves are to be subject to an inter-communal state" (p. 166).
So far the process of building small enclaves of community life and work has been successful only to a limited degree. Communities show much vulnerability in the face of societies with greater political centralization and concentration of force. On the other hand, the progressing reification of mutual relations between people in the modern societies leads to so many negative consequences that there is a growing demand to foster and deepen reciprocity, diminish political specialization by shortcutting the offices of the state and widening participation, as well as to stimulate less specialized relations between people.
The promotion of community is not limited only to the nature of human relations. From the point of view of the growth of community the nature of the product of cooperation is important, too. Depending what people actually

contribute to the society by their joint effort, they become more or less useful in a broad social sense. This important factor is quite often missing from the concern on organizational effectiveness. Useless or even socially harmful products undermine any deeper sense of human cooperation and spoil the moral content of work.

There are several obvious advantages of *community* in comparison with the modern mass society based on fragmentation, depersonalization, and manipulation. Our preoccupation with efficiency and organizational effectiveness leads quite often to the neglect of such fundamental values as mutual trust, the service factor in leadership, cooperation, goodwill to each other, the culture of human relations, and so forth. The tradition of community has been overshadowed by formalized organizational manipulation devoid of a genuine human concern.

As long as the majority of the population is ready to abdicate responsibility to big organizations, and particularly to the government, there is not much chance to overcome the inhibition of human cultural development within the bureaucracy. On the other hand, the pressure of conformism may limit the individual freedom even under conditions of self-government. Humans can be creative under quite dissimilar circumstances: the effective techniques of maintaining order, even if they are very democratic, do not necessarily contribute to a higher culture.

There is an obvious value in self-regulation, mutual help and the minimalization of frictions by socializing people to play games of cooperation. However, it would be naive to assume that the decentralized and debureaucratized order is a perfect answer to all basic socioeconomic and moral problems. The dictate of a majority may be painful for individuals and their well-being may be harmed by the practice of consensual politics.

In the beginnings of state formation it was the interdependent development of government and social class tied to an economy that was able to provide the means to sustain an elite class. However, a division between leaders and led does not appear from the anthropological data as a historical necessity. There are other alternatives available and it is a historical question why they are taken or not.

There is not much reason to overestimate the strength of the present-day bureaucratic structures and underestimate the need to look for alternatives. The perspective to introduce much more elements of spontaneity into the existing organizational structures looks in the present time quite promising. There is much organizational hope in a communal spirit based on the common beliefs and values, direct and many-sided relations between members, as well as reciprocity, fraternity, friendship, and mutual acceptance.

The fulfillment of *community* is limited to relatively small and stable groups of people. "It is easiest where the population of the maximal effective social group is small—probably up to 200 individuals. In it 'face to face' relations prevail and thus the typical diffuse sanctions of gossip, ostracism and the like can operate most effectively" (Barclay, p. 110). Community is easiest where the population is homogeneous and undifferentiated. "Among other things, this means there is only a minimal division of labor and specialization of tasks. Such a situation where people are much the same, reduces or minimizes the opportunities for differences of opinion, sharp cleavages, and conflict, and maximizes what people have in common so that even if there is disagreement there is still immense pressure to conform and keep the system going. Numerous bonds of commonality bind the dissident to the group and prevent total alienation" (Ibid., p. 110).

The gross inequality undermines community and therefore it is generally avoided by communities which bother mainly about the *quality* of mutual relations among people. This is done involuntarily (Taylor, p. 101).

> It is true that all the experience of primitive and peasant communities, intentional communities, and collectives and communes in "socialist" societies—even those whose members have grown up and have been well socialized in the community—does not prove that there can never be societies where "human nature," appropriately socialized, will be such that equality is maintained voluntarily; but certainly this evidence gives no grounds for optimism (Ibid., p. 101).

MICRO-STRUCTURE

The issue of a *primary group* is much sensitive. "It is the particularly intense and complex interplay among pressures from the outside society, the emotional dynamics of the group, and the selves of the members that lie at the heart of primary group existence" (Ridgeway (1983:351).

It is widely accepted that the development of small intimate groups is of vital importance for the well-being of the society and for the growth of organizations. "They are the supporting structures in which individuals root their self-identities and on which they rely for satisfaction of their need and for the feedback about the social world" (Ibid., p. 354). On the other hand, the dynamics of small groups is quite often in disagreement with the transformations of organizations and this leads to tension, feeling of dissatisfaction, loneliness, and frustration.

With the intensified social mobility, people become uprooted and lose some skills of dealing with others which become obsolete in the new environment. More and more, people hold several jobs, marry more than once, change friends, and live in many neighborhoods over the course of their lives.

In the modern market societies there are several factors leading to the disintegration of primary groups. Data show a progressing reevaluation of the family patterns in the United States which has something to do with the growing economic independence of women, the practice of cohabitation, and the flexible marriage arrangement. The median household income has remained approximately the same (in constant 1981 dollars) during the period 1967–81 but the share of relatively rich households ($35,000 and over) has grown from 14 percent to 19 percent, and the share of the middle-income households ($15,000 to $25,000) has diminished from 28 percent to 24 percent.

Families as the basic primary groups in the U.S. society are still materially well-off on the world scale (only 23 percent of the average family budget goes on food) but they face many pressures coming from the expectations instigated by the market economy as well as by a high territorial mobility; in the period 1975–80 almost a half of the population has changed location. In addition, it is necessary to take into consideration the *vertical mobility* achieved mainly due to the educational channels: among those in the age group 25–29 the percentage of those with four years of high school or more has grown in the period 1950–81 from 38 to 86, and the percentage of those with college education (4 years or more) has grown from 8 to 21 (Statistical 1982).

As may be seen from the above facts, there are several trends in modern society that undermine the tissue of primary groups and weaken the basic sociomoral bonds on which the society is based. Artificial small groups are created for the therapeutic purposes in order to help people who are under stress, resocialize the delinquents, create a better communication between the supervisors and the subordinates, achieve higher productivity, and so forth. Artificiality has its costs and dysfunctions, and at the same time contributes to the manipulative nature of modern society empoverishing the moral content of social bonds.

Under such circumstances it becomes difficult to maintain the sense of security, belonging, and identity. Personal attachments are much more superficial, the socialization process is not smooth enough, the new specialized institutions are not an adequate substitute for the
missing traditional bonds.

Many modern institutions suffer because of an inadequate contact with the already existing *small groups*. It is
very difficult to assure the loyalty and effort of people
when the primary human bonds are totally neglected. The
conflictual nature of the modern societies prevents to promote the spirit of cooperation when most of the people are
entrenched in their vested interest groups that remain
mutually antagonistic. "The future effectiveness of our
major business, government, and educational institutions, as
they grow larger and more bureaucratic, will be strongly
affected by their ability to balance growth against more
significant links with their constituent small groups, and,
through them, with their individual participants"
(Ridgeway, p. 357).

Social culture has a fundamental impact on the nature of
small groups. Different cultures treat intimacy in a different manner and the meaning of *social distance* varies profoundly. On the other hand, culture is closely linked to
the socioeconomic basis of society.

In the developed market societies with their highly
commercialized mass culture and a strong dependence on
mutual manipulation there is very little room for a sophisticated type of intimacy characteristic for the old traditionalistic social cultures. The atomization of society and
the exaggerated significance given to individualism is well
entrenched in the program of a manipulatory society which
constantly appeals to the egotistic elements of human
psyche.

Social relations in a small group become much more
complicated not only with the addition of new members but
also with the growing exposure to the external pressures
and temptations that are harmful to intimacy. People constantly running for their *own* success and completely ignoring a genuine self-growth are not good candidates for the
small-group intimacy. They need others only in an instrumental sense and not for an in-depth mutual communication.

The small-group encounter very often reflects only what
happens in the society without the preservation of its own
unique character. The emotional relationships between the
small-group members may become so much subordinated to
the *vested interests* that everything in the group serves
some instrumental purpose. This danger appears even in

the self-growth movements when people enroll in them to accomplish the perfection but limit their commitment to paying fees, keeping each other happy, and attending meetings.

The sophisticated kind of emotional attachment in a primary group in the modern societies can be achieved quite often only by rejecting the dominant sociocultural trend, withdrawing from the rat race, and accepting the marginal position. The cost is so high that very few individuals are willing and able to pay it.

In the analysis of small groups it would be necessary to look closer into the subtle differences appearing in *power* (or control) as well as in *affection,* treated as the two fundamental dimensions in the emotional lives of groups. The cultural context plays an important role in this respect and it is not proper to treat small groups in a total isolation from the surrounding. There are "warm" cultures which reinforce the involvement of people into close relations with each other, and there are "cold" cultures which gratify an emotional withdrawal.

All phenomena appearing in small groups are culturally conditioned and it is very unfortunate that so far the whole research in this field is almost exclusively North American, and even the studies done outside North America do not pay enough attention to the cultural distinctions. It is quite obvious that people in their daily life obey more or less consequently certain sociocultural norms inherited from their own families and communities. Why not pay attention to this practice as applied to small groups? Bonds existing among people due to their personal attraction, interlocking roles played by them, as well as due to the shared norms and beliefs are far from being culturally neutral.

The small-group *culture* may be understood as the group's organized system of information about itself, its environment, and what it does. This system exists in its truest sense in the interaction among the group members. Small groups may be approached in a completely different manner depending how is understood their primary constructive role in shaping the society: as vehicles of emotional satisfaction or as keepers of sociomoral standards.

When *social structure* is the pattern of relationships among the members that emerges from their interaction, culture is "the ordered system of ideas group members use to guide and interpret their interaction together" (Ridgeway, p. 248). The claim that small groups evolve their distinctive culture in relation to the larger social network and offer a distinctive "commentary on the culture of society as a whole" (Ibid., p. 277) is justified as long as it does not overshadow the opposite argument that small groups are much influenced by the dominant cultures of the environment.

The rules for behavior, values, beliefs, and symbols—all of which constitute the elements of specific cultural systems; these systems compete with each other in the society. People more or less consciously follow certain patterns and represent them in their encounters in small groups or elsewhere. From this perspective, we do not have enough scientific testimony on the religious and ethnic diversification and its impact on mutual relations among people in small groups. Also we do not know enough how much small groups differ at the level of various national and class cultures.

A small group treated as a part of the complex organization functions best when it uses it skills, efforts, and strategies in a way that matches the demands of its task. A common difficulty in complex organizations arises in the attempt to define precisely enough the nature of group task. Various power centers within an organization may differ profoundly on what to expect from the task group and how to operationalize this expectation. Task groups may be efficient or inefficient depending upon which aspect of their performance is treated as basic. All of the *group-level* factors affecting task performance, namely group's norms, status relations, communication patterns, leadership structure, size, and cohesiveness, play a secondary role to the necessity to clarify the nature of the task.

MACRO-STRUCTURE

Organizational structure as "the relatively enduring allocation of work roles and administrative mechanisms that creates a pattern of interrelated work activities and allows the organization to conduct, coordinate, and control its work activities" is obviously a part of a reality historically given (Jackson and Morgan, p. 81). All the structural variables such as organization size, complexity or differentiation, formalization, control, administrative component, bureaucratization, centralization and levels of authority, can be abstracted from this reality but the question should be asked in this respect how much we are losing in insight by undertaking such an operation.

The study by the Aston group is very significant in this respect. On the basis of data from 46 work organizations located in the Birmingham, England area the authors of this study came to the conclusions that an organization with many specialists tends also to have more standard routines, more documentation, and a larger supportive hierarchy, as well as that the organizations high on specialization, standardization, and formalization tend to be low on centralization.

It is always useful to confront our commonsense knowledge with the empirical data in order to avoid being wrong. However, the reduction of these 46 work organizations to the sets of six components (specialization, standardization, formalization, centralization, configuration, and traditionalism) and later on to the four components (structuring of activities, concentration of authority, line control of work flow, and supportive component) obviously contains a certain cognitive cost which should be at least recognized.

In the Aston studies the best predictor is size but the following studies continued later on show that the size is not alone in its importance. *Both* technology and organization size have important effects on the structural pattern of organizations but by themselves do not determine the pattern.

The mutual relationship between the broader social structure and the organizational structure is quite complicated and any deterministic reasoning does not seem to be helpful in this respect. The environmental/structural match is actually crucial for the survival of organizations. The strategic decisions have to be taken by the organization leaders in order to achieve an adequate domain and to defend the *core technology* on which the organization is based.

It is possible to conceptualize the *adaptational process* in the terms of differentiation and integration. As external environment changes, uncertainty, and time span for receiving feedback increased, internal differentiation would also increase. The progress of differentiation creates a demand of integration at a higher level of development. The effective organizations are good on differentiation as well as on integration.

The basic organizational properties derive from the collective structure but at the same time they influence this structure. In the process of *organizing* several collective properties become evident. Organizational forms are limited by the existing knowledge of alternative forms available at the point in time when they are conceived. The existing objective and subjective resources limit the scope of organizations and influence their shapes. Depending how effective organizations are in finding for themselves some suitable opportunities in the society, they have more or less chance of success. The life-cycle of a given organization is very much influenced by the external conditions.

When the modern society becomes more and more organizationally dense, there are several new problems that arise out of it. One of them is the potential tension between organizations which are lacking a common denominator and struggle with each other to the detriment of public good. Another problem is the vulnerability of private life penetrated by organizations and becoming an object of their unscrupulous manipulation. Still another problem arises from the fact that the mutual relations between various organizations become more and more complicated and diversified. Boundary spanners are necessary as mediators between the organizations which need one another. There is a strong tendency to create coalitions which would be beneficial enough to keep organizations intact. The interests of the dominant coalition influence very much the structure, and the same is valid for the cause/effect belief systems as well as to the most appropriate means to achieve the goals and strategies. The managerial factors should be considered together with contextual factors in order to construct a realistic model of structural determination.

Unfortunately, there are not yet enough empirical studies dealing with the coalition formation and survival. Probably one of the reasons is that coalitions promoted by the private business are under the suspicion from the point of view of public interest. The control of coalitions is not easy and there are many problems related to it: How to control without harming the autonomy of partners involved in the coalition? Who is qualified to exercise the control? How much of the results of control may be useful for the general public?

Being a part of society any organization has some *uniqueness* but at the same time also some *universality* taken from a broader system. All research which is based on such universal concepts as "size," "technology," "control," and so on, may miss easily the social uniqueness as well as the social universality—as long as it uproots the organizational phenomena from their historical, cultural, political, and economic context. Weber constructed the model of bureaucracy as a helpful component of his broad humanistic studies based historically. We are now involved more and more in a very specific research on abstracted data taken out of the context under the assumption that historicity does no count because we can overcome it by acquiring a universal knowledge liberated from the time and space limitations.

Of course, this does not mean that the existing amount of research is necessarily useless but something very important is definitely missing in it. Organizations are constantly established and re-created in the acts of specific people under the specific historical circumstances. By reducing all organizations remaining under our investigations just to the general categories we may falsify the reality so much that the utility and adequacy of our knowledge may become endangered. For example, the model of bureaucracy as a universal concept may be very confusing when applied to various organizations taken away from their context. The Soviet bureaucracy is an entirely different thing than the British civil service.

The superficial similarities may be much more misleading than explanatory. The participatory system advocated by Likert may be "similar" to the totalitarian control system imposed by the Chinese communists under Mao but in reality they are totally different.

It is true that the ability of "size" to predict the level of structural characteristics was later on verified across societies; the relationships between context and structure remain relatively stable. However, what really counts are not universal categories but the *local* practice of doing something with them. Differences between units *within* an organization or a country are often greater than differences between organizations and countries (Jackson and Morgan, p. 93).

The choice given to the organizational leadership may be utilized in this or another way. Depending on the circumstances it may be proper to use a broad or narrow span of control, make the organization smaller or larger, and so forth. Of course, it is worthwhile to study how much various coordination types correlate with various organizational interdependencies and technologies (see the studies by J. D. Thompson) but the reduction of alternatives, done for the purpose of clarification, should not close us to the potential variety of alternatives.

In the social world the survival and change is the common problem of all organizational systems. This is a problem of a balance between the driving and the restraining forces; both of them are needed for the organization to survive and develop. The organizational life-cycles show a great need of organizational renewal based on learning and experimenting.

Functions and dysfunctions of power relations are one of the main objects of the sociological analysis, which tries to explain how organizational systems react to forces of change in an adaptive manner, why the social order persists despite internal and external pressures for change, which are the functions and causes of conflict (as well as of a relative equilibrium), how systems arrange their internal states and processes to be consistent with external demands, how the process of selective response to environmental change actually functions, and so forth. It is of crucial importance from this perspective to study how complex organizations achieve "a state that includes the acceptance of legitimate authority and compliance with its requests, a compliance that for many people extends to acts that they do not understand and that may violate many of their own values" (Katz and Kahn, p. 194).

The concept of ideal types is particularly useful in all considerations mentioned above. The more sharply and precisely the ideal type has been constructed—thus the more abstract in this sense it is—the better it is able to perform its functions in formulating terminology, classifications, and hypotheses (Weber).

The social science of organization has a great future in the modernized world characterized by a high organizational density and a rapid change. However, our present-day knowledge in this important field is too much limited only to the developed countries that follow the market economy. The sociocultural contingencies of organizational phenomena are still not adequately explored. There is not enough understanding how much organization differs depending on various branches of the economy, the level of national development, the ethnocultural characteristics of the population, and the influence of various vested interest groups located inside the organization or outside.

The comparative studies of organizations so far have not reached enough depth and they miss the socioanthropological perspective. The humanistic coefficient (Znaniecki) is quite often neglected and the social culture of a given organizational environment is missing in the dominant research perspective. The conflictual nature of organizations is now recognized at least at the theoretical level but the empirical studies of organizational conflicts remain relatively scarce. Generalizations formulated within the framework of organizational theory are not adequately qualified for time and place; their universality very often is highly questionable.

ORGANIZATIONAL STRUCTURE

The nature of organizational structure is approached by Richard Hall in the terms of three basic functions played by it: provision of a guarantee that organization will more or less fulfill some basic expectations regarding the output, minimalization of the potential individual variations, and creation of a basis for the exercise of power-making decisions and promotion of activities. Within the structure, tasks are allocated, control is exercised, the rationalization is formulated, people are socialized, forms of cooperation and conflict resolution are implemented.

Technology is one of the key determinants of structure, and this is also related to the raw material that the organization manipulates. Depending how many exceptional cases are encountered in a given work, and which is the nature of the *search process* involved, the organizational structure will differ accordingly (Perrow 1979). However, technology acts mainly at the level of work flow and the administrative element in large organizations remains relatively unaffected by technology. In addition, each of the various segments of an organization can have a structure quite different from those of other segments. Different units of the same organization often have different structural forms (Hall, p. 67). Probably various determinants affect structure in an interactive, rather than additive fashion (Ibid., p. 69).

It seems futile to treat technology from a deterministic perspective. As "the concept of technology is expanded, it becomes increasingly difficult to distinguish technology from other aspects of management and organization" (Jackson and Morgan, p. 208). The impact of technology does not seem to be all pervasive. There is little support to treat technology as an imperative. It is fruitful to pursue technological impact at the organizational subunit level, as well as to view technology as a moderator between other variables and structure.

Another problem is how to answer the question: what is technology? It is not easy to delimit and distinguish technology from other organizational variables. Technology is not just one thing. It has multiple dimensions which have to be taken into consideration.

Power is extremely difficult to identify and measure objectively. How to compare the different power relations existing between various organizational units? The scarce resources being available to some and not to others are the source of power as long as there is a demand of them and the organizational behavior can be controlled accordingly. These resources which are in excess of the minimum required to get the work done (slack resources) are an important factor of control. The appearance of power in one part of organization quite often provokes the establishment of power in other parts. For example, people exposed to power existing at the higher levels of the organizational hierarchy try to balance it by forming coalitions or building their own statuses. As regards individual subunits in an organization, their relative power is a function of the number of strategic contingencies controlled by each sub-unit.

Control is the link between the inputs, processes of conversion, and the outputs of the organization. With the growth of the total amount of control in a given organization, the effectiveness becomes adequately higher, and therefore there is an important organizational problem how to establish the conditions favorable for a high level of control. Both the *behavioral* control as well as the *output* control are needed in order to achieve an optimum. However, there may be a conflict between them. For example, too much of a behavioral control may influence negatively the outputs. The democratization of control may provide some positive results but not necessarily.

Rules, procedures, and policies are needed to keep an order but their stabilizing and objectifying effect may go too far. In the struggle between various forces of stability and flexibility the role of rules is to mark the compromise. This is not a passive role. The implementation of rules has an important socialization function within the limits of acceptance given them by the people. Vulnerability to the rules encourages the violation of them, especially when the sanctions are not strong. "A rule will be observed when the organizational or individual benefits (stability) derived from adherence exceed organizational or individual costs (tensions) associated with adherence; a rule will be ignored when the costs exceed the benefits" (Jackson and Morgan, p. 304).

Instead of looking for one structural determinant (technology, size, local tradition, and so forth) it seems more useful to treat organizational structures as *situationally* conditioned, and at the same time internally differentiated and remaining under the impact of a whole set of factors. For example, the hostile environment will inspire a different organizational structure than a friendly environment. The strategic choices made in organizations in the consequence of decisions agreed upon within a given organization (bounded rationality), also much influence the shape of the structure.

How "complex" are complex organizations? They become *complex* due to the horizontal differentiation, division of labor, vertical differentiation, and spatial dispersion. Organizations differ among themselves in their complexity depending on which field it appears. For example, organizations with an intense subdivision of labor tend to have less vertical differentiation. Those with horizontal differentiation due to the employment of specialists usually have rather tall hierarchies.

Regardless of the form of complexity, a high degree of it introduces to the organization problems of coordination, control, and communication (Hall, p. 93). In general, complexity depends on several factors, and its degree has to be adequate to the existing circumstances in order not to influence negatively the organizational effectiveness. Environmental and technical factors, together with the related consideration of the nature of the personnel, traditions, decision making, and other internal conditions, determine the form of an organization at any particular point in time (Ibid., p. 94).

Organizational *differentiation* may be measured according to such criteria as: the number of occupational specialties, the professional activity, the professional training, the number of different positions and different units, and so on. The *spatial dispersion* is related to the delegation of power, autonomy versus centralization, and several other organizational problems. *Vertical* differentiation is based on the depth of the hierarchy which influences very considerably the functioning of the whole organization; there are difficulties in control and communication in the case of tall hierarchies.

All three factors of complexity mentioned above vary independently of each other. Most organizations are complex in one of the various configurations. There is a strong tendency for organizations to become more complex as their own activities and the environment around them become more complex (Ibid., p. 86). In order to survive and succeed, organizations have to acquire such a measure of complexity as to fit into the challenges met by them. Organizations that survive become more complex. On the other hand, complexity is related to an intensified program change and this exposes the organization to several tensions, conflicts, and adaptational problems.

With the growing mutual involvement of organizations on the basis of joint programs the vulnerability becomes more acute. Organizations with many joint programs usually are more complex; that is they are more highly professionalized and have more diverse occupational structures.

THE METHODOLOGICAL PROBLEMS

The amount of organizational studies is rapidly growing in modern times due to the great interest in the application of them to the practice of structuralization. This does not mean that the scope and level of these studies is necessarily satisfactory. Several theories are not substantiated in their claims. For example, the open systems theory is organization-wide in its formulations but specific and testable only at the level of motivations, leadership, the work group, the job, and the like. Its true domain is in fact much more circumscribed than its generalizations (Miner, 1982:432).

The same is valid for several other theories. A limited set of variables is very helpful in making a theory really successful, as is evident with control theory or several subtheories focused on decision making and (primarily) on programmable decisions. Developing really specific, testable hypotheses in each limited domain is much more profitable than mere speculation.

It is also methodologically inefficient to focus on the normatively superior component of the domain to such a degree that little else can be learned (Ibid., p. 435). In many instances the research progress has proved that a given "macro" theory in reality occupies a smaller domain than initially anticipated. The main question is how much narrower a given generalization should be. This is valid, among others, to the role of core technology as a determinant of the total structure of large organizations.

The inability of theorists to formulate sufficiently valid constructs is a common weakness: there are many logical inconsistencies, formulations are mutually conflicting, statements are ambiguous, significant aspects are not adequately specified. For example, "technology as construct does not look powerful enough to advance knowledge of organizational structure and process, even if construct validity could be assured" (Ibid., p. 437). The looseness, ambiguity, and abstractness of constructs is particularly evident in various systems theories. "It is the essence of the systems approach that everything interacts with everything else, and accordingly these theories attract large numbers of variables, often to the point of threatening parsimony" (Ibid., p. 438). Several constructs are not operationalized consistently and precisely. The utilization of statements that are conflicting and imprecise leads to confusion.

The development of measures is much facilitated by the utilization of more precise constructs free from ambiguity and logical inconsistency. The more general concepts—for example, the concept of bureaucracy—become much more clearly recognizable when their methodological foundation is well made. For example, formalization, standardization, specialization, size, and hierarchy as the components of bureaucracy are very helpful.

The neglect of adequate measures is a major weakness.

Without constructs that are adequately and precisely defined and illustrated it is just impossible to generate measures that would guarantee an adequate reliability and validity. For example, the reports of respondents on their organizations may lack validity when the respondents know what the researchers want to hear.

The basic instrument has to remain the same over time in order to secure the reliable measurements. There is a clear connection between good constructs and good measures. Vague constructs tend to give birth to poor measures, as in the case of contingency theory, or to no measures at all, as in the case of classical management theory.

The lack of testable constructs makes the theories very weak. The systematic accumulation of knowledge and the progress toward the unification of the whole field are difficult to achieve as long theoretical weaknesses are widely tolerated. "Overlapping domains, uncharted areas, and numerous constructs with unknown relationships to each other assure the failure of any such unifying effort at the present time. Clearly, the theory of organizational structure and process has not as yet achieved what we would like from it" (Ibid., p. 453).

A good theory needs to settle on a limited set of directional, causal hypotheses of maximum explanatory, and/or predictive power. Some theories in the organizational field, particularly the systems theories, are very far from any methodological perfection. So far the field of organizational behavior shows a larger number of better theories than the field of organizational structure and process. "It may well be that a difference in the resistance of the subject matter to theoretical penetration constitutes the major factor" (Ibid., p. 456).

Much more has to be done in the organizational field.

There is a need to tie the various theories, with their different domains, together in some manner to yield the kind of "big picture" that general managers, corporate strategists, and even broadly concerned scientists desire. At the present stage in the development of the science, this is not possible. There is a clear need for research at the boundaries of theories and of their domains, and for more comparative analyses in which one theory is pitted against another to see which will do best in handling a particular problem. Some such research has been conducted; we need much more (Miner, 1980:417).

How strong are theories in predicting the performance of people? In several instances performance has not been predicted at all. Or other theories have proved successful but not under all circumstances. Motivational theories are better in this respect than those dealing with leadership. Achievements have been recorded by motivation theory, equity theory (for short periods of time), and goal-setting theory (not for everyone, or under all circumstances). The behavior modification techniques appear to work best in improving performance in the highly controllable contexts and with variables of an independent and separate nature, such as absenteeism. In more complex situations they work less well. The performance effects tend to peak and then taper off. The leadership theories work some times but not others. "There is no such thing as a general theory of performance at present, and there is little reason to believe one will emerge in the near future" (Ibid., p. 405).

As for predicting work satisfaction, not all theories focus on this subject. The best predictions of satisfaction come from expectancy and equity theories (Ibid., p. 406). Also the motivation-hygiene theory and the job characteristics theory both have proved to be useful.

REFERENCES

Barclay, Harold. 1982. *People Without Government: An Anthropology of Anarchism.* London: Kahn and Averill, with Cienfuegos Press.

Hall, Richard. 1982. *Organizations.* Englewood Cliffs, NJ: Prentice-Hall.

Jackson, John H., and Cyril P. Morgan. 1982. *Organization Theory: A Macro Perspective for Management.* 2nd ed. Englewood Cliffs, NJ: Prentice-Hall.

Katz, Daniel, and R. L. Kahn. 1978. *The Social Psychology of Organizations.* New York: Wiley.

Matejko, Alexander J. 1983. *Social Organization: A Dialectic and Existential Perspective.* Edmonton, Canada: University fo Alberta Bookstore. Mimeo.

Miner, John B. 1980. *Theories of Organizational Behavior.* Hinsdale, IL: Dryden Press.

————. 1982. *Theories of Organizational Structure and Process.* Chicago: Dryden Press.

Ridgeway, Cecilia L. 1983. *The Dynamics of Small Groups.* New York: St. Martin's.

Statistical Abstracts of the United States 1982/83. 1982. Washington: U.S. Bureau of the Census.

Taylor, Michael. 1982. *Community, Anarchy and Liberty.* Cambridge: Cambridge University Press.

3

ORGANIZATIONAL OPENING
TO NEW TECHNOLOGIES

WHAT IS MODERN ORGANIZATION?

An adequate coordination of activities and motivation of
those who are supposed to make their contribution is the
essence of any organization. Any social structure needs a
reinforcement in moral beliefs as well as in the collective
mutual dependencies and even pressures. As long as the
subordination of individual good to the common good remains
seen as an external, inevitable and impersonal condition,
people remain loyal. The disruption of social structure is
due to the split of loyalties as well as the growing conviction that the spirit of discipline and commitment are
objects of an external manipulation harmful to people
(Giddens and Mackenzie).

Expediency and coercion are not enough to keep the
organization going. The *internal* constraints of conviction
are badly needed in order to achieve any meaningful cohesiveness. The external observance of certain fixed rules of
outward conduct may be enough in the *static* societies but
are definitely inadequate when the society has to develop,
change, and adapt (Kumar 1978). This is one of the main
reasons why in modern societies the functioning and loyalty
of the "service class" becomes a question in several cases.
Modern bureaucracy has a very limited moral appeal and
this prevents it from fulfilling an integrative function.[1]
Organizational loyalties developing inside bureaucracies are
too conformistic and even fatalistic to prepare people
adequately to face change.[2]

Fatalism is based on the ideological constraints inherent in the structures of specific belief systems which prevent people question the nature of the system, for example, the caste structure of India. The acceptance of what is unavoidable limits the scope of choice and allows at most the *rebellion* remaining within the framework of a given system but excludes any major structural transformation. In the modern societies fatalism is treated as historical anachronism but at the same time the assumption taken for granted that *everything* may be changed makes the system very vulnerable to internal and external disruptive pressures.

The "service class" in this respect is in a very sensitive situation. On one hand, the traditional spirit of bureaucracy imposes on this class strong elements of conservatism, conformism and even fatalism. On the other hand, rapidly changing historical circumstances make it necessary to reform, question, and pursue new ways of thinking. Exposed to controversial expectation, members of the "service class" face the dilemma that is very difficult to handle effectively (Giddens and Mackenzie).

Functionaries depend on higher authorities to develop a system of practical behavior (recipe rules) for getting the job done. This system has to be in agreement with an *appearance code* of a given organization in order to avoid penalties. It is in the vested interest of the functionaries to avoid the penalty rules being selectively used against them. For example, police officers "know that if they fall from official grace they will be out on a limb on their own, or treated as a rotten apple fallen from the tree" (Shearing, p. 90). In order to avoid major trouble they follow the rules that keep them relatively safe:

1. Keep the working rules apart from the official rules; follow those rules that are under your direct control.[3]
2. Keep the working rules submerged and manipulate the official rules for your benefit.
3. One should take any precaution to avoid being found out; keep up appearances, even while engaging in practices that would belie them.
4. The formal rules provide the functionaries a discourse helpful to prepare the case fitting into the existing channels of communication and decision making (the construction of facts for a case).
5. The appearance of keeping the situation under control is crucial for organizational survival. People become expendable when they endanger the organizational image. Therefore, the manipulation of appearances is very important (Ibid., pp. 90–102).

There are many difficulties in complex organizations regarding priorities (what should be done first), competence of those who lead and those who are expected to follow, programming of action, execution of decisions, power games, and so forth.[4] There are various ways of approaching complex organizations and understanding their problems. A historical perspective on organizations helps to understand how they have developed and have met challenges of various kinds (Mouselij; Matejko).

The organizational intelligence is of a growing importance with the progress of modernization. Without this intelligence it would be impossible to deal with many problems that become more and more complicated. It is up to present-day managers of the public and private sector to appreciate the importance of adequate and reliable *information*. Organizational intelligence is an institutionalized mechanism of collecting such information and supplying it to the managers (Matejko; Wilensky). Any complex organization which faces the challenge of modern technology needs more *intelligence* than the traditional organizations. One of the aspects closely related to this problem is the matter of *creativity* and its place in an organization. Unfortunately, many managers still are not familiar with the character of the creative process and depend mostly on conformism.

The steps in the creative process are essentially the same as the steps in ordinary problem solving. "The difference lies in the degree of originality of the product" (Hare 1982, p. 11). If taking into consideration that "the creative person is essentially a nonconformist with the capacity to pursue nonconforming and creative ideas in the face of societal pressures to see things as others have seen them and leave things as other found them" (Ibid., p. 157) then the immediate small groups surrounding the individual has much to do with his or her creativity. In order to have the courage to look at things in another way it is necessary to be free from constraints which are particularly strong in a small intimate group. Adverse criticism devastates creativity. The individual quite often is unwilling to take a risk to appear to friends as different. As long as the small group subdues its members there is not much chance for any independent behavior, including creativity.[5]

Complex organizations are located within specific *cultures* and when estimating the adaptational capacity of these organizations to modern technology it is necessary to take this into consideration. The factor of culture is particularly strongly emphasized in the French studies of organization (Crozier and Friedberg 1980). For example, O. Kuty (1975) in his research of dialytic units (*les unités d'hemodialyse renale*) emphasizes that technology becomes to a considerable extent *reinterpreted* by the actors involved and therefore it would be very hazardous to take it in terms of a face value. A *strategic* analysis is needed in order to understand mutual relations between structure, culture, and technology. A comparison of four French units of dialysis of the same technological nature has shown the appearance of major differences among them originating from the basic approaches taken by people responsible for these units.

There is a major difference between a purely manipulatory approach to the patients and the arrangement under which the patient plays a participatory role. In some units all patients are admitted when other units are very selective in their admittance of people. The treatment of patients as a group makes much difference in comparison with the treatment of them primarily as individuals. The hierarchically oriented units much differ from the task-oriented units in the sense that in the former a strict division of labor is maintained and in the latter all team members cooperate closely, and even the patients are included in this cooperation. As regards the relative openness of a unit, the latter may be more or less willing to accept inputs coming from outside, and particularly from patients.

O. Kuty tries to show that the differentiation of organizational units will appear even under the same technology, and it is related mainly to the *orientation* of people responsible for a given unit; this orientation is founded on the cultural background of people who take the decisions. In the case of an authoritarian culture the situation will look differently in comparison with a democratic culture. The patient treated by a permissive medical doctor will react differently than the patient treated by a paternalistic doctor, even when both doctors follow the same kind of treatment (in a technological sense).

Doctors differ profoundly in their philosophy of medical treatment. Some of them want to control the patients and have a vested interest in keeping them passive. Others appeal to the cooperation of patients and act more as consultants than patrons (Kuty 1975, p. 211).

CONFLICT AND COOPERATION IN THE INNOVATIVE PROCESS

Labor process contains elements of cooperation as well as conflict, and it is necessary to consider the relative significance of both these strands in various settings. Legitimation may be organization-based or culturally based. The achievement of consent is a matter of modus vivendi between management and shop floor which may have little to do with generating, or reflecting, large-scale legitimations.

> Actual shopfloor behavior and relationships must be seen than not as consequences of the unilateral imposition by management on a passive work force of specifications and prescriptions, but a two-way exchange in which an accommodation concerning the meaning and relevance of such prescriptions is achieved in exchange for some level of commitment to the existing distribution of authority, and to working objectives (Littler 1982, p. 42).[6]

There is a historically rooted tradition of the managerial staff to be jealous about their prerogatives and hesitate to delegate power. A much more enlightened and progressive approach should be expected from the managers of public and private enterprises. They badly need an adequate training how to promote integration, as well as conflict resolution, without depending on the traditionalistic authoritarianism, which becomes obsolete in the modern times.

There are thousands of good reasons for keeping our mouths shut when seeing something wrong around us. Do not rock the boat! Smile at everybody because all people around you are your potential enemies! Do not open your heart because others will take advantage of your naiveté. If you want to enjoy the luxury of being moralistic just mail a few dollars to hungry people in Africa, criticize Reagan or Gorbachev, but do not try to advise your boss. Be always like others but at the same time deeply distrust people—even those who are supposed to help you as your teachers, medical specialists, politicians, and so on.

It is so comfortable to be expedient all the time and look for any occasion to achieve a success. Is it not our goal to outsmart others and in the final outcome achieve a total independence? Let others depend on us and not us depend on them. The ideal is to be alone in a big house surrounded by a high wall.

This *practical* reasoning has at least one important loophole. We want to have a nice feeling about ourselves and, exactly for this purpose, from time to time, we go beyond mere expediency. A student genuinely committed to learning will be ashamed at exercising pressure on the professor to obtain a better grade. People participating in the pursuit of a dignified social cause will sacrifice the concern about the "pecking order" for the sake of mutual appreciation and cooperation. A professional in a true sense of this word will defend the ethical standards of his or her job even at the expense of the reward.

THE RATIONAL MODEL OF ORGANIZATION

The spread of a rationalized mode of organization has contributed to the progressing depersonalization. By designing compulsion into the organization of the workplace it was possible to achieve more order and predictability but at the same time the diversity of interests between various partners of the production process became even more accentuated. Low mutual trust is now a matter of fact in the capitalistic enterprises as well as under state socialism. The system is highly vulnerable to tensions and shows low adaptability to changing circumstances. A genuine cooperation becomes something unnatural because partners follow blindly their own self-interests and are not open to the public good. When facing difficulties with employees, the employers prefer to substitute machines and transfer the responsibility for the discharged workers on the welfare state. The art of management has acquired a manipulatory character devoid of ethical considerations. The notion of a community of interest including all partners remains only a myth suitable for the sake of public relations but being very far from the daily reality of industrial relations.

Application of rationalized control management has reached its limits within the growing power of trade unions, interference of the public sector, the higher level of expectations among workers, and the failure of the system to fulfill its promises under captialism as well as under socialism. Several alternative social relations of production have gained in attractiveness: humanization schemes at the shop-floor level, job redesign, job enlargement and enrichment, new career opportunities, enlightened personnel management, team building practices following the Japanese patterns, permanent employment, the decentralization of decision making and the autonomization of the small work groups, encouragement of the individual and group initiative coming from the bottom, improvement of safety conditions, and so forth (Matejko).

However, any genuine humanization necessitates a much deeper reform based on communal ownership and workers' control. Is it a practical alternative to the unsatisfying status quo? There are several arguments in favor of this thesis: specialization is not incompatible with worker control; task fragmentation is not necessary for productive efficiency; self-management works well in many cases (Israeli kibbutzim, Swedish autonomous work teams, some workers councils); many cooperatives function very effectively on the free market; the much improved loyalty of partners reduces waste and tension; workers' control may be well reconciled with the professional management; the oligarchic rule is not unavoidable; the process of socialization occurring in the framework of industrial democracy is beneficial for the awareness of public interest among partners.

The anonymous control from the outside is definitely growing with the dominance of the economy by big corporations and governments; this leads to the alienation of immediate producers and consumers from the decision-making centers. Organizational policy is a weapon to subdue the lower level of the hierarchy to the wishes and interests of the highest levels without much concern to those at the bottom. In the name of rationality, people are deprived of the autonomy and have to follow orders which do not have much in common with the local circumstances and considerations. Bureaucracies show a vicious circle of decreasing efficiency and effectiveness.

THE INFORMATION REVOLUTION

The microelectronics revolution brings a declining labor intensity in several sectors of the developed economies (In the Chips . . .).

> The service sector, which has been such a bountiful supplier of new employment opportunities over the last twenty years, seems to be reaching a plateau in term of employment. In fact, with informatics eroding its clerical labor component and intensifying employment at the more senior levels, the entire sector could be entering a state of relatively static employment, although there are indications that the demand for domestic services will continue to increase (Menzies 1981, p. 77)

The labor content of clerical functions in becoming much reduced in banking, insurance, retail trade, secretarial work, and so on. Fewer clerical functions are provided for each type of service. Several clerical jobs formerly distinct become amalgamated. More clerical functions are completely eliminated. Performance supervision and staff training are taken over to a growing extent by computers, and therefore the supervisory requirements are reduced. There is an overall reduction in the clerical-labor content of information-related administrative and other functions. The multiple access to a common telecommunications work (*telematique*) makes possible a very considerable productivity gain, much higher than in the case of a diffusion of many independent informatics loci (*privatique*).

The problem is what to do with the large number of clerks, mostly women, who have a diminishing chance to enter the professional ranks, needed at the new technological level but recruited mostly from outside. The skills gap between clerical-type information work and professional- and technical-type information work is widening and the chance for the employee to move from the first to the second is very limited. The high-skill demand is filled by graduates of professional schools, and the clerks are forced to remain in the low skill-level jobs. More technical knowledge as well as sharper technical skills are in demand all over the developed countries, "As available jobs increasingly move beyond the skills reach of the average clerical worker, the skills barrier to occupational mobility will tend to aggravate the even more intractable problem of chronic unemployment if no changes elsewhere in the economy are assumed" (Ibid., p. 61).

The consumption-oriented expectations and ambitions of people relatively well educated (at least formally) inspire the growing demand for jobs among married women. However, where will they find these jobs when the clerical positions are diminishing in numbers and work content, and the professional positions are mostly occupied by men? The microelectronics revolution is potentially highly divisive at the social level by pushing a large number of people, especially women, to permanent unemployment, strengthening the professional-clerical gap, and practically eliminating the in-house promotion up the hierarchical ladder. A major effort of governments, federated employers, and trade unions is needed to promote computer literacy, retrain a large number of people for potential jobs, and take care of the negative consequences of the omnipotent computerization.

There are several savings from the introduction of information technology: lower spending on communication, office space, paper, and so forth; much higher white collar productivity, staff reductions, elimination of certain layers in the organization; replacement of the work of middle managers as information gatherers, filterers and analyzers; less need of data processing people. However, in order to obtain these savings it is necessary to have an adequate management of information resources. Data processing, communications, and office systems need to be adequately coordinated. Sometimes the data-processing and technical staff do not have enough understanding of their service function and are too jealous to share their competence. The wide introduction of microcomputers has abolished this data monopoly. Therefore, even more coordination of mutual services is badly needed in order to gain the full advantage of the existing needs and resources. Human aspects have to be taken into consideration: lighting, heat, glare, effects of video display terminals, work in isolation from others, the work load, adequate communication between the supervisors and subordinates, and so on (How to Deal, p. 53).

The wide application of standardized computer programs ("packages," "turnkey") leads to deskilling as well as to the tighter methods of control. The separation between conception and execution leads to deskilling. The direct-ness of immediate supervision is substituted by the direct-ness of output data. High purchasing and installation costs have so far limited the application of robots but the already existing technological conditions make many people feel like robots. On one hand, modern technology gives some people more job control. On the other hand, there is a growing gap between gainers and losers, regarding job content (Thompson, p. 115). The attempts of workers to retain control of job tasks and rewards meet some distinct limita-tions under the conditions of modern technology. The growth of the professional-managerial class leads to the tensions between various decision-makers (Ehrenreich and Ehrenreich 1979). However, even at the workers level there is much reason for disagreements, contrary to the traditional Marxist image of a united working class.

> Deskilling does *not* result in the homogenization of labor, but in an internally differentiated structure of dexterities and rewards with a variety of conse-quences for class formation. . . . The division of labor does not obliterate the existence of class, but it does structure the experience of class in such a way as to limit its oppositional character (Thomp-son, p. 232).

It is in the vested interest of employers to engage and control the work force simultaneously (Ibid., p. 255). This becomes much easier to achieve under the new conditions of the microelectronics revolution. However, a different problem is with involvement. People who are forced by circumstances to accept the working conditions may remain loyal but at the same time much dissatisfied. (For example, the work dissatisfaction has considerably grown in Canada during the last ten years, mainly because of the limited promotion opportunities, inadequate treatment by supervisors, and little chance to change jobs under the highly unfavorable labor-market conditions.) There is a perpetual struggle between supervisors and subordinates for the job controls but under the condition of computerization and the economic recession employees are quite often on the losing side, especially when they are not supported by the trade unions. "The strategy of refusal may be a 'luxury' no longer available" (Ibid., p. 245).

This negativism among employees is a commonplace which is quite uncomfortable for the employers who invest capital into the modern equipment and may lose much due to the lack of rank-and-file support. Some employers try to establish a cooperation with trade unions, as has been seen in Japan. However, the unions themselves have only a limited influence on their members (Crouch 1983) and even a much willing union is not able to make employees happy about jobs that have been deskilled. Some employers move their production to regions where a cheap and docile work force is available. It is quite common for many high-technology employers to avoid unionization, employ part-time workers, reduce unskilled and semiskilled manpower to a minimum, reward employees in a way conducive to loyalty (profit-sharing plans). All these measures promise only a limited success and the struggle for work controls probably will continue even under conditions of the most sophisticated technology. As long as humans are involved in the production process, and they much differ in power, privilege, rewards, or control, the industrial peace may be always upset by collective conflicts.

POWER AND MODERN TECHNOLOGY

Power considerations play a major role even in the field of technology. There are certain managerial assumptions in any piece of technical equipment but this does not necessarily mean that the shop-floor reality fits into them. The social and moral order existing in the workplaces is the outcome of confrontation among opposing vested interests and concerns; there is much of an effective resistance against the managerial orders at the lower levels of the hierarchy. The selling of a given technology as the best and therefore unavoidable is very often not effective because people are aware of vested interests hidden behind the smokescreen of rational argumentation. "Unless the underlying economic basis of alienation is removed, the attempt to bind management and labor into a unitary community is unlikely to promote industrial harmony for any length of time" (Hill, p. 102).

Within many existing technologies it is possible to choose how the social organization of production is to be arranged within the limits of what is feasible; also the market pressures do not determine managerial choice as closely as might be assumed. Technological determinism may be a handy camouflage of vested interests promoted by people of power and influence who want to manipulate their subordinates into a situation of dependence. "Attempts to use technology as an independent explanatory variable risk mystifying its nature by their failure to analyze the social processes that lie behind productive technique" (Ibid., p. 106). "There is no necessary logic of industrialism which creates one particular form of the division of labor or the trend of replacing human control by machines" (Ibid., p. 110). The massive deskilling of jobs is not just an automatic effect of technological progress but the conscious promotion by the managerial circles of a new status quo in which workers as partners would be eliminated (Thompson).

Why does the computer fascinate us? According to S. Turkle, "Behind the popular acceptance of the Freudian theory was a nervous, often guilty preoccupation with the self as sexual; behind the widespread interest in computational interpretations is an equally nervous preoccupation with the self as a machine. Playing with psychoanalytic and computational theories allows us to play with aspects of our nature that we experience as taboo" (p. 299). The machine aspects of our natures are not less interesting for us than our sexual and aggressive dimensions. At the same time there is something terrifying in the fact that computers upset the distinction between things and people. "It can no longer be simply the physical as opposed to the psychological. The computer too seems to have a psychology—it is a thing that is not quite a thing, a mind that is not quite a mind" (Ibid., p. 61).

Being an extension of our own mental and physical capacities, computers with their growing sophistication painfully reveal to us our own limits and incapacities. In this sense they "liberate" themselves from our control and impose upon us the feeling of incapacitation. They appear very often to be "smarter" than us, more reasonable and much more consistent in their functions. Their rules are projected upon us and much limit our freedom, even if at the same time we are able to achieve more by using computers.

The models on which computers are based have a great influence upon our present-day perception of ourselves and society. The nature of our brain may be understood much better than before on the basis of computers and the coexistence inside them of various programs. As formal systems, computers are necessarily "incomplete" and "imperfect" (Godel's theorem). If the formal system is really powerful there will be a question that can be posed within it which it cannot answer. If you are sufficiently strong you are by definition vulnerable and incomplete (Ibid., p. 304). Therefore, the growing power of computers and us as users of them brings the growing awareness how limited, vulnerable, and weak are our inventions. This is something contrary to the spirit of the nineteenth century when many thinking people had a very strong feeling of power and potential related to human reasoning.

The computer is for us a new mirror, the first psychological machine. People who are more and more lonely find the computer a peculiar companion without emotional demands. "You can interact, but need never feel vulnerable to another person" (Ibid., p. 307). In addition, it is a provocative companion, who claims that our mind is an imperfect machine. "The computational model of mind is another blow to our own sense of centrality. . . . The computer takes up where psychoanalysis left off. It takes the idea of a decentered self and makes it more concrete by modelling mind as a multiprocessing machine" (Ibid., p. 309) The fact that the place of instrumental reason in our culture becomes much magnified probably will reinforce a flattened, mechanical view of human nature and therefore expose all of us even more to omnipotent manipulation. On the other hand, the moral resistance to such a model may lead to the assertion that the human is the uncodable (Weizenbaum). "We may be machines, but it is our morality that unyields us to search for transcendence—in religion, history, art, the relationships in which we hope to live on" (Ibid., p. 311). Love and affection, spiritual urges, sensuality, warmth and familiarity of friendship, all of them make us definitely different from computers.

What will happen with our "rational" civilizational heritage when reason becomes the domain of machines and to us is left sensuality and emotion? "The computer presence gives new legitimacy to a set of values that many people did not find comfortable as long as they were associated with the East and opposed to science and reason" (Turkle, p. 312). Reasoning becomes the matter of computers but the spirit of our actions and their outcomes remain our own responsibility. The outcome of wars may be decided by the quality of computers but the moral essence of hostile actions belongs only to us. "Under pressure from the computer, the question of mind in relation to machine is becoming a central cultural preoccupation. It is becoming for us what sex was to the Victorians—threat and obsession, taboo and fascination" (Ibid., p. 313).[7]

The informational revolution (National Research Council) happening in our times opens not only new opportunities but also undermines several traditional structures of power (Abrahamsson 1977). The control of vital information was always a source of privilege. The managerial hierarchy is, among others, the instrument of people located at upper levels knowing more about the issues of a strategic importance than people down the ladder (Feldman and Arnold). Of course, this is more or less valid for the situation today. But computerization potentially makes possible to contact the sources of knowledge very easy and very fast (Dorf). What is more, superiors keeping important information to themselves act often against the vital interests of their institutions. The slowdown of decision making arising from the fact that each time the boss has to be personally contacted looks as an anachronism. And who really wants to appear as an enemy of efficiency? In the rapidly changing circumstances and the expensive modern equipment expected to prove itself as worth its high cost, decentralization of many decisions is a matter of necessity. The sophisticated labor power can be trusted. Bosses are too busy with other matters most of the time to be able to control what their subordinates are actually doing. Delegation of power is practical, under the circumstances, when communication with information sources is fast; it becomes more and more difficult to justify the fact that the decision has to wait until the boss will have enough time to deal with the case (Weiss and Barton).

ORGANIZATIONAL RIGIDITY
AS AN OBSTACLE TO INNOVATION

One of the major organizational difficulties arises from the fact that the traditional hierarchical structure does not fit into the technological realities. The successful companies depend more and more on flexible and better motivating forms: matrix organization, autonomous work groups, flextime, and so forth. Hierarchy is a device to reduce the uncertainty in the field of power and control; as long as technological innovations reshuffle this field, they contradict the hierarchy and lead to tensions. Therefore, very often, in order to accommodate major technological changes, top executives have to act against their own hierarchies by firing subordinates, reallocating power from the managers to the experts, transferring people from one place to another, and so on. It becomes more and more attractive just to change the whole system of management instead of being forced to inspire from time to time some "organizational revolutions."

The rigidity of organizational schemes has several social sources (Gendron). One of them is the fact that complex organizations are not only purposive units (rational, goal-oriented entities) but also they constitute the vital parts of a broader social structure. There are several vital reasons why several people want to keep this structure as stable as possible: vested material interests, fear of loss of power due to its redistribution, defense of status, fear against the unknown, negative feelings against the innovators, lack of self-assurance, and so on. It is much easier to pay lip service to the need for change than actually to face its consequences, especially when only some of the latter can be predicted. In addition, people may have an ambivalent attitude toward what they actually want: the fear of the unknown may be subconscious, it may be difficult to admit to oneself a lack of skills, imagination, and necessary courage, people may manifest a want of one thing but actually desire another thing.

The technical innovation quite often changes substantially circumstances under which things are being done (Bernard and Pelto; Marcson). New people have to be hired and their skills, as well as their aspirations, may be much different from those to which management is accustomed. Retraining of the personnel has to go together with the retraining of supervisors; the problem is that superiors are particularly sensitive not to reveal their weaknesses. There is usually the necessity of a major investment and the risk related to it imposes much stress upon the managers. The line-staff ratio also changes and this has several consequences for the style of management: experts have to be trusted and the control of their performance should be rather indirect than direct; inspiration and coordination functions have to be executed with the acknowledgment of the staff specificity; the professional values and aspirations of the personnel need to be recognized and incorporated into the system of incentives (Abrahamsson and Broström).

People belonging to a given workplace usually differ in the general orientation related to work. Some of them are more innovation-oriented than others and their status within the workplace has impact on the chance of success. As long as these people remain too much subordinated to the conservative centers of power and influence, there is not much chance for them to push effectively for innovation. Therefore, one of the organizational problems of strategic importance is ways and means to establish the *innovative target groups*. Some organizational forms—for example, the matrix organization—are in this respect more suitable than others. Change needs an organized power center willing and able to promote it. On the other hand, any rigid organizational forms and traditions create obstacles to change. The strategy of innovation necessitates resources, people, and clearly elaborated plans of what, when, and how it should be done. In several institutions there are units particularly dedicated to organization change. This may be much effective as long as they have enough power and capacity to promote innovations indirectly, by providing information, inspiration, and guidance. The direct involvement in innovation may have a discouraging effect on the remaining parts of the institution. A monopoly of innovation, limited to some people against all others, is not a suitable organization arrangement. It leads to conflicts of interests and a distance between those people who claim for themselves the status of innovators, and the rest.

The diagnosis of resistance to change is badly needed in order to establish adequate promotional policies (Johns). This resistance may come from a variety of sources. Some part of management is usually dedicated to the status quo and shows anxiety about any innovation. Enthusiasm about change may be a cover for keeping things as they are for as long as possible. There may be a conscious effort to make innovation harmless by accommodating it as much as possible to the current organizational practices and configurations of power. Such action quite often weakens very considerably the innovative project by making out of it just a repetition of the same traditional pattern that should be changed. Pseudo-innovations are pretended changes, which in reality represent the window-dressing devices.

A long-range perspective is badly needed in any serious attempt to make the innovation longitudinally useful (Dickson; Clark). Something of a considerable immediate utility may become a nuisance and a waste in the long run. Therefore, an innovation plan has to be designed, taking into consideration several manifest and latent consequences of a given change. Without such a perspective, organizational resources are improperly allocated and the innovation remains at the window-dressing level, instead of contributing to the organizational well-being.

With the technical innovation, a new spirit of human relations is needed in the workplace (Schaller; Shanks; Teich). Trust relations are often a necessity as long as it is organizationally difficult, inconvenient, and expensive to exercise a rigid control of performance. The innovative forms of social organization are badly needed and management is pressed to look for them as an alternative to the traditional organization, mainly bureaucracy (Matejko). However, new forms will not work as long as the management follows the old line, treating subordinates only as its tools.

In the conditions of a technological innovation there is a room for organizational experiments to activate subordinates in a participatory capacity. The *collegial arrangement* makes much sense as long as there is a demand for professional or at least semiprofessional commitment. The joint interest of various ranks in the excellence of a given project provides an appropriate room for a genuine cooperation. Any effort to make a "good climate" and "cooperation" working for their own sake is doomed to failure because a sound organizational and material basis has to be provided for teamwork. Only an involving and exciting joint work project may commit people at an adequate level. The trouble with many "workers' participation" projects is that they are not properly rooted in their mobilizing tasks. Any declaration of goodwill on the side of management has to be accompanied by a specific proposal what and how is expected to be done jointly. Of course, all the partners in a given project must have some stake in it. As long as they do not see this stake there is not much hope to involve them at the level beyond verbal declarations of goodwill.

Another question is how well management itself is prepared to face innovation. Lack of knowledge and understanding on the side of management may paralyze many good projects. Managers occupied with the current operation of the business quite often have neither time nor patience to gain an adequate expertise. They delegate this task to their assistants and the lower-ranking personnel but at the same time they themselves do not have enough authority to give the innovation an adequate push and support. Under such circumstances it is better to delegate the whole responsibility for innovation to the team of knowledgeable and responsible people.

The risks of innovation have to be recognized by all sides. Failure may originate from several organizational units quite distant from the main location of the innovation. For example, when the repair and maintenance services are not adequately prepared well in advance, the purchasers of a given new gadget would be exposed to much disappointment, not due to the inadequate quality of this gadget but due to the nuisance in obtaining an appropriate service. Several aspects of the innovation have to come into consideration and need a careful scrutiny.

THE IMPACT OF LABOR-MANAGEMENT RELATIONS

Changes provoked by technical innovations have to be accommodated within the framework of labor-management relations (System Organization . . .). As long as "antagonistic cooperation" prevails not much is needed in order to provoke a conflict. Collective bargaining as practiced so far in the West remains a relatively rigid arrangement and it is not easy to make it more flexible. Trade unions have several good reasons to take a defensive attitude; many of their members become unemployed due to the introduction of labor-saving devices; there is not enough foresight in planning what to do with the surplus people; management quite often takes advantage of any formal excuse not to take responsibility itself for what happens with people.

There is in the innovative enterprises an obvious need, or even a necessity, to open the channels of communication with employees in order to prepare them adequately for change. Management, with consultation by experts, takes the initiative to introduce innovative forms: quality circles, information committees, briefing groups, problem-solving teams, autonomous work groups, and so on. One touchy question is how much the innovations may change the power balance between the basic groups involved: various management levels, experts, manual workers, clerks, union stewards and leaders, activists of the internal self-governmental bodies, and so forth. Each of these has its own vested interests, specific points of view, idiosyncrasies of various kinds. Much sophistication and tact is needed on the side of management in order to avoid tensions and misunderstandings, which may make the innovation impossible (Crosby; Dubois; Mars; Littman).

With the growing democratization of the workplaces it is

highly probable that the *social organization* of the employees will grow in power independently of management as well as unions. This organization has traditionally existed at the informal level but now more and more it takes a formal shape. Unions tend to treat this organization as a potential danger to their control and also are afraid of the influence exercised by management. As long as there are strong common interests between various formal employee groups and the managerial ranks, the mobilization power represented by the union remains limited by several external factors. Unions in their policies are not able to focus mainly on a specific workplace but have to follow the interests of their membership at large. As long as the local employees depend only on the union and do not have their own institutionalized power, it is relatively easy to keep them under control. On the side of management two different considerations play a role. On the one hand, management is much tempted to weaken the union by helping establish another local partner. On the other hand, it may be easier to bargain only with the union (or a coalition of unions) than with several partners representing highly diversified interests.

The pluralistic arrangement is the product of various trends. The highly skilled personnel differs internally and externally in the whole variety of aspects and is internally divided into various subgroups. Introduction of new equipment creates teams of a more or less evident identity (project groups, and so forth). People who are jointly appointed to a new technical task quite often develop a spirit of comradeship badly needed in order to face the uncertainty. In order to achieve the success, management has to delegate, at least temporarily, much of its power to people directly involved in the project. Professionalism of the personnel tends to make pluralism much more probable than the traditional hierarchical arrangement (Giddens and Mackenzie).

Even when control remains centralized it differs from the *personal dependence* characteristic for the low level of technology. People communicate with each other utilizing some technical equipment and they remain separated territorially. Of course, even under such circumstances tensions and personal unpleasantries are still possible, but at least the stress of staying close together is not there.

One of the problems with the new social organization is its orientation. Whether or not the new groups are positively or negatively oriented to jobs, partners, superiors, subordinates, and the employer depends on the number of

circumstances. As long as the volume of necessary investment grows, there is more and more danger of waste arising
from mutual misunderstandings, negative attitudes, differing
vested interests, and so forth. It is enough for a small
part of the labor power acting negatively (sabotage, slowdown, strike) in order to paralyze all the rest. Therefore,
good management-labor relations are a particularly sensitive
issue. Responsible management is aware of the fact that
machines do not work by themselves and it is worthwhile to
invest into the good climate of human relations.

THE SOCIAL ASPECTS OF
HUMAN ENGINEERING

In the literature on social consequences of modern technology quite often there is a tendency to exaggerate the
dependence of people on machines (Marcson; Moore).
Behind the sophisticated pieces of technical equipment there
are always individuals and organizational arrangements.
Persons can spoil the machines. Due to an inadequate
organizational solution, technical investment may be wasted
because of the machines remaining idle or not loaded heavily
enough. The foresight and the sense of duty both are
badly needed and both of them depend much on the climate
of industrial relations.

A special issue is work safety (Reasons et al.). In
several cases we are still far from knowing the actual
impact of modern equipment on human health. However, we
know enough to warn people and enterprises against using
machines in a way dangerous to people who serve them or
remain close to them in any other capacity. Cooperation
between management, unions, and employees is of a crucial
importance in this respect. Joint safety committees meet
some difficulties arising from the fact that management feels
endangered in its prerogatives in the case of the union or
the employees being able to formulate some demands and
recommendations that are either expensive, or even stop-
ping the production.

Here is a very sensitive issue which cannot be solved
without a good measure of mutual trust. Excessive demands
may endanger the rentability of production. On the other
hand, lack of external control may endanger human lives.
The power struggle developing under the guise of safety
concerns is a very important aspect of technical modernization.

This is an additional reason to take seriously the quality of working life (QWL) activity as a joint project of management and labor. It is a very important task of the public authorities to promote QWL and offer facilities suitable for the growth of this activity. For example, in Canada since 1984 there is the Canadian Labor Market and Productivity Center initiated by the federal government but administered jointly by management and organized labor.

There is a practical question how far collective bargaining (Morici et al.) may be extended to the QWL field without unnecessary formalization and even bureaucratization of projects that should remain spontaneous, free from any rigidity, and based primarily on local initiatives. It is obvious that the collective-bargaining mechanism is necessary to open room for QWL and at least allow initiatives to be recognized. However, not much more may be expected. The management-union contract has a legal character and this may become an obstacle for such projects which are impossible to plan much in advance. Any attempt to squeeze QWL into the channels of collective bargaining may be negative because the main purposes of both of them much differ.

There is always a potential danger that both management and unions may do much harm to the QWL by patronizing the actions which in their true nature have to be initiated, implemented, and evaluated by people themselves. Bureaucracies, including the management and union forms, do not tolerate anything growing outside their established channels. Modern technology often grows so fast that any formal channeling may have only a damaging effect. A very considerable field of free activity has to be left alone in order to mature gradually to some future regulation. It is a well-known fact that bureaucracies are usually very slow to innovate because they are too much oriented toward safety.

HANDLING OF STRAIN AND STRESS

By the introduction of new technology the organization exposes itself to several strains. The task performance may slow down temporarily quite substantially. Communication and cooperation among various organizational units meets resistance arising from the fact that something unknown is introduced into mutual relations. Personnel has to adapt to new schedules and new duties. Usually it takes a considerable time to adapt to new conditions and incorporate the technical innovation into the existing framework.

It is always an open question how much novelty the organization has to introduce in order to be effective under the changing circumstances. Would it not just be better to start another organization which would be more suitable? The existing tradition may appear to be such a heavy burden that it is even not worth to be bothered with overcoming resistances arising from the simple fact that the "old" organization was arranged for different purposes. In any case, it is usually advisable at least to designate a specific new organizational unit focused on a new project and autonomous enough to be free from resistance.

To achieve the necessary organizational cooperation is always a sensitive issue (Vaughan). There are various ways to establish necessary action groups (target teams) responsible for a given project and enjoying a green light in this respect. It is important not to dilute personal responsibility.

The establishment of rules and adherence to them is basic for the process or organizing (Robey). It is a valid question under which circumstances people are willing and able to take both conditions for granted: the rule of order, and the subordination of private good to the common good. *Value systems* have much to do with it as well as a *situation* more or less conducive to obedience. *Reduction of uncertainty* achieved thanks to the existence of organization happens due to identification of this uncertainty and the removal of the latter by: enactment (creation of a necessary information), selection (organization muddles through the alternative itineraries of action overcoming difficulties), and retention of the information or experience (Weick). The organizational potential depends much on the conditions under which the mobilization of necessary resources (people, technology, information, and so on) happens. In their growth, organizations meet several *crisis situations* related to the quality of leadership, autonomy, control, red tape, and so forth. The survival of the organization and its success depend much upon the way the organization handles a given crisis.

The proper design of organizational structures has much to do with the ability of a given institution to handle adequately the innovation (Peters and Waterman). Organizational structure is treated as "the relatively enduring allocation of work roles and administrative mechanisms that creates a pattern of interrelated work activities and allows the organization to conduct, coordinate, and control its activities" (Jackson and Morgan, p. 81). The Aston's group research has stated that structures have four independent dimensions: structuring of activities (specialization, standardization, formalization, vertical span of control); concentration of authority; line control of work flow; and supportive component. The following research studies have introduced some corrections into this image. The main factor seems to be that the more effective firms do a better job of contingently matching their structures to the demands of their situation (Ibid., p. 89). It is clear also that cultural differences do not affect the relationships among the structural characteristics, or those between structure and size, or technology and autonomy.

There is a need to treat structures only as vehicles of performance and success instead of taking them as *fixed entities*; it seems better not to be overtly committed to a given structure only because it does exist. On the other hand, some continuity is also needed and the unjustified move from one structure to another may disrupt the harmony, in addition to the cost.

New technology may be a source of stress for employees as well as for management (Karmous et al.). As long as personal expectations and needs do not harmonize with the reality, there is always a possibility of tension. Quite often the modern pieces of technical equipment make necessary the development of sharp attention and precision, which was not so much needed before. The logic of machines imposes demands upon the human mind. Another aspect is the new relation to clients dictated by the "professional smile," characteristic among others for the flight attendants (Hochschild) as a supplement of the "friendly" machine. The standardization of human behavior goes together with the standardization of technology. For humans it is not easy to carry the emotional cost of business smiles. The business of "processing" people expects from workers to show smiles being *on* them but not necessarily *of* them.

A relaxed approach of management may help much to absorb modern technology by the employees without necessarily experiencing stress. Many pressures may be released by creating a good atmosphere of human relations. Leisure may enter and there is not necessarily a conflict between a relaxed, leisurely attitude and a serious approach to duty (Parker).

There are several general problems arising when the new technology enters a given workplace. It is up to innovators to be aware of them as well as pay attention to several locally specific issues, which may not appear somewhere else. Innovative sensitivity is needed not only for managers but also for the trade-union activists.

THE POLICY FOUNDATIONS

The concept of "evolving" is essential in order to understand the flexible and multidimensional process of planning
technological change, remaining flexible but also consistent
at the same time, recommending solutions to the problems.
There is a need to upgrade the quality of policy forming
and execution. Another task is to provide intelligence data
needed for various policies. Still another problem is related
to the training and consultation needed in order to upgrade
the skills of policy agents. How to get oriented to the
policy process? How to locate problems with respect to
their status or maturity somewhere within the policy process? How to organize, compare, and accumulate knowledge
about the policy process itself? How to coordinate the roles
of various persons, groups, and institutions in the policy
process? What goal values are sought and by whom? What
trends affect realization of these values? What factors are
responsible for the trends? What is the possible course of
future events and development? What can be done to
change that course to realize or achieve more of the desired
goals, and for whom? All such questions have to be answered within the framework of policy analysis.
     Policy analysis is seriously disadvantaged by social
complexity, uncertainties about the future, and the diversity of human values. In addition, policy analysts themselves
bring into the picture their own preferences.

> Human values are the crux of policy sciences;
> problems for analysis are generated by the society
> at large, not by the theoretical inquiries of the
> scientific disciplines; and analyses must include
> many individual perspectives and should aim to be
> practical while striving to improve the policy pro-
> cesses responsible to and benefiting humankind
> (Brewer and deLeon 1983, p. 6).

There are four basic types of policies (distributive,
competitive regulatory, protective regulatory, and redistributive). These policies differ much in the likelihood of
generally accepted stable implementation routines, degree of
stability of identity of principal actors and the nature of
their relationships, degree of conflict and controversy over
implementation, degree of opposition to bureaucratic implementation decisions, degree of ideology in debate over
implementation, and the degree of pressures for less government activity (Ripley and Franklin). Various organizational bodies react to policies according to their vul-

nerability, competence, and vested interests.[8]

Initiation of a policy starts with the problem recognition or identification. Next comes the estimation of various policy options, in terms of costs and benefits. This leads to the selection of most beneficial options (beneficial for whom?). The execution of the chosen option is the next stage after which comes evaluation what has been actually achieved. Finally, come the concerns for adjustment of policies, programs, and organizations that have been dysfunctional and redundant.

A faulty problem definition may damage the whole policy process. "A dereliction of responsibilities during the initiation phase can postpone, impair, or even negate the rest of the policy process" (Brewer and deLeon 1983, p. 32). There are four basic elements of initiation: recognition of the problem, identification of the problem context and its time constraints, determination of goals and objectives, and the generation of alternatives. One of the valid questions is how sensitive are organizational agents of a given policy. Bureaucratization quite often lowers this sensitivity because institutions follow their own programs without paying attention to the changing environment and various setups in it (bounded rationality). Their reactions are lacking rapidity, selectivity, validity, and comprehensiveness. In bureaucracies, internal goals take priority over external goals and this creates several problems, among others, the difficulty to terminate programs which are inefficient or obsolete.

Diagnosis should be focused on the root causes of the problems but quite often is actually limited only to some manifest aspects. "The complexity of the subject matter; on the one hand, and our limited intellectual and operational capacities for analysis, on the other, require us to simplify; yet the implications of doing so are seldom considered by analysts and decision-makers" (Ibid., p. 88). It is necessary to sense and assess the variety of time and place dimensions; loads, lags, leads, and gains have to be taken into consideration. "Control in a system varies inversely with the degree of load and lag, directly with the amount of lead, and, up to the point of overcontrol or overresponse, directly with the amount of gain" (Ibid., p. 95). Diagnosis has been done very often on the basis of scant information, under constricting time pressures, with only a limited ability to consider the variety of consequences related to several alternatives.

The complexity of policy situations has to be dealt with in order to reduce it to a manageable amount. One useful procedure is to model the complexity in order to reconfigure the given system; for instance, to apply the model of conditioned organizational behavior. Another procedure is to formulate policy alternatives in order to gain a perspective. Problem diagnosis and rediagnosis (concentration on structural certainties, focus on changes, establishment of priorities among competing problems) is a third possible procedure. The aggregation of information is another procedure; also aggregation of preferences.

THE SOCIOTECHNICAL PATH

Every policy has its critical path which has to be analyzed not only from the perspective of ordered, component tasks or alternative means but also values, time, distance, cost, or another metric. However, "at best, any analysis provides a single perspective on a problem, one that is sensitive to and qualified by the steps taken to create it" (Ibid., p. 124). Therefore, there is always a need of complementary analyses to formulate the diagnosis according to various distinct capabilities, biases, perspectives, and expectations.

In the contradiction between *simplicity* and disorganized *complexity* there should be a room for a reasonable compromise: an organized complexity. It is necessary to take for granted that every analysis represents a simplified, abstracted, incomplete, and inadequate view of the problem. This does not eliminate the usefulness of making analyses but leaves enough room for doubt and criticism.

The stage of selecting one from the available policy alternatives is the most overtly political stage in which bargaining between several involved interest groups plays an important role. "The political process requires consensus, but the very act of exploring options and trying to attain consensus heightens awareness of the many interests and values at stake" (Ibid., p. 181). There is a question how to reconcile various pressures and demands imposed on the policy makers and implementers. Various expectations have to be recognized without necessarily making the whole policy dependent on them. One problem is to keep people happy. Another problem is to serve the company and public good in the best possible way. There seems to be too much preoccupation with the manipulatory aspect of policies to the detriment of the broader utility.

Evaluation of policies has to be understood within a broad concept of system performance: systemic standards on which judgments or decisions may be applied, various tools, techniques, and approaches. The classification of operating goals is necessary to formulate the criteria of its performance. Which values are foregone and sacrificed in the process of goal fulfillment? How are benefits related to costs? Is it possible to establish the reliable criteria or performance? How to locate inputs and outputs? Which measurement strategy should be applied? How to specify the impact evaluation? How to locate the deficiencies of a given policy? There are many questions of such a kind that need to be answered in relation to the specific time and place.

The success of policy implementation may be measured by the compliance of policy executors to the established program, smoothness (lack of disruption) of policy implementation, impact of the program, and satisfaction of clients. Quite often the effect of a given policy may be measured only in a long time perspective, and the positive or negative reaction to the program arises mostly from the short-term gains or losses of people involved. The impact of the policies should be assessed much in advance but it does not work this way even in the U.S. government. [9]

> Congress usually contents itself with a few anecdotes if it asks very serious questions at all. Many bureaucratic agencies content themselves with the same fare, and that is all they are required to pass in to Congress. . . . Attention to implementation as a separate phenomenon is not a high priority or conducted at a very high level by most of the political actors. . . . The major congressional concern having to do with implementation is simply seeing that money is spent and that it is done so in timely fashion . . . and without inordinate theft (Ripley and Franklin 1982, p. 202).

Sometimes policies may be products of events remaining beyond the control of people who are supposed to make decisions and selections. The incremental decision making obscures the fact who, when, and why takes responsibility for a given policy and which are the implications of this fact. The context of the problem, points of leverage (variables which can be manipulated by the decision-maker), importance of the problem, availability of information, and the personalities of participants—all these factors have to be recognized and be adequately considered. Local values, importance of time factor and its effect on the context of an issue, level of analysis (individual, group, general system, interaction between major systems), political culture, timing and sequencing of events, the power of the public mood, countervailing powers—all of them have to be considered. The priorities of decision-makers may be much biased. The necessary information may be missing. The sources of insight may be misleading. The intelligence source may be confidential. Personal indiosyncrasies may much influence the decision-making process. All these factors and circumstances complicate the policy making.

Bargaining and making compromises is an important part of any policy. There is a need to build coalitions in order to make possible certain achievements. "The total number of issues pressing for attention must be kept small, and for those treated, their importance must be minimized or diligently focused" (Brewer and deLeon 1983, p. 215). Usually there is a whole variety of alternative ways to handle a given problem and the final choice of which of them to implement depends on many factors.

Implementation used to be quite often neglected in analytical policy studies but recently there is a growing interest in it. General goals and objectives must be identified and specified in operational terms. Specific, realistic contexts in which decisions are made and results are sought, have to be sensitively appreciated. Past practices and procedures have to be acknowledged. The following factors deserve a particular attention: source of policy, clarity of the policy, support of the policy, complexity of the administration, incentives for implementers, resource allocation. There are various phases of policy implementation: initial introduction, reaction, partial incorporation, acceptance, and routinization. Depending upon the level of certainty, level of knowledge and goals searched for, the implementation of policy may happen by calculation, judgment, adjustment, or inspiration. There is much stress on implementators and its nature has to be recognized.

The resistance against the program being terminated usually is quite strong and it is necessary to take this factor under consideration. People react by resigning from their jobs and privileges; clients expect the services to be continued; decision-makers have their stake to continue what they have done so far. Functions may continue under a different organizational set. Organizations are deliberately designed for long-term operations. Programs and policies are relatively easy to terminate but the consequences of their elimination have to be acknowledged from the beginning. Partial termination is quite common in the form of replacing, consolidating, splitting, decrementing, or discontinuing.

NOTES

1. Bureaucracies quite often do not perform at the necessary level of efficiency because of their avoidance of any risk, political pressures, favoritism, red tape, and financial security (Ripley and Franklin 1982).

2. This is already a good reason to question the adequacy of bureaucracy to the exigencies of the post-industrial society.

3. The principle "never squeal on a fellow officer" is widely used in the police force. With the organizational system becoming more complicated and exposed to contradictory expectations there is a tendency of "service class" people to depend on each other more than on the code of professional ethics. This defensive orientation contributes to the growing gap between the formal system and the informal arrangements dominated by local coalitions of interests. Formal structures which are not realistic enough encourage and even legitimate the violation of norms.

It seems necessary to mention that the impotence of the functionaries within their organizations, and not only their unlimited power, may breed corruption. For example, it happens quite often to the police force that in order to fulfill duties they are put into a situation where it is necessary to exceed operational capabilities by using illegal measures. According to J. P. Brodeur, therefore "the proliferation of desirable legal checks upon the behavior and operations of the police will only add to their impotence, thus generating more deviance" (Shearing, p. 152).

4. Organizational behavior is, according to Mintzberg (1983), a power game in which various influencers see the control of the organization's decisions and actions. The configuration of organizational power is an outcome of that game. There are several bases of power (resource, technical skill, knowledge, legal prerogatives, access) but *will* and *skill* are needed in order to make a full use of them. There are internal and external *influencers* who act individually or in coalitions. In the first category are top managers, operators, line managers, analysts of the technostructure, the support staff, and ideologists. In the second category are owners, suppliers, and clients, employee associations, publics and directors.

5. The model of group analysis applied by Hare (1982) is taken over from T. Parsons. Values, norms regulating role relationships, the leadership and the utilization of resources are considered at the four major system levels: cultural, social system, personality, and biological. Hare

tries to reconcile the dimensions of behavior in groups formulated by Parsons with the dimensions formulated by Bales. He suggests that when a group is working on a problem of *pattern maintenance,* the conforming-nonconforming process dimension will be the most salient; when the problem is *integration,* the positive-negative dimension will be salient; when the problem is *goal-attainment,* the dominant-submissive dimension will be salient; and when the problem is *adaptation,* the serious-expressive dimension will be salient (Ibid., p. 42). This is a suggestion where to focus attention depending what is at stake.

When the social interaction takes the form of a *drama,* the dramaturgical analysis is applicable. Various roles in the drama are identified: director, protagonist, antagonist, supporting member, audience members. There are various stages of drama development and they have to be taken into consideration.

6. Littler makes a distinction between three levels of work structuralization: the area of work design, the formal authority structure of the factory, the relation of job positions to the labor market. "Whilst there is a tendency for changes in job design, control structures and employment relations to go together, this is only a tendency and not a necessity. . . . The introduction of new technology formed the base for the erection of bureaucratic structures of control, nevertheless the bureaucratization of the administration of production does not *entail* deskilling" (Ibid., p. 43).

From this perspective, the bureaucratization of the structure of control and the bureaucratization of the employment relations are two different processes. The dependency of workers is at a maximum when the employer has much to say in every aspect on their lives and when there is a little chance to organize a collective opposition against him. On the other hand, the *indirect* employment and control, based on domestic system or an internal contract may make workers even more dependent than the direct employment and control.

7. The conclusions summarized above were formulated in an empirical study which included, among others, interviews with 200 children and more than 200 adults who had a variety of reasons for using the computer.

8. For example, the United States Congress is most likely to intervene in those policies in which the tangible benefits are going to influential constituents, or when there is a coalition between bureaucrats and congressional constitutents. Consumer groups so far are able to exercise

only a sporadic influence, and therefore they do not count much.

9. It is up to the experts to judge the ultimate facilitating or nonfacilitating impact of various policy-implementation options. It happens that for the sake of political convenience the real impact of a given policy is consciously neglected. There is a need of better management, delegation of power to the other bodies whenever this is suitable, offering of responsibility-sharing to the local branches, coordination of various programs, networking of supporters at the local level, refinement of program design and expectations. All these things become particularly important in the public sector, especially when this sector becomes so large as now this happens in several industrial democracies. The growth of government (in the United States from 26 percent of GNP to 38 percent in the period 1950–77) is a common fact in industrial democracies particularly at the middle and lower level; in the United States, the share of the federal level in the total government civil employment has diminished from 38 percent to 18 percent in the period 1951–81. The number of governmental programs multiplies all the time and it is of great importance how effective they really are. "Goals are vague to accommodate multiple points of view, and translating that vagueness into specific concrete implementation actions renews the potential for conflict and compromise" (Ripley and Franklin 1982, p. 28).

The governmental policies need effective controls not only of a formal nature (auditing) but also from the general perspective of their effectiveness. Social sciences have much to offer in this respect, and social technology has a distinct future.

REFERENCES

Abrahamsson, Bengt, and Anders Broström. 1980. *The Rights of Labor*. Beverly Hills, CA: Sage.
Abrahamsson, Bengt. 1977. *Bureaucracy or Participation. The Logic of Organization*. Beverly Hills, CA: Sage.
Bernard, H. Russel, and Pertti J. Pelto, eds. 1972. *Technology and Social Change*. New York: Macmillan.
Braverman, H. 1974. *Labor and Monopoly Capital: The Degradation of Work in the Twentieth Century*. London: Monthly Review Press.

Brever, Garry D., and Peter deLeon. 1983. *The Foundation of Policy Analysis*. Homewood, IL: Dorsey.

Clark, Peter A. 1972. *Action Research and Organizational Change*. London: Harper and Row.

Crosby, Faye J. 1982. *Relative Deprivation and Working Woman*. London: Oxford University Press.

Crouch, Colin. 1982. *Trade Unions: The Logic of Collective Action*. Glasgow: Fontana.

Crozier, Michel, and Erhard Friedberg. 1980. *Actors and Systems: The Politics of Collective Action*. Chicago: University of Chicago Press.

Daniel, W. W., and Nell Millward. 1983. *Workplace Industrial Relations in Britain. The DE/PSI/SSRC Survey*. London: Heinemann Educational Books.

Dickson, David. 1974. *Alternative Technology and the Politics of Technical Change*. Glasgow: Fontana.

Dubois, Pierre. 1979. *Sabotage in Industry*. Harmondsworth, England: Penguin Books.

Dorf, R. C. 1974. *Technology and Society*. San Francisco: Boyd & Frazer.

Edwards, P. K., and Hugh Scullion. 1982. *The Social Organization of Industrial Conflict. Control and Resistance in the Workplace*. Oxford: Basil Blackwell.

Edwards, R. 1979. *Contested Terrain: The Transformation of the Workplace in the Twentieth Century*. London: Heinemann.

Ehrenreich, B., and J. Ehrenreich. 1979. "The Professional-Managerial Class." In *Between Labour and Capital*, edited by P. Walker. Brighton, England: Harvester.

Feldman, Daniel C., and Hugh J. Arnold. 1983. *Managing Individual and Group Behavior in Organizations*. New York: McGraw-Hill.

Gendron, Bernard. 1977. *Technology and the Human Condition*. New York: St. Martin's.

Giddens, Anthony, and G. MacKenzie, eds. 1982. *Social Class and the Division of Labour. Essays in honour of Illya Neustadt*. London: Cambridge University Press.

Gospel, Howard F., and Craig R. Littler, eds. 1983. *Managerial Strategies and Industrial Relations. A Historical and Comparative Study*. London: Heinemann Educational Books.

Hare, A. Paul. 1982. *Creativity in Small Groups*. Beverly Hills, CA: Sage.

Hill, Stephen. 1981. *Competition and Control at Work. The New Industrial Sociology*. Cambridge: The MIT Press.

Hochschild, Arlie Russell. 1983. *The Managed Heart.*

Commercialization of Human Feeling. Berkeley and Los Angeles: University of California Press.

"How to Deal with the Impact of Information Technology." *The Financial Post,* 13 October 1984, p. 53.

In the Chips: Opportunities, People, Partnerships. Report of the Labour Canada Force on Micro-Electronics and Employment. 1982. Ottawa: Minister of Supply and Services.

Jackson, John H., and Cyril P. Morgan. 1982. *Organization Theory. A Macro Perspective for Management.* 2d ed. Englewood Cliffs, NJ: Prentice-Hall.

Johns, E. A. 1973. *The Sociology of Organizational Change.* Oxford: Pergamon.

Karmous, Wilfried, Verena Müller, and Gerd Schienstock. 1979. *Stress in der Arbeitswelt.* Cologne: Bund-Verlag.

Kumar, Krishnan. 1978. *Prophecy and Progress. The Sociology of Post Industrial Society.* Harmondsworth, England: Penguin.

Kuty, Olgierd. 1975. "Orientation culturelle et profession medicale. La relation therapeutique dans les unites de vein artificial et son environment." *Revue Française de Sociologie,* 16 (2): 189–214.

Littler, Craig R. 1982. *The Development of the Labour Process in Capitalist Societies. A Comparative Study of the Transformation of Work Organization in Britain, Japan and the U.S.A.* London: Heinemann Educational Books.

Littman, Deborah. 1984. *Bliss or Destruction: The Impact of Technological Change on Women's Work.* Toronto (a paper).

Marcson, Simon, ed. 1982. *Automation, Alienation and Anomie.* New York: Harper and Row.

Mars, Gerald. 1982. *Cheats at Work. An Anthropology of Workplace Crime.* London: Allen and Unwin.

Matejko, Alexander J. 1984. *Beyond Bureaucracy?* Cologne: Verlag für Gesellschaftsarchitektur.

McMillan, Charles J. 1984. *The Japanese Industrial System.* Berlin and New York: Walter de Gruyter.

Menzies, Heather. 1982. *Women and the Chip. Case Studies of the Effects of Informatics on Employment in Canada.* Montreal: Institute of Research on Public Policy.

Mintzberg, Henry. 1983. *Power In and Around Organizations. The Theory of Management Policy Series.* Englewood Cliffs, NJ: Prentice-Hall.

Moore, Wilbert E., ed. 1972. *Technology and Social*

Change. Chicago: Quadrangle Books.

Mouselis, N. P. 1975. *Organization and Bureaucracy.* London: Routledge and Kegan Paul.

Morici, Peter, Arthur J. R. Smith, and Sperry Lea. 1982. *Canadian Industrial Policy.* Washington, DC: National Planning Association.

National Research Council. 1982. *Outlook for Science and Technology. The Next Five Years.* San Francisco: Freeman.

Parker, Stanley. 1983. *Leisure at Work.* London: Allen and Unwin.

Peters, Thomas J., and Robert H. Waterman, Jr. 1982. *In the Search of Excellence.* New York: Harper and Row.

Reasons, Charles E., Lois L. Ross, and Craig Paterson. 1981. *Assault on the Worker. Occupational Health and Safety in Canada.* Toronto: Butterworths.

Rees, Albert. 1977. *The Economics of Trade Unions.* Chicago: University of Chicago Press.

Ripley, Randall B. and Grace A. Franklin. 1982. *Bureaucracy and Policy Implementation.* Homewood, IL: Dorsey.

Robey, Daniel. 1982. *Designing Organizations: A Macroperspective.* Homewood, IL: Irwin.

Schaller, Lyle E. 1972. *The Change Agent.* Nashville: Abingdon Press.

Shanks, Michael. 1967. *The Innovators. The Economics of Technology.* Harmondsworth, England: Penguin Books.

Shearing, Clifford D. 1981. *Organizational Police Deviance.* Toronto: Butterworths.

System Organization: The Management of Complexity. Block 3. Organizations, 1980. Milton Keyes, England: Open University Press.

Teich, Albert H., ed. 1981. *Technology and Man's Future.* 3d ed. New York: St. Martin's Press.

Thompson, Paul. 1983. *The Nature of Work. An Introduction to Debates on the Labour Process.* London: McMillan.

Turkle, Sherry. 1984. *The Second Self. Computers and the Human Spirit.* New York: Simon and Schuster.

Vaughan, Diane. 1983. *Controlling Unlawful Organizational Behavior. Social Structure and Corporate Misconduct.* Chicago: University of Chicago Press.

Weick, Karl. 1965. Experimentation with Organizations. In *The Handbook of Organizations,* ed. by J. G. March. Chicago: Rand-McNally.

Weiss, Carol H. and Allen H. Barton, eds. 1980. *Making*

Bureaucracies Work. Beverly Hills, CA: Sage.
Wilensky, Harold L. 1967. *Organizational Intelligence: Knowledge and Policy in Government and Industry.* New York: Basic Books.

4

A PERSPECTIVE
ON WORK COOPERATION

TWO BASIC TYPES OF WORK COOPERATION

People who are expected to cooperate with each other in the
process of production or service offering may be coordinated either in an authoritarian manner or a cooperative one.
In the first case they depend mainly on the authority of
somebody equipped with power over them and they are
expected mainly to obey what he or she orders them to do.
In the second case people jointly constitute the authority
and exercise it through the channels of participation in the
decision-making process. Of course, most real cases represent a mixture of both types. For example, people under
some situations are expected to obey and under other
situations are sovereigns. However, polarization between
the two types allows, at least, an understanding of the
nature of the dilemma between obedience and conscience, so
typical in many work situations. This dilemma has been
dramatized in modern times by the revolution of rising
aspirations of people who become more difficult to satisfy
under the conditions of unemployment, limitation of human
freedom under monopolistic organizational pressures, and
the focus on mass manipulation.

Until recently, authoritarian cooperation has been
widely treated as a necessity and no chance was given on
any large scale to participatory cooperation, except the
marginal cases of intentional communes, the work cooperatives, and various voluntary groups (Matejko 1984, pp.

279–412). However, in modern times new circumstances have arisen which not only favor participatory cooperation but even make it almost unavoidable as a historical solution adequate to growing mass education, the democratic spirit of modern social relations, the climate of questioning the traditional authorities, and so forth. We move gradually from a model of *unidimensional* society, based on ideological-moral unity, to the *multidimensional* society in which plurality is a matter of fact. Marcuse (1964) with his concept of a one-dimensional man is much further from the modern socioeconomic reality than D. Bell (1976) with his conflictual model of a developed market society full of internal contradictions among the *economy, polity,* and *culture.* However, both of these studies neglect the fact that modern societies with their socioeconomic growth become more and more pluralistic thanks to increasing division of labor, articulation of various segmental interests, great enrichment and diversification of social structure, the growth of consumer power, and so forth.

There has always been some internal contradiction involved in the whole concept of authoritarian cooperation and it has become even more acute with the progress of democratization—much faster in some fields than in others. Authority based on tradition, power, privilege, or personal attraction is now much more open in public questioning than before, when the sociomoral bond remained strong and the dependence of people on others was mainly of a sociopersonal nature—whereas now it is mainly of an objectified nature (reification of socioeconomic relations). As long as the external pressures on people remain strong and very specific, the society functions more or less according to the expectations of the elites. However, bureaucratization, in general, depersonalizes these pressures and leaves people in a sociomoral limbo. The formalized order appears in the collective consciousness of societies as a dehumanized reality full of irrationalities, basically inefficient and even counterproductive, but always able to be a nuisance to common people. The more a system becomes bureaucratized the worse it is for the well-being of those who have to maintain it by their own work.

With the progressing dilution of authority, the stimuli functions more and more in a highly depersonalized manner and the material incentives, fear of being fired, and the fear of oppression (especially strong under authoritarian political regimes) dominate over any moral and social concerns. As long as the above-mentioned stimuli are effective, the work structures do not disintegrate whether the personal prestige of supervisors is high or not. However, particularly in the developed countries there are several factors which gradually undermine the stimuli here under discussion. First of all, the aspirations tend to grow faster than the ability of socioeconomic systems to satisfy them. In several societies the buying power of the working population has diminished due to inflation, depletion of natural resources, the growing difficulties of export allocation on the foreign markets, and so on. However, the growth of the welfare state has provided the population with a security which lowers, very substantially, the previous fear of losing a job, being exploited, being discriminated against or persecuted. With the growth of plural forces in society there is relatively more opportunity to counter the power of some traditionally dominant social, economic, and political institutions by the collective bodies, for example, trade unions or leftist political parties, empowered to exercise an effective pressure.

Under such new circumstances the participative cooperation becomes more a matter of necessity than a moralistic appeal on behalf of a more humanitarian approach to collective work. In order to stimulate people to work it is not possible to depend mainly on money, fear, and supervisory authority—in general, on the carrot and the stick. On the other hand, the manipulatory nature of modern mass societies disintegrates social bonds so much that reintegrative measures are badly needed. The relative success of various countercultures may be at least partly explained by the fact that they appeal to the moral solidarity of men and women. (The practice of extreme leftists and extreme rightists, various religious sects, hippies, and so forth, is very illuminating in the respect.) More exactly, the solidarity to a large extent is missing in the manipulative mass societies and makes them vulnerable to anomie, segmentation, alienation, dissension, and finally disintegration. Participative cooperation becomes one of the most important measures in reintegrating modern societies by the establishment of basic units of sociomoral cohesion and at the same time of an effective socialization. Instead of the dehumanized bureaucracy, people face each other within their autonomous work groups. Social reality regains its human character and mutual relationships among working people acquire a new moral meaning.

Of course, the success of autonomous work groups (AWGs) depends, among other things, on their effective integration into the broader work structures. As long as there remains a conflict of interests and concerns among the organizational units located at various levels, there is a strong chance for the autonomous work groups either to fail and disintegrate or to become microcenters of the power struggle. Therefore, the concept of autonomous work groups makes sense only as long as it is clearly related to the broader concept of work democratization in the whole institution: an enterprise, an office, a school, or the like.

The bargaining process among the client (for instance, the government) and various teams eager to accept a given task must be adequately regulated within the broader framework of collective bargaining. Evaluation procedures must be developed in order to achieve the performance of tasks according to mutually accepted conditions. (In bureaucracy the evaluation is neglected or heavily biased by the necessity of the apparatus to appear successful.) Members of autonomous work teams should have full opportunity to participate in decision making and share in the results of their work. In order to achieve this, the teams should consist only of a few people who would be able to establish face-to-face relationships (Matejko 1962, pp. 149–85; 1973). Various teams should cooperate with one another on the principles of a multilevel federalism (Matejko 1973). The life of a team should be limited to the length of time needed in order to perform a given task; this will prevent teams from becoming ossified and more status-oriented than task-oriented.

The teamwork approach has become quite popular among several promotors of a humanized work organization such as Bennis (1966) and Likert (1966). In the communist countries, Yugoslavia first offered an evident trend in that direction, even if she is still far from achieving the satisfactory results. The Israeli kibbutzim offer several very good examples of effective teamwork performed within a fully democratic setting. However, probably most may be learned from the experience of teams which consist of highly skilled people who perform work of a creative nature (Matejko 1966, 1970, 1973). The professional success of these teams depends upon the effective reconciliation of task-orientation with person-orientation. We should carefully study the experience of such teams in order to formulate practical conclusions that may help to promote the new social organization of work.

THE CONCEPT OF AUTONOMOUS
WORK GROUPS (AWG)
AND ITS APPLICATION

Specialization, formalization, and even regimentation are a necessity in all complex organizations. However, bureaucratized bodies have their own dysfunctions which sooner or later lead to an organizational crisis. This is exactly what becomes evident—for instance, in the modern hospitals—and leads to a very substantial deterioration of medical care (Matejko 1984, pp. 413–34).

There are several obvious advantages of primary group and community feeling that are evident not only in the intentional communities such as kibbutzim but also in the regular workplaces as long as the autonomous work group principle becomes incorporated into the socio-organizational structure.

The feeling of "we-ness" is the major socializing factor that penetrates the individuals deeper than the bureaucratized manipulation, and the appearance of this feeling is much more possible—for instance, in primary nursing and in team nursing than in the functionalized model of the nursing service. This latter model provides anomie and discourages any deeper concern in the patient as well as in the quality of medical care. It has been transferred mechanically into the hospital from the traditionally bureaucratized institutions and does not satisfy the growing demand of a better medial care. In addition, this model discourages any deeper commitment of the hospital personnel in their jobs (Ibid.).

The task team should be "enriched" as a human group by giving its members the joint opportunity to share jobs and responsibilities, organizing their mutual support, gaining together from the results achieved through a collective effort. The team should usually have not fewer than three or four members and not more than eight; larger groups are more prone to emotionalism and elitism. However, teams consisting of ten to twenty people can also be very effective if they share a deep-rooted culture and if the parts of the group are highly interdependent (Emery and Thorsrud 1976, p. 163). Members of the team "must know that they can aim at targets that are explicit, realistic and challenging to them; and they must have a feedback of group performance" (Ibid., p. 164).

There is always a problem how to establish the optimal length and variety of tasks, how to integrate them into meaningful units (inclusion of auxiliary and preparatory tasks), how to determine the standards of performance and achieve a feedback, how to make the job socially identifiable and respectful. In any job reform experimentation is necessary; it is worth remembering about such obvious conditions as making jobs challenging and promotional (learning), offering people recognition and reward for their efforts, opening some broader chances and leaving at least some decision to the discretion of the individual.

Within the work teams cooperation among members will be much strengthened by providing of interlocking tasks, job rotation, mutual contact and mutual help, collective decision making in the fields vital to members, delegation of power to the whole team, limitation or even total withdrawal of the direct interference by the supervisors (management by objectives), application of the collective incentives for good performance (departmental bonus), and integration of the formal structure into the broader social organization of the team as a human group.

"The establishment of semi-autonomous groups is strongly dependent on the ability of management to shift its primary attention from internal coordination and control to the regulation of the company's boundaries" (Emery and Thorsrud 1976, p. 136). Within the changing environment the main task of management is to keep in touch with the world outside and to innovate the necessary modifications, as well as to take care of the coordination between various organizational units. Internal affairs may be left to autonomous groups of employees looking after their own affairs collectively. This kind of division of labor fits the best the modern conditions of dynamic markets, relatively sophisticated employees and specialized managers who do not necessarily have to practice the power plays all the time (on the historically changing role of power and authority, see Martin 1977). "Authority is becoming a question of influence through competence, through information and through an ability to motivate people to pull together" (Emery and Thorsrud 1976, p. 138). Emphasis in the sphere of values and norms is now on freedom and justice, not as before on diligence, obedience, and frugality.

Introduction of the AWG principle leads to the personalization of work and simultaneously to the much higher socialization of people into their occupational and institutional roles. As much as people gain more say within the framework of their specific AWGs, they become motivated and stimulated to fulfill the expectations. There is here also an element of mutual control, encouragement, and inspiration among the group members. Working people are bombarded by conflicting forces pushing them either to solidarity or to an individualistic isolation (Wilson 1978, pp. 26–48); in the AWGs people gain a strong incentive to move towards solidarity.

The interdependence of members with the team modeled according to the AWG principles may be well understood within the following basic elements of group life:

- Interation of members in the process of fulfilling the joint tasks. It is a question of how much this inter- action is stimulating and rewarding for all AWG members (job rotation, personal growth through work, and so on). Maximalization of interaction outcomes by some AWG members should not be achieved through the minimalization of interaction outcomes by other members.
- Acceptance by members of common group norms. Here the question is how valid are those norms to the quality of services and to the professional growth of AWG members. The group conformism may become harmful for the members and may influence their performance negatively. The normative group order helps to maxi- mize the outcomes of joint activities but at the same time it may alienate individuals and lower their con- tribution. Any AWG has to find its own solution to the dilemma between the normative regulation of its activ- ities and the acceptance of deviation.
- Status structure of the patterned differences among the members in the team. Status rights are not always adequately related to status obligations and this may lead to confusion and mutual disillusionment, especially when the person in a leading position does not behave according to expectations. The status consensus is very much needed in the AWG and an adequate clarific- ation of this factor is a necessity.
- Goals of an interdependent nature, facilitating recon- ciliation of the interests of individuals with the collective good. In the AWG it is important to create such a situation in which members would be facilitated in their personal goals performance by their group belonging but, on the other hand, the group interest would become a priority. The greater the extent to which members are aware of and can articulate the group's goals, the greater the interdependence among them (Deutsch 1949).
- Cohesiveness of the team is attractive to its members, reinforces their loyalty, social and instrumental inter- dependence of them within the AWG, and interpersonal attraction. In the management of AWGs it is important to strengthen all mentioned above factors of cohesive- ness.
- Awareness of group belonging and group identity among the members of the AWG. Without a clearly defin- ed—inside and outside—identity of members of this team, it would be difficult to achieve all expected advantages of the AWG.

To summarize, it is suggested that the teams functioning in their AWG capacity will be at the high level of internal solidarity when having a frequent, equally distributed and friendly interaction, an elaborated system of accepted and implemented norms, a high status consensus (not much challenged inside or outside), well-accepted and clearly stated goals of a cooperative nature, strong general cohesiveness in all its basic dimensions, high awareness of membership and a good esprit de corps (Wilson 1978, p. 49).

INTERHUMAN RELATIONS IN THE AWG

The internal relations within the AWG are based on such ingredients as attitudes of members toward each other, their mutual contact, acceptance and interaction, activities exercised by members and their mutual interdependence. Members of the team build up and elaborate the whole system of interrelationships, develop the group norms (and follow them more or less consistently), establish a status structure. How the ingredients of group life are related to each other has been explained in the theoretical frameworks elaborated by Homans (1950) and Bales (1950). In general, it is possible to say that people are more or less inclined to be loyal to the group, in this case the AWG, depending what is more rewarded and accepted: an interdependent orientation or an individualistic orientation (Thibault and Kelley 1959).

It is up to the team to promote the collective spirit without necessarily damaging the individual freedom. The harmonious, well-organized and satisfying instrumental or socioemotional interaction leads to the positive attitudes which on their side reinforce the cooperation within the team. On the other hand, any disorder and conflict of interests at the instrumental or socioemotional level will lead to a negativistic orientation at the levels of group and individual consciousness. The awareness of it is very important for the success of the team. By establishing collective norms and by supporting them through the group commitment, the AWG helps to preserve an internal peace and order as well as stimulates the socialization of individual team members to the group values (Calgart and Samovar 1974).

Another question is how much the internal normative order of the team is in agreement with the external conditions. For example, the nursing team may have the best will and ability to improve the medical care but the external conditions are such that this improvement is extremely difficult to achieve. This is a very common situation in the case of organizational innovations introduced under the experimental conditions when the environment remains lukewarm or even hostile to the innovation.

Members of the AWG depend in their statuses on each other. It is impossible to retain a high status without being accepted and appreciated by those lower in status (Homans 1974). "By curbing their power, which is potentially disruptive of solidarity, the powerful members are provided a high-ranking status in the group" (Wilson 1978, p. 136). There is some exchange of services among group members: those claiming for themselves high-ranking statuses have to provide rewards for their fellow members in order to gain their approval (Blau 1964).

The status differentiation within the team is the natural product of cooperation and the inequalities that reveal themselves. The ideal of absolute equality is unnatural (Andreski 1975) and, therefore, it would be impractical to treat it as a necessity. The main problem in this respect is not how to keep the AWG members completely equal but how to prevent the inequality from becoming a privilege endangering the team spirit.

The external status characteristics brought to the AWG may play a major role in the relations between members. It is necessary to avoid tensions which may arise because of status ambiguities or the status rejection. During the process of work performance new status hierarchy will develop and this again may be an asset or a handicap, depending on the relationship between the spirit of team members and the team goals. For example, an authoritarian person may gain dominance over the whole team at expense of the participatory spirit. Members of a low status may become and remain shy, discouraged from showing initiative. The status configuration based on inequality may be detrimental to the team performance when some members lose motivation and feel exploited by others.

It is necessary to recognize the contribution of anybody who belongs to the AWG and has a goodwill. The high level of general status consensus and status congruence is an ideal for the AWG; then the members are much less vulnerable to worries and tensions. The homogeneity of AWGs may be assured by their voluntary nature. Self-selection allows the AWGs to admit into their own ranks persons most suited for a peaceful and fruitful cooperation.

It is natural for any small group, including the AWG, to have an internal competition. The AWG members compare themselves regarding their abilities and achievements.

Lower ranks grow less confident in comparison with the higher ranks who enjoy an assured status in the group. The collective spirit may be a very useful integrative factor in the AWG as long as there is no substantial conflict of interests.

The interdependence of members within the AWG is important for their solidarity but should not go too far because of the possible danger for the individual growth and satisfaction. There is a delicate balance in the AWGs between their instrumental functions and the socioemotional functions. Both these types of functions have to be balanced adequately within the team in order to avoid the appearance of disequilibrium. Too much attention paid to only one of these functions at the expense of another may be harmful for the whole team. "Social systems are caught between two sets of problems (instrumental and socioemotional), and the way a system solves one set influences the solution of the other. Furthermore, the level of solidarity maintained by the system depends on how successfully these two sets of problems are solved. . . . Two aspects of solidarity—positive socioemotional interaction and cohesion—tend to go hand in hand" (Wilson 1978, pp. 52, 68). Teams tend to balance between both types of system problems and depending on several external and internal circumstances the problem solution applied to a given case may be more or less satisfactory.

There is a mutual reinforcement between the instrumental realm and the socioemotional realm: the instrumental success reinforces the social emotional solidarity and satisfaction of the team members. On the other hand, the high level of solidarity, mutual acceptance, and status consensus help the team members to achieve their instrumental goals. In the AWG it is necessary to make a distinction between the task leadership and the socioemotional leadership. People who are good in task performance are not necessarily very good in the socioemotional influence and it is better to distinguish between these two roles.

The nature of tasks done by the AWG has a great impact on the social organization of the group: whether the correctness of a decision can be adequately verified (there are tasks and circumstances which are not open to verification), task requirements are clear and known to members, whether there is one or more than one path to the goal, and whether the solutions are specific or not (Shaw 1963; Susman 1976). The tasks may be more or less structured, specific, and urgent. The allocation of people and resources within the AWG, the whole process of decision making, as well as the informal network of human relations, are under the influence of all factors mentioned above. There are several specific studies of working groups in hierarchical organizations which describe in detail the environmental conditioning of the social group organization (Wilson 1978). It is possible to learn much from them and the AWGs may also benefit.

The formal, nonformal, and informal aspects of organization (Dubin 1958, pp. 65–73) are easier to be synchronized in the AWGs than in the hierarchical organizations (Matejko 1980), in which the diversity of vested interests makes a reconciliation very difficult. In such a group which consists of face-to-face relationships between people simultaneously involved in the variety of structures, the social bonds are personalized enough to integrate these structures adequately. On the other hand, the clearly formulated task orientation of the AWG provides a solid basis for group identity and justifies the existence of all its structures.

The formal structure of the AWG includes its total size, mechanism of decision making, span of control, pervasiveness of rules, distribution of jobs, standardization of roles and activities, interdependence of components, and so on. Size as such is a critical variable in this sense since depending on it, contacts and relations between the team members may be more or less developed and close. Decision making in the AWG should be of a collective nature but the implementation of this principle may give the team leader more or less power and responsibility. In many cases it would not be practical to arrange meetings of all AWG members for any minor decision. The span of control does not count in the AWG when the joint responsibility is taken for granted.

In the AWG there is no need to multiply rules in order to keep order and push people to do what is expected from them. The cohesion of the AWG should guarantee that tasks would be implemented properly and punctually. The decision-making function and the implementation function in the AWGs are not separated in such a distinctive way as is the case in the traditional division of labor. The individual and group organizing processes adhere in the AWG to those in the whole workplace and there is a problem how to synchronize them in the most efficient way.

THE SMALL GROUP RESEARCH
AND AUTONOMOUS WORK GROUPS

The effective promotion of autonomous work groups within the general framework of the quality-of-working-life movement needs a sound psychosociological basis. The small-group theoretical framework based on a very substantial empirical research provides such a basis. Some general conclusions have been formulated in this vast field and the emphasis here will be on the set of hypotheses brought together by M. E. Shaw (1976).

Mutual Compatibility Among Members

In voluntarily selected groups, including the autonomous work groups, there is supposed to exist a mutual attraction of members, need for compatibility, mutual acceptance and recognition—all of these factors play a very important role. Working together in a group allows people to gain an additional motivation from the fact that they are not alone, except when the nature of tasks gives preference to the individual commitment, for example in the brainstorming situation. Of course, similarity of views and mutual attractiveness make working together a much easier task, especially when group members share their devotion to the group and its goals (Shaw 1976, pp. 87–91, 106–9).

Groups offer a social facilitation in the sense that people mutually inspire each other, the presence of others increases motivation to perform well (except with tasks that require higher mental processes), and the evaluation by others is an important stimulus. Groups learn faster than individuals, encourage the taking of risks by the accumulation of mutual support, produce more and better solutions to problems than do individuals working alone, and arrive at superior judgments in tasks that involve random error and therefore can be built up from a number of individual judgments (Shaw 1976, pp. 58–81). Of course, these are conditional statements and several interfering factors have to be here considered.

The human content of an autonomous work group has to be taken carefully into consideration. For example, women usually are less self-assertive and less competitive in groups than are men; they also conform more to majority opinion. People with special skills or more intelligence than others show more activity but are also less conformist. (However, individual differences have not predicted conformity well.) Socially sensitive individuals have ways to enhance their acceptance in the group membership and group effectiveness.

Groups that appear to individuals as instrumental in satisfying their needs, attractive and rewarding directly or indirectly have much more chance to succeed than the groups that are less attractive. The similarity of back-ground among the group members contributes much to mutual compatibility but on the other hand may be in some respect harmful to the group because of too much sociability at the expense of task orientation. This danger will be avoided when the group, going through various stages of its growth (from the preliminary orientation through the stage of evaluation to the full control of all external and internal factors) incorporates adequately some additional tasks that enrich the collective challenge (Shaw 1976, pp. 293–334).

There is in groups something that may be called a collective maturity—a product of changes in feelings, atti-tudes, and behavior of members as a consequence of the growing group experience. By participation in a group, people have a chance to gain more self-awareness vis-à-vis others. How they perceive themselves and what they want (the reflected self versus the ideal self) gives a better or worse chance of coming closer together. The group plays the role of a mirror in which people can watch their own image better, and correct their behavior accordingly. Depending on the quality of group life, people either gain or lose in their personal growth. For example, in a group full of tensions and excessive pressures individuals may become exposed to severe psychological disturbances. The "mature" group is able to handle tensions successfully and open enough room for its members to grow in harmony with others, and not necessarily against them (Wilson 1978, pp. 262–72).

Environment and Space

Being within a certain environment, an autonomous work group perceives it in a specific way and adapts according-ly. This perception may be positive or negative and the way of adaptation depends very much on the group. For example, a negative perception will lead to a defense-oriented adaptation.

There is a certain "space" available to the group, and within it there are also personal "spaces" of individual members. The scope of each space and the delimitations between them change depending on various factors located within the group and outside of it. There is always a question whether all group members are comfortable with the space available to them, recognize the existing spatial delimitations, and are willing and able to accommodate each other in this respect.

The allocation of space to group members and the availability of a mutual contact among them influence significantly the communication patterns and mutual dependence (Holmstead and Haire 1978, pp. 103-4). Even the seating arrangement influences the quality of group interaction. Depending on whether the communication network is centralized or decentralized, a leader is more or less likely to emerge, organizational development occurs more or less rapidly, group members have higher or lower morale, complex problems are more or less difficult to deal with, and the task overload is more or less probable. It is an important question how and under which conditions centralization and decentralization influence the morale and efficiency of groups.

The allocation of the whole group and of its individual members within a given space develops in a more or less organized way and the boundaries become established depending on status, "proprietary" rights, the personalness of the situation, and so forth. Any intrusion from outside or inside against these boundaries usually meets a negative reaction, upsets the internal equilibrium in the group, and leads to intergroup tensions. There are significant differences in this respect, depending on the age, sex, and cultural background of the group members (Shaw 1976, pp. 131-37).

The Group Structure

The structuralization of groups is not only a function of tasks and external circumstances but also of needs of the group members and their perception of how organization may facilitate goal achievement. The distribution of status among the group members influences accordingly the structuralization of a communication network (Wilson 1978, pp. 159-60; Shaw 1976, pp. 137-216). The group pressure keeps members within the structure and prevents individual members from deviating from group norms, especially when they are outside the high-status positions.

The mechanism of conformity works particularly effectively when there is unanimous agreement among members. In the cohesive groups the decentralized communication networks promote even greater conformity than centralized networks where pressure can be exerted by some members on some others only through intermediaries. Conformity introduces order into the group process and provides for the coordination of individual behavior (Olmstead and Haire 1978, pp. 68-73). Behavioral consistency has to be implemented in groups in order to achieve internal order and predictability. The creation of adequate group norms and their acceptance by an appropriately large number of members, especially by those who occupy the strategically important positions, it of great importance for the success of any group.

Extreme role differentiation in groups disrupts them, due not so much to the extended division of labor as to low status consensus (Shaw 1976, p. 249). It is an open question in groups as to how much the problem of status may interfere with the problem of group efficiency based on an efficient and well-coordinated role performance by the group members. For example, in airplane crews, differential influence by individual crew members goes traditionally very well with the role—as well as status-ranking—and therefore there are relatively few tensions which would negatively influence performance. The status consistency plays a major role in groups.

The distribution of power within a group has several important consequences. In general, a dispersal of power makes the individual more attractive, influential, and approved. The more power a group member has, the greater the probability that he may use it.

High group cohesiveness has several advantages. There is much communication and interaction in general; much influence is exercised by the collective body over members; the goals are more or less effectively implemented; there is much satisfaction; people who have diverse, relevant abilities are able to contribute effectively; social heterogeneity of members is not particularly dangerous for the group and even becomes a positive factor. All these advantages are usually missing in the low cohesive groups in which any diversity becomes an obstacle.

The group cohesion helps the teams to keep their level of aspiration on an appropriate level despite failures, whereas isolated individuals are much more vulnerable in this respect when the group reinforcement is missing.

Group Goals and Tasks

There may be several problems in relation to the goals held for the group. Firstly, group goals may be heterogeneous and perceived differently by different members. Secondly, the consciousness of group goals and their acceptance by group members usually varies quite substantially among various members. Thirdly, there is always a gap between the private goals of individuals and the group goals. Fourthly, in the process of group thinking and group acting, there are several factors which endanger an adequate selection of group goals, their serious recognition and an efficient implementation (groups very often are in action slower than individuals); especially when the internal tensions occur within a group. Fifthly, deindividuation, when it happens in the group situations, leads to the diffusion of responsibility as to who should fulfill tasks and when and how they should be fulfilled.

The performance of tasks by groups leads to more or less success and afterwards this influences the selection of the next tasks. Members of the group in this respect compare themselves with the performance of other groups, take into consideration their own abilities and external circumstances, look into the various aspects of risk taking. The quality of performance often decreases with increasing task demands. On difficult tasks, the free exchange of judgments among group members is particularly important.

When time is concerned, individuals are very often faster in problem solving than groups, and therefore it is necessary to avoid absorbing the whole group with tasks which may be completed much more effectively by an individual. Criticism and competition arising in a group situation may slow down the search for new solutions and divert attention from the task; in "brainstorming" the temporary suspension of the critical evaluation of ideas is widely used to stimulate the creativity of people.

Group size is an important limiting factor. Increased size decreases the participation of individual members, there are more differences in the amount of this participation, and the emergence of a leader becomes more probable. At the same time the group loses intimacy and becomes more open to manipulation and conformity.

The effect of group size upon group performance depends on the nature of tasks. If the outcome is the result of some combination of individual contributions or mainly of the most competent group member then the group performance increases with increasing group size up to a certain level. However, when the outcome is the result of everyone in the group making his or her contribution (a conjunctive task) then the performance depends on the least competent group member, and with the growth of group size there is more probability that incompetence will interfere negatively.

Leadership

The most effective kind of leadership in groups varies with tasks faced by the group and other contingencies located inside and outside the group. For example, group performance is better when the task is disjunctive than when it is conjunctive. The quality of group performance, as measured by time investment and errors, is negatively correlated with the cooperation requirements of the group task. Goal clarity and goal-path clarity are positively related to the motivation of group members and to their efficiency. Homogeneous group goals facilitate effective group functioning, whereas heterogeneous group goals hinder effective group functioning.

The leadership style of people who are in charge of groups depends on their own orientation (other-oriented versus task-oriented) as well as on the situational contingencies. For example, it was observed that in unfavorable circumstances other-oriented leaders tend to behave in a relationship-relevant manner whereas task-oriented leaders tend to the task-relevant behavior. A task-oriented leader is more effective when the group-task situation is either very favorable or very unfavorable for the leader, whereas a relationship-oriented leader is more effective when the group-task situation is only moderately favorable or unfavorable for the leader.

Both task-orientation as well as the other-orientation are needed for the survival of the group and its success. One should not be sacrificed for the other but the goal orientation should be clearly emphasized in order to make the group structures subservient to goal fulfillment. Ascendant individuals are dominating and self-assertive in groups and generally facilitate group functioning. The well-adjusted members, those free of anxiety and who accept group norms, are necessary in order to keep the group functioning well. However, some dissent is also constructive as long as it does not assume too much effort and attention.

Depending on the circumstances, the style of leadership should be more or less directive. For example, when the group-task situation is only moderately favorable or unfavorable for the leader, it is better for him or her to adopt a nondirective leadership style. The permissive style of group leadership usually improves morale but productivity may suffer when there is some loosening of discipline and the order is not adequately maintained.

In the AWGs the conditions for good leadership and good performance are particularly suitable when the motivation is high, people are experienced, there are few internal tensions, the leadership function does not give room for objections, and intelligent people are selected to the leadership functions (Fiedler and Liester 1977). The group setting is favorable for the fulfillment of all conditions mentioned above—more than the setting of a hierarchical organization.

Management participation in the AWGs is not a goal in itself but serves the specific purpose of making decisions as comprehensive as possible, mobilizing the contributions of group members, achieving a satisfactory level of mutual agreement and integrating all members around common goals. The functional nature of the AWG participation excludes the practice of playing participation as a power game or having often the long and boring meetings devoted to petty problems. When there is too much participation in the AWG then it becomes easily adversive to the group members.

In the AWGs several traditional functions of management are taken over by the group but this does not mean that the new collective leadership is of less importance or that individual responsibility becomes totally diluted in the vague concept of "groupness." There remains a need to structure group tasks and group roles, plan ahead, formulate and implement adequate procedures, control the results, allocate people and resources, integrate group members, give attention to their needs and motives, and encourage group loyalty and group effort. Individual contributions play a role in all these aspects and any neglect of it may be very harmful for the group.

Initiating structure and consideration are both based in AWGs on a nonconflictual foundation and there is no reason why leadership should rely on privilege and power. The justification of leadership within the AWGs is of a functional nature only. It is taken for granted that group management has to be beneficial for the whole group and therefore the basic contradiction between "initiating structure" and "consideration," so characteristic of hierarchical organizations, has no place in the AWGs. Where there is a high level of consideration, as in the AWGs, there are usually also the structural arrangements suitable for the ad hoc changes.

There is a great need in the AWGs for flexible leadership which can be adjusted adequately to the changing circumstances. The leadership function within the AWGs should be understood as a cycle of planning, allocation, stimulation, coordination, integration and feedback—all related to specific tasks and subordinated to them. Leadership may be fulfilled by one or more persons and is of an instrumental character dictated by specific contingencies of situations, task, people involved in it, time pressure, allocation of resources, and so forth. To be a leader in the AWG is not a question of power and authority but a question of a specific responsibility, which is exercised within the group on a rotational basis.

In the AWG model there is a place for leadership but at the same time the strict segregation of functions is abolished. The same people who make decisions are also involved in the implementation, feedback, and evaluation. This does not mean, however, that there is no specialization. People move from one job to another in order to be qualified for virtually all responsibilities available within the AWG.

The Sociotechnical Directives

On the basis of the above-mentioned hypotheses, some of which have been verified in process of research, the following directives will be here proposed as valid for autonomous work groups (AWGs).

1. The voluntary character of the AWG should be safeguarded and promoted in order to allow for the spontaneous selection of group membership, free exchange and mobility of people between various groups, and the adequate matching of characters and personalities. The AWGs, in order to fulfill their destiny, should not be just administrative units but first of all they should constitute viable social groups of a high humanistic quality in which the process of individual and collective growth would develop.

2. Groups have several advantages as well as disadvantages and it is necessary to expand the former and to avoid the latter. Tasks which may be performed more effectively by individuals than by groups should be appointed on an individual basis. It is necessary to keep the AWG free from the dominance of an uncritical conformism, "groupthink," and mediocrity. The minority should be defended from too much pressure by the dominant majority. Freedom of individual expression must be preserved under any circumstances.

3. In the selection of group members and in managing the AWG it is important to take into consideration various characteristic features of people who constitute the membership. On one hand, it is necessary to recognize these features and to organize teams accordingly. For example, supervision and control may be more or less penetrative, depending on how much of them people need and expect. Group meetings may happen more or less often and their character may be more or less businesslike depending on

the preferences of members. The AWGs should be flexible in their social organization in order to adapt the latter as well as remain open to the sociocultural nature of a given human surrounding and its specificity. However, this does not mean that the social organization of the AWG should be based on the uncritical acceptance of a given sociocultural reality. The purpose of the above-mentioned social organization is to achieve a smooth group functioning, but also to upgrade a given AWG to a higher level of maturity and growth. The educational aspect has to be recognized and implemented adequately. For example, if the female members are shy it is worth trying to activate them and to encourage a higher level of self-confidence.

4. The question of what members are really gaining from belonging to the AWG is one of the most important ones. Is it enough to keep them in the AWG and to achieve an adequate motivation? Does the social character of the AWG promise that the task-orientation will be strong? It would not be good for the AWG to promote sociability at the expense of work performance. On the other hand, the purely work-oriented calculative preoccupations would impoverish the content of group life and impose some limits on its growth toward maturity. As long as several important resources of the group are not mobilized for the sake of growth, the group remains at the immature level.

5. Decentralization within the AWG is advisable as long as this encourages individual members to take initiative, feel responsible, make meaningful contributions to the well-being of the whole group. At the same time it makes sense to centralize such tasks which may suffer by being decentralized (for example, the maintenance functions, planning, and so forth). Centralization in the AWG should be avoided only when it leads to elitism and to the gap between those with power and those who remain powerless. As long as the AWGs remain small, face-to-face groups, there is relatively little danger in this respect, especially when the leadership function is rotated. With the growth of group size this rotation becomes more and more difficult and the face-to-face relationships gradually diminish in importance. It is better to keep the AWGs at the level of five to nine persons.

6. Status-orientation and task-orientation are very often in mutual disagreement in groups. Power related to higher status may be misused, which is harmful for task performance. Status preoccupations divert the attention of members from doing things toward the issue of prestige and relative position to one another. Group cohesion may become a goal in itself at the expense of achievement. It is

important to keep status subservient to the goal performance and prevent it from being a goal in itself. Whenever the group cohesion starts to dominate over task considerations it is better to dissolve the AWG and to start a new group. The variation of tasks and organizational conditions should be followed by the variation of the AWGs. Any ossification of the AWGs as social units will endanger the task performance, and lead to a gap between the reality of a group and its surrounding.

7. The socioeconomic value of tasks performed by the AWGs should be reconciled with the well-being of the AWG members as individuals as well as collectivities. It makes much sense for the AWGs to share in all benefits achieved from their individual and collective contributions. It is also important to avoid any harm to the AWG members due to the fact that they participate in the implementation of specific tasks. Competition between various AWGs in the performance of their tasks remains useful and even advisable as long as there is not any specific damage to the well-being of the group members, their health, spirit of collective solidarity, and so forth. It is necessary to avoid such a competition, which would endanger the common well-being.

8. The leadership function remains very important in the AWGs, even if this function is rotated among the group members and a large part of it is practiced on a participatory basis. It is necessary to safeguard the responsibility related to leadership, the competence associated with it and the foresight in planning the future of the AWG. Leadership style is based on several changing contingencies and this factor becomes of crucial importance under the new circumstances when power and leadership are no longer closely related. Authority, traditionally supporting leaders in their organizational functions, gradually becomes a matter of the past, and this is especially valid for the AWGs. Leadership training loses its elitist nature and becomes one of the subjects of a general education. It seems necessary to develop leadership training programs on a mass scale for the benefit of AWGs, emphasizing strongly leadership as a function of changing circumstances.

CONDITIONS OF AN EFFECTIVE FUNCTIONING OF AUTONOMOUS WORK GROUPS

There is already a considerable amount of experience regarding the functioning of autonomous work groups and it is worth summarizing. The following factors are here proposed as of crucial importance:

1. Existence of a clearly defined team: stable membership; univocally designed scope of activity; specific goals; well-defined responsibility; elementary mutual trust and acceptance inside and outside. Participation and the team identity are expected to reinforce each other.

2. Validity of decision-making matters to the team members: a clear relationship between these matters and the needs of team members as well as their aspirations; common values and goals provide an adequate level of team cohesion; the differentiating factors kept well under control; the prestige and privilege hierarchy evolving from the goal performance does not undermine the unity of the team as a communal body.

3. The reinvigorating impact of the team functioning on the decision-making process: the leadership does not counter the participation; successes as well as failures do not undermine the democratic character of the team; encouragement prevails over discouragement. The monotony and pettiness of daily functioning does not lead to great discouragement.

4. The practice of collective decision making should become the matter of a broader culture; people on the team become socialized to the new style of mutual coexistence not only in their behavior but also in their general life orientation; the human environment of a given team learns to accept the uniqueness of what the team represents; teams become willing and able to continue in the same direction as well as to spread the message; the tradition of democratic spirit becomes a heritage.

5. A basic harmony should be achieved between the team and its environment: technology does not prevent the team from continuing its democratic culture; competition between team and other organizational bodies does not lead to disastrous effects; there is not much interference from outside into the internal team functioning.

6. The challenge confronting the team should not be too easy but also not too difficult: in both cases there is a danger that the team members may lose their motivation and the authority of leadership will be undermined.

7. Distinction between the nuclear role of each individual member and his or her extended role. In addition to the basic scope of his or her activities the individual from time to time should commit himself or herself to other obligations, dictated both by the group demands and his or her own ambition to grow as an individual and a citizen. There is a problem of how meaningfully the nuclear role is related to the extended role and if there are any contradictions between them.

8. The dynamics of both roles mentioned above should be adequately planned and coordinated in order to fit into the life the individual, life of the group, and the transformations of the tasks as dictated by changing technologies, market demands, administrative structures, and so forth. This is the problem of treating all the above-mentioned factors as interrelated processes which influence each other.

9. The group provides a microenvironment for the evolving process of mutual relationship between each member individually and his or her work environment. It is a problem of critical importance if and to what extent the group helps (or prevents) each individual to cope successfully with his or her problems and to achieve a positive adaptation. Of course, in this respect, individual differences and preferences have to be considered and appreciated.

10. Mutual relations between individual group members have to remain within the general framework of group concerns and interests but at the same time the climate of freedom should not be endangered. It is a question of the group's internal tolerance not necessarily becoming a license for everything. The personal friendship bonds may contribute much to the group cohesion and attractiveness but these bonds in some cases may lead to the establishment of cliques which promote their own interests at the expense of the group.

11. Group values bring people together but the climate of conformism is a danger for the quality of group life. When people in the group lose interest in the problems external to the group and when they become self-satisfied in their own group setting, the content of group life may remain on a mediocre level. Therefore it is always important to look for some inputs from outside to enrich the life of the group and prevent it from remaining at a mediocre level.

12. Tensions within the group can be used to benefit the group rather than damage it. The question is what to learn from them and how to channelize them to worthwhile purposes to inspire useful changes within the group. The distinction should be made between tensions which result from the internal development within the team and tensions which are imported from outside and should be located within the framework of the external communications. It is quite often very difficult to locate the genuine sources of several more complicated tensions happening in the group: how much they are of a purely individual nature and to what extent they arise from the group as such?

13. Aspirations of individual members quite often go beyond group limits and the question is how to meet them adequately without damaging the vital group interests. Suppression of these aspirations may be very damaging to the individual. On the other hand, an adequate socialization of the individual necessitates some appeasement on his or her side in order to accommodate the group well-being.

FACTORS OF CONFUSION

The basic task in the field of participatory cooperation is to get rid of several confusions, naïvetés, and misunderstandings. First of all, participatory cooperation is *not* a universal answer to all possible difficulties in the field of labor relations. On the contrary, it seems necessary to be well aware in advance that the novelty of participatory practices will lead to some at least transitory additional difficulties which are worth being risked only under the assumption that in the long run our trouble, effort, and investment will be productive.

Secondly, participatory cooperation consists of some general directions and intentions rather than of ready-made universal schemes of how, when, and in which order things should be done. The practices of participatory cooperation have to be tailored adequately each time to the specific conditions. People differ very much in their ability and willingness to engage themselves in the collective efforts. It does not make sense to enforce participation under the circumstances of an open lack among people of any genuine interest in it. Certain social environments and their specific cultures may be so foreign to the spirit of participatory cooperation that it would be better to wait quite a long time for a suitable occasion to propagate some novelties. For example, in Israel the Oriental Jews so far show in general little interest in kibbutzim and this may be explained at least partly by the fact that most of them only recently have entered modern economy.

Thirdly, participatory cooperation in order to become meaningful has to be based upon some common characteristics and values shared by the potential participants. Without this minimum there is no promise of a success adequate to invested efforts. Therefore, it does not make much sense to promote participatory cooperation in the human settings characterized by a very high turnover, a far reaching diversity of backgrounds, or profoundly contrasting vested interests. Of course, this does not mean that under adversary circumstances it is not worthwhile to promote the participatory cooperation. Anyway, it is necessary to know in advance that the promotion of the AWG idea under these circumstances becomes particularly difficult. Instead of wasting effort for projects that are too risky it is better to create positive patterns somewhere else and allow them to radiate on the more difficult environments.

Fourthly, participatory cooperation in order to succeed has to undermine the existing stratification among people regarding power, status, and prestige. Instead of the previous inequality, a new type of hierarchy is supposed to take place appealing not to power but to moral values and achievements. This is very evident in the kibbutzim where the new "elite" gains its esteem mainly from the devotion to collective goals, high work performance, friendly attitudes to other people, and so forth. Mutual trust, missing very often in authoritarian cooperation, usually goes together with the clarity of performance criteria, the validity of performed tasks to all involved agents of joint action, the establishment of a smooth procedure of work, an evident justification of rewards by the actual inputs of people, and justice applied in the daily functioning of a given team. There is nothing more crucial in the climate of work relationships than mutual trust (Fox 1974), but there is also nothing more vulnerable to upset through negligence, injustice, and bad will.

The identification of justice with equality leads to a confusion that contaminates participatory cooperation. Equality does not necessarily mean justice when the contributions of various team members remain unequal and those who do more are not rewarded accordingly. The sacrifice of distributive justice for the sake of equality has been practiced many times in history, for instance until recently in People's China, but failed in most cases when the best workers became discouraged because they were rewarded the same way as the worst workers.

Fifthly, participatory cooperation means a new order, but not a lack of order. Successful organizational projects usually lead to such structures in which too much rigidity, and not necessarily too much freedom and spontaneity, becomes a critical problem. Coordination and motivation remain under participatory cooperation the two basic dimensions of leadership and any project in this respect which fails to recognize these both dimensions is condemned to fail. The management of autonomous work groups and of any other forms of participatory cooperation is not easier than the management of authoritarian cooperation and probably even much more difficult. A completely different approach is needed, based on the perfect understanding of human relations and factors which motivate human beings.

Dialectics of leading participatory teams have to deal effectively with several strategic choices: spontaneity versus formalization, elasticity versus rigidity, innovation versus conservatism (continuity), freedom versus discipline, individualism versus collectivism, and so forth. It is a specific problem of participatory teams to limit the managerial functions mainly to the external relations but at the same time to achieve for the benefit of team growth a collective leadership not necessarily of an impersonal character. The "dilution" of individuals in the collectivity is a highly deceptive solution which may lead to moral irresponsibility.

Sixthly, there is a need of continuity and tradition in the teams that would help build an adequately stable social organization. On the other hand, the changing organizational demands of the task-fulfillment process have to be recognized so that the sociocultural factors should not fully dominate over the productivity considerations. It may easily happen that the social organization suppresses task fulfillment, as is particularly evident in bureaucracies. An effective control of sociocultural aspects and their utilization for the benefit of the team (and not to its detriment) is one of the main leadership tasks. On the other hand, the aspects mentioned above need to be adequately recognized.

Continuity of teams and their identity are justified both by the will of members and their well-being as well as by the nature of tasks to be fulfilled. Both these criteria need to be appreciated because without them there would be no justification to expect from teams all potential benefits arising from participation. With the fulfillment of tasks or their substantial transformance the team loses its sense of existence and continuation. This has to be recognized as a problem.

Teams have their uniqueness as well as their communality and both conditions need to be diagnosed by the leadership in order to act adequately, avoid policy errors and all unnecessary hazards. The existence of an autonomous work team has its logic dictated by external and internal circumstances. The team should be prepared adequately for changing circumstances dictated by technological transformations, the motivational readiness of members, level of socialization, and challenges of various kinds. In the current literature there is, so far, little understanding about the dynamics of working group life and the process of collective problem solving. The idealization of participatory cooperation is still very common and misleads many people.

THE GROUP MORALE

The social climate of the AWG depends primarily on the attractiveness of a given AWG as a specific human environment and only afterwards on the satisfaction of members' needs, positive reinforcement of their actions, reduction of cognitive discrepancies (the reduction of tension between inputs and outputs), and the match between expected and obtained rewards (instrumentality). It is in the nature of any close face-to-face group that it is potentially able to offer members a unique encounter. In addition, the social group environment provides individuals with some stability and support of a highly personalized nature, and therefore is much different from the depersonalized world of bureaucracy. The Hawthorne studies carried out over a half-century ago showed that the small group may exercise a very considerable influence on the work behavior of its members, an influence that could be either positively or negatively related to productivity depending on the group values (Roethlisberger and Dickson 1939; Landsberger 1958). In the small and tightly knit work-group there is a likelihood that the individuals will become socialized effectively; the realization of common goals will become for them the source of satisfaction. Both types of needs, hygiene needs and motivators (Herzberg et al. 1959; Herzberg 1966), become absorbed into the group goals and start to play a different role than in the individual situations.

The models of work motivation based only on the individual do not apply adequately to the group situations in which the collective functions as a filter and as a shock-absorber. Members of the cohesive group perceive their own needs and the external stimuli from the perspective of the whole group's well-being and not only from the perspective of their own satisfaction. They calculate their own reactions in the terms of the acceptance by the group, and this is a factor of at least the same importance for them as the direct individual gain or loss.

Group belongingness changes the hierarchy of importance quite profoundly: what is of primary importance for an isolated individual may be of secondary importance for the group member. On the other hand, group belongingness provides a much higher stability of satisfaction that is more unstable in the individual situations (Landy 1978). The emotional states of individuals are under more control in a small group and this is one of the major advantages of the AWGs.

The emotional balance of workers is of great importance for harmonious industrial relations. Small groups keep the emotionality of its members from getting out of control and protects them as well as their performance. The rotation of tasks in the AWG, from interesting to boring and vice versa, is a very useful instrument in the preservation of emotional balance.

An obvious obligation for the AWGs—but very often neglected in hierarchical organizations—is to provide challenging but not too demanding tasks, to promote active personal interest, to provide rewards which are just and informative, and to create working conditions that are at least satisfactory and facilitative. In the AWGs people gain self-esteem, help each other, ambiguities become eliminated, and there is an atmosphere of mutual trust. All these conditions are crucial for the high level of work satisfaction and a good work morale in general (Locke 1976; Fox 1974).

A good group morale has positive impact on absenteeism, because of the effective group pressures; people who are satisfied are also willing to attend work more regularly. People are ashamed to leave their colleagues alone by missing a day of work. Group membership diminishes the perceived opportunity of workers to stay at home instead of going to work. The same is true, to some extent, with the labor turnover that usually is much lower in the AWGs than in hierarchical organizations.

The fact that the AWGs are cohesive helps them to organize work. The growing productivity reinforces the group morale and vice versa. Mutual reinforcement in this respect functions very well in the AWGs as long as the potential interfering factors are kept effectively at bay.

The positive impact of good AWG morale should not be exaggerated. The fact that people are satisfied with their jobs does not necessarily mean that they feel happy about their lives (London et al. 1977). However, the influence of the small group means much more than an influence upon the job. Work in modern society is only a fragment of total life but it is not the same with a team of close companions. Of course, companionship in the AWGs does not necessarily mean friendship and there is no particular reason to encourage the AWGs to go in that direction. The preservation of some emotional distance between the group members may be sometimes more beneficial than close emotional ties.

It is not an ideal of the AWG to make work a central life interest, promote job satisfaction over and above other satisfactions, give priority to job commitments before the nonwork commitments, and sacrifice the individual for the benefit of the AWG collectivity. First of all, this approach would be unrealistic if the present-day sociocultural trends in the modern Western societies are taken into consideration. It would be much more realistic to treat the AWGs as a collectivistic correction of the highly individualized values on one side and of the reified realities of the manipulatory mass society on the other side.

THE VEHICLES OF SOCIALIZATION IN AWGs

Order and security are factors of a particular importance for the positive motivation of group members. The tension at the individual level is quite often related to cognitive dissonance (Festinger 1957) and to the awareness of members that there is some imbalance in their work situation: colleagues have easier and more rewarding jobs, the rate of pay is not adequate to the performance, the principle of distributive justice is upset, and so forth.

In AWGs the rotation of jobs and the commonly accepted system of payment allow members to avoid tensions mentioned above. There is a general tendency in the AWGs to solve the problem of payment in the manner acceptable to all group members (Matejko and Rubenowitz 1980).

The conciliation of the AWG goals with the goals of the individual group members is more probable than in the hierarchical organizations. The hierarchical model of organization leads very often to several conflicts and irrationalities arising from the fact that the local needs and potentialities are not adequately mobilized, and sometimes even totally neglected. The power struggle of vested interests at the individual and group level develops behind the scene and the latent organizational functions (or dysfunctions) nullify the manifest organizational achievements.

The AWGs have the opportunity to eliminate many annoying routines and obvious errors because they dispose of social power. The element of spontaneity inherent in the AWGs makes it possible to correct many things which are otherwise very difficult to change. The innovative power involved in the AWGs allows for the development from a mechanistic to an organic model of organization based on elasticity, informality, and initiative.

Therefore, the organizational climate of the AWGs is usually much better than in the hierarchical organizations, thanks to participatory structure (collective decision making, job rotation), the high level of individual involvement, the large scope of rewards (which are not limited only to the material gain), sharing of risks and responsibility, warmth and mutual support among team members, and a much better conflict resolution. In the AWGs there is less probability than in the hierarchical organizations that people will feel overloaded with work, be much different in their perception of justice, tasks will be allocated in an incompetent manner, and there will be a tendency among group members to do their work differently than expected. Role ambiguity is very common in the hierarchical organizations but rare in the AWGs.

The AWG group is vitally interested in energizing its members, keeping them at the optimal level of arousal and preventing them from feeling lonely, depressed, afraid, and discouraged. The fact that the AWG group is a very human environment, and not only an organizational unit, makes all group members equally valuable and worth appreciation. This factor allows the AWG group to stimulate its members in the social field to a much higher degree than usually occurs in modern mass societies.

Members in the AWG not only have much more chance than is usual with hierarchical organizations in choosing their own goals, but in addition they can depend on the whole group in the implementation of these goals. The risk involved in accepting hard goals is lower for an individual in the AWG than elsewhere, and in this respect the situation is similar to that existing in a sporting group. The AWG not only encourages its members to select hard goals but also offers them recognition for the successful accomplishment of these goals. In the AWG, members become sensitized in a natural way to each other, the group, and the whole workplace without necessarily moving to the more artificial methods of sensitization.

The differentiation which accompanies the division of labor leads to several adaptational problems (Lawrence and Lorsch 1967) and the AWG concept is particularly suitable to solving them successfully. The rigidity of hierarchical organization has made almost impossible the type of flexible solution offered by the AWG concept. This may be well illustrated by the difference between the assembly line and the paralleled group assembly in Sweden (Matejko and Rubenowitz 1980).

The work situations differ depending on the core job dimensions (skill level, completeness of tasks, impact of tasks on other people and jobs, discretion, feedback), expectations and abilities of performers, organizational framework, and so forth (Hackman and Oldham 1976). It is reasonable to expect that, depending on various combinations of the factors mentioned above, the perspectives of success will be either higher or lower for the AWG. For example, the repetitive tasks done by people who have a low level of expectations will provide a much different work situation than the highly variable jobs done by people who have a high level of expectations.

Various factors play a role in the AWGs in motivating people to work. Conditions responsible for the variations in the intensity, quality and direction of group members' behavior may be located in their individual needs. For example, the need for achievement may be a very important factor in promoting people to act in a certain direction. The achievers enjoy tasks of a challenging character.

The needs of workers are not necessarily arranged at a predetermined level as Maslow (1943) imagined. Needs from various levels may appear simultaneously and also do not always lose importance when they have been satisfied. The needs related to existence, relatedness, and growth may differ in their level of concreteness (Alderfer 1972) and this factor also plays a certain role. The intensity of various needs and their selection depend very much on the directions of individual growth as well on the group climate. The impact of the group on individual needs may vary, depending on the loyalty of members, their commitment to the group goals, and so forth.

WORK SATISFACTION IN THE AWGs

In the AWGs, everything should be done in order for people to feel well at work instead of them feeling tense and uncomfortable. The distinction should be made between challenging tasks and unpleasant tasks. The challenge may make people uncomfortable but as long as it makes sense for them there is nothing particularly unreasonable in it. It is quite obvious that people are in the AWG not just to have fun together but to do the work in the most effective way. The fact that they are satisfied is definitely beneficial for work attendance and freedom from tardiness but not necessarily for productivity.

There are many aspects which make people temporarily dissatisfied but have to be tolerated and overcome for the long-range benefit. The worry about work satisfaction should not be of primary importance in the AWG as long as the members gain in the long run and therefore are willing to remain with the same AWG for a prolonged period of time. There is great wisdom in keeping channels open in the AWGs for mobility of members among various groups.

If somebody is dissatisfied with a group he or she should be encouraged to look for another AWG willing and able to accept him or her. In this way the maladaptation would be kept to as low a level as possible by allowing people to try again under different circumstances. The necessity of staying with the same group all the time may be uncomfortable and should be avoided as much as possible.

The level of work satisfaction naturally should be higher in the AWG than in the hierarchical organizations. The difference between expected and actual rewards (Landy and Trumbo 1976, p. 338) does not necessarily have to be higher in the AWG, but what counts much more is the general acceptance of the state of affairs in the group which is voluntarily selected by its members and remains under their control. The general satisfaction in the AWG is not necessarily positive; for instance, if it does not go together with the commitment to group goals. People who are dissatisfied often have a stimulus to act in order to change the state of affairs in a positive direction. Instead of trying to keep the AWG in a good mood all the time, it seems better for the sake of common well-being to face courageously the challenges of group life and group effort.

It is not difficult to keep people satisfied if at least their few basic expectations remain satisfied. What seems to be much more difficult to achieve is a high level of performance that depends only to some extent on how people feel about their jobs in terms of recognition, reward, treatment, promotion, working conditions, and so on. The motivators do not help very much under circumstances which objectively prevent the job from being done well due to the lack of an adequate coordination, inadequate instruction, and so on.

CONCLUSIONS

The AWG model promises success in keeping needs and expectations of members at the realistic and constructive level, allowing individual workers to experience a harmony between their desires and achievements, gaining for all members the satisfaction arising from the fulfillment of their goals within the predictable set of conditions, and reinforcing the achievement orientation within the limits of common well-being.

The combination of extrinsic and intrinsic reinforcements in the AWGs may create some difficulties. It has been observed that extrinsic reinforcement diminishes the intrinsic motivation and vice versa (Deci 1972) and that the relation between various rewards is not additive anyway. With the growing social maturity of the AWG the intrinsic rewards usually grow in importance and the extrinsic rewards lose their previous priority. It does not necessarily mean that the latter stop to function as "hygiene" factors (Herzberg 1966).

There are several factors which play a major role in the orientation of group members to the work tasks. The odds of receiving a particular outcome are considered by people, together with the attractiveness of the job. The value of a given reward will differ among various group members. Effort which people are willing and able to invest into the particular tasks depends not only on their capabilities but also on the stimulative power of the potential rewards, as well as on the reinforcement offered by the immediate group environment. The perception of one's role by the group member, as well as one's self-perception, influence orientation towards the work tasks. Intrinsic and extrinsic rewards differ in their impact on people, depending on the taxation systems, personalities, rate of inflation, and so forth. People usually compare their own rewards with these available to "significant others," or what they had themselves in the past.

In the AWG situation there are several reinforcements which may be very beneficial for the work motivation of individual members but they have to be consciously applied and utilized for the common benefit. Mutual trust and mutual dependence among the group members give them a relatively high amount of security. Close interrelationships based on the joint commitment to common tasks (and to the common well-being) lead to the team spirit that constantly reinforces the work commitment of individual members. They encourage each other and exchange various services helpful for the task performance. The acceptance by other group members becomes for an individual member a very important motivational factor.

The self-image of individual members and their perception of roles played by them within the group are distinctly shaped by the face-to-face relationships between group members. Probably the most important factor is the immediate availability of "significant others" within or close to the boundaries of the group (the supervisor, the staff members, and so on).

Of course, all the group advantages mentioned above appear in the autonomous groups to various degrees, depending upon the quality of group life. No positive outcomes come merely from the fact that people work in a group. Under the conditions of a low quality of group life, some negative outcome of "groupness" may manifest themselves. Therefore, it would be very superficial and naïve to treat the phenomenon of autonomous work groups as necessarily beneficial. It is up to people responsible for a given AWG to mobilize all available group resources for the common benefit (Janis 1971, 1972).

There is the general problem of how to reconcile work roles with the self-evaluations or self-recognitions of the workers. In the hierarchical organization this problem has been almost unsolvable because individual growth has remained in constant contradiction to organizational growth. In the AWGs self-growth develops within the group framework where it becomes a very important part of the group growth. The process of mutual accommodation between the individual and the group is quite often painful but always contributes to socialization. The positive self-image of the individual is encouraged by the group, because, among other reasons, it would be difficult to elicit a continuous effort and loyalty from the people who have a negative self-image. On the other hand, a positive self-image which is not against the group and does not have a purely egoistic character is promoted by AWGs. It is the basic socializing function of the group to impose on its members all necessary corrections and demands dictated by considerations for the common well-being.

In the AWGs the promotion of job-enrichment projects is the natural way of improving the well-being of members and their performance. However, the dimension of job enrichment and its scope in the AWGs have to be adapted to the particular circumstances and not treated as a generally valid recipe. For example, it does not make sense to enforce a type of job enrichment that would discourage group members instead of encouraging them. The process of job-enrichment implementation should be, in general, less painful in the AWGs than in hierarchical organizations in which mutual trust is lacking (Cooper and Mumford 1979).

There is a growing practice in several developed countries of improving the quality of working life by giving small teams of workers considerable autonomy. A major sociological problem of a theoretical and practical nature arises in this respect: The systemic characteristics of autonomous work groups under the conditions of participatory management should be carefully analyzed from a comparative perspective. The small-group research provides us with the data and insights that should be applicable to the sociotechnics of AWGs. Differences in the environmental conditions depending upon the peculiar characteristics of various societies, economic branches, and individual enterprises have to be taken into consideration. Mutual compatibility among the AWG members depends on several external and internal factors. The AWG internal structures vary under the impact of several circumstances which should be carefully ascertained. The leadership style in the AWGs has to be adapted to the democratic character of these very specific organizational units that differ profoundly from their bureaucratic surrounding. The motivational balance in the AWGs is based on the combination of extrinsic and intrinsic reinforcements. The whole problem of job enrichment and job rotation looks differently in the AWGs than in the traditional hierarchical units.

So far there is a clear tendency to idealize the AWGs, but a much more constructively critical and analytical approach is needed. The purpose herein is to provide a systematic review of the basic AWG problems from the social-system perspective, as well as from the praxiological perspective (social praxiology/sociotechnics). Special attention was paid to the problem of socialization of AWG members (reconciliation of various roles and the satisfaction of various demands), the issue of leadership versus supervision (a new type relationship between the elected leader, functioning on a rotational basis, and the AWG membership), and the adaptation of the AWGs to the hierarchical complex organization (the transformation of bureaucratic setup under the impact of the innovative structures). The aim is to cover the preparation stage for modeling AWGs as social systems.

DILEMMAS IN THE FIELD OF WORK PARTICIPATION

The concept of participation

1a The structure of organization, the nature of its technology and the means of gaining the compliance of members of it (Etzioni 1961), all of these, as well as other factors (pattern of ownership, degree of specialization, formalization, and so forth) condition the perspectives of employees toward participation. In hierarchial organizations most of these perspectives are just excluded. The same applies to organizations based on coercion imposed by human power or by machines.

1b In the task-oriented organizations, in normative situations which favor the sense of involvement, and under conditions which in general favor creativity, there will be much room for participation. However, the task-oriented organizations lack, up to now, an adequate organizational theory and social technology of universal validity.

2a The concept of basic solidarity of interests among all occupational groups participating in the workplace (functional interdependence versus the cleavage of interests) provides the justification for industrial democracy.

2b The conflict of interests between various pressure groups in the enterprise makes it extremely difficult to achieve any changes in the balance of power without exercising some strong external pressures.

3a It is assumed in the general model of industrial democracy that all levels and categories of employees have some obvious stake in the participatory decision making.

3b The identification with the institutional goals grows with the level of skills, education, and power (executives have the highest sense of participation). The lower levels show a high level of frustration and low level of participation, identification, satisfaction, and so forth.

4a The interests of a workshop community are clear and attractive enough to integrate employees around them. The progressing division of labor quite often makes it difficult to bring people together. However, the common work tasks provide a common denominator.

4b The local interests on the workshop level are not the same as the broader interests of particular industrial branches, specific occupations, territorial communities, and so forth. Therefore, there is always a problem of how to reconcile workshop interests with other interests.

5a The appointment of people who would represent a specific class of employees (for instance, blue-collar workers) on the boards of directors is treated as one of the basic characteristics of industrial democracy. These representatives are supposed to be from the ranks of a given class, and to be controlled by the class institutions.

5b The boards of directors in the private and public enterprises are expected to be able and willing to fulfill specific tasks, and not just to represent divergent interests. The duty of managing may be in disagreement with the duty of representing and advancing workers' interests.

Social Conditions of Participation

6a   There is an evident historical development of democratic ideals which favor participation of citizens in making decisions of vital importance for them personally and for the society.

6b   There is an alienation of people from their own products and the authoritarian reality of modern complex organizations. The highly specialized function of modern management is justified by the developed division of labor. Social distances have been created. There is the growing complication of modern society and the danger of upsetting its very delicate internal equilibrium. Both of them make any substantial changes very difficult. There is the necessity of producing goods and services on the basis of swift and expeditious decisions.

7a   Some new solutions must be found when considering that even in the developed countries there is a growth of pessimism.

7b   The short-range perspective dominates in many societies, and is justified either by poverty and traditionalism (developing societies) or by the market mechanism (developed capitalist societies) or by the ossification of the internal power balance (developed socialist societies). There is a strong resistance to change dictated by the whole variety of factors.

8a   There is a growing estrangement of vital decisions from people who execute them—due to the progressing division of labor, mechanization, improvement of organization, and the like. The peripheral importance of work in the life of many people becomes an important problem.

8b   There is a social urgency to make working people loyal to the institutions which employ them, better informed and committed (a contented and efficient labor force).

9a   It is maybe too optimistic to assume that people want to participate; that the management role may be limited to the encouragement in creativity; that the improvement of human relations leads to higher productivity. On the other hand, it would be terribly pessimistic to accept the opposite view.

9b   The realistic approach leads us to the distinction between factors which make work just bearable, factors which make people happy, and factors which allow people to grow. However, management represents a normative factor imposed on the social reality. It makes a difference if management just controls others or it stimulates people to achieve growth based on their own latent potential.

Limits of Participation

10a   The degree of people's interest in participation differs widely and it is an oversimplification to claim that organization members in general want to exercise control (Tannenbaum 1966, p. 94). "The number of nonmanagerial workers who are able and ready to participate in management decisions, other than those that directly affect their immediate jobs and work-loads, would in fact appear to be limited" (Clarke et al. 1972, p. 19).

10b   It is true that some people like to be independent, gain personally from participation and reduce their own frustrations because of it. However it is not always so, and not everybody really has interest in participation. The potential in this respect differs widely among various cultures and various socio-economic circumstances.

11a   People are mostly interested in their specific tasks and issues; much more than in broader issues of running the whole business.

11b   The task-based participation (job enlargement, job rotation, job enrichment, autonomous group work, and so forth) puts people into an active situation in which they are expected to identify themselves with the authentic and motivational tasks. In this way people overcome the previous limits of their interests.

12a   There is a particularly high level of estrangement among lower class people; it is related to the small responsibility of the employer for lower ranks of people who are wage and salary earners.

12b   Among unskilled and uneducated people there is a limited propensity to participate; also a narrow scope of commitment and its limitation only to certain aspects of work situations. Rewards are remote and too small.

13a   Employees are traditionally interested only in managerial decisions concerning discipline, organization of work, but primarily wages (Clarke et al. 1972, p. 5). The progress of inflation and tensions related to it may make necessary a genuine sharing of managerial authority in much broader scope. The problem is how to reconcile the task-oriented aspect of this issue with the problem of power-sharing.

13b   The dual allegiance of the labor directors and other appointees who are supposed to represent interests of the blue collar workers, leads to several adaptional problems for them. They may become totally alienated from the rank and file. They may be manipulated by external bodies, for example the ruling party or trade unions. They may also develop their own tactics of out-maneuvering all other partners. Inside appointees become parochial; outside appointees are not familiar enough with local problems.

The Management Participation

14a   Depending on the style of management, of the supervisor's "tell," "sell," "consult" or "join," there is more or less room for participation by employees in the decision making.

14b   The style of managing people depends not only on the goodwill of managers, but also on their personalities and several external factors.

15a   The authority based on power or tradition loses its appeal among people. They are willing to accept only such authority which originates from the demands of the situation and which has some objective justification. The functional requirements legitimize the modern authority.

15b   The crisis of authority becomes also the crisis of organization. It is not possible to effectively coordinate and stimulate the activities of people without depending on at least some common values shared by people.

16a   There is a hesitancy of management as well as unions to experiment with new participatory schemes which would allow employees to gain some control in work places. There is an unwillingness of unions to tolerate the participatory schemes outside of their direct control.

16b There is a spontaneous development of semiformal and informal pressure groups at workplaces. They exercise a widespread control over the behavior of working people and over the functioning of work places.

17a It is necessary to make a distinction between the freedom of management to make decisions within certain acceptable limits of risk-taking, and the unlimited liberty of managers from any external controls, particularly from those coming from the rank and file, unions, representatives elected to the participatory bodies.

17b In order to be successful in its main task, the management must reconcile the conflicting interests of various groups which participate in the workplace or have some stake in it. The cooperative nature of the workshop community must be respected by the management.

Participation in Bargaining

18a The workplace is a joint enterprise in which several vested interests are involved. The dominance of only one of these interests may upset the balance and lower the effectiveness of the whole workplace. Unless adequate attention is paid to each one of the vested interests, the workplace will not utilize its whole internal and external potential.

18b The primary function of the board of directors is to conserve and ensure the growth of the company's capital per se. The representation of workers' interests in this respect is of no critical importance. The division within the boards of directors according to the diversive interests may considerably weaken the ability of the board to deal effectively with its primary task.

19a Participation is effective only when all partners have some strength to bargain, thanks to their secure position in the division of labor, advantages of the technology controlled by them, favorable market conditions, education, and so forth.

19b Any substantial imbalance between partners in their

relative bargaining power may undermine the process of participation.

20a   There is a common practice for unions to arrange with the employers the conditions of work and employment on the basis of collective bargaining (the antagonistic cooperation). Development of the joint consultative machinery (especially in the nonprofit sector) is welcome.

20b   There is the hesitancy of unions to share responsibility for the economic effectiveness of the workplaces under the assumption that it may weaken the power of unions to bargain with employers. The management insists that nobody should encroach on its prerogatives. Unions are committed to the rules of trade.

21a   Consultation without negotiation leads to the discussion of trivial issues only, and loses its attractiveness to the partners.

21b   Preoccupation of management with the encroachment upon managerial rights degrades the meaning of joint consultation.

22a   The mutual adjustment of antithetical interests in the process of collective bargaining is particularly effective in securing the industrial peace if promoted on a continuous basis (speedy settlement of problems by shop stewards on an informal basis). It is particularly true in the productivity bargaining.

22b   The institutionalization of the face to face task-oriented contacts shared by management and the representatives of the employees leads to the set of joint vested interests and the gradual abolition of the existing group loyalties.

23a   The unilateral decision making by management and union bosses separately or jointly together eliminates the rank and file as the participatory factor in industrial relations. The restrictive practices concerning manpower utilization represent an answer to it.

23b   The consultation and involvement of the rank and file becomes a necessity in the productivity bargaining. The willingness of the management to discuss to the full length the implications of its proposals is of crucial importance in this respect.

Formalization versus Spontaneity

24a   The opposition within the framework of participation
        must be based on such contradictions which are
        solvable within certain framework, it means which are
        based on at least some evident common interests,
        elements of knowledge and goodwill. The play of
        oppositions exercised within the participatory bodies
        must be adequate to the play of oppositions within the
        broader constituency.

24b   The development of common interests within the
        participatory bodies leads to the gradual elimination of
        opposition and to the complacency with the status
        quo. There appears a progressing alienation of
        participatory bodies from the broader constituency.

25a   Voluntary and nonformalized bodies of participation
        are highly effective in the climate of a collective
        bargaining tradition, where there is a balance of
        power between bargaining partners.

25b   The formalized and compulsory bodies of participation
        are the only possible solution when there is an evi-
        dent imbalance of power between bargaining partners.

26a   The network of rules and customs mutually agreed by
        employees and employers is a guarantee of an efficient
        functioning of the whole.

26b   The nature of demands and necessities changes in
        relation to the bargaining between various partners in
        the field of industrial relations.   The fixed rules are
        the source of difficulties in improvement of the indus-
        trial relations.

27a   Formal participation is more common in large work-
        places where the informal channels would not be able
        to secure an adequate flow of information and nego-
        tiation. The participation of employees in the finan-
        cial decisions must be based on adequate information
        offered by management (index of labor cost per unit
        of output, number and type of workers employed,
        payroll, financial standing of various types of pro-
        duction, structure of sales, broad disbursement as
        percent of total income of the company). The issue
        of opening the books.

27b   The formalization of participation eliminates the
        face-to-face contact and the positive values of inte-
        gration in the field of human relations. There is also

a loss in the information flow. Management as well as unions, for quite different reasons, are against the involvement of employees in the financial decisions. Joint regulation and joint determination leads to mutual involvement, and both partners are unwilling to go into it.

28a Subcontracting work to autonomous groups of employees on a lump-sum basis (a collective contract) provides not only an opportunity for them for self-actualization, but also offers an opportunity to foster participation at the bottom of the organizational structure.

28b The parochial commitments of people versus one another may limit their scope of interests to such extent that it undermines the unity of the whole organization.

REFERENCES

Alderfer, C. P. 1972. *Existence, Relatedness and Growth: Human Needs in Organizational Settings*. New York: Free Press.

Andreski, S. 1975. *Reflections on Inequality*. London: Croom Helm.

Aronson, Elliot. 1980. *The Social Animal*. San Francisco: W. H. Freeman.

Atkinson, J. W., and J. R. Raynor, eds. 1974. *Motivation and Achievement*. Washington: V. H. Winston.

A Review and Evaluation of RPSLMC Nursing Workload Staffing Systems. 1978. Chicago: Medicus System Corporation.

Bakke, K. 1974. Primary Nursing: Perception of a Staff Nurse. *American Journal of Nursing,* 74:1432–38.

Bales, R. F. 1950. *Interaction Process Analysis*. Reading, MA: Addison-Wesley.

Bell, Daniel. 1976. *The Cultural Contradictions of Capitalism*. New York: Basic Books.

Benjamin, Alfred. 1978. *Behavior in Small Groups*. Boston: Houghton Mifflin.

Bennis, Warren G. 1966. *Changing Organizations*. New York: McGraw-Hill.

Blau, P. M. 1964. *Exchange and Power in Social Life*. New York: Wiley.

Calgart, R. S., and L. A. Samovar, eds. 1979. *Small Group Communication*. Dubuque, IA: William C. Brown.

Cang, S. 1977. "An Alternative to Hospital." *The Lancet,* April 2:742–43.

Cang, S., and F. Clarke. 1979. *Hospital at Home.* London: Croom Helm.

Cang, S., and R. Rowbottom. 1978. *National Health Service Reorganization.* Uxbridge (U.K): Brunel Institute of Organization and Social Studies.

Cartwright, D., and A. Zander, eds. 1968. *Group Dynamics.* New York: Row and Peterson.

Christensen, K., and J. A. Lingle. 1972. "Evaluation of Effectiveness of Team and Non-team Public Health Nurses in Health Outcomes of Patients with Strokes or Fractures. *American Journal of Public Health,* 62:483–90.

Christman, L. 1978. Book review of A. J. Davis and M. A. Aroskar, *Ethical Dilemmas and Nursing Practice, Nursing Forum,* 17:2.

————. 1980. "An Organizational Perspective for Nursing Practice." Paper for the American Nurses Association Convention, Houston, June 9–13.

Clark, M. J., R. T. Hartnett, and L. L. Baird. 1976. *Assessing Dimensions of Quality in Education.* Princeton: Education Testing Service.

Clarke, R. O., D. J. Fatchett, and B. C. Roberts. 1972. *Workers' Participation in Management in Britain.* London: Heinemann.

Clayre, Alasdair. 1977. "Tomorrow's Industry," *The Economist,* March 5.

Cooper, C. L., and Mumford, eds. 1979. *The Quality of Working Life in Western and Eastern Europe.* Greenwood Press.

Crowden, Peter. 1978. "Dissatisfaction and the Changing Meaning and Purpose of Nurse's Work," *Nursing Forum,* 17(2):202–9.

Cummings, T. 1978. "Self-Regulating Work Groups: A Socio-technical synthesis," *Academy of Management Review,* 3:625–34.

Davis, James H. 1969. *Group Performance.* Reading, MA: Addison-Wesley.

Deci, E. L. 1972. "The Effects of Contingent and Non-contingent Rewards and Controls on Intrinsic Behavior," *Organizational Behavior and Human Performance,* 8:217–29.

Democracy in the NHS. 1974. London: Department of Health and Social Security.

Deutsch, M. A. 1949. "An Experimental Study of the Effects of Cooperation and Competition Upon Group Process," *Human Relations,* 2:199–231.

Donahue, P. 1978. "The Nurse. A Patient Advocate?" *Nursing Forum,* 17:143–51.

Dubin, Robert. 1958. *The World of Work. Industrial Society and Human Relations.* Englewood Cliffs, NJ: Prentice-Hall.

Elling, Ray H., and M. Sokolowska, eds. 1978. *Medical Sociologists at Work.* New Brunswick, NJ: Transaction Books.

Emery, F. E., and E. Thorsrud. 1976. *Democracy at Work: The Report of the Norwegian Industrial Democracy Program,* Leiden: Martinus Nijhoff.

Etzioni, Amitai. 1961. *A Comparative Analysis of Complex Organizations.* New York: Free Press.

Festinger, L. 1957. *Theory of Cognitive Dissonance.* Stanford: Stanford University Press.

Fiedler, R. E., and A. F. Liester, 1971. "Leader Intelligence and Task Performance: A Test of a Multiple Screen Model," *Organizational Behavior and Human Performance,* 20:1–14.

Fox, A. 1974. *Beyond Contract.* London: Faber and Faber.

Garant, Carol A. 1978. "The Process of Effecting Change in Nursing," *Nursing Forum,* 17(2):152–67.

Georgopoulos, B. S., and R. A. Cooke. 1978. *A Comparative Study of Hospital Emergency Services.* Ann Arbor: Institute for Social Research.

Georgopoulos, S. D., and A. Matejko. 1967. "The American General Hospital as a Complex Social System," *Health Services Research,* 1:76–112.

Gerson, M. 1978. *Family, Women and Socialization in the Kibbutz.* Boston: Heath.

Glasser, P., R. Sarri, and R. Vinter, eds. 1974. *Individual Change Through Small Groups.* New York: Free Press.

Gordon, E., and P. Adams. 1971. "You Can't be a Team by Yourself," *International Nursing Review,* 18:76–79.

Group Care—An Alternative? 1978. *Spri rapport,* 4 Stockholm, Sweden: Sjukvardens och socialvardens planerings—och rationalisirungsistiut (in Swedish).

Hackman, J. R., and G. R. Oldham. 1976. "Motivation Through the Design of Work: Test of a Theory," *Organizational Behavior and Human Performance,* 16:250–79.

Hardie, M., and L. Hockey. 1978. *Nursing Auxiliaries in Health Care.* London: Croom Helm.

Haire, A. P. 1976. *Handbook of Small Group Research.* New York: Free Press.

Haire et al. 1965. *Small Groups: Studies in Social Interaction.* New York: Knopf.

Herzberg, Frederic. 1959. *The Motivation to Work.* New York: Wiley.

—————. 1966. *Work and Nature of Man.* Cleveland: World Publishing.

Homans, G. 1950. *The Human Group.* New York: Harcourt, Brace and World.

—————. 1974. *Social Behavior: Its Elementary Forms.* New York: Harcourt, Brace, Jovanovich.

Janis, I. L. 1971. "Groupthink," *Psychology Today,* No. 5.

—————. 1972. *Victims of Groupthink.* Boston: Houghton Mifflin.

Jacques, E., ed. 1978. *Health Services.* London: Heinemann.

Jelinek, Richard J., et al. 1974. *A Methodology for Monitoring Quality of Nursing Care.* Bethesda, MD: U.S. Department of Health, Education and Welfare, DHEW 76–25.

Jones, Nancy K., and Jack W. Jones. 1979. The Head Nurse: A Managerial Definition of the Activity Role Set, *Nursing Administrative Quarterly,* 3(2):45–57.

Haussman, R. K. Dieter, Sue T. Hegyvary, and John F. Newman. 1976. *Monitoring Quality of Nursing Care,* Part II. Assessment and Study of Correlates, Bethesda, MD: U.S. Department of Health, Education and Welfare, DHEW 76–77.

Haussman, R. K Dieter, and Sue T. Hegyvary. 1977. *Monitoring of Nursing Care,* Part III. Professional Review for Nursing: An Empirical Investigation, Bethesda, MD: U.S. Department of Health, Education and Welfare, DHEW 70–77.

Katz, D., and R. L. Kahn. 1978. *The Social Psychology of Organizations.* New York: Wiley.

Kneedler, J. A. 1979. "Perioperative Role in Three Dimensions," *ARON Journal,* 30, 5:859–75.

Kogan, M., et al. 1971. *Working Relationships Within the British Hospital Service.* London: Bookstall Publications.

Kramer, M. 1974. *Reality Shock.* St. Louis: C. V. Mosby.

Landsberger, H. A. 1958. *Hawthorne Revisited.* Ithaca, NY: Cornell University Press.

Landy, F. J. 1978. "An Opponent Process Theory of Job Statisfaction," *Journal of Applied Psychology,* 63:533–47.

Landy, F. J., and D. A. Trumbo. 1976. *Psychology of Work Behavior.* Homewood, IL: Dorsey Press.

Lawrence, R. R. and J. Lorsch. 1967. *Organization and*

Environment. Cambridge: Harvard University Press.

Likert, Rensis. 1967. *Human Organization*. New York: McGraw-Hill.

Lindzey, G., and E. Aronson, eds. 1969. "Group Psychology and the Phenomena of Interaction." In *Handbook of Social Psychology,* Vol. 4. Reading, MA: Addison-Wesley.

Lio, A. M. 1973. "Leadership and Responsibility of Team Nursing," *Nursing Clinics of North America,* 8:267–81.

Locke, E. A. 1976. "The Nature and Causes of Job Dissatisfaction." In *Handbook of Industrial and Organizational Psychology,* edited by M. Dunnette. Chicago: Rand McNally.

London, M., et al. 1977. "The Contribution of Job and Leisure Satisfaction to the Quality of Life," *Journal of Applied Psychology* 62:328–34.

Manthey, M. and M. Kramer. 1970. "A Dialogue on Primary Nursing," *Nursing Forum,* 9:356–79.

Manthey, M., et al. 1970. "Primary Nursing," *Nursing Forum,* 9:65–83.

Marcuse, H. 1964. *One-Dimensional Man*. Boston: Beacon Press.

Martin, R. 1977. *The Sociology of Power*. London: Routledge and Kegan Paul.

Maslow, Abraham. 1943. "A Theory of Motivation," *Psychology Review,* 50:370–96.

Matejko, Alexander J. 1962. *Kultura pracy zbiorowej* (Culture of Collective Work). Warsaw: Wyd. Zwiazkowe.

—————. 1966. "Les Conditions psycho-sociales du travail dans les groupes scientifiques," *Sociologie du Travail,* 1.

—————. 1970. *Uslovia Tvorczeskogo Truda* (Conditions of Creative Work). Moscow: Izdatelstvo Mir.

—————. 1973. "Institutional Conditions of Scientific Inquiry. Survey of Research Teams in Poland," *Small Group Behavior,* 4,1:89–126.

—————. 1977. "Management Participation," *International Review of Sociology,* 13:3.

—————. 1980. "The Obsolescence of Bureaucracy," *Relations Industrielles/Industrial Relations,* 35, 3.

—————. 1984. *Beyond Bureaucracy?* Cologne: Verlag für Gesellschaftsarchitektur. Chap. 11, on teamwork in hospitals.

Matejko, Alexander J., and Sigvard Rubenowitz. 1980. "The Sociotechnics of Working Life: Experiences from Sweden," *Europa,* 3:2.

—————. 1980. "The Optimalization of Sociotechnical

Conditions," *Newsletter* (Research Committee of Socio-technics I.S.A.) 5:14–39.

Miles, M. B. 1973. *Learning to Work in Groups*. New York: Teachers College Press.

Miles, Theodore M. 1967. *The Sociology of Small Groups*. Englewood Cliffs, NJ: Prentice-Hall.

Minzberg, H. 1973. *The Nature of Managerial Work*. New York: Harper and Row.

Napier, R. W. 1973. *Groups: Theory and Experience*. Camden, NJ: Nelson.

Nicolson, N., et al. 1976. "Absence from Work and Job Satisfaction," *Journal of Applied Psychology,* 61:728–37.

Nursing Research Abstracts. Department of Health and Security. Index of Nursing Research. Room A324. Alexander Fleming House. London: Elephant and Castle.

Ofshe, R. J., ed. 1973. *Interpersonal Behavior in Small Groups*. Englewood Cliffs, NJ: Prentice-Hall.

Olmstead, M. S., and A. P. Haire. 1978. *The Small Group*. New York: Random House.

Pembrey, S. 1978. "The Role of the Ward Sister in the Management of Nursing." Ph.D. dissertation, Edinburgh University.

Phillips, G. M., et al. 1979. *Group Discussion*. Boston: Houghton Mifflin.

Porter-O'Grady, T., and J. A. Carter. 1979. "Bringing the Nursing Process into the OR," *ARON Journal,* 30, 5:898–995.

Pryma, R. 1978. "Primary Nursing," *The Magazine Rush—Presbyterian—St. Luke's Medical Center* 2, 2:3–17.

Roethlisberger, F. J., and W. J. Dickson. 1961. *Management and the Worker*. Cambridge: Harvard University Press (first published in 1939).

Rowbottom, R., et al. 1973. *Hospital Organization*. London: Hospital Educational Books.

Rowbottom, R., and A. Hey. 1978. *Collaboration Between Health and Social Services*. Uxbridge (U.K.): Brunel Institute of Organization and Social Studies.

Schumacher, J. 1975. *Small is Beautiful*. London: Sphere Books.

Sharp, B. H., and E. Cross. 1971. "Rounds and Rounds," *Nursing Outlook,* 19:419–20.

Shaw, M. E. 1963. *Scaling Group Tasks*. Gainesville, FL: University of Florida.

————. 1976. *Group Dynamics*. New York: McGraw-Hill. (1981. 3d ed.).

Shils, E. A. 1951. "The Study of Primary Group." In *The Policy Sciences,* edited by D. Lerner and H. D. Lasswell, Stanford: Stanford University Press.

Slocum, J. W., and H. P. Sims, Jr. 1980. "A Typology for Integrating Technology, Organization and Job Design." Southern Methodist University. Manuscript.

Staff Mobility on Hospital Wards. 1978. *Spri rapport,* 5 (in Swedish) Sjukvardens och socialvardens planerings—och rationalisirungstitut, Fak 10250 Stockholm.

Steers, R. M., and L. W. Porter, eds. 1975. *Motivation and Work Behavior.* New York: McGraw-Hill.

Stimson, David H., and Ruth H. Stimson. 1972. *Operations Research in Hospitals: Diagnosis and Prognosis,* Chicago: Hospital Research and Educational Trust.

Susman, G. 1976. *Autonomy at Work: A Sociotechnical Analysis of Participative Management.* New York: Praeger.

Tannenbaum, Arnold. 1966. *Social Psychology of the Work Organization.* London: Tavistock.

Theis, G. 1974. "A Change From Team Nursing," *Nursing Outlook,* 22:258–59.

Thelen, H. A. 1954. *Dynamics of Groups at Work.* Chicago: University of Chicago Press.

Thibault, J. W., and H. H. Kelley. 1959. *The Social Psychology of Groups.* New York: Wiley.

Wilson, S. 1978. *Informal Groups.* Englewood Cliffs, NJ: Prentice-Hall.

5

THE SWEDISH CASE

THE SWEDISH MODEL OF SOCIOTECHNICS

Work becomes more and more organized and we urgently need not only a reflection on the real effectiveness of work organization but also an active experimentation in this field. The Quality of Working Life (QWL) movement (Davis and Cherns 1975) has opened some new perspectives in this respect and Sweden has become world-known as so far the most suitable ground for genuine job reform. The teleological paradigm proposed by A. Podgorecki as the methodological basis of sociotechnics, for instance, the theoretical reflection on the effectiveness of practical social actions (Podgorecki 1975, pp. 112–13) seems to suit particularly well the Swedish QWL scene.

Swedish society faces several practical problems related to the common well-being and to the progressive humanization of various fields of joint activities, mainly work. In this respect, in Swedish society there is relatively more consent, mutual trust, and cooperation than in most other free-market societies. The large scale of Swedish QWL commitment allows a broad experience valid not only for Sweden but also for many other countries.

The material in this chapter was collected and analyzed in cooperation with Professor Sigvard Rubenowitz from the Institute of Psychology, University of Gothenburg in Sweden.

150

The social mechanism of value clarification and the establishment of priorities is based in Sweden on joint consultation among management, trade unions, and the state. Diagnosis needed for the QWL activities is largely provided by the academia and various consulting services. The global evaluation of specific conditions existing in the workplaces is done by the joint bodies established ad hoc for this purpose and consisting of all interested parties: management, consultants, trade-union functionaries, representatives of various categories of employees. The decision to carry out the QWL innovation is taken in such a way as to assure the consent and involvement of all major partners. The anticipation of positive and negative results of innovations may be done much more effectively when the broad participation of employees is achieved from the beginning and when the potential worries and insecurities are eliminated, or at least greatly limited. The projects borne out inside the workplaces, with some external help but without the total dependence on experts from outside, are critically analyzed and the follow-up becomes something obvious.

The origins of sociotechnics are related to various practical applications of scientific studies in law enforcement, industrial relations, public policy, social welfare, and so forth. The rigorous theoretical thinking has only recently started to enter the fields of applied sociology and applied social psychology (Cherns 1979), which so far constitute a chaotic collection of various projects uncomparable with one another and therefore not allowing a systematic accumulation of knowledge. With the growing "organic solidarity" (Durkheim 1893) of the modern societies and the danger of overbureaucratization, due to the growth of big corporations and the welfare state (the public sector in the developed non-socialist countries takes in some cases even a bigger share of GNP than in such a communist country as Poland), there is an urgent need to develop an adequate theory of shaping and transforming complex organizations (Katz and Kahn 1978; Matejko 1980a). For several years we have known many important things about the structural properties of the hierarchical organizations but we have learned much less about the praxiological properties of practical actions, their successes as well as failures (Podgorecki 1975). The current much more mature state of sociotechnics allows us to study the nature of practical actions in a more systematic way than before.

The value of Swedish sociotechnical experience is unique in many respects. Technology until recently has been widely accepted in the study of industrial complex organizations as the independent variable and the Swedish experiments in reshaping technological conditions have been a major breakthrough in this respect. For the first time, social scientists have become fully aware of the fact that the technological ramifications of sociopsychological micro-systems may be treated not only as flexible but in addition as highly adjustable according to social concerns (Dahlström 1978).

The development of modern work sociotechnics in Sweden should be understood in the framework of the traditionally peaceful relations among labor, management, and government, as well as the mutual acceptance among all three partners. It seems quite natural why in Sweden, and not in Italy or in France, management was first to start—with the consent of organized labor—the massive experiments oriented toward the reconciliation of social microsystems with the technoeconomic and administrative systems (Job Reform . . . 1975). In comparison with the Norwegian contribution, in Sweden there seems to be less sociotechnical conceptualization of a theoretical armchair nature as, for instance, the Norwegian concept of "matrix organization" (Elden 1978; Bolweg 1976), but much more awareness of the industrial realities, for example, the impact of sociotechnical conditions on absenteeism and labor turnover. Swedish social scientists are busy studying such issues as resistance to change, not only among managers and trade union leaders but also among blue-collar workers, analysis of small-group functioning, the systematic studies of specific technological constraints, and so forth.

The sociotechnics of technological changes is influenced by broad social concerns much more evidently in Sweden than in other developed countries. Differences between the tradition of ergonomics and the new sociotechnical engineer-ing practiced in Swedish industry are quite substantial. Why is the assembly line put into question in the big Swedish enterprises? Various alternatives of the production flow have been considered in Sweden and implemented with more or less success. This undermines the still widespread thesis that the assembly line represents the most efficient form of organizing people and machines. It is not only the question of various technological improvements oriented toward making work easier, more pleasant and more sociable, but even to a much greater extent the question of how to incorporate such improvements into the existing system of the factory, the union, the company, and so on. The Swedish experience shows that the implementation of such innovations remains quite difficult even under the basically cooperative system and that the resistance to change has various sources, sometimes quite unexpected. The conflictual nature of Western industrial systems outside Sweden is so evident that this factor makes major innovations almost impossible from the beginning; but they still remain possible in Sweden, even under the adversary economic conditions. This additionally makes Sweden a particularly suitable place for drawing sociotechnical conclusions from the study of innovative changes.

The creation of autonomous production groups and the incorporation of them into work organization has been done in Sweden on a much larger scale than in other countries—except the Soviet bloc where, however, these groups are manipulated by the ruling party and by management. Swedes already have an awareness of basic conditions under which these groups manage to survive and succeed. It is very important to compare the semiformal rules of Swedish group dynamics with the experimental knowledge based on laboratory research mostly in the United States (Shaw 1981). It is also an important question how much the Swedish group experience matches the group experience of other countries. Another question is if and how the rules valid for the industrial blue-collar workers may apply also to other occupational environments.

Awareness that managerial styles and patterns have to be constantly modernized is strong in Sweden. In the developed modern societies there are several trends that make obsolete the traditional management in general, including the authoritarian management. According to the new trends that have developed, the managers or supervisors should focus mainly on the boundary functions, leaving the internal coordination to the autonomous group itself (Herbst 1976). The move from the old to the new managerial pattern is intrinsically linked to the sociotechnical changes, and the Swedish experience is of primary validity. Sweden has been the first Western country in which the traditional managerial prerogatives have become the matter of formal bargaining between management and trade unions. How does the Swedish industry prepare its managers to the new pressures, anxieties, and responsibilities? To what extent does the management as well as the trade-union leadership cooperate in the gradual change of management style? How do managers adapt to the new situation? What is the role of social scientists in shaping the new management style? All these questions are of vital importance.

The organizational innovations and work reforms constitute, in present-day Sweden, a major factor of general change. The whole content of Swedish complex organizations has been considerably changed because of the transformations occurring in the industrial relations system. What are the implications of it for the internal and external socioeconomic hierarchy, commitment of employees to the workplace, work motivation and life satisfaction of people, mutual relations among various people participating jointly in the work process, distance between people occupying various positions, productivity, inventiveness, and so forth? There are several Swedish studies which provide at least the fragmentary answer to all these questions.

Many changes happening in Sweden have to be related to its long historical process of the welfare-state growth much different from other Western countries. This fact imposes some limitations on the sociotechnical validity of practical directives which have succeeded in Sweden but may not fit into other national realities. It is necessary to make a clear distinction between what is sociotechnically unique for Sweden and what may be generalized and applied elsewhere.

THE PARTICIPATORY PROJECTS

Under the conditions of the welfare state and a very strong impact of organized socialism there is a climate favorable to a new approach to work organization. In the Swedish industrial relations system, based on union-management cooperation, equalization of net incomes, the limited role of material incentives, the security of employment (even in the case of high absenteeism), and the limited management prerogatives, it becomes almost unavoidable to look for a new management style. Of course, this new style is also a part and parcel of the sociotechnical organizational forms. There is a great potential for goodwill and knowledge among the employees that so far has not been explored adequately. On the other hand, any enlargement of participation at the lower levels of complex organizations makes sense only when there is enough delegation of power down the managerial hierarchy (Rubenowitz 1974, p. 6). The middle- and lower-level managers may rightly be afraid of such a pattern of participation in which they are expected to share power with their own subordinates, when at the same time they do not obtain an adequate delegation of power from the higher echelons.

According to the position taken by the Swedish Federation of Employers (SAF), the primary desire of employees is to influence their own jobs. Board representation is a less important issue. Anyway, in all limited liability Swedish companies with at least one hundred employees there are usually on the board of directors two employee representatives in addition to three executive directors and three nonexecutive directors. The major concern of SAF is how to preserve the character of boards as decision-making bodies instead of bargaining bodies in which various categories of members represent different positions. "There should be no special rules for worker board members, such as for example, the right of veto in special cases or the right to postpone business" (Board Representation 1976, p. 3). Only employees in any particular company should be eligible for election to its board (the law permits exceptions but they rarely happen). According to SAF all employees, and not only the trade-union members, should be allowed to elect board members. There should not be much turnover among employee board members. The owners must retain the dominant influence on company boards (Ibid., p. 3).

Many of the Swedish enterprises face, as has been previously mentioned, the necessity of reforming their organization in order to mobilize resources which so far have remained dormant. The organic shop-floor participation has proved itself to be more desirable and fruitful for both the employees and the organization than other forms of participation: the financial participation of employees in the enterprise's profits, or the formally structured company participation in the form of representatives of employees in the management boards, or top-level participation, or the formally structured shop-floor participation through representatives at the shop-floor level itself.

Under the inspiration of management circles and the consultants, mostly from academia, hundreds of participatory projects have been experimented on in the Swedish factories since the 1970s.

For example, in the AB Astra pharmaceutical factory several autonomous work competence groups deal with daily matters of the packaging process. Five to ten members rotate the jobs among themselves, plan production, solve problems without the assistance of the supervisor, plan the budget, take courses together, and so forth. Because of the job enlargement, their remuneration has been upgraded adequately. In AB Casco factories of industrial adhesives and resins the work environment groups have been formed which consist of the foreman, safety officer, and workers. The groups are kept small and informal and they move gradually from diagnosis to specific practical actions.

In several other cases, employees are invited to join the consultative groups dealing with such problems as the induction system for new employees, new systems of payments, the improvement of administrative routines, training schemes, personnel planning systems, and so forth. The companies help members of the consultative groups gain adequate additional information or even develop training needed in order to promote the consultative work. According to the experience gained in these projects, large committees take too much time. For example, in the Esseltepac AB consumer packaging factory, the experience of committees established for the detailed planning of the new factory building was

> that consultations of this nature are rather time-consuming. The decision-making process takes longer and very many working hours have to be set aside for meetings. The committees appointed small project groups to discuss special limited problems. Experiences from these small groups are very good. The members personally felt they were more involved in the work. They worked quickly and efficiently (Participation . . . 1975, p. 13).

From the many cases of autonomous group application, the factory of ethylian amins of the Berol Kemi AB in Stenungsund deserves particular mention (the description deals with the situation of mid-1979) as a carefully prepared participatory project in which the success is due to the very good cooperation between management, particularly the production manager, and the blue-collar crew. The production of ethylian amins was started by Beril Kemi in 1977 and this was the only place in the world in which this particular technology was applied. People work on five shifts, changing every eight hours, with each shift consisting of five persons. The production manager is helped by the training instructor, an analyst and two other white-collar workers. In each shift group people rotate among all jobs. One of them is the job of a shift coordinator, who is expected to have at least one-and-one-half or two years' experience. He has to know well all the jobs on the shift. He stays on his job as a coordinator for two to four months. The whole shift group shares the decisions and the responsibility related to the current production: allocation of people to various jobs, help offered to other shifts if necessary, dealing with various current problems, and so forth. The cooperation within the shift groups has developed very well; absenteeism is relatively low; there is a friendly atmosphere; people stick together.

The production manager is in close touch with the shift groups and enjoys their trust. People working in the amins factory are carefully selected; 30 percent of them are engineers and the average age is around 24 years. They do not earn much over the Swedish average. They work on an average of 35 hours per week. The income difference between blue-collar workers and white-collar workers is small. Even if the shift work has some disadvantages, people want to be employed in the amins factory, due to the good atmosphere in the autonomous work groups, rotation and an effective management.

The decline of work morale among the lower and middle levels of managers is a realistic danger when such participatory democracy is introduced and these managers become forced to share decisions with people who are incompetent and not adequately motivated. In some cases democracy comes to be treated as a substitute of efficiency.

> One should pay an appropriate amount of attention to the situation of supervisors and middle managers. These categories should be given a fair chance in the organization to get stimulating and challenging tasks and responsibilities. It might be disastrous to the whole organization, if these categories find their possibility of performing good and qualified contributions seriously limited (Rubenowitz 1974, p. 10).

It is in their vested interests, according to many supervisors, to maintain a maximal specification of the tasks performed by their subordinates, assigned individually to the clearly definable, easily performed and limited subtask. For the supervisors, "The fact of their promotion to a position of special influence and individually assigned responsibility puts them in a situation where they are among the ones who receive the benefits from this way of organizing" (Edlund 1978, p. 180). This is the reason why the lower and the middle level supervisors quite often have great difficulties in adapting themselves to the new situation in which managers "are no longer the only ones to know, they are no longer the only ones to give orders, they are no longer used to expect obedience. On the contrary, their decisions, their values, are questioned" (Halden 1976, p. 12).

Workers and supervisors, according to the research done by Edlund (1978) in a Swedish shipyard and other places, differ greatly in their actual amount and perception of information, influence, and responsibility. For example,

> To the *workers,* responsibility is something that is preferably shared among all involved. It is an

> important component of solidarity and therefore of
> group cohesion and of the climate of cooperation.
> To the *supervisors* responsibility is a concept that
> focuses on the individual and the consequences he
> has to take individually for his actions. The formal
> and legal aspects of responsibility lie close at hand
> for the supervisor (Edlund 1978, p. 182).

Taking into consideration that supervisors surveyed by
Edlund were mostly former blue-collar workers, it was
rather surprising that they acquired so fast a new "supervisor consciousness" determined by the content of their
work roles.

There are several basic leadership functions which do
not become automatically obsolete under the conditions of
participatory democracy. Motivation and coordination may
be shared jointly by managers, participatory groups, and
experts from outside, and so forth, but good work discipline remains valid under any circumstances. Without an
adequate leadership there would not be enough progress in
work, and participatory democracy makes sense only as long
as it contributes to the better fulfillment of tasks, inspires
people to work more efficiently, and allows the cooperating
people to gain more mutual trust and respect. The instrumental character of participatory democracy should be fully
acknowledged.

It is an important question whether the participants are
well integrated in all four ways: functional, socioemotional,
normative, and ideological. Meaningful work and a smooth
cooperation with others allow people to find a place for
themselves satisfying enough for their ambitions and aspirations. The effective attachment to the members of the same
participatory unit allows them to find a common language
with others. The clarity and legitimacy of norms shared by
the group members shapes the behavior of people according
to the expectations of the environment. The acceptance of
the basic principles on which participation is based furnish-
es the additional reinforcement.

Shop-floor participation has become more and more
popular in Sweden and unions accept it as long as it does
not diminish the authority of the trade-union bodies.
"Participation by the employees in the company administration will help to contribute to a healthier operation of the
firm with more to divide among employees, help to make
jobs more secure in the future and make a contribution
towards a stronger economy for the country as a whole,"
states the report of the working party set up by the Executive Board of the Swedish Federation of Trade Unions

(LO) in 1972 to consider the questions arising in connection with the direction and assignment of work (Work Organization 1977, p. 41). On the other hand, LO expects the participatory projects not to interfere with the workers' solidarity (this is the reason why people in the autonomous work groups are expected not to earn much more than others,)[1] adjust to the human needs, give participants equal rights, allow for continuous improvement, avoid any interference with the union authority. It seems that in the long run the Swedish trade unions will provide a growing support to the participatory schemes.

Many of these schemes are directed toward the improvement of the working environment and they have been quite successful. The general rules for working environment activities in the Swedish companies are formulated as follows:

1. The employer has primary responsibility in this field but the employees share this responsibility through the safety delegates pertaining to various safety areas. They are appointed by the trade union and are entitled to the time off;

2. Employer is obliged to keep safety delegates well informed on all matters related to safety;

3. The safety committee is the central body in this field and it consists of the representatives of employees and of the employer. The latter are less numerous by one than the former. The employees' representatives are appointed by the local trade union. The chairman and the secretary are appointed by the employer. The members of the safety committee shall always strive to achieve unanimity in their decisions. If unanimity cannot be reached, decisions shall be made by a simple majority. The debatable matters may be referred to the union-management company health services council for the binding final judgment (Working Environment . . . 1977).

SOME GENERAL FINDINGS AS TO PARTICIPATION AND SOCIOTECHNICAL SOLUTIONS IN SWEDISH PLANTS

The transition from a technical job design toward a sociotechnical job design policy is, among other things, supposed to bring about a better adaptation of technical equipment to human needs and capacities and a higher degree of participation. In Sweden, as in many other

Western countries, participation is considered by most people as something positive and desirable. However, it is evident from discussions and studies on this matter, that there exists a rather widespread confusion on the use and operationalization of the participation concept.

A distinction should be made between kinds of formal participation based on rules, laws, and/or negotiations concerning frameworks of participation in decision-making processes. There are the following three basic kinds of participation:

1. Formally structured *company* participation, for example, structured participation through representative bodies on the plant level.
2. Formally structured *shop-floor* participation, for example, structured participation through representative bodies on the workplace level.
3. Organic *shop-floor* participation, for example, line-related procedures with codetermination by all concerned in the daily planning and job decisions.

As will be illustrated later on, the organic shop-floor participation has proved to be much more profitable (from both the workers' and the management point of view) than the other kinds of participation. One of the most suitable design policies for promoting organic shop-floor participation is the sociotechnical job design.

The long tradition of collaboration between the organizations of the labor market has provided in Sweden a suitable ground for industrial experiments in order, among other things, to give the individual more influence over his or her job and vest the individual with responsibility. The prolongation of schooling has given young people increased resources and heightened aspirations and expectations as to broader influence at the workplace.

The firms are also greatly induced to interest themselves in environmental issues as they are suffering from the widespread tendency among the young people to shun factory employment because the industrial environment looks unacceptable to them on physical and social grounds. The interest of management in a sociotechnical production design can also be traced to such advantages as fewer absences and easier balancing when the pace of production is altered. Besides, managers have experienced more and more that it is easier to establish a well-defined production goal for a more extensive production unit than for a specific job or individuals. The combinations of production factors and sociotechnical systems are getting more and more advanced and complicated. As a consequence, it is getting more difficult to break down complicated production goals into jobs for the single individual employees and to define clearly individual tasks. Instead, the need increases for close contact and collaboration between the employees within a work unit. The new production forms must prove to be able to increase productivity in order to be fully accepted not only by management but also by employees. As a consequence, experiments with autonomous groups and other organizational transformations are today common in Swedish firms.

In these experiments, applied psychology and sociology have had a significant direct impact both through the general theories about job satisfaction which have been introduced into the higher education and industry, as well as through an active role of the scientists in the change processes. The main features of sociotechnical change efforts may be summarized as follows:

- The objectives of work reform are generally expressed not only in terms of increased productivity and efficiency but also in the terms of increased job satisfaction and more interesting and more stimulating tasks as worthwhile ends in themselves.
- There should be an increased participation between managers and those farther down in the hierarchy. The design of work organization and work routine should result from a group effort.
- Monotonous and boring work can be attacked by changing the division of work.
- Wage systems are being changed. Individual piece-rate systems are being replaced with more stable wage systems.
- Considerable attention is being devoted to the physical design of the workplace and the engineering production equipment. Often the completely new production systems have been created.

Autonomous production groups often appear in Sweden as an end product of the sociotechnically conditioned transition. According to the general experiences at Swedish plants, the rules of an effective functioning of the above-mentioned groups may be summarized in the following way:

- The production group should function within a well-defined and limited work space.
- The production group should have a well-defined com-

mon production goal.
- The members of the production group should, if possible, have the competence to carry out all tasks performed in the group.
- Wages should be similar for all members. Any differentiation should be linked to competence rather than to individual productivity.
- The groups should have a say over their own composition, for example, over the recruitment of new members.
- The work pace does not have necessarily to be determined by the production rate of the surrounding technological system; the group should have, in other words, a certain autonomy in relation to the production system, which implies considerable buffers at both sides of the production (input-output).
- The group should also have a certain autonomy in relation to the administrative system, including among other things collective responsibility as to the quality, economy, and work assignment; a prerequisite for this is a well-functioning productivity feedback keeping the group informed about its performance.
- There should be a variety of tasks for the group in order to assure the multidimensional character of its activities.
- If a coordinator is needed, the position should circulate between the group members.
- The production goal should be so formulated as to allow a good collaboration between all group members without the risk of ostracism (removal of members who have a working capacity below average).

Later on in this chapter, an example of a well-functioning sociotechnically designed unit will be given. Before that, some general views and comments on sociotechnical conditions will be discussed.

THE OPTIMALIZATION OF SOCIOTECHNICAL CONDITIONS

In the field of labor relations sociotechnics is definitely growing in popularity because, while remaining within the general spirit of a welfare state at the same time it offers an opportunity of a group initiative, contrary to the authoritarianism of bureaucracy.[2]

The general trends of organizational development in Sweden and its practical applications in the shape of, for example, autonomous production groups are well in line with what has been argued by scientists in other countries. There is a common agreement as to the principle that a joint optimalization of systems: technical, administrative, social and economic is aimed at in the sociotechnical approach. They are expected to complement each other (van der Zwaan 1975, p. 150). It is up to sociotechnics to find an organizational choice assuming the optimal combination of various designs and concerns, any of them focusing on the different aspect of the work reality. Modern production systems may improve their efficiency by: substituting a series of connected processes (assembly line) by parallel or reciprocal connected process, a changeover from central control to a decentralized control, with an increased amount of discretion for the system elements, a high inter-changeability rate of individuals with regard to tasks, as well as the better adaptation of technical equipment to human needs and capacities (van der Zwaan 1975, p. 161).

A study of effectiveness of participation in ten Swedish plants, done by Rubenowitz (1979a), shows a high level of correlation between freedom from technological constraints (diversification of tasks, ability to have some breaks, personal dependence on machines) and liking to work for a given employer. The psychosocial quality of the work milieu (job content and design, freedom of controlling the work process, availability of social contacts) was evidently correlated with the level of absenteeism. It means that the humanization of the technoeconomic surrounding should be treated as a necessary condition of any significant sociotechnical reform.

Another survey by S. Rubenowitz (1977) of employees in seven Swedish manufacturing plants (metal, food, plastic) shows that they desire much more influence within these areas which seem vital for them and in which they already have influence: working conditions, work assignment, type of payment, supervision. Most people express a wish to get more influence primarily on questions related to their own daily work or work situation (Rubenowitz 1977, p. 7).

> The more the individual is enabled to exercise control over his task and to relate his efforts to his work group, the more likely he is to experience job satisfaction and to accept a positive commitment. . . . A certain amount of freedom at work, allowing the individual to have a great deal of say regarding his job and collaboration, is an important factor behind his satisfaction and productivity (Ibid., p. 18).

The general satisfaction with work and its place does not necessarily exclude the fact that people differ in their subjective evaluation of their work situation depending on the position in the hierarchy. The survey of more than 5,000 employees of a Swedish ball-bearing company done by S. Rubenowitz (1976) shows that only 13 percent were, on the whole, dissatisfied with their company (little difference between various categories of employees). However, the differences in the evaluation of jobs as interesting and stimulating were very evident when taking into consideration the level of activity (70 percent to 90 percent among the different categories of managers and only one-third among blue-collar workers) and the educational level (80 percent among people with academic degrees and only 27 percent among people with elementary education). The opportunity to use their ability, capacity, and knowledge at work was open to four-fifths of managers and only 18 percent of the production workers (Ibid., p. 9). It might be added that at the time of the investigation the company had adapted a sociotechnical job design policy, but only to a very limited degree.

There is a great need of sociotechnical consultation in Sweden, particularly in the enterprises which face the limits of growth under the existing circumstances. In several cases the expectations of people have grown much faster than the ability of the enterprises to meet the demands of the employees. Sweden in some fields experiences labor difficulties typical for the well-to-do nations. For example, despite good working and wage conditions in the shipping industry, there is a shortage of seamen. More than one-third of all persons employed in the Swedish shipping industry in 1972 were foreigners, mostly from Finland, Denmark, and Spain. At the same time the average time spent at sea by seamen was only five years and the turnover was 17 percent. About a half of all seafarers were contemplating leaving their occupation even if the attitude toward management was mostly positive (Rubenowitz and Gleerup 1977, pp. 6–10).

With the rising standard of living, working people in Sweden demand better working conditions and a higher level of participation. For example, the collective bargaining in the shipping industry includes more and more such items as an active and meaningful leisure abroad, free travel to the home country, and more time off to spend ashore (Ibid., p. 26). The ship-level representation of employees' interests works quite well in the framework of disciplinary and safety committees; the unions and management are able to agree on basic things but much more seems to be needed in order to make room for a genuine participation by employees.

There is a growing practice in Sweden whereby the sociotechnical consultants are approached by the enterprises in order to gain some professional help in problem-solving.

For example in Teli, one of the very few state-owned factories, there was a problem in 1979 of changing market priorities, due to the new development in electronics. The factory produced the telephone equipment, as well as other types of equipment, but it had to extend the production of printed-circuit assemblies. The factory was located in southern Sweden; it employed around 800 people and was the main employer in its municipality. It was attractive to stay with this factory and the workers were willing to become retrained to other jobs just to be able to stay with the same employer. Absenteeism was low. The earnings were comparable to incomes in manufacturing in the large industrial centers. The wage consisted of a fixed part (80 percent), and a bonus depending on the volume of production (20 percent). People worked on flextime: they started between 6:15 A.M. and 8:15 A.M. and finished between 3 P.M. and 5 P.M., depending on how much time they took for lunch (maximum 2 hours). They also had two coffee breaks.

Under the earning and tax system of that time the purchasing powers of people positioned at various levels were quite similar. The graduate engineer started from a monthly income only a few hundred crowns higher than the income of a manual worker and any further raises were largely consumed by progressive taxation.[3] The main difference was that the interest payed on the housing mortgage was tax deductible and better paid people were therefore encouraged to buy houses, yachts, and so on. The income equality was even more evident among the blue-collar workers, who differed among themselves only a little after tax. Skilled workers were in a disadvantageous position and in several cases earned even less than production workers. For example, in the Teli factory, the maintenance workers employed in the tool and repair shop generally earned about 15 percent less than the production workers, even if their work was much more demanding in terms of skill.

Teli was in 1979 just starting to build a new electronic factory, which would be based on the sociotechnical principles of job enrichment (already practiced to some extent previously). Cooperation with Chalmers Technical University in Gothenburg was established and the government provided an additional grant in order to cover part of the total consultation costs.

There are now several academic centers in Sweden directly involved in the remodeling of technical structures and processes in order to make them more suitable to human needs. Material and object handling is one of the main objects of concern: how to hold to a minimum repacking of materials; how to move objects from one place to another with the minimum of effort and cost (cheap wagons and small handy lifters attached to them); how to standardize the containers according to the direct needs of the people assembling the objects; how to design the object of assembly in order to limit the waste of time to a minimum;[4] how to reorganize the process of product development in order to eliminate unnecessary delay;[5] how to reorganize the management structure adequately to the specifities of the parallel system of assembly and how to train the management personnel accordingly; how to transfer more load to the preassembly processes that are particularly suitable for autonomous groups; how to promote for the autonomous groups within the technical system an adequate opportunity for autonomy, variance, responsibility, and feedback; how to adapt the administrative system to the needs and necessities of autonomous groups.

The technological line-out system of parallel assembly assures the autonomous groups their autonomy and freedom on the basis of big buffers[6] (40 minutes or more) which allow the team to organize the work process in their own way, rotation of team members every week between jobs of various quality and physical demand, as well as joint participation in the decision-making process.[7] The functions of management at the shop-floor are taken over by the autonomous groups themselves. The role of a foreman has changed considerably by releasing him or her from the daily direct control of working people; workers control themselves and even take over successfully the responsibility for better quality of their products (technical control).[8]

There are several important consultant's problems of a technical nature which have to be solved satisfactorily in order to open enough room for the parallel system and autonomous groups. First, is the question of buffers; easy to solve in the case of small objects but becoming more and more difficult with the growth of their size. Without adequate buffers the technical constraints make the group autonomy quite illusory. The matrix organization principle is applied to large objects; various teams are allocated to the same objects and work in coordination. In this case there are three major difficulties: (1) The sequence of jobs may be a limiting factor (for example, in the bus assembly from 18 hours of total work only the half of an hour is free from sequency); (2) There are limits of training (the job cycle of more than two to three hours becomes difficult and expensive to learn); (3) The variance of assembled objects (this is the reason why in Sweden all variance of assembled cars is allocated to the end part of the assembly line).

AN EXAMPLE OF A SUCCESSFUL SOCIOTECHNICAL CHANGE

The reform of the technological system directed by socio-psychological considerations is, according to Swedish experts in this field, one of the basic conditions of the work humanization. In this respect, they differ widely from their colleagues in other countries who take technology for granted. The action research done in the period 1975–77 at the body shop of the Saab-Scania car factory in Trollhättan may be a good example (Karlsson 1979a).

In 1975 most of the assembly lines at the body department of the Saab–Scania plant in Trollhättan were replaced by work stations where eight workers carried out final welding, grinding, adjustment, and inspection, while the automobile was stationary. The reason for the transition was various problems linked to the assembly line's human costs. When the employee turnover rate amounted to more than 50 percent in the beginning of the 1970s and the absenteeism grew to about 25 percent, one began to investigate other techno-organizational alternatives. Already in 1971, SAAB had scrapped the assembly lines at the engine factory at Södertälje and this experiment proved to be successful.

By abandoning the assembly line the possibilities for each employee to influence his or her own work situation would be enhanced. Another objective was to render the various production tasks more attractive and meaningful. A further aim was to reduce susceptibility to disruption and to increase production efficiency through greater flexibility and adaptability. Thus, in sum, the object was to strive for increased productivity accompanied by higher job satisfaction.

As in most other Swedish plants, the collaboration between the management and the unions was good. In the course of time, and backed by several basic agreements between the Swedish Employers' Confederation (SAF) and the Swedish Trade Union Confederation (LO), a valuable mutual trust had developed among managers, foremen, and workers. This "confidence capital" proved to be most helpful during the transition period. Even if there was some suspiciousness to overcome, not least from the foremen's side, most people at the department, from the shop floor to the department manager, worked with commitment for the change once the decision was made. The fact that the people affected by the change were engaged in the planning of the change compensated for much of the feelings of threat that often appear when people have to leave ingrained work methods, even if the new ones have obvious advantages. The changeover was accomplished during the summer of 1975 at a cost of about $2.5 million.

The initiative for the work organization change was taken by the department manager, who established a steering committee, the members of which were the production director, two other management representatives, and two union representatives. On the shop-floor level, production groups with foremen and affected workers were established. The steering group was responsible for the policy questions dealing with the work organization, while the autonomous production groups were more engaged in the practical job task questions.

The New Setup

Before the change, the car bodies were made on a traditional assembly line with a cycle time of 3 to 6 minutes. The workers were directly steered from above with a detailed control system and without their own responsibility for the quality or other parts of the task. Under the new arrangement the autonomous work groups became entrusted with responsibilities related to quality and quantity of production, maintenance, and even their own budget.

The autonomous groups (or self-controlling groups, as they are called by Saab) are responsible for several types of tasks. At the work stations, where the bodies are stationary, the production group members are carrying out welding, grinding, and adjustment, and in addition to these production tasks they are responsible for equipment maintenance, transport, cleaning, controlling of own work and administration. The cycle time is about 45 minutes (all these data are for the state of affairs in 1979). The goal for the group is to produce 52 bodies a week. A higher production does not give a higher wage, so the group need not experience stress arising from piece rates.

Depending upon the technological setup of each group, the proportion of the various tasks can vary from group to group. In principle, each individual group member should have the opportunity and obligation to work at all tasks of the group. The coordination of the tasks is made by one of the group members, "the contact man." This function rotates among all group members. The rotation time varies from group to group but usually is one week. Most of the coordinator's time is devoted to administration, with some also to transport and equipment maintenance. The coordinator visits from time to time another production section in order to estimate the production quality of the group in relation to the demands of the next section in the process of production.

The responsibilities of the autonomous production group can be summarized in the following ways: planning and accomplishment of the production program; control of arriving material; transport; maintenance, cleaning; introduction and teaching of new members; permission to individual members to be absent from work for valid reasons (1 day maximum); control of the product; feedback of sample control of the product; budget. The groups have worked out together with the foreman, rules for behavior inside the group. These rules have been confirmed by the groups and the steering committee (management and the union). Formal rules exist for all groups on the role of the coordinator, recruitment (the groups have veto rights), job rotation, control, and so forth. The fulfillment by production groups of their responsibilities is judged by the management as well as by trade unions. The reward to the group is limited to some small addition to the hourly wage (approximately one-thirtieth).

The establishment of autonomous production groups and the incorporation of them into the sociotechnical and administrative system of the factory is the major fact which in the long run may have many consequences for the whole industrial relations system. The identity of these groups is mainly based on the manner according to which they function. The rules of group daily functioning are a blend of formal regulations and informal accommodations.

Autonomous groups in Trollhättan have the following general rules which help them to maintain a high level of performance, harmony, and satisfaction: every job is rotated among the group members including the contact man (he or she spends half of their time in administration and the other half working in production); jobs are exchanged among members every week; members of the team are expected to work not too fast but also not too slow, help one another and stay up to the end of the daily task; members relieve one another temporarily in the case of any urgency; the work has to be left well prepared for another shift; all external affairs are dealt with by the contact man exclusively; autonomous groups in the case of any need temporarily delegate their own members to another group but only in the positions where replacement is available; the delegated member is expected to be appointed to the easiest jobs; newcomers to the team start from easy jobs and progress gradually to the jobs which are more difficult.

Productivity

What gains and drawbacks have been registered in Trollhättan since the new organization was introduced in 1975? Has the new organization, offered an increased possibility for people to decide upon matters that directly affect them, and finally resulted in an increased job satisfaction and better productivity?

As to the productivity, it can be noted that considerable production gains have been made until 1979. When the new system was planned, Saab estimated a payoff time of investments at 3.8 years, but the goal was reached much earlier (2.63 years). According to the traditional view, modern car production makes necessary assembly lines, from the profitability point of view, even if this might be disastrous for the physically and psychologically frustrated assembly line worker. The experiences from Saab-Scania contradict this widespread opinion. The autonomous working group organization has proved to be superior in comparison with the traditional assembly line. A comparison between the two systems as to the efficiency losses clearly favors the new system, according to thorough analyses made at the plant.

In the production systems there are always efficiency losses in the sense that more time is needed than would be theoretically necessary. First there are the *system losses* related to the time needed for control and adjustment. Secondly, there are the *balance losses,* due to the fact that it is impossible to keep all operators busy to the same degree. At assembly lines these losses can be of a considerable size; around 20 percent is not unusual. Thirdly, there are *handling losses,* appearing especially at short-cycle times, owing to the fact that the handling of tools and material can be considerable in comparison with assembling and fixing.

The total time losses at the new line-out group system have proved to be 21 percent of the production time compared with 61 percent for the old assembly lines. The large difference between the two systems is attributable mainly to the diminished number of quality controllers in the line-out system. At a production rate of 60,000 auto bodies per year, a saving of 15 controllers was obtained. A statistical sample control on about 5 percent of the finished auto bodies proved that the quality was increased significantly after the change. In addition, the unplanned stoppages proved to occur much less than previously in the new line-out system.

On the debit side may be mentioned an increase in the expenses due to the need for relatively large buffers, for changes in the technological structure, and for the considerable training investments. However, the production gains by far outweighed these expenses. As the department manager puts it:

> A common view on work organization changes toward autonomous groups is that this is something that you can take up under good times, when you can afford some money in order to increase the job satisfaction. Had it not been profitable with autonomous groups, it would have been beyond our means to carry on with such activities. Fortunately, the fact is that if the activities are run in the right way, it is a profitable investment.

Job Satisfaction

Three different measures were used in order to learn about the general job satisfaction among the employees working in the autonomous groups; the rate of absenteeism, the turnover rate, and attitude survey data. As to *absenteeism,* the figures for 1976 and 1977 can be compared between workers in the autonomous groups and workers on the traditional assembly line. Total absenteeism was clearly higher at the assembly line than at the line-out unit. However, it appeared that sickness mainly accounted for the differences. Absenteeism "for other reasons" proved to be of the same magnitude. The production group was allowed to give its members the permission to be absent for personal reasons. This possibility was well received by workers.

In regard to the *turnover,* it was hoped that a substantial decrease would appear among the workers in the line-out system. The expectations were already fulfilled within one year after the change, and later the turnover remained on a low level. However, changes of the market and in shift work affected the turnover figures. Perhaps most interesting to notice is the direction of the manpower flow. When workers leave the traditional organizational units, they either go to the autonomous working groups or to other companies. Among workers leaving the autonomous groups, hardly any go to the traditional units. They either go to qualified service departments within the Saab plant, or to a smaller degree to other companies.

> No worker has left autonomous groups for line-jobs. Most of the people who left the system did so to assume a more qualified job (often maintenance) or returned to Northern Sweden or Denmark where they got jobs in their home areas. Only 5 percent left the groups because they did not like group work. These workers went to jobs where they could work alone, for example, as forklift drivers, operating their own machines, etc. (Karlsson 1979b).

A diagnosis of *job satisfaction* was obtained through group discussions and attitude surveys. According to the group discussions, job satisfaction was considerably higher in the autonomous groups than in the traditional assembly line. Its level became equal to the relatively high level of job satisfaction typical for the maintenance workers. However, in the changed work situation it was not the job content that was of greatest importance but rather the general job conditions that lay behind the increased satisfaction and especially the possibility to decide over one's own working pace and the feeling of group cohesiveness. Comparison of the difference in the minimum time actually used to perform a day's job and the time available found there was no difference between the assembly line and the line-off system. In both cases it amounted to about one-and a half-hours a day. But the important difference was that in the assembly line people were paced by the system and forced to take the time off repeatedly in fractions of minutes. In the line-off system, workers were free to dispose of time at their own convenience. In many autonomous production groups workers tended to work eagerly in the mornings in order to get an hour off in the afternoon to rest before leaving the plant. The sufficiently large buffers before and after the production group constituted the basic prerequisite for the freedom of collective decision in the autonomous production group how to allocate time for work and leisure.

The Changing Role of Supervisors

It is often (and sometime with good reason) feared that the role of foreman may be seriously undermined as a result of organizational changes from the traditional to a more participative pattern. How did the Swedish foremen react during the innovation process at Saab, and in what way had their role changed? From the beginning the foremen were directly engaged in the planning of the project. They rather soon changed from a wait-and-see policy to a more positive attitude. As a matter of fact, many of them acted as the eager change agents during the whole transition period. They were not dismissed, but rather got a new and more stimulating role. In the new production group organization the supervisors discussed with workers all changes or adjustments, and for this purpose a considerable theoretical and practical knowledge was needed. In order to encounter the new role, the supervisors get a substantial additional training within the fields of organization, personnel administration, production technology, economy, and so forth. It may be added that the majority of the foremen were in favor of this new role but there were a few exceptions, primarily among older supervisors.

CONCLUDING REMARKS

The autonomous production groups, in the way they are planned and function at Saab-Scania in Trollhättan, have proved to be an economically profitable alternative to the traditional assembly line. The change has resulted in both increased productivity and increased job satisfaction, and the new organizational principles are expanding more and more within the company, in spite of some drawbacks and problems. These are primarily linked to the costs of rebuilding the technological production system, increased costs for training, and capital costs related to the creation of an increased number of buffers. The material-handling problems were not great at the body shop but proved to be considerable at the final assembly of cars.

On the positive side should be mentioned the decreased costs of quality control, fewer and shorter stoppages, more reliable material handling, decreased costs for instructors, decreased turnover and decreased rationalization costs. Besides, the personnel can be better utilized in various jobs, they tend to become more positive and engaged in their work, and better prepared for an increased organizational development.

In several Swedish industrial plants, successful attempts have been made to establish autonomous production groups. Is it possible to find some general characteristics in the change process itself toward enlarging the work content of the individual, either separately or by creating autonomous or semiautonomous work groups? Yes, at least according to experiences in Swedish plants. Among all factors, the change agents probably play the most important role. In plants where line managers, supervisors, and well-qualified skilled workers assumed an active role in the change process, the sociotechnical success was much more evident than in such plants where the external consultants played a major role, or where the reorganization had been planned by staff members or elected committees working as a separate adjunct to the established organization.[9] The major question in the strategy of innovation is how to activate the rank and file at the shop-floor level and within the scope of issues of vital importance for them.

The most successful attempts have been made in small-scale innovations located in relatively few organizational units where there has been found a willingness to try new ideas, rather than in the large-scale innovations, covering a whole plant. The elasticity and flexibility of the timetable was also of great advantage for the innovations.

Besides, on the whole, it has been found that the possibilities of achieving comprehensive changes in the factories are more limited by technological and economic considerations than most people would expect. Thus, possibilities for more radical sociotechnical solutions are more applicable to new plants than to the already existing workshops. In old factories with rigid steering (assembly lines, and so forth) the only possible alteration is at best to change the function of the assembly line from pacer to a transport line.

Another problem is linked to the traditional attitudes at the work place. If a relatively tough authoritarian atmosphere has prevailed at a workplace for years, the likelihood that the workers will collaborate in autonomous groups is relatively small. A positive attitude cannot be expected toward job enlargement among workers who for years have had individual tasks of a repetitive nature. They show, among others, that it is good to start with a limited self-steering group and an authorized leader. The newly hired workers, especially if they have a relatively solid education, should be gradually introduced to the line-out system.

Social research on participatory projects in Sweden may and should help to clarify how things may be done in order to improve the sociotechnical quality of these projects. Social science may contribute to policy making by providing practitioners with the basic concepts and theories about man and society, delivering data and devising technical solutions to problems. According to Cherns, "by increasing the policy-maker's knowledge an understanding of the system in which he is operating and the characteristics and potentialities of its human components, social science knowledge can clarify and increase the options available to him" (Cherns 1979, p. 45). In practice the relations existing between research institutions and users of research are full of problems depending on the nature of research (pure basic research, basic objective research, operational research, action research) and the openness of practitioners to learn from research. Options available to decision-makers become much clearer and more reliable when they are formulated on the basis of research. On the other hand, even the best research will not help much if the client system does not have adequate channels for diffusion of the valid knowledge. Very often by changing the mutual perceptions of policy-makers and social scientists it is possible to improve the research application. The utilizing organization and the research team usually operate on different time scales; the learning ability of the utilizing organization is quite often very limited; research application fails when the mutual interdependence between various parts and power levels of the organization are not taken into consideration; practitioners have difficulties in the adequate selection of research projects actually needed by them at various stages of decision making.

Social scientists devoted to sociotechnics may be helpful to the practitioners who implement the participatory projects in a number of ways. Research is only one of them. Another important service is the diagnosis on the sociotechnical quality of practical projects which are expected to modify the work reality. The principles of sociotechnical design formulated by Cherns (1979, pp. 310–20) may be very helpful in this respect.[10]

The Swedish participatory projects in many cases follow the principles mentioned above without their promoters being necessarily aware of the methodological advantages of the sociotechnical model subconsciously implemented. For example, the facilitating role of external experts and the heavy dependence on local initiatives has been probably much more dictated by the balance of social powers in Sweden and the nature of her democracy than by a conscious methodological choice. In the country where the trade unions have so much to say the imposition of job reform arbitrarily from above through the management channel becomes just impractical and unrealistic. Anyhow, as a matter of fact, so far, almost all sociotechnical initiatives have come from the managers and consultants, and not from unions. On the other hand, it would not be possible to implement the sociotechnical projects if the unions would object.

The consent of trade unions and employees in general is absolutely necessary. The organic nature of new organization also becomes a necessity under the Swedish conditions where the employees have much freedom and choice; the power of new organization to strengthen the motivation of people is of crucial importance for its success. The same may be said about the necessity to keep to a minimum the strains of the changeover period from one model of organization to another. The danger of encapsulation and erosion of innovations seem to be lower in Sweden than in other free-market societies as long as these innovations fit well into the problems and needs of a society vitally interested in the socialization and humanization of collective work. The traditional individualistic spirit is much lower in Sweden as, for example, in France or in the United States. The participatory projects move in the direction of social development started many years ago and allowed persistently even under the changing political conditions.

NOTES

1. In this respect the view of SAF differs very substantially from the view of LO. According to the position taken by the Technical Department of SAF, a premium component of 15–30 percent of the income may function well as an additional incentive to the system, based primarily on the social unit of enough strength and attractiveness to preserve the steady state of the whole socioeconomic system (Lindestad and Norstedt 1973, p. 52).

2. It is known from research in management training that the large differences in job experience, educational level, and intellectual ability make it difficult to get the message across (Jerkedal 1967, p. 228). The communality of background in small groups may substantially help in an autonomous group to inspire the punitive attitudes of the group members toward one another and toward the group goals.

3. The share of taxes and social charges of total income had increased in Sweden during the period 1950–78 from 17 percent to 40 percent. The public sector owned in the late 1970s 35 percent of the total net wealth. In 1977, even with the progressive taxation, 2 percent of the population owned 60 percent of total taxable wealth.

4. For a good example in this respect see "GM Front-Drive Compacts," *Popular Science,* April 1979.

5. Swedish experts mention the fact that new-car models absorb too many decision-makers who, instead of helping one another involve themselves in power struggles and become insulated from the reality of production. The first very successful model of Saab involved only 40 decision-makers, in comparison with five times more of them in the late 1970s and almost 60 times more in Volvo.

6. The storage of things to be done and another storage of things already finished.

7. One of the savings expected is the time (and money) allocated for the replacement man: usually one man for seven team members. It is assumed that this man should not remain idle for more than 30 percent of the time (on the assembly line it is 40 to 50 percent) and it is up to the team to allocate people accordingly.

8. The managerial hierarchy in the automobile plants starts at the bottom with the foreman, who has under his care around 40 people and earns 15–20 percent over their average income. The department manager has around 200 people under him and the body-plant manager administers around 600 people.

9. The well-known Kalmar plant of Volvo is based on the assembly wagons, instead of assembly lines, which circulate between various working groups, carrying auto bodies or chassis; these wagons wait in the parking spaces reserved for the buffer inventory between two work areas. However, the pace of work is relatively fast and the individual teams, by working faster and more effectively, manage to earn no more than five minutes' break after each 20 minutes of intensive work. The principle of a mechanically paced process of work remained intact in Kalmar and this was widely criticized in Sweden in the late 1970s. In addition, in Kalmar a large number of battery-powered assembly wagons were in daily use and these were very expensive.

10. According to Cherns, "organizational objectives are best met by the joint optimization of the technical and the social aspects, exploiting the adaptability and innovativeness of people in attaining goals, instead of over-determining technically the manner in which these goals should be attained" (1979, p. 311). The process of sociotechnical design must be compatible with its objectives, accordingly modified and based on the voluntary consent of the people involved. No more should be specified in the sociotechnical design than is absolutely essential, and this essence should be specified very clearly. The correction of variances and

deviances should be done on the spot, and not only much later. "The fewer the variances that are exported from the place where they arise, the less the levels of supervision and control required and the more 'complete' the jobs of the people concerned to whom it now becomes possible to allocate an objective and the resources necessary to attain it" (1979, p. 313). Organization should be designed according to the multifunctional principle (organism versus mechanism), in order for it to be able to fulfill the whole variety of changing demands and achieve the high level of flexibility and adaptability. The boundaries drawn between various parts of the organization should not interfere with the effective functioning of the whole workplace. Information systems should be designed to provide information in the first place to the point where action on the basis of it will be needed. Sophisticated information systems can "supply a work team with exactly the right type and amount of feedback to enable them to learn to control the variances which occur within the scope of their spheres of responsibility and competence and to anticipate events likely to have a bearing on their performance" (Cherns 1979, p. 317). The systems of social support should be designed so as to reinforce the behaviors which the organization structure is designed to elicit. An objective of organizational design should be to provide a high quality of working life to its members. The strains of the changeover period from one model of organization to another should be carefully taken into consideration. The whole sociotechnical design should be treated as a reiterative process; instead of looking for a perfect final solution it is much more reasonable to be open to constant improvements.

REFERENCES

Agreement on Rationalization between SAF and LO 1972, 1974. Stockholm.

Asplund, Chister, and Casten van Otter. 1978. "Codetermination by Own Efforts." Stockholm: Arbetslivscentrum. Mimeo.

Backhaus, Jürgen. 1979. *Okonomik der Partizipativen Unternehmung.* Tübingen, West Germany: J.C.B. Mohr.

Backhaus, T. Eger, and H. G. Nutzinger, eds. 1978. *Partizipation in Betriebs und Gesellschaft.* Frankfurt-am-Main: Campus Verlag.

Bartlett, Lailie E. 1976. *New Work/New Life.* New York: Harper and Row.

Batstone, Eric, I. Boraston, and S. Frenkel. 1977. *Shop Stewards in Action: The Organization of Workplace, Conflict and Accommodation.* Oxford: Basil Blackwell.

Bayart, P. 1979. *Les Relations Sociales dans Enterprise.* Paris: Chotard.

Beer, S. 1975. *Platform for Change.* London.

Bell, Daniel. 1976. *The Cultural Contradictions of Capitalism.* New York: Basic Books.

Berlind, Hans. 1976. "Pension or Work? A Growing Dilemma in the Nordic Welfare States." The Nordic Welfare States, *Acta Sociologica,* 21:181–92.

Bergström, Villy. 1978. *The Political Economy of Swedish Capital Formation.* Stockholm: Arbetslivscentrum. Mimeo.

Bergström, Villy, and Hans Melander. 1978. Production Functions and Factors Demand Functions in Post War Swedish Industry. Stockholm: Arbetslivscentrum. Mimeo.

Beskow, Jan. 1979. Suicide and Mental Disorder in Swedish Men. *Acta Psychiatrica Scandinavica,* Supplementum 277, Copenhagen: Muksgaard.

Beynon, H. 1975. *Working for Ford.* London: EP Publishing.

Blackler, F. H. M., and C. A. Brown. 1978. *Job Redesign and Management Control.* Studies in British Leyland and Volvo. Farnborough, England: Saxon House.

Board Representation. 1976. Stockholm: SAF.

Bolweg, Joep F. 1976. *Job Design and Industrial Democracy: The Case of Norway.* Leiden: Martinus Nijhoff.

Brandes, O. 1971. *Supply Models: An Empirical Study of Adaptation and Innovation in the Firm.* Göteborg, Sweden: Elanders Boktryckeri Aktiebolag.

Brannen, P., et al. 1976. *The Worker Directors: A Sociology of Participation.* London: Hutchinson.

Bratt, Christian. 1977. *The Development of Workers' Participation in Sweden.* Stockholm: SAF (Document No. 139).

————. 1978. *Workers' Participation in Sweden: A Survey.* Stockholm: SAF (Document No. 131).

Carby-Hall, J. R. 1977. *Worker Participation in Europe.* London: Croom Helm.

Cherns, Albert. 1979. *Using the Social Sciences.* London: Routledge and Kegan Paul.

————, ed. 1976. *Sociotechnics.* London: Malaby Press.

Clark, Alfred W., ed. 1976. *Experimenting with Organizational Life.* New York: Plenum.

"Co-determination in Sweden. An up-to-date analysis of developments and the reforms implemented in the 70s." 1979. Stockholm: LO. Mimeo.

Crispo, John. 1978. *Industrial Democracy in Western Europe.* Toronto: McGraw-Hill Ryerson.

Dahlström, Edmund. 1976. *Efficiency, Satisfaction and Democracy in Work: Ideas of Industrial Relations in Post-War Sweden.* Göteborg, Sweden: University of Göteborg.

——————. 1977. "Efficiency, Satisfaction and Democracy in Work: Conception of Industrial Relations in Post-War Sweden," *Acta Sociologica,* 20, 1:25–53.

——————. 1978. "The Role of Social Science in Working Life Policy: The Case of Postwar Sweden." In *Sociology of Work in the Nordic Countries.* Oslo: Scandinavian Sociological Association.

Dalton, G. W., P. R. Lawrence, and J. W. Lorsch. 1970. *Organization Structure and Design.* Homewood, IL: Irwin-Dorsey.

Davis, Louis E., and J. C. Taylor, eds. 1972. *Design of Jobs.* Harmondsworth (U.K.): Penguin.

Davis, Louis E., and A. Cherns, eds. 1975. *The Quality of Working Life.* 2 vol. New York: Free Press.

Deming, D. D. 1977. "Reevaluating the Assembly Line," *Supervisory Management,* 16:13–16.

Democracy at Work. 1977. London: BBC.

Diverrez, J. 1971. *Practique de la direction participative.* Paris: Enterprise Moderne d'Edition.

Durkheim, Emile (1893). 1947. *The Division of Labour in Society.* Glencoe, IL: Free Press.

Edlund, Claes. 1978. *Influence and Responsibility at the Place of Work: A General Interpersonal Perception Model for Organizational Development and an Empirical Study.* Stockholm: Swedish Council for Personnel Administration.

Elden, Max. 1978. *Three Generations of Work Democracy Experiments in Norway: Beyond Classical Sociotechnical Analysis.* Trondheim (Norway): Technical University of Trondheim. Institute for Industrial Social Research.

Elements subjectifs du bien-être. 1974. Paris: OECD.

Elliott, John. 1978. *Conflict or Cooperation? The Growth of Industrial Democracy.* London: Kegan Paul.

Experiences Suedoises de Gestion Participative des Ateliers. 1977. Paris: Editions Hommes et Techniques.

Fair Pay. 1979. Stockholm: SAF.

Forsebäck, Lennert. 1976. *Industrial Relations and Employment in Sweden.* Stockholm: Swedish Institute.

Fredriksson, Lennart. 1974. "The Use of Self-Observation and Questionnaires in Job Analysis for the Planning and Training. *Studia Psychologica et Pedagogica,* Series Attera 22. Lund, Sweden: CWK Gleerup.

Fry, John A. 1978. *Limits of the Welfare State: Critical Views on Post-War Sweden.* Farnborough, England: Gover Press.

—————. 1979. *Industrial Democracy and Labour Market Policy in Sweden.* Oxford: Pergamon Press.

Gardell, Bertil. 1963. *Social Implications of Automation in Sweden.* Stockholm.

—————. 1977. "Psychosocial Aspects of the Working Environment," *Current Sweden,* 160, 4.

Gardell, Bertil, and Bjorn Gustavsen. 1978. *Work Environment Research and Social Change—Current Developments in Scandinavia.* Paper for the 9th World Congress of Sociology, Uppsala, Sweden. Mimeo.

Golomb, Naphtali and Daniel Katz. 1969. *The Kibbutzim as an Open Social System.* Ruppin Institute.

Gomez, P., F. Malik, and K. H. Oeller. 1975. *Systemmethodik-Grundlagen einer Methodik zur Erforschung und Gestaltung Komplexer Sociotechnischer Systeme.* Bern.

Grevenmeyer-Korb, Viktoria. 1978. *Die Polnische Diskussion um die Arbeiterräte.* Berlin: Osteuropa Institut at the Free University of Berlin.

Groere, J. P. and P. Stern. 1979. *33 Fiches d'Analyse des Relations de Groupe.* Paris: Editions d'Organisation.

Guest, David, and Kenneth Knight, eds. 1978. *Putting Participation into Practice.* Farnborough, England: Gover Press.

Gumbury, Doran. 1978. *Industrial Democracy Approaches in Sweden: An Australian View.* Sydney: The Productivity Promotion Council of Australia.

—————, ed. 1975. *Bringing Work to Life: The Australian Experience.* Sydney: The Productivity Promotion Council of Australia.

Hackman, J. K. and J. L. Suttle, eds. 1977. *Improving Life at Work.* Santa Monica, CA.

Halden, Folke. 1976. *Co-determination—A challenge to Management.* Stockholm: SAF.

Halebsky, Sandor. 1976. *Mass Society and Political Conflict. Towards a Reconstruction of Theory.* Cambridge: Cambridge University Press.

Hall, Phoebe, et al. 1975. *Change, Choice and Conflict in Social Planning.* London: Heinemann.

Hammarsten, Bengt. 1978. *Rätten till arbete.* Lund:

Student Litteratur.

Hammarström, Olle. 1978. *Negotiation for Co-Determination: The Swedish Model*. Stockholm: Arbetslivscentrum. Mimeo.

—————. 1978. *On National Strategies of Industrial Democracy*. Stockholm: Arbetslivscentrum. Mimeo.

Heathfield, David F. 1977. *The Economics of Co-determination*. London: Macmillan.

Hedberg, Bo. 1979. *How Organizations Learn and Unlearn*. Stockholm: Arbetslivscentrum. Memeo.

Herbst, Ph. 1976. *Alternative to Hierarchies*. Leiden: Nijhoff.

Hettlage, Robert. 1979. *Genossenschaftstheorie und Partizipationsdiscussion*. Frankfurt-am-Main: Campus Verlag.

Horn, Norbert. 1978. *Pro und Contra Arbeitpartizipation*. Königstein: Peter Hanstein.

Ingham, G. K. 1974. *Strikes and Industrial Conflict: Britain and Scandinavia*. London: Macmillan.

Jerkedal, Ake. 1967. *Top Management Education: An Education Study*. Stockholm: Svenska tryckeri bolagen.

"Job Reform in Sweden." *Conclusions from 500 Shop Floor Projections,* 1975. Stockholm: SAF.

Johnson, Carol P., M. Alexander, and J. Robin. 1978. *Quality of Working Life*. Ottawa: Labour Canada.

Karlsson, Ulf. 1979a. "Alternative produktionssystem till line-produktion" (Production Systems Alternative to Line Production). Ph.D. dissertation, University of Göteborg.

—————. 1979b. *Evaluation of Alternative to the Traditional Assembly Line at the Body Shop of Saab-Scania in Tröllhattan, Sweden*. Gothenburg: Chalmers University of Technology.

Katz, D., and R. Kahn. 1978. *The Social Psychology of Organizations*. New York: Wiley.

Knight, K., and D. Guest. 1979. *Putting Participation into Practice*. Farnborough, England: Gower Press.

Knight, K., ed. 1977. *Matrix Management*. Farnborough, England: Gower Press.

Kolvenbach, Walter. 1978. *Employee Councils in European Companies*. Klower, Deventer (the Netherlands).

Kornhauser, Arthur. 1968. "Mass Society," *International Encyclopedia of Social Sciences*. New York: Free Press.

Korpi, Walter. 1978. "Social Democracy in Welfare Capitalism—Structural Erosion, Welfare Backlash and Incorporation?" The Nordic Welfare States, *Acta Sociologica,* 21 (Supplement):97–111.

Krejči, J. 1976. *Social Structure in Divided Germany.* London: Croom Helm.

Kuhnle, Stein. 1978. "The Beginnings of the Nordic Welfare States: Similarities and Differences." The Nordic Welfare States. *Acta Sociologica,* 21:9–36.

Laaksonen, Oiva. 1977. *The Power Structure in Chinese Enterprises.* International Studies of Management and Organization. *A Journal of Translations.* Spring: pp. 71–90.

Labor Market Reforms in Sweden: Facts and Employee Views. 1979. Stockholm: Swedish Institute.

Labour Relations in Sweden. 1975. Stockholm: Swedish Institute.

Lager, Carl. 1974. *Pilot Reliability: Reliability of Human Components in Technical Systems Discussed as a Function of Overload, Provocations and Individual Differences.* Stockholm: Royal Institute of Technology.

Lansbury, Russell D. 1978. *The Scandinavian Experience in an International Perspective: A View from Downunder.* Paper for the 9th World Congress of Sociology, Uppsala, Sweden. Mimeo.

LaRosa, M., and M. Gori. 1978. *L'Autogestione, Autonomia Politica e Democrazia Industriale.* Rome: Editrice Citta Nova.

Lepage, H. 1978. *Autogestion et Capitalisme.* Paris: Institute de L'enterprise.

Levinson, Klas. 1978. *Power Structure and Decision-Making Process: A Case Study of Multinational Corporations in the Swedish Flat Glass Industry.* Stockholm: Arbetslivscentrum. Mimeo.

Liljeström, Rita, et al. 1978. *Roles in Transition: Report of an Investigation Made for the Advisory Council on Equality between Men and Women.* Stockholm: Liber-Forlag.

Lindestad, Hans, and Anders Kvist. 1975. *The Volkswagen Report.* Stockholm: SAF.

Lindestad, Hans, and Jan-Peder Norstedt. 1973. *Autonomous Groups and Payment by Result.* Stockholm: SAF.

Lindestad, Hans and Goran Rosander. 1977. *The Scan Vast-Report.* Stockholm: SAF.

Lindholm, Rolf. 1979. *Towards a New World of Work.* Stockholm: SAF.

Lindholm, Rolf, and Jan-Peder Norstedt. 1975. *The Volvo Report.* Stockholm: SAF.

Long, Richard J. 1977. "The Effects of Employee Ownership on Job Attitudes and Organizational Performance: An Exploratory Study." Ph.D. thesis, Cornell University.

Löwenhard, Percy. 1978. "Die Gleichheit, die Verzweifeln Last," *Bildung, Der Report,* 43:6.

Mabon, Hunter. 1975. *Job Analysis: Measurement Problems and Applications.* Stockholm: M & B Fackboksforlaget AB.

Marris, Robin. 1979. *The Theory and Future of the Corporate Economy and Society.* Leiden: North-Holland (Elsevier).

Matejko, Alexander J. 1979. "The Crisis of Authoritarianism in Eastern Europe," *Canadian Slavonic Papers* 21(2):197–224.

——————. 1980a. "The Obsolescence of Bureaucracy," *Relations Industrielles* 35(3):467–92.

——————. 1980b. The Manipulated Freedom in Mass Societies (West and East). *International Review of Sociology* 16(213):238–76.

Matthöfer, Hans. 1978. *Humanisierung der Arbeit und Produktivität in der Industriegesellschaft.* Cologne: Europaische Verlagsanstalt.

Meidner, Rudolf. 1974. *Co-ordination and Solidarity: An Approach to Wages Policy.* Stockholm: Prisma.

Meidner, Rudolf. 1978. *Employee Investment Funds: An Approach to Collective Capital Formation.* London: George Allen and Unwin.

Mohan, Raj. P., ed. 1979. *Management and Complex Organizations: A Comparative Perspective.* Westport, CT: Greenwood Press.

Muechielli, E. 1978. *Le Travail en Equipe.* Paris: Enterprise Moderne Edition.

Müller, Jürgen C. 1978. *Humanisierungsanforderungen an die Unternehmung und Partizipationskonzepte als Organisatorische Lösungsmöglichkeiten.* Bad Honnef, West Germany: Bock und Herchen.

Myrdal, Hans-Goran. 1979. *The Swedish Model—Will it Survive?* Stockholm: SAF.

Norén, Anders E., and Jan-Peder Norstedt. 1975. *The Ørrefors Report.* Stockholm: SAF.

Norstedt, Jan-Peder, and Stefan Agurén. 1973. *The Saab-Scania Report. Experiment with Modified Work Organizations and Workforms.* Annual Report. Stockholm: SAF.

Occupational Accident Research: Papers Presented on a Seminar in Stockholm, 1975. Stockholm: Arbetarskyddsfonden.

Ortsman, Oscar. 1978. *Changer le Travail.* Paris: Dunod.

Öhlman, Berndt. 1974. *LO and Labour Market Policy since the Second World War.* Stockholm: Bokförlaget Prisma.

Participation in 25 Swedish Companies. 1975. Stockholm: Development Council for Collaboration Questions.
Pay Reform in Sweden. 1977. Stockholm: SAF.
Pejovich, Svetozar, ed. 1978. *The Codetermination Movement in the West: Labor Participation in the Management of Business Firms.* Lexington, MA: D. C. Heath.
Pfeffer, Jeffrey. 1978. *Organizational Design.* Arlington Heights, CA: AHM Publishing.
Podgorecki, Adam. 1975. *Practical Social Sciences.* London: Routledge and Kegan Paul.
Primary and Secondary Education in Sweden. 1976. Stockholm: Swedish Institute.
Ross, J. P., ed. 1978. "The Nordic Welfare States" (special issue), *Acta Sociologica,* 21.
Report on Labour Market Policy. 1978. Stockholm: LO.
Research for a Better Work Environment. 1975. Stockholm: SAF, Swedish Work Environment Fund.
Rubenowitz, Sigvard. 1974a. *Experiences on Industrial Democracy and Changes in Work Organization in Sweden, 1974.* Göteborg: University of Göteborg, Department of Applied Psychology, 1, 2.
——————. 1974b. *Motivational Factors Afecting Manager's Attitudes Towards Industrial Democracy.* Göteborg: University of Göteborg, Department of Applied Psychology, 2, 2.
——————. 1976. *Planned Change Based on Survey Feedback: A Field Project in a Metal Works Industry.* Göteborg, University of Göteborg, Department of Applied Psychology, 4, 1.
——————. 1977. *The Impact of Members Participation in Swedish Industrial Organizations: Some Research Results.* Göteborg: University of Göteborg, Department of Applied Psychology, 7, 2.
——————. 1978. *Quality of Working Life: QWL—The Individual Job and the Production Group.* Manuscript.
——————. 1979a. "The Effectiveness of Participation in 10 Swedish Plants." Manuscript.
——————. 1979b. "What do we Mean by the Concept of Participation?" Manuscript.
Rubenowitz, Sigvard, and Alf Gleerup. 1977. *The Shipping Industry in Sweden.* Geneve: International Institute for Labour Studies. Research Series, No. 25.
SAF and the Swedish Labour Market. 1976. Stockholm: SAF.
Sari, R., et al., eds. 1979. *Management of Human Services.* New York: Columbia University Press.
Sawyer, M. 1976. "Income Distribution in OECD coun-

tries," *OECD Economic Outlook,* Occasional Papers. Paris: OECD.

Scase, Richard. 1977. *Social Democracy in Capitalist Society: Working Class Politics in Britain and Sweden.* London: Croom Helm.

——————, ed. 1976. *Readings in the Swedish Class Structure.* Oxford: Pergamon Press.

Shaw, M. E. 1981. *Group Dynamics.* New York: McGraw-Hill.

Simeray, J. P. 1971. *La Structure de l'Entreprise.* Paris: Entreprise Moderne d'Edition.

Slack, Nigel D., and Ray Wild. 1975. "Production Flow Line and 'Collective' Working: A Comparison," *International Journal of Production Research* 13, 4:411–18.

Smith, Cyril. 1977. *Industrial Participation.* London: McGraw-Hill.

Some Data About Sweden. Stockholm: Skandinaviska Enskilda Banken. (Published annually.)

Starbuck, W. H., A. Greve, and B. Hedberg. 1978. "Responding to Crisis." Stockholm: Arbetslivscentrum. Mimeo.

Statistisk Årsbok. Stockholm: Statistiska Centralbyran. (Published annually.)

Stokes, Bruse. 1978. "Worker Participation—Productivity and the Quality of Work Life," *Worldwatch Papers,* 1975.

Susman, G. I. 1979. *Autonomy at Work.* New York: Praeger.

Susman, G. I., and Roger D. Evered. 1978. "An Assessment of the Scientific Merits of Action Research," *Administrative Science Quarterly* 23:582–603.

Swedish Laws on Security of Employment, Status of Shop Stewards, Litigation in Labour Disputes. 1977. Stockholm: Ministry of Labor.

Swedish Legislation on the Working Environment. 1978. Stockholm: Ministry of Labor.

Swedish Trade Union Confederation. 1978. Stockholm: LO.

Tannenbaum, Arnold, et al. 1974. *Hierarchy in Organizations: An International Comparison.* San Francisco: Jossey Bass.

Therborn, G., et al. 1978. "Sweden Before and After Social Democracy: A first Overview." The Nordic Welfare States, *Acta Sociologica* 21 (Supplement):37–58.

"This is How an Agreement Comes into Being." 1978. Stockholm: LO. Mimeo.

Tinbergen, J., ed. 1976. *Reshaping the International Order.* New York: Dutton.

Towards Democracy at the Workplace: New Legislation on

the Joint Regulation of Working Life. 1977. Stockholm: Ministry of Labor.

Törner, Pär. 1976. The Matfors Report. Stockholm: SAF.

Turner, A. N., and P. R. Lawrence. 1965. Industrial Jobs and the Worker. Boston: Harvard University, Graduate School of Business Administration.

Van der Zwaan, A. H. 1975. "The Sociotechnical Systems Approach: A Critical Evaluation," International Journal of Production Research 13, 2:149–63.

Vanek, Jaroslav. 1970. The General Theory of Labor—Managed Market Economics. Ithaca, NY: Cornell University Press.

Weiss, Dimitri. 1978. La Demokratie Industrielle. Paris: Editions d'Organisation.

—————. 1979. Les Relations du Travail. Paris: Dunod.

Westländer, Gunnela. 1976. Arbetets Villkor och Fritidens Innehall. Stockholm: Personal-administrativa radet.

—————. 1977. Rapport om Kvinnor i Fabriksarbetete. Stockholm: Personal-administrativa radet.

White, Terrence H. 1979. Human Resources Management: Changing Times in Alberta. Edmonton, Canada: Alberta Labour.

Wiio, Osmo A. 1975. Systems of Information, Communication and Organization. Helsinki: Helsinki Research Institute for Business Economics (LTT).

Wild, Rag. 1975. "On Selection of Mass Production Systems." International Journal of Production Research 13, 5:443–61.

Wilensky, Harold. 1976. The New Corporation, Centralization and the Welfare State. Beverly Hills, CA: Sage.

Wissen und Gewissen in der Technik. 1964. Vienna: Styria Verlag.

Work and Society. 1976. Milton Keynes (U.K.): The Open University Press.

Work Organization. 1978. Stockholm: LO.

Working Environment Agreement. 1977. Stockholm: SAF-KI-PIK.

The Working Environment in Sweden. 1977. Stockholm: Ministry of Labor.

Yanowitch, Murray. 1978. Social and Economic Inequality in the Soviet Union. New York: M. E. Sharpe.

Yearbook of Nordic Statistics. Stockholm: Nordic Council and Nordic Statistical Secretariat. (Published annually.)

Youngblood, Kneeland. 1978. "Safety Delegates and the Working Environment Act." Current Sweden 204, 4.

6

PROFESSIONAL ETHICS
AND BUREAUCRACY:
THE CASE OF SOCIOLOGISTS

MORAL PROBLEM AREAS

There are several virtues that facilitate the life of any
professional or other community: reciprocity of services
and commitments, feeling of solidarity, repayment good for
good, readiness to give and not only to take, mutual aid
(as long as there is a room for it),[1] readiness to become
involved (and the opportunity of it), rejection of privileges
for the sake of equality, empathy to each other,[2] good
morale,[3] ability to overcome the spontaneous egoism, ability
to cooperate, sense of responsibility for the life of the
community, readiness to forego one's own affairs for the
sake of others. Sociologists as a professional group have
an objective interest in the reinforcement of the above-
mentioned virtues in order to improve their bargaining
power at the professional market, as well as to gain personal satisfaction.

Behind professional decisions and actions are certain
values which have to be adequately recognized. The moral
assumptions quite often remain unnoticed and this distorts
our picture of the social reality. The black/white approach
is damaging. "We would be happy if the things we consider

This is the paper presented at the session of the
Department of Sociology at the University of Alberta on 30
January 1985.

good resulted only from the facts that also seem good and we would like evil to have only evil consequences" (Ossowska 1980, p. 4). The dangers to the reliability of scientific thinking are quite obvious when we take a one-sided approach.[4] In this respect, dialectical reasoning seems to be superior.

Sociologists, like others, have to worry about their existence and survival as a professional community but this concern may become a goal by itself. Student enrollment numbers and research money may divert our attention from the basic sociomoral parameters of our profession. The question is about the final *purpose* of our professional activities, and depending on our answer, the maturity of us as *professionals* may be adequately judged. In any profession there is a vital moral issue of whom professionals serve primarily: themselves, their sponsors, a selected public, or public interest in a broad sense?

The ability of a collective self-criticism is a very important measure of moral maturity. People have obvious reasons to defend their dignity but it is always a good question what they are actually trying to defend. It is typical for the newly established professions to be oversensitive regarding their standing. The acknowledgment of the limits of a given professional competence is a very important factor. Ignorance is not only a matter of lack of knowledge but may be the product of exaggerated claims based on a too-narrow basis. People who mentally stay all the time within the framework of one particular discipline may be blinded to other perspectives; they acquire an incapacity to grasp the alternative ways of approaching a given subject; they are preoccupied with their own professional dignity and deny it to others.

Professional honor consists in the defense of values which are of a basic importance, and therefore are worth some sacrifice. It is up to each profession to agree collectively which are these basic values and how to defend them effectively. There is no reason to claim some demands as long as the contribution is not well articulated. There is a problem of false dignity and a wrong sense of honor tied to a specific kind of distorted values. Much power may be derived from the professional dignity but there is also the danger of misinterpretation. For example, there is a possibility of claiming more implications from a given set of research data than is justified on an empirical basis.

The inner-directedness would be better for sociologists than the other-directedness. It is in the nature of the sociological discipline to emphasize the importance of social bonds and group considerations, but this does not necessarily mean that it is good for a sociologist to be primarily a social animal. The quality of intellectual growth depends on many concerns other than how to cultivate good human relations. The accumulation of facts may become an empty exercise when it is not reinforced by an in-depth analysis of phenomena under study.

The climate of professional exchange depends much on the ability and willingness of people to cultivate their own minds. Work as such is not the only condition of professional success. Pride and shame are personal characteristics much needed to make young sociologists sensitive to the core values of their profession. When we teach history of sociology it would be important to let students know what kind of individuals where our classics: their virtues and human weaknesses. One important characteristic was a willingness to be morally strong and supporting to those who needed their support. Personal strength and the sense of responsibility toward others is a very important virtue.

The ideal of a "reliable protector," somebody who practices protectiveness as a central moral virtue is valid also for sociologists (Ossowska 1980, p. 207). Not to let others down is a great asset of any leader, including a department chairperson. Egotistical inclinations are not uncommon among social scientists and they are only partly justified by a need of privacy and concentration on professional tasks.

How really socialized are sociologists? Some among us are particularly eager to play an active social role, not necessarily only on our own expense (armchair politicians). Some others become cynical about any social duties and take the position of an observer. To be a "reliable protector" means much more than to be a good buddy to students or to attend regularly all departmental meetings; a deeper and more professional approach to people around us is here included.

The sense of *independence* is something worth appreciating. People who move all the time from one fashion to another, who are dominated by market considerations, will not be good sociologists. It is up to our professional institutions to elaborate norms which protect our independence, but the final responsibility in this respect is on each among us individually. An uncritical absorption of the truth formulated by others is harmful for the whole profession. It is not enough to digest thought originated by somebody else. The art of inspiring independent minds is a precious skill highly valuable for sociology departments all around the world. According to J. S. Mill, "Nobody can be a great thinker who does not recognize that as a thinker it is his first duty to follow his intellect to whatever con- clusions it may lead" (Ossowska 1980, p. 79). The truth can triumph only through the confrontations of different opinions. We have the duty to ourselves to be open and not indulge in an unjustified belief in our own infallibility. It is also important to cultivate the right to be different.

Tolerance is one of the conditions for people to be creative and not prevent each other to grow. In sociology, tolerance is particularly necessary due to the fact that especially in the democratic countries various world-views coexist. However, more in nondemocratic conditions, much harm is done by lack of tolerance. Any academic discipline deteriorates when some paradigms enjoy much official sup- port at the expense of other paradigms (Matejko 1986).

The recognition of other people's right to think and behave in the way they actually do is not an easy thing. Views which differ from ours act against our own vested interests, undermine our self-assurance, question our integrity, shake our peace and order. It is not surprising that people take a defensive attitude. Pluralism is easy to pronounce but actually very difficult to practice. The disposition to tolerate others, similar to the disposition to love, needs cultivation and a suitable climate. It is an open question how much of such a climate is available in various departments of sociology. Definitely, the cross- cultural exchange helps to cultivate tolerance. Nationalist protectionist policies do not help in this respect.[5]

On the other hand, there are some obvious limits of tolerance. The spectrum of authorized kinds of behavior is not unlimited and each profession necessarily tends to develop appropriate criteria. In sociology there is more diversity than in other disciplines but the cost of the potential moral ambiguity is also higher.

There is a need to make a distinction between freedom *from* and freedom *to*. In the concerns of sociologists the first concept prevails and much may be found in the socio- logical literature on human rights. The respect for the autonomy of an individual or a group makes sense only when it goes together with some duty, because the freedom for one side usually goes together with the limitation of freedom of another side. Freedom *to* is, according to E. Fromm (1966) the possibility and willingness to express our own identity. This activity originates in our self and is carried for its own sake.

It seems that in sociology so far freedom *to* is not adequately appreciated because of the cult of the average. In the process of growth tendencies are much more impor- tant than the averages. In the more sophisticated societies, people probably will need more and more of the freedom to. On the other hand, actually only freedom *to* may allow for positive growth of the humanitarian values.

Privacy is one of the most important resources which allows one to apply freedom *to*. There is much to say in favor of our right to be left alone occasionally, not being exposed to a constant external control, against unwanted familiarity and rudeness. The respect of the *private* person deserves much more attention in sociology than has been the case.

There is a sensitive issue here, inasmuch as the neutralization of values is one of the professional traditions of such sociology, which takes distance to the phenomena under study. A doctrinaire approach, represented, among others, by Marxists (Jain and Matejko 1984), eliminates the possibility of being "neutral," but even in this case there is a room for various interpretations of "commitment" and its application to the sociology study (Parkin 1979). Universal moral norms function as a lubricant, which reduces friction in the mechanism of the profession. Mutual trust is one of the basic social bonds among people. Constant watchfulness is tiring and unpleasant. Lies make impossible a meaningful communication. Truthfulness makes people mutually dependable.

In conclusion, professional ethics of a sociologist is worth some attention. Respect for the human person in general is valid for sociology as well as for any other scientific discipline dealing with people. There is something very dignified in a "chivalric" ideology making people better because of personal or ornamental virtues (courage, truthfulness, modesty, self-restraint, dignity, loyalty toward oneself), as distinguished from civil virtues: humanity, compassion, gratitude, tendency to forgive those who repent, and so forth. (Ossowska 1980, p. 243).

Both of these kinds of moral virtues have some relation to such practical virtues as accuracy, methodicalness, enterprise, precaution, prudence, perseverance, frugality, temperance, providence, conscientiousness, and continuance (Ibid., pp. 244–47). The instrumental character of practical virtues gives them a lasting value only when they are subordinated to something much above them. There is no reason why sociologists should treat themselves different from others and miss Kant's imperative: Only directives which can be generalized should be adapted as guidelines for action.

The utilitarian approach, which holds that moral judgments should be based upon the amount of suffering spared or pleasure enchanced,[6] is too narrow because it misses the importance of human *dignity* as a value in itself. Sociological concerns are not open enough to moral norms appealing to dignity, and this has some negative repercussions regarding the moral self-definition of sociologists themselves.

The hierarchy of professional values upon which one insists and which one can defend in case of emergency seems to remain among sociologists much less crystalized than in the older professions; for example, physicians, lawyers, and so forth. Righteousness will go hand in hand with brutality when the value of tactfulness is not allocated highly enough in the hierarchy of professional values.

Moral norms are the matter not only of principles but also of *expediency*. In order to achieve some stability of human relations, it is practical to obey some rules of human relations. A proverb from Zaire gives this advice: "You can lie to a mouse, because a mouse will come and go. But you should not lie to a cockroach for a cockroach stays on" (Ibid., p. 124). With the much-declining institutional mobility of sociologists the message of this proverb is particularly appropriate.[7] We need to trust professional colleagues in order to feel secure. Believing people is necessary if we want to believe *in* people (Ibid., p. 126). Hypocrisy,[8] double-thinking,[9] cheating, delation, stealing and other wrongdoing make impossible mutual trust, loyalty, and the feeling of security.

The sense of justice will flourish only when people are given what they deserve (suum cuique), distribution of rewards and penalities is legitimate,[10] rules are consistently executed (identical cases are treated in an identical manner),[11] charity softens justice,[12] not much difference is given in treating oneself in comparison with treating others,[13] the stronger do not claim too much for themselves,[14] indivisible values are allocated in a nonconflictual manner, a peaceful solution is substituted for fighting, divergent interests and beliefs are harmonized, aggressions are channeled into harmless outlets, goodwill is available in an adequate quantity and quality.

The sociotechnical task to construct human communities of good moral quality is open, among others, to sociologists as deliverers of an adequate professional expertise. Of course, sociologists may be rightly expected not only to serve outside interests in this respect but also to clean up their own professional institutions. So far we do not pay enough attention to the question of how to establish conditions helpful to our own growth as moral entities. Current expediencies take most of our time and effort, we push forward our own careers, but actually how much we are dedicated to improving our own professional community?

SHAPING PROFESSIONAL COMMUNITY

In doing anything, including teaching or research in sociology, we have to follow more or less consistently some moral norms. They guard our existence in the terms of elementary safety in relation to each other (do not kill, do not harm) and therefore at least allow us not to spend much time and effort just only on survival. In any intellectual pursuit this seems to be quite basic because safety measures are prior to anything else and the preoccupation with them may be a major burden in the individual as well as group dimension. In general, it is difficult to work systematically and follow a long time perspective in the situation of much exposure to the danger of persecution, expulsion, and so forth. Fear paralyzes the thought and makes life miserable even under relatively comfortable material conditions. The concept of academic tenure is the device to eliminate fear by making academics free from external pressures in their pursuit of their professional duties.

It is also a matter of dignity as

> an attribute of those who know how to defend the values they recognize, whose sense of self-worth is associated with the defense of those values and who expect to be respected for it by others. Lack of dignity is demonstrated by those who will degrade themselves by giving up such values or will allow themselves to be humiliated for the sake of personal gain. . . (Ibid., p. 54).

Dignity functions as a protective shield against personal humiliation and at the same time against lowering of social standards, particularly important in the professional practice. People who are justly proud of their values and norms are guardians of public interest.

Both honor and virtue are related to specific values and imply an acute sensibility to our image in other people's eyes (Ibid., p. 58). The process of socialization is based on shaping exactly this sensibility in order to make sure that under critical circumstances people will act according to the established standards and not follow their own expediency. The reward is in a good feeling of self-worth and the consciousness of power originating from it. There is here also an important factor of sensibility to the opinion of others; any substantial decline of this sensibility is the evidence of desocialization.

The personal and civic virtues may be in mutual disagreement when the personal sense of justice differs much from the social rules which people are expected to follow (Ibid., pp. 64–65). Under a despotic rule there is not much room for personal virtues. According to B. Russell, "without civil morality societies perish; without personal morality they do not deserve to survive" (1958, Ibid., p. 73).

Moral norms as applied to the field of professional ethics function in a variety of ways. They secure some independence from the external intrusion. A member of a profession is expected to remain free within the specific framework of matters related to the execution of his or her skills. The growing bureaucratization of several traditionally "liberal" professions leads to the potential limitations of freedom and the incapacitation of professionals in their free judgment. The case of Soviet psychiatrists is an extreme example but any company physician even in the Western democracies faces the moral dilemma: Should he or she follow primarily the interest of his or her patients or the interest of his or her employer?

As long as there is not social and legal guarantee for conscientious objectors to express themselves freely, there is always a chance for public bodies to indulge in follies that cost the society much and are based on the misuse of resources for the pursuit of wrong policies.

The prototype of a folly is for Tuchman (1984) the case of Trojans taking the wooden horse within their walls on their free but misguided choice against all warnings and by the rejection of the feasible alternative just to destroy the horse. Afterwards she discusses how popes provoked the Protestant secession (the period 1470–1530). "Theirs was a folly of perversity, perhaps the most consequential in Western history, if measured by its result in centuries of ensuing hostility and fratricidal war" (Tuchman 1984, p. 52).

The pursuit of policy contrary to self-interest is not uncommon, not only among individuals but also among public bodies. Tuchman has selected several cases of policies perceived as counterproductive already in their own times, accepted and pursued even if feasible alternatives were available, and promoted not only by individuals but by some authorities.

Wooden-headedness, the source of self-deception, is a factor that plays a remarkable large role in government. It consists in assessing a situation in terms of preconceived fixed notions while ignoring or rejecting any contrary signs. It is acting according to wish while not allowing oneself to be

> deflected by the facts. . . . Wooden-headedness is
> also the refusal to benefit from experience (Tuch-
> man 1984, p. 7).

Policies demonstrably unworkable or counterproductive are
promoted without much resistance when the rulers are able
and willing to suppress the opposition to them arising from
the people who have courage and enough insight to question
the judgment of those in power (Matejko 1986).

Professionalists do not want to be humiliated by being
subjected to the power of those who sponsor them. Much
depends in this respect on the professional consciousness of
people who work in a given profession, actual dependence
on sponsors, level of moral sensitivity, values of a given
society, situation on the market, and so forth. Professions
differ much in their collective awareness of rights and
duties of their members. The sociological profession is in
this respect in a much worse position then the more-estab-
lished and better-organized professions which managed to
obtain some guarantees for themselves.

One of the major handicaps of sociologists is the fact
that in order to practice the profession they need a major
institutional sponsor: a university, a research institute, a
governmental agency, and so forth. Individual clients or
small business usually are neither interested in sociological
services nor willing to pay for them. In countries which
recognize human rights sociologists in general at least have
some universal freedoms to call for. Under the despotic
regimes the dependence is particularly evident in the case
of sociologists because the rulers have a strong vested
interest to claim that society is in good shape and for the
sake of social harmony any criticism should be eliminated.

Several despotic rulers have eliminated sociology as a
discipline (for example, in the Soviet bloc under the rule of
Stalin and his followers) or at least have made it harmless
by censorship, imprisonment and layoff of university sociologists, grants given only for projects of no critical importance, promotion policy giving advantage only to the opportunistic sociologists, and so forth.

In the developed countries there are enough financial
resources and problems related to diversification and integration of society to create an evident need of sociological
expertise. Even the countries which before did not tolerate
sociology, primarily the Soviet Union, now are willing to
promote teaching and research in social fields, even if it is
still limited and heavily censored. In the developing countries the situation remains much worse. First of all, the
omnipotent ruling parties and governments are anxious to

keep intact their monopoly of power and actually do not tolerate an independent expertise. Quite often a sociologist who differs in his or her views with the local rulers does not have a chance to apply himself or herself. Secondly, there is no choice regarding the jobs for sociologists; if they are lucky to find one they have to keep it at almost any cost. Thirdly, there is not much liberal tradition and the views which differ from what is "proper" are much suppressed.

With the growing mass education in developed as well as developing countries there is a tendency to lower the standards of education. The publicly financed educational institutions have a vested interest in keeping students happy (and easy good grades are one of the most important conditions of student happiness), and convinced that not much effort is needed in order to obtain diploma. In many developing countries the mass social advancement is treated as the most evident proof that the local ruling elites are actually doing something for people. It is much easier to offer an illusion of educational advancement than to improve substantially the ailing economies vulnerable to corruption, mismanagement, nepotism and dependence on foreign markets. In the developed countries the extension of highly subsidized higher education functions as one of the ways to reduce the high unemployment indicators, reduce the conflict of generations, improve the image of the government in the eyes of the young people and their parents, offer some inducement to capital investments, and prevent the opposition from taking advantage of mass dissatisfaction.

Sociology has very often the image of something easy in comparison with more professionally oriented disciplines. It puts academic sociologists into a peculiar position of teachers who owe their income and credentials more to popularity than to an in-depth approach. In North America personal attractiveness of a sociology teacher influences directly his or her merit rating and it is almost impossible to obtain a tenure without being fully accepted by students.

POSITION OF SOCIOLOGISTS IN UNIVERSITIES

The popularity of sociology is gradually diminishing with the saturation of professional market, especially in North America, unemployment among the graduates, shortage of research funds, and the dissatisfaction with a discipline that is unable to fulfill exaggerated past promises. In the United States, "salary gains among sociologists have been less than among other faculty"[15] (*Footnotes*, American

Sociological Association, 1985, 13, 1, p. 5). Sociology definitely shares in the difficulties of a declining growth of universities and problems related to it.[16]

The quality of humanities and social studies, including sociology, depends much on the cultural and educational background represented not only by teachers but also by students. Any major crisis of the postsecondary education has its impact on the chance of sociology applying itself within the framework of university studies.

In social sciences, history and geography are particularly important as the foundation of any sophisticated knowledge of society. The analytical skills, ability to speak and write well, aspirations going much beyond grade hunting, some basic orientation in the main world issues, some sophistication in local affairs—all these qualities should be definitely shaped already at the middle-school level.[17] Teachers themselves being interested in issues going much beyond the material success may inspire their students and open the new horizons.

The intellectual and moral quality of the middle school, and primarily of its teaching staff, is crucial for the quality of the whole educational system. At the postsecondary level there is not much time and opportunity to do later on what has not been done before. In addition, the relatively high expense related to the postsecondary education makes it economically inefficient to apply remedial courses at this level.

In North America today there are many ambitious and enlightened teachers who are far from being happy with the educational system identified by S. Hume with "a sausage machine that mindlessly processes graduates who can't read, write or do basic math."[18]

The basic problem is not so much additional *money* or even *computers* but first of all how to allow these good teachers to implement their aspirations: authentically *teach* instead of manipulating or entertaining, focus on basics instead of following changing fashions, help students to understand the nature of things instead of a cheap simplification, exercise *analytical* thinking instead of a futile memorization, prepare young people to overcome difficulties instead of pretending that everything is easy. It is up to the educational policy-makers to create in the schools conditions allowing teachers to teach better, stimulate students to achieve intellectual and moral maturity, develop a climate of mutual cooperation between teachers and students. It is very difficult to be a good teacher without being exposed to students who want to learn instead of only chasing good grades for as little effort as possible.

Any really good educational system has to be based on inspiration, systematic learning, discipline, and a genuine evaluation of performance. Teachers are paid not just to keep students happy right now, without bothering about the educational output in the long run. It is not good educational economy to use the expensive postsecondary education as a remedy for an inadequate secondary education (remedial courses, and so forth). An in-depth public discussion is needed about the actual quality of education and the best use of taxpayers' money in this sensitive field where the whole future of young generation is at stake.

The high number of first-year students failing writing competency at the university level shows the evident weakness of secondary education in North America. Undergraduate studies suffer much from the lack of knowledge and motivation among students. Universities are too expensive to function as mere temporary shelters for unemployed young people. When quality of education is sacrificed for the sake of expediency, the public good becomes endangered. Gifted students suffer and higher education is vulnerable to mediocrity.

The educational system treated as "a sausage machine" is not only useless but also harmful. Too much preoccupation with keeping students happy and shaping learning requirements in order to please them misses the basic purpose of the educational process. Mastery may be achieved only through painful but rewarding effort. When taking into consideration the fact that most of university costs are covered by society and not by students as "clients," there is a good reason to condemn any cheap popularity contest among the teachers. The evaluation of teachers by students makes good sense but it never should function as the main criterion of academic performance.

One of the basic problems is how to achieve a progressing maturation of students. Andragogy is more proper than pedagogy in dealing with adults.[19] Knowledge and experience should accumulate gradually and this will not happen as long as the choice of courses by students remains chaotic. There is an urgent need to strengthen consultation and tutorial services, as well as improve the discipline of studies. Too much liberalism in this respect leads to mediocrity in studies and in the long run is very harmful to students.

It is a vital question how much universities in general, and sociology teaching in particular, are able to resist the tendency towards mediocrization. According to Bercuson et al., "the universities of Canada became educational supermarkets, grovelling for government grants, selling their souls in return for public approval and simultaneously selling the value of higher education for a song" (1984, p. 8).[20] It is nonsense to leave to the uneducated the selection of their own personal route to knowledge in the academic "supermarket." Students who are expected to learn are not the best judges of the standards which teachers are expected to follow. Quality education is crucial for the future of any country and the easy diplomas actually diminish the chances of the young generation to find jobs.

The question whether the quality of universities is good enough[21] and how much this quality may become endangered by the current shortage of funds seems to be quite appropriate. Bercuson et al. claim that "Incompetent students, students who should never have gone to a university, have nearly destroyed the system" (Ibid., p. 28). There is too much leniency in accepting the candidates, as well in the discipline of studies. The vested interests of organized pressure groups play too much role at the expense of the main purpose of university teaching: to deliver to the society well-qualified and constructively oriented human beings. "Nothing is more important in the building of a qualified staff at a university than the decisions to grant tenure, to reward meritorious performance, and to provide job security for the best teachers and scholars" (Ibid., p. 46). The growing adversary relation between organized teachers and top administrators spoils these decisions. The best among academics do not have much say in the governmental bodies.

> Democracy must now be tempered with a strong dose of elitism in the determination of academic policy and, in its trade union guise, democracy must be limited before it homogenizes the teaching staff, undermines programs, and turns universities into glorified high schools. . . . A strong dose of elitism and genuine shared authority are the best way to run a university (Ibid., p. 56).

Anything worthwhile is difficult to get and in order to turn out a really good product the discipline of studies must be tightened up. Low entrance standards open room to mediocrity. The same is valid for the good grade inflation and the very lenient approach to the work load of students. In the system where everyone gets in and almost everyone passes there is no room for excellence. The weakness of the core curriculum or its total absence prevents the student from gaining a necessary basic knowledge in a given field. A chaotic collection of more or less accidental courses does not lead to any specific skill.[22]

The traditional conceptualization of a student is all too often that of a passive recipient of knowledge who is totally dependent upon an instructor for his or her learning experience. Malconceived teaching evaluation reinforces this passivity and dependency. There should be a chance given for an alternative to the bureaucratic, instructor-controlled format established by many instructors by creating a democratic milieu in which students are asked to assume responsibility for some of the control, which is usually the instructor's prerogative, and wherein authority is of the group. This may be done consistently in many ways—by allowing the class to decide what format exams would take, having students choose their own topics for class presentations from those available, having students grade the class presentations, and asking students to make administrative decisions re, for example, whether a class member should be allowed to write the final exam early, be given an extension on the term paper, and so forth. Also, with the approval of the class, the grading sheet may readily be available to students whenever they wish to see it. This sheet identifies students by I.D. number and contains grades for the mid-term exam, the case presentation or term paper, and the class presentation; and so students are readily able to see how they have been evaluated by both their instructor and peers. It is up to the teacher to effect a mutuality of responsibility in planning and conducting activities and evaluating them. This process wherein students are given an opportunity to assume some responsibility for their own learning experience is very different from most courses in which paternalism, regimentation, restriction of information, and enforced dependency on authority prevails.

The status of sociology at the university depends ultimately not on the number of students taking courses but on the academic standing of the discipline (research, publications, entrepreneurship, public appeal) and quality, long-term return on educational investment. The nature of sociology makes it vulnerable to a potential denounciation as a "Mickey Mouse discipline" and this is already a good reason to make everything possible to reinforce the basics. Popularity is something highly misleading in this respect and definitely should not be used as the main criterion. In this respect the "marketing" of sociology is a delicate issue and some serious errors may be committed.

For example, promotion and rewarding of sociology professors depends in some cases too much on student evaluation. This is a very unreliable criterion due to the fact that quite often students are inadequately prepared and take courses either accidentally or as a required nuisance. In reviewing staff performance, what actually counts are: teaching, research and scholarly work, knowledge of the discipline and specialization, professional conduct, contribution to the administration of the department, faculty and university, public service, and contribution to academic and professional bodies.

The theoretical orientation needs much preparation and may be very boring to those students who have neither motivation nor adequate background to appreciate a discursive style of lecturing.[23] Many of them become disappointed when memorization does not promise a high grade and they have to think independently. J. Barzun is right in saying that we should train students not only in analytical skills but also in intuitive understanding. It should be the personal ambition of a sociology teacher not to limit himself or herself only to the minutial and analytical methodism but also to the cultivation of the "activities of the mind along the path of the finesse" (1984, p. 104).

Much depends on the ability of the teacher to focus upon conceptual issues which students can integrate into their world-view rather than focusing on disjointed bits and pieces of information which are quickly forgotten soon after—if not before—the final exam. The teacher is supposed to understand and convey the importance of integrating conceptualizations rather than focusing on isolated facts and statistics which can readily be looked up in a text or reference book. It is up to a good teacher to facilitate adeptly the ability of students to think for themselves. It is up to the teacher to show respect for the student's opinion. His or her concern and responsiveness to questions and comments is demonstrated by his or her willingness to share decision making and the leadership role with the class. He or she also makes himself or herself readily available to meet with students individually to discuss concerns, class presentations, and case studies.

In North America we should offer the best to our young people but nothing can be done without their active cooperation and full realization of what learning is about. There is an obvious immaturity of students to select courses which are relatively easy as well as to push teachers to give good grades for a mediocre performance. The emphasis on bargaining spoils education because the main purpose of teaching should be to expose young people to difficulties. Something which we take for granted in sports is still neglected in education. The entertaining factor is an obvious aspect in good teaching but we should be careful not to overemphasize it. A good teacher should not be identified with a clever manipulator who knows how to keep his students happy because he or she makes everything very easy (and superficial).[24]

It is not proper to be poetic about the institution's strengths while ignoring its weaknesses. For a university to act as the "conscience of society" by seeking truth and knowledge it is necessary to keep high standards. There is nothing basically wrong in universities trying to be attractive to students in giving them the opportunity to evaluate teachers, take part in running the institution, and so forth. It is also a very good idea to please local communities and be on good terms with the mass media. However, all these fully justified concerns should not be promoted at the expense of academic excellence.

Good teaching and scholarship would be sacrificed in the case of keeping students happy at any cost, by focusing on "fashionable" courses at the expense of basic knowledge, lowering the standards of evaluation, entertaining, instead of a genuine training. The pursuit of lucrative grants and political supports may happen at the expense of good teaching, contribution to the university community, and intellectual interests.[25]

FOR QUALITY LEARNING IN SOCIOLOGY

Learning of sociology is much different from buying goodies in the supermarkets; however, in this sophisticated field there is room for a "consumer" awareness. Is it really a good bargain for a student to be lost in a crowded class when at the same time there is a choice of much smaller classes in which there is more opportunity to study in a direct contact with the professor? Does it make sense to fight for lower demands when this makes the learning much less substantial and handicaps the university graduate later in the labor market? Is it really good for the student not to write papers and have this way "easier"? What is really wrong in the teachers being treated at equal footing with coaches who are useful for people in practicing sports only when they are much demanding?

Also at the university level of teaching sociology there is an urgent need to concentrate on basics and not to allow fashionable or marginal courses to dominate. It is true that sometimes the basic courses are somewhat boring[26] and do not look as directly useful, but a university is supposed to offer students universal guidance valid not only for today but also for tomorrow. Without skill of *reasoning* within the framework of sociological discipline there is not much purpose to spend time and money to study.

There is no reason to deny that professors and graduate students should cooperate to decipher the puzzle of graduate training. The essence of this "puzzle" is in common sharing of the commitment to intellectual mastery and professional duty.

From the author's perspective, there is too much hunting for high grades and easy terms of obtaining degrees. Professors are expected to be nice to students and keep them in good spirits. This may lead to too much leniency which becomes harmful for students in the long run. The matter of a scientific degree is a much more serious issue than just a convenient arrangement between consenting individuals. Young people who look for a professional career need to be exposed to difficulties—this is helpful to gaining self-control. Permissiveness in sports as well as in academic training is not an asset but a liability.

In the past, there was too much struggle for easy terms of training and various privileges and not enough concern for professional mastery. It is possible to understand the intentions of teachers who, by improving the grades of students, help them in obtaining scholarships and other material benefits. However, with the decline of the discipline of graduate studies, their main purpose becomes undermined.

The role of a responsible professor is at least the same as the role of a good coach. A very lenient coach becomes a failure, as is a professor who wants to be popular at any cost. It is in the common interest of professors and graduate students to share jointly in the promotion of mastery, especially when the market value of academic degrees declines. There is no good reason to treat university learning less seriously than training in sports. A good coach is appreciated not for what kind of a good buddy he or whe is or according to his or her entertainment capacity but primarily for what kind of skills he or she is able and willing to offer.[27]

Any skill is largely based on knowledge, the unity of conception and execution, as well as a considerable amount of autonomy exercised by the skill holder. The university education makes sense only when it is targeted on high skills. The exercise of temporal memorization (mostly only until the date of the final exam) of some amount of data is in basic disagreement with the traditional spirit of excellent universities which provide their graduates with a high professional-career potential. Especially in the higher level sociology courses, students should be exposed to the exercise of their creative skills in writing *original* papers, taking a very active part in debates, being able to oppose *constructively* what the teacher says, learning how to make excellent oral presentations, and so forth. A sociology teacher who limits himself or herself only to the exam material and emphasizes rote learning does not fit into the profile of an ambitious university. A modest amount of knowledge available, neglect of an in-depth liaison between theory and practice, acceptance of the fact that students remain passive absorbers of digested and vulgarized interpretation of a given discipline, are the evidence of mediocre sociology teaching. Only very naïve and immature students will be satisfied with learning which does not actually lead to any meaningful skill.[28]

The passivity of students is not so much a matter of their personalities and an inadequate high-school background, but often the traditional system of course enrollment.[29] For a student it is almost impossible to gain much from the more advanced courses without taking before some preparatory steps: lower courses, individual reading, informal contact with the specialists in a given field, and so forth. Students who are not offered a qualified guidance waste their time and effort picking up a chaotic collection of courses which taken together do not constitute a cohesive whole. Exactly for this reason we need more *core curricula* which would constitute the systematic programs of a general study, far from a narrow specialization but organized enough to constitute a well-grounded study.

We need in sociology less memorization and more reasoning, debate and creative learning in general. With the present-day easy availability of information sources, the main task of postsecondary education is to provide students with the high intellectual skill to make reasonable choices, follow well-provided procedures of data gathering, analysis, interpretation and making conclusions. The fact that most of teaching time is wasted on facts and their mechanical memorization is shocking when taking into consideration the unfavorable labor market situation, highly competitive character of international market conditions, and the growing reliance on computers. We have an urgent need to produce people who know well how to reason effectively and not human substitutes for data banks. Universities will fail by not encouraging students to formulate valid questions, become aware of the limits of each discipline, gain human skills of empathy and cooperation, accept the difficulty of coping with the unknown.

Our function as a university is very much different

from a community college, which is much cheaper to maintain but at the same time has a focus of a nonacademic nature. There is not reason for us to compete with community colleges in enrollment numbers and to resign from our professional aspirations in order to bring as many students as possible to the courses related to specific skills or to the popularization of some new subjects. Community colleges can make popularization much better than we are doing at the university level, and at the same time they cost the taxpayer and students much less. Our main role is either to produce the highly skilled specialists in sociology or to offer a very good *general background* for the personal growth in specific fields of sociology. Only an in-depth approach to learning can justify in the long run the heavy public expenditure on sociology studies. Any involvement into the popularity contest denies the basic mission of a genuine university. We should take for granted that university learning is not a joke but a difficult process based on a close daily cooperation between professors and students.[30]

In the democratic society everyone must be encouraged to give his or her opinions. However, the traditional role of students and teachers still stands. In case the student fails to harmonize his or her difficulties, he or she has the option to leave the course if the disagreement with the teacher is impossible to resolve. The student is there to learn, the professor is there to instruct. This is not demeaning to anyone; it is the natural order as exemplified for centuries. Undermining this basic concept erodes anyone's stability and undermines the basic purpose of university studies.[31]

It is in the vested interest of students to defend the high market value of their future diplomas by insisting on quality learning of sociology. The progress of understanding has to be well based on a harmonious progress from introductory courses to more difficult subjects. Entertainment and buddy relations with teachers may be good additions to the learning process but not substitutes of it. There should be available a tutorial help offered by people who have necessary skills. *Explain* and *understand, interpret* and *formulate meaningful conclusions* should count more than *remember* and *repeat* at the exam.

Much goodwill is needed on both sides: students and teachers. As long as students prefer the easiest way by expecting no much from their teachers in the intellectual sense, no progress in sociology may be expected. The academic staff should be fully aware of the fact that by allowing the standards to deteriorate (easy grades, vulgar-ization of course content, low level of expectations) they undermine the main purpose of university learning. It would be much less expensive for the public bodies to support community colleges, rather than those universities that offer nothing much different. In the tough, present-day economic situation it is not possible to survive on the basis of pretensions. Only close cooperation between teachers and students for the sake of quality learning may be a positive answer to the present-day financial and intellectual crisis of universities in the Western world.

Of course, we should not return to elitist universities. They must be open to everybody as an opportunity but not as the assurance of an easy diploma (with no market value). Gifted and hard-working people should be generously granted as this happens in several countries. However, it would be an illusion to expect *everybody* to succeed in the studies, especially at the adequately high level of expectations. Students' interests need to be defended by a well-functioning grievance system. On the other hand, teachers should be free in the critical judgments. *Tutorials* may help students who have difficulties to grasp things. We should not be slow or hesitant in learning from the experience of the best universities which have much tradition in the tutorial system (Oxford, Cambridge, Harvard, and so on). The chance of opening many good jobs on the expanded scientific and technological basis depends much on quality learning and everything should be done in this respect by universities.

PROBLEMS OF SOCIOLOGISTS UNDER COMMUNISM[32]

The rapid development of sociology in countries of the Soviet bloc is dictated to a large extent by the necessities of a modern economy. The search for satisfactory new solutions to several managerial problems has to be supported by the adequate development of social studies. The awareness of this fact seems to be now common to all communist countries except Albania. Especially in the Soviet Union, Poland, and more recently in Czechoslovakia, a vital interest has developed in sociology and in finding some practical application for this discipline. In Poland, for example, a group of sociologists, inspired to some extent by the development of praxiology (Kotarbinski 1965) and cybernetics, initiated in the 1960s its own original approach to social technology. The founder of that group, A. Podgorecki (now at Carleton University in Ottawa), describes the sociotechnical approach as an attempt to translate systematically verified hypotheses into practical rules of effective action. "Socio-technique is an applied (or practical) social science which serves to inform the practitioner on how to find effective means to realize intended goals when a given set of values is accepted and a given body of tested propositions describing human behavior is accessible" (Podgorecki and Schulze 1969, pp. 142–43).

While we are fully aware of wide differences among the various versions of the nationalized economy in the various countries of East Europe, it is possible to characterize some general traits of the model which so far prevail; Yugoslavia is, of course, a special case. "The basic institution in the socialist economy is the socialized enterprise, run either by the government employee or by a cooperative director," writes Szczepanski.

> The one and the other are bound in their decisions by the central plan. The privately owned enterprises in small industry, the handicrafts, retail trade, the services and agriculture (in Poland) are connected with (the) planned economic system. And government policy determines the range of their decisions, output limits, prices, etc. In a word, the operation of the market is determined by the government's economic policy, shaped by the targets set in the plan. . . . In this economic system there arises a special type of economic career-man. This career is not only directly dependent on the economic results obtained, but on the fulfillment of the targets set for the planned functioning of the economy. It is a career of an administrative type . . . (Szczepanski 1964, pp. 6–7).

The total subservience of every individual enterprise to the needs of a centrally planned economy has been taken by top decision makers as the basic advantage of the model presented above. On the other hand, one may say that the far-reaching curtailment of initiative not only at the bottom of the hierarchy, but also at many intermediary levels, is presumably the most unfavorable consequence. A second consequence is mentioned quite often, the not fully realistic goal of subordinating individual needs and interests to those of the total society.

> The aims of the economy are fixed by the plan and most by individual motivation. Income is decided by a system of remuneration. The plan is law and

its fulfillment is implemented by legal sanction. It is consequently accepted that the individual in this type of economy is on the one hand guided by social motivations—since he identifies himself with the aims of society as a whole—and on the other hand, by the fear of repression. Two different qualities must be distinguished here. One is the ideal socialist man, who subordinates his individual desires to the general objectives of society and to the principles governing society as a whole, and (who) expects that society will remunerate him with a just share of the social income. The second is the actual shaping of the human personality as it is expressed in reality (Szczepanski 1965, p. 15).

It is this human reality which sociology aims to study. Even without questioning the existing political system, sociological studies of an empirical character discover some weak points, areas of social life underscored by problems, such as conflicts between supervisors and subordinates, maladjustment of peasants to industrial life, low employee morale and low levels of work satisfaction, difficult conditions for working women, housing difficulties, prostitution, cultural lag affecting certain strata of the population, and so on (Matejko 1974, 1986).

In several communist countries sociology is beginning to play an important role in introducing an empirical correction to the prevailing models. However, another role of sociology is becoming even more important. It consists in the sociotechnical function of social sciences in the planned economy. Among sociologists in the communist countries there is a strong conviction that empirical sociology should contribute to the social change. In Poland, Adam Podgorecki has made a substantial contribution to the establishment of a sociological interpretation of practical sciences. He approaches these sciences as a set of general statements on how, depending on the connections between facts, a state of affairs desirable according to the accepted evaluations can be brought about. Developing this approach, Podorecki has progressed in building a social technology of law. One can observe similar attempts to the Polish sociology of work (Matejko 1969b). There is among the leading Marxist sociologists a growing inclination to emphasize the importance of sociology as a scientific basis for rational social action.

In addition, contacts between Western sociologists and the sociologists in the Soviet-bloc countries have developed greatly since the 1960s. The evident interest in Western industrial sociology and even in Western human relations techniques has its source in the similarity of some difficulties and problems which have to be solved in both worlds.[33]

INTELLECTUALS OR ORGANIZATION MEN?

Social researchers in the modern world of complex organizations face several different choices, which are particularly acute under communism. One of them is the choice between being an intellectual (Parsons 1970, p. 4) and being an organization man (Whyte 1956). It seems necessary to remember that the autonomy of an empirical scientist is, historically speaking, a relatively new phenomenon. In traditional societies even if from time to time some accumulation of valuable empirical knowledge developed successfully, "sooner or later science was always subordinated to other concerns and, as a result, lost its validity" (Ben-David 1971, p. 23). In modern societies, empirical research has developed not only because of growing need for fact finding and reasoning based on it, but also because some people started to see themselves as scientists (Ibid., p. 45).

Social researchers are particularly close to the whole business of "myth" production. It is not only an issue of the impact of value judgments and moral motives on human actions, but also an issue of the contribution which social researchers make to the current or future image of society. It is a question for philosophical and methodological debates as to how close various images are to social reality. What seems unquestionable is the fact that cooperating directly with big and influential organizations, the social researchers shape the social image, by imposing upon the society at least to some extent, their own "scientific" myths. By stating their own positions, social researchers can at least warn their potential clients against biases which are contained in value-distorted information data (Nettler 1968, p. 203, Myrdal 1944, p. 1043). However, how much of such honesty and self-criticism can be expected from people who become servants of a dominant power?

In France, Germany, Japan, and the Soviet Union science has developed to a very large extent because of the direct support of the state (Ben-David 1971). On the American continent it is primarily the dependence of scientists as individuals on grants which exposes them to temptations and internal conflicts characteristic of "organization men." It appears quite clear from several studies dealing with American professors (Anderson and Murray, eds. 1971) that commitment to influential organizations outside of the university setting may look like a tempting solution to several tensions and troubles which characterize their professional roles.

The career of an "organization man" is particularly attractive for a social researcher, among others, because of the uncertainty of effects more typical for social sciences than, for example, for natural sciences, as well as because of a still-limited applicability of research conclusions to social and political practice. There are so far relatively few cases in which social scientists have proven to be successful as social technologists. The basic issue still is not how corruptible social scientists are but if there is anybody really interested in corrupting them.

Social researchers, as long as they apply objectified techniques of collecting data in studying social reality fit relatively well into the role of "technicians." Exactly in that capacity they are acceptable for modern complex organizations as intelligence experts (Wilensky 1967). There are several moral issues which follow acceptance of such a role (Baritz 1960). There are also several significant hardships (Matejko 1986).

It would be quite naïve to assume that empirical orientation absolves social researchers from any social and moral responsibility. Whether he or she likes it or not, the social researcher takes part in constructing a certain image of social reality which delimits, to some extent, the horizons of his or her potential clients. Specialists in the field of human relations focus the attention of managers on certain issues, and at the same time discourage them from paying attention to remaining issues. People who evaluate applications for research grants shape to a considerable extent the choices of candidates.

Social research, in order to be qualified as scientific, has to fulfill general principles of explanation, verification, simplicity, and consistency. The most touchy issue, in comparison with research in natural sciences, is the impact of nonscientific considerations on the whole process of social research (Gouldner 1970). Selection of topics and fields for research may be heavily biased, for example, by the fact that some of them seem to social scientists to be more lucrative than others. Collection of facts may be heavily influenced by idiosyncrasies of researchers. Choices of explanatory hypotheses may be more influenced by current fashions and vested group interests than by anything else. The frame of reference accepted by researchers may be very much dictated by their positions in complex organizations, for example, by the position of a party activist in communist countries.

Social sciences in their general approach are located somewhere between the cosmocentric and the anthropocentric orientations. The first of these orientations allows one to see social reality in an integral way but on the other hand it must neglect the variety introduced by subjective differences. The second orientation pays tribute to the multitude of human experiences but does not provide room for a unified and generalized approach. [34]

Social research should be always accompanied by intellectual self-awareness, which would be free enough from formal restrictions. It is the task of intellectuals to conceptualize social reality far beyond limits of current empirical knowledge. The main function of intellectualism consists not only in producing "myths" but even more in making people aware that: (a) There are many ways of seeing reality, (b) These various ways are more or less mutually exclusive, (c) It is reasonable to preserve some skepticism in commitment to all kinds of "myths," (d) There is always a certain calculation in the case of choosing some "myths" and rejecting others, (e) Trained incapacity is a danger related to any kind of specialization, (f) People in their choices are under the impact of some vested interests (is impartiality possible?).

Irony and skepticism are main weapons of intellectuals. How much success is it possible to achieve with these weapons in a bureaucratized world? All kinds of complex organizations, especially in the communist bureaucracy, are "serious" in their nature and they are vitally interested in getting rid of any frivolity and even more of any irony. Organizations as artificial machines created by people are more or less static but the reality which they deal with is dialectical. Research sponsored by complex organizations tends to be establishment-oriented. It is in the nature of organization in general that it has to bring all items to one common denominator (one social reality) in order to coordinate them smoothly. Social research by—(a) being Aristotelian in its philosophical sense, (b) being organized, (c) serving organizational goals, (d) developing within the framework of huge organizations—has to accept a certain single concept of social reality as given. No confusion and dialectical thinking are allowed.

There are some important arguments against such a state of affairs. First of all there is the above-mentioned question of whether it is justifiable to limit the number of possible images of social reality to only one. Would it not be eventually more justified to approach objects of social investigation on the assumption that several realities (or better to say several *images* of realities) always do exist and are in some conflict with one another? Is it not a terrible simplification to assume that our facts are the only possible facts? In many cases sociologists are aware of conflicting images; for example, in industrial sociology the managerial insight obviously is not easily reconcilable with the insight of workers. Sociologists quite often tend to deal in an eclectic manner with the whole problem of conflicting images. However, it would be better just to accept the existence of conflict than to try to hide it under the cover of a positivistic common denominator.

Another question deals with the function of research conclusions in the organizational framework. The scientific myth produced by researcher is not socially neutral. Of course, depending on the whole variety of circumstances, the social researchers will be taken more or less seriously by their own sponsor. If they are just obedient servants of power, as in some East European countries, or despised "eggheads," as used to be the case in the United States, their influence appears rather limited. However, any kind of a deep ideological crisis in society creates a growing demand for "objective" images of social reality. This "objectivity" at present time is based in all developed countries, including the Soviet Union, on scientific criteria of investigation. People just take for granted that what is "scientific" at the same time is "objective."

Problems discussed above are of a universal validity in social sciences all around the world; therefore they provide a suitable starting point for the analysis, among others, of the East Central European sociology. It is necessary to learn about the specific role sets and the role pressures typical for sociology in Eastern Central Europe. It would be an oversimplification to reduce the whole issue just to communism and its totalitarian nature. Even under the present system there are still several local traditions which managed to survive under all political changes. It is also necessary to take into consideration the demand-supply ratio. As long as there are more applicants than available attractive posts, the competition has to appear and shape human behavior. The authoritarian nature of professorship is not just an innovation introduced by communists, but seems to be deeply rooted in the local tradition. The habit of looking for informal ways of dealing with issues did exist before and it subsequently grew to a large extent under the communist bureaucracy.

Social scientists when playing roles of empirical researchers expose themselves to several expectations and social standards which may be far beyond their professional ability. Most vital questions in the society are of a normative nature: what to choose and why? A social scientist when limited only to the framework of his or her empirical knowledge is not able to provide meaningful answers to those questions. A "myth" producer has to be morally committed and it is not possible to imagine any narrow-minded professional transformed into an intellectual without taking a moral stand.

Being a part of a highly organized communist world the social researcher has to appear (at least) as consistent, reliable and telling the officially accepted truth. He or she is expected not to confuse his listeners and readers but to offer them a highly digestible message. All organizational bonds and pressures give the highest premium to "reliability" and penalize "confusion." On the other hand, the researchers are expected to be knowledgeable and therefore they have to present all kinds of facts. What, however, if these facts just belong to different versions of reality and represent different levels of depth? What if confusion is just in the nature of a particular reality and the only reasonable solution would be to acknowledge this kind of situation?

Social researchers in the totalitarian systems replace previous court jesters who had to be successful in their gimmicks in order to maintain kings' favors. The open question is how much of what sociologists really do are gimmicks and how much, on the other hand, is dictated by search of truth. What is the difference between an organizational truth, the truth of a sponsor, the truth of professional colleagues, the truth of a client, and finally one's own truth?

We know so far relatively little about the distortion of truth in social research which occurs under communism. Modern sociologists in the Soviet bloc are parts of complex organizations and it has a very significant impact on the whole image of them as well as on the kind of truth which they pursue. It would be necessary to study carefully all such cases in which the intellectual tradition and the organizational commitment have to confront one another. The research grant policy may provide many such cases. The situation of university teachers is also very significant in that respect (Matejko 1969a). The case of sociology under communism seems to be particularly interesting. The strong tradition of East European intelligentsia as the stratum devoted to promotion of intellectual and moral values met the system based on the principle of a total organization and ideological commitment. How do they go together?

What kind of conflicts have to appear in the case of such a confrontation? What kind of compromises become possible and agreeable for both sides: political manipulators and intellectuals? What kind of strategy do intellectuals develop in order to reconcile the organizational loyalty imposed upon them from the top with their devotion to intellectualism? What are the pitfalls of being between apparatchiks on one end and the mass of intelligentsia on the other end? What are the ways and means of self-deception which seems almost unavoidable in such a situation?

TWO CONFLICTING ORIENTATIONS IN EAST CENTRAL EUROPE

Sociology has developed in Eastern Central Europe from two entirely different positions. On one hand (at least in some countries, such as Poland and Czechoslovakia) there has been a long tradition of treating liberal sociology as an intellectual exercise. On the other hand, in the late 1950s several communist regimes in Eastern Europe recognized the possibility of using sociology as an ideological weapon against the so-called Western ideological infiltration. This was then the new attraction of sociology for party officials and their followers. Several party functionaries and people employed in the ideological sector found it attractive to switch to sociology as a new discipline. Their place in sociology gave the party the assurance that the discipline would develop according to party interests and that any political and ideological deviants would be kept under control. For many politically reliable people sociology provided opportunities to establish themselves as scientists (which was more secure than being apparatchiks) and university professors, to enter attractive professional careers, travel abroad, publish (in Eastern Europe scientists receive royalties for anything they publish), and in addition to gain some personal autonomy from the party.

Depending upon the local political tradition, there is more or less a tendency among sociologists to deal with touchy issues and to challenge the establishment. In the Soviet Union, Czechoslovakia, East Germany, Bulgaria, and Romania sociologists are in general very loyal to the party. Most of them come from party ranks and sociology offers them an attractive opportunity to be secure in their professional careers. They do have no reason to question the political status quo since their whole existence is based on the preservation of the current political and social system. Most of the sociological writings (almost all in the Soviet

Union) are oriented toward exemplification of ideological and political items, with some empirical data, and glorification of the regime as the end result. In this sense what sociologists are doing is very similar to the services rendered to the regime by journalists and mass media people in general.

In countries with a strong tradition of a democratically oriented intelligentsia—Poland and Hungary—sociology to a large extent continued its historical traditions under the new regime. New people joining the ranks of sociologists feel obliged to take over the intellectual inheritance of the older professional generation. Some of them simply pay lip service to intellectualism, relying primarily on their political power and the support of party officials. However, in order to become fully accepted within the professional world, as well as to develop contacts with Western sociologists, new people had to accept professional standards. With the passage of time the party becomes less and less useful to them after offering them everything they need: power and privilege, personal connections, political security. But professional standards and values are yet to be gained; and in this respect the party allegiance appears more of a liability than a real asset. Several sociologists with strong party backgrounds soon find the ruling party officials to be people of narrow perspectives and very limited social knowledge.

In the countries still strongly influenced by intelligensia (Poland, Hungary and in Czechoslovakia during the 1960s), party sociologists are strongly tempted to question the ideological and intellectual monopoly of the ruling elite. They feel that some basic changes are necessary and that the establishment cannot meet modern needs. On the other hand, political old-timers of the establishment feel increasingly endangered by new party intellectuals who have gained influence and become very outspoken. It finally becomes impossible for the ruling elites to control effectively those party intellectuals who are quite independent of the party apparatus. An ever-increasing conflict develops between these two influential groups. This led to the firing of several prominent party sociologists in Poland and in Czechoslovakia during the late 1960s, and again in Poland in the early 1980s.

Constant development of the intelligensia and the evident ineffectiveness of the old style of management contribute to tensions within East European societies. Those sociologists who pretend to be unaware of tensions expose themselves to public contempt, are treated as blind doctrinaires or cynical careerists, and in the final outcome become a burden, even for the party.

DISSIDENTS AMONG EAST CENTRAL EUROPEAN SOCIOLOGISTS

It was stated before that sociologists all around the world are located between intellectuals and organization men. On one hand they want to be accepted as inheritors of traditional intellectual values and pursue their interests just for their own sake and not primarily for material profit. On the other hand, sociologists have to be realistic in dealing with bureaucratic organizations as sponsors of all kinds of social and research activities. Some sociologists are inclined to sacrifice almost everything in order to preserve their own freedom. Others prefer to serve organizations, gaining all kinds of benefits and constructing rationalizations to justify their actions.

Whereas in the West it has become very fashionable for modern sociologists to practice a professional self-criticism, in the Soviet bloc they are still very far from any kind of a critical self-awareness. There are several reasons why the tide of self-criticism has not yet come to East Central Europe. One of them is of an ideological nature. Eastern European Marxism is so much bureaucratized that it no longer allows for a real self-evaluation (Kolakowski 1978). Whereas in the West the dialectical critique is in fact welcomed, in the East there is still enough ideological rigidity to prevent any meaningful debate. This is one reason that several prominent Polish Marxists had to leave the country and settle in the West. Their Marxism may be criticized meaningfully only by people who are internally or externally free from organizational constraints imposed upon them in the East. Even G. Lukacs had to repudiate half-heartedly his early production. "Dialecticians from Marx to Lukacs have vigorously argued for the necessity of keeping all inquiry open-minded. That is, dialecticians have continually pointed out the dogmatic character of any claim that purports to have grasped the one true set of problems, by means of the True Methodology" (Hansen 1967, p. 2). But dialecticians put under control of the party bureaucracy stop being real dialecticians and defeat their own purpose.

Another factor is that sociology in East Central Europe consists, to a large extent, of status seekers. In the 1960s the party started to support sociology in order to use it as the bridge to the West and as the new propagandistic tool for internal and external use. It was in this framework that many party activists and also careerists outside the party found it profitable to join the ranks of professional sociologists. It is in the common interest of all these people to accept the status quo of the discipline and not to question any of its basic assumptions. The dissident wing is still far from becoming established among East European sociologists, except in Poland and, to some extent, also Hungary. There are too many among them who still feel professionally insecure and do not want to risk anything. Young people find sociology suitable for making a relatively easy career, especially when it is supported by belonging to the party. Even for people outside of the party the joining of sociology ranks is attractive as long as there are job openings in the discipline.

The peculiar situation of sociology in the countries in which orthodox Marxism is still the official doctrine provides an easy justification for sociologists to just keep quiet. In private conversations, the leading personalities in sociology, regardless of whether they belong to the party or not, are often quick to take a defensive attitude. According to them, sociologists have to be particularly careful not to do anything to harm their discipline. But this may be only a justification of opportunism. Political oppositionists in the communist countries come relatively rarely as yet from the ranks of sociologists, except in Poland. It is more common for a natural scientist, journalist, writer, television commentator, or party functionary to show independent political judgment, than for a sociologist.

On the other hand, in their dealing with empirical data, the sociologists are close to social reality. It is always a very delicate problem for them as to what they will do with the facts of reality. They can only register them honestly and try to publish, overcoming the difficulties created by censorship. They can select some facts, abandoning others. They can also simply falsify facts in order to offer a rosy picture of the social reality which would be welcomed by the party bureaucrats.

In order to manipulate data according to the expectations of the party, the sociologists have to create for themselves some suitable rationalization. However, at the same time they are eager to avoid any public and private criticism for being mere opportunists. In some of the communist countries where the intelligentsia have a very great deal to say, as in Poland and Hungary, the pressure of an informal public opinion is very strong and it is dangerous for the intellectual, from the standpoint even of his or her future career, to become too involved in opportunistic activities.

The selection of topics for research is very much influenced by the above-mentioned circumstances. There are several topics which are politically more secure than others: methodology of empirical investigations, history of sociology, sociography, and so forth. On the other hand, several careerists who come to sociology directly from the party apparatus even prefer to study touchy issues, as, for example, the problems of political sociology, criticism of Western sociology, issues of the so-called ideological struggle, and so forth. There are several problems which have to be abandoned totally by honest sociologists; for example, problems of the power elite. There are also several approaches which would be totally unacceptable for censorship; for example, the dialectic approach to the social and political structure of the communist countries. There is an obvious premium for sociologists who limit themselves to safe issues only, avoiding the others.

All the above-mentioned behavior patterns of East European sociologists may be explained in terms of their status incongruence. They are in the traditional position of intellectuals, highly esteemed; but at the same time, their intellectual freedom is very much limited by the authoritarian party rule. They are expected by public opinion to be nonconformists, but they would risk just too much if they made this commitment. They are vitally interested in maintaining contacts with the West; but at the same time, they are expected by the party to condemn the West. They want to be on good terms with the party and the governmental bosses who make all crucial decisions (promotions, research grants, travel grants, and so forth), but they do not want to appear publicly as being opportunists. Pretentiousness is an attractive escape for many sociologists (Matejko 1974. The chapter on intelligentsia. 1986. The chapter on social scientists).

CONCLUSIONS

The sociological profession is particularly vulnerable to external and internal pressures undermining its professional and moral integrity. In the nondemocratic systems sociologists are an easy game of the rulers, who are unwilling or unable to make a distinction between indoctrination and an objective diagnosis. They need sociologists mainly to justify their own decisions and policies by empirical data and insights carefully scrutinized regarding their acceptability. Research, conference, and travel funds are widely used in order to keep sociologists under control.

However, the sociological "industry" has been growing, even in the nondemocratic conditions, and this is a new fact of a major importance. Instead of nonverifiable insights sociological data, more or less reliable, enter the scene. It is an open question how much the sociological profession will be able and willing in the future to implement on a world scale some criteria of reliability. The difficulty in this respect comes not only from outside but also from inside: sociologists differ so much in methodology that it seems almost impossible for them to agree on the universal criteria. On the other hand, this pluralism is exactly the main source of growth in the discipline.

The main load of sociology remains in the field of general education at the undergraduate level and precisely in this area some problems arise. How much do the sociological courses really contribute to the growth of students as citizens and individuals? To what extent do students serve as a "captive audience" exposed to an ego trip of a teacher? How much learning does sociology actually offer people to construct their own world-view and reinforce their independent thinking? The analytical skills and the discursive approach seem to be sacrificed for the benefit of the pseudoscientific indoctrination and the memorization of insignificant facts. Sociology treated as a mass discipline based on recycling a great number of students is vulnerable to become a shallow discipline. The progressing multiplication in sociology of subdisciplines endangers the unity and homogeneity of the discipline. But it is not too late to return at least from time to time to the basic questions: What is exactly the sociological reasoning? As sociologists, how much "scientific" we can be and should be? How much room is left within the discipline for the views which differ profoundly from the dominant ones? Do we as sociologists recognize adequately the civilizational roots and limitations of facts studied by us?[35] Do we show in our teaching enough appreciation and sensitivity to other disciplines, particularly history and anthropology?

It is not our role to give others a world perspective but to help them acquire it by themselves. Our own biases should be clearly recognizable and distinguishable from the scientific authority of our discipline. We must be modest in our claim that the truth presented by us is authentic. In the democratic countries sociologists are relatively free from direct political pressures. Our intellectual role is to fulfill duties in quality teaching, doing constructively critical research, offering students freedom of an intellectual choice, and cultivating our own self-growth.

NOTES

1. In the state socialist countries, the state has a monopoly of aid and therefore the spontaneous collective

initiative of citizens extinguishes.

2. According to Ossowska (1980, pp. 224–25), a bond of analogous work is more important than the bond of dependence posited by Durkheim (similarity versus dependence)

3. The ability to withstand deprivations.

4. There is a tendency to treat norms and opinions we ourselves use as valid everywhere (Ossowska 1980, p. 6).

5. According to R. Lipsey and D. Purvis, at the Canadian universities much harm has been done since the early 1980s by policies making it impossible to hire foreigners to fill academic posts. (*Financial Post,* January 26, 1985, p. 9). The same may be said about many other countries, especially in the field of sociology, this particular discipline does not make much sense without a comparative cross-cultural approach.

6. Usually it is accompanied by conviction that not only should moral judgments take utilitarian effects into account, but they are actually based on these effects and even exclusively on these effects (Ossowska 1980, p. 254).

7. On the other hand, the uncalled-for truthfulness may be nothing more than compensatory aggression which stems from frustration.

8. The masking of one's true feelings and beliefs for some personal gain harmful to others.

9. Forceful adjusting of one's beliefs to one's interests leading to malconscience.

10. According to Aristotle, people who are not alike should not be given like shares and those who are alike should not be given unlike shares.

11. Nobody is entitled to anything just because of being this particular individual and not another. One should treat in the same manner all beings which belong to the same principal category.

12. According to E. Dupreel, justice is not merciful, mercy is not just.

13. According to an English saying, "People who live in glass houses, should not throw stones."

14. According to Aristotle, the weaker are always asking for equality and justice, but the stronger care for none of these things.

15. However, data deficiencies prevent one from being certain of this conclusion.

16. For example, in Canada during the last 35 years the situation of universities has changed quite dramatically. Fees and endowment income have declined from around 40 percent of cost coverage to around 15 percent—as regards fees (see *University Affairs,* 1984, vol. 25, no. 10:12).

Attendance of universities has become a mass phenomenon among young Canadians. The number of faculty members has grown more than four-fold and their economic status has much improved. Sociology has shared in this growth in the number of students as well as faculty. However, there is not any promise that in the future the situation will be much improved for sociology, or at least remain as it is now. Fashions may change and sociology is vulnerable, due to the claims of several other disciplines that share the same field with sociology. There is always a chance that any of the neighboring disciplines may grow at the expense of sociology.

17. For example, in Alberta there is a growing concern with the quality of education, which in the long run, may have some important consequences. It was stimulated by Provincial Premier Lougheed, stressing a back to basics approach. According to the editorial commentary of the Edmonton *Journal,* January 4, 1984, "There is something inherently unfair in depriving students of the right to a challenging curriculum. Why waste precious time and public money to turn out students whose competency in reading, writing and arithmetic is often marginal?"

18. *Edmonton Journal,* December 31, 1983.

19. A teacher who takes an andragogical approach cares about a classroom climate in which students communicate in a friendly and informal fashion. He or she fosters a sense of mutuality between himself or herself and class members by adopting a "spirit of joint inquiry." He or she conveys in many ways an attitude of interest in and respect for students, rather than viewing students as receiving sets of his or her transformation of wisdom.

20. See the criticism of this book by Max von Zur-Muehlen in *University Affairs,* 1984, vol. 25, no. 10:12 and in *CAUT Bulletin,* 1984, vol. 31, no. 8:3–7.

21. Is it really so that universities are sliding into mediocrity? According to Bercuson et al. (1984) in Canada, teaching people how to think must be stressed, student fees have to be at least doubled, entrance standards should be substantially raised, the enrollment-driven university financing has to be abandoned, tenure must be eliminated, the waste of governmental money allocated to various fancy programs has to be stopped, full professors should regain influence at the governing level, the nonsense of students deciding arbitrarily about the quality of their teachers should be stopped, core curriculum for students has to be definitely imposed. "All these suggestions, if instituted, would begin the process of reform. Higher education in Canada has to be restored to health" (pp. 159–60).

22. Excessive specialization and narrowness is the trap characteristic for several special programs. Students are not stimulated to choose wisely in selecting among various courses. "We are allowing university students to equip themselves with the knowledge tools of their own choosing instead of forcing them to acquire a set of skills that others, more experienced and more knowledgeable, know are necessary" (Bercuson et al. 1984, p. 73). There is no order and direction in the pursuit of knowledge. When students and professor become buddies, grades are better but the actual quality of learning suffers. Professors who depend on their evaluation by students lower the criteria. "The idea that uninformed opinion is not valuable is now a heresy" (Ibid., p. 83).

23. We should expect from our sociology students that they communicate well, be able to use analytical reasoning in order to problem-solve and make informed judgments, show a questioning attitude with a sound basis; that they be self-confident enough to be innovative and risk-take when appropriate, be energetic, be adaptable, and able to apply basic core skills in a variety of situations. This is exactly what we should do in sociological courses in order to encourage students to discuss issues, make oral presentations, write papers and improve them under our personal guidance, and so forth. Good teaching should not be identified with keeping students happy at the cost of lowering the professional quality of training. Teaching performance shall receive special scrutiny, but in this respect peer evaluation seems to be more reliable than student evaluation. "Student evaluations do not measure the most important thing in the teaching-learning process, namely the account of learning achieved by the student. . . . Student evaluations should be used in conjunction with other forms of rating" (*Procedures* . . . 1979, p. 2).

24. We depend too much on the mature decisions of young people when in the reality they need much sophisticated help. My ideal is the education offered in Oxford and Cambridge, where the tutorial system allows the students to integrate knowledge under the supervision of experienced staff members. We are spending in Canada more per capita on education than Great Britain but we remain much behind the British level. Something is basically wrong when the young people entering universities do not read and write well enough but are ready to involve themselves in tough bargaining with professors for the relaxed criteria of grading. There is not much sense in providing an expensive postsecondary education to people who are not prepared morally and intellectually to take full

advantage of sophisticated learning facilities sponsored by society. There is no good reason just to keep students happy by lowering adequately the learning expectations. Anyway, students pay only a small part of the educational cost at the university level and the rest is covered from the taxpayer's pocket. I am very much for the education offered to everybody, even at the postsecondary education. However, there is something absurd and immoral in the tolerance of "free riders," who take advantage of the institutions originally designed primarily for people who are really gifted and dedicated. When the teacher has to serve mediocre students primarily we are doing injustice to the talented and hard-working people. There is also something degrading in a teacher being pushed to the wall by the students who deny him or her a satisfactory evaluation in the case of his or her not being lenient enough. The educational system has to be selective. There is nothing wrong in redirecting students who are not able or willing to achieve certain standards. There are various kinds of education and a good counseling should help people to be educationally allocated according to their specific potentials. Standards are badly needed at all levels of education, from the bottom to the top. Only standards high enough may allow the education to function for the benefit of the whole society. It is nonsense to treat schools as a temporary shelter for the unemployed without taking into consideration the negative consequences of lowering the standards. Of course, there is a good reason to help generously those who really deserve it by offering educational grants and loans. However, there is also a good reason to apply the strict criteria of selection and given full support to teachers who have the courage and dedication to defend professional standards. Popularity contests among teachers must lead to the deterioration of education and in the long run harm the welfare of students.

25. As university teachers we have a very important and responsible mandate to help students to make progress toward maturity. We are sponsored by *society* and only to a very minor extent directly by our "customers." I am not sure whether all of us are fully aware what kind of responsibility this is, in the moral and intellectual sense. Competition for popularity among students is evidence of academic irresponsibility and should be treated as unethical. For an academic teacher to please the "grade hunters" and to withdraw the critical judgment of poor performance may be good for student enrollment (and the university budget) but very bad for the welfare of society. There is definitely not enough accumulation of knowledge in some most

popular fields of university training. The assumption that it is up to the student which courses he or she takes and whom he or she wants to have on his or her graduate supervisory committee may look from the outside as very liberal but in reality it is harmful for everybody: the student who does not study systematically enough, the teachers who have to deal with the students inadequately prepared to learn something more sophisticated, the university which lowers its standards, and the society which is not able to trust the half-educated graduates. We need badly a reform that would open room for a *tutorial system* helping students to integrate the knowledge and gain some analytical abilities instead of useless memorization of the multitude of facts completely forgotten after the exam. We need a genuine evaluation of teaching instead of a popularity contest among students who are not necessarily the best judges of the academic qualities. In medicine, law, and sports we accept the fact that to be a good professional is more important than anything else. People teaching in these disciplines do not have to be popular in order to be appreciated. Why not apply the same reasoning to other disciplines? Why not to strive for a real excellence? There are several difficult ethical dilemmas for the university teacher who wants to be up to the academic standards and at the same time is expected by the university administration to keep students in a good mood. This is one of the important subjects in the ethics of higher education.

26. I am against teachers being primarily expected to keep students happy. Yes, I want to please my students but without lowering the demands which may look as a nuisance today but provide a useful preparation for the future. Some students are much misguided by the overemphasis on memorization, which may be just an empty exercise as long as the student does not grasp completely the true nature of a given subject.

27. At universities sometimes we have a tendency to treat the learning process of sociology more as a necessary nuisance than a professional and intellectual adventure. Uninterested students are after the teacher who "bothers" them with the whole variety of additional sources of information, tries hard to explain the complicated nature of things instead of delivering ready truths for an easy digestion and memorization, who expects student to be active and committed. Who actually wants to rewrite the same paper several times? Who enjoys delivering oral presentations? Who is eager to spend additional hours in the library in order to enrich the amount of information offered in the class? Many students enter the university with the

very definite idea what is work and what is leisure. Learning, according to them, is only in the first category. They attend classes as a boring necessity to make the substantial investment of time and effort in order to obtain sooner or later a diploma. A demanding teacher is a nuisance for them because he or she insists on something which is opposed to having fun (watching television, sports, dating, having a glass of beer, and so forth).

28. I am not far from retirement and all my life I have had much fun learning and teaching. It is difficult for me to imagine my daily existence without constantly searching for something new, looking into the books recently published, writing papers for the conferences, as well as discussing professional subjects with the few people who share with me my interests. I would like to contaminate students with my own enthusiasm for the fascinating intellectual adventure of my beloved discipline but I know how much resistance and distrust may be met in this respect.

29. In my personal experience of several years I had to teach many students who found themselves in my courses more or less accidentally.

30. I am strongly against the use of graduate students instead of professors in teaching any high-level courses. It is true that in individual cases a graduate student or a young scholar with no substantial knowledge and research may be much more popular among students than the experienced expert in the field. Our main function is, however, to teach and not just to entertain or be a good buddy. The expert may have his or her personal shortcomings but the direct contact between him or her and students is much more rewarding for students in the long run.

31. Peer evaluation of teaching should be taken much more seriously. The research and publication record is an adequate proof that a given teacher has a necessary intellectual background. Of course, there is always a room for the improvement of specific teaching skills and in this respect teachers may learn much from student evaluation. On the other hand, personal popularity of the teacher is not the proof that he or she is a real expert in the subject and that he or she is a real asset in the academic sense. Community colleges necessarily have to be very sensitive to the fact of just how happy are their clients. For a university *the quality* learning should be the only factor which actually counts.

32. This is a revised version of A. J. Matejko," Sociologists in Between," in *Studies in Comparative Communism* (1972) 5, 2–3:277–304.

33. For example, the foreman in a communist factory is,

like his or her American or British counterpart, caught in conflicting role-prescriptions. The management expects him or her to be effective instrumentally, and the workers would like him or her to be loyal first of all to them. For the foreman it is difficult to practice leadership, and in this respect his or her problems are similar to the problems of an American foreman, even if the communist foreman seems to have relatively more in common with the workers. His or her bonus depends on their efficiency. They may leave the workplace if they are dissatisfied with the foreman's treatment of them. It is quite easy for them to sabotage on a small scale, which penalizes the foreman. Slowdowns, absenteeism, insubordination, disparaging the foreman to higher supervisors, are weapons which workers may use against him or her.

34. It seems that the substance of social phenomena is located somewhere between these two approaches. It is in the nature of the above-mentioned phenomena that they are experienced and shaped by people in their activities. One should accept the fact that the nature of social phenomena consists of the whole variety of subjective realities and approaches. It would be necessary to distinguish several levels which are interrelated and influence one another. One may raise serious objections to reductionism in social research going so far as to say that the only acceptable phenomena are measurable phenomena. Even if the researchers are obviously able to measure only those facts which are in the framework of their own concepts, the total rejection of everything outside of what may be measured leads to the reduction of the whole social variety to just one reality, chosen more or less authoritatively by the researcher. Such a manipulation is particularly dangerous if social scientists are dependent on their political and bureaucratic bosses.

35. In this respect some studies done by non-sociologists may be instructive. See among others, a profound critical analysis of Indian civilization by V. S. Naipaul. 1977. *India: A Wounded Civilization* (New York: Knopf).

REFERENCES

Aron, R. 1964. *German Sociology*. Glencoe, IL: Free Press.

Anderson, H., and J. D. Murray, eds. 1971. *The Professors*. Cambridge: Schenkman.

Baritz, L. 1960. *The Servants of Power*. Middletown, CT: Wesleyan University Press.

Barzun, J. 1984. "Scholarship versus Culture," *The Atlantic* 254, 5:93–112.

Bauman, Z. 1971. "Twenty Years After: The Crisis of Soviet-type Systems," *Problems of Communism,* 20:6.

Ben-David, J. 1971. *The Scientist's Role in Society.* Englewood Cliffs, NJ: Prentice-Hall.

Bercuson, David J., Robert Bothwell, and J. L. Granatstein. 1984. *The Great Brain Robbery: Canada's Universities on the Road to Ruin.* Toronto: McClelland and Stewart.

Bienkowski, W. 1966. *Problemy Teorii Rozwoju Spolecznego* (Theoretical Problems of Social Change). Warsaw.

————. 1970. *Motory i Hamulce Socjalizmu* (The Driving and Inhibiting Forces of Socialism). Paris: Institut Litteraire.

Conquest, R. 1967. *Industrial Workers in the U.S.S.R.* London: Bodley Head.

Drewnowski, J. 1970. "Socjalizm w Polsce (Socialism in Poland)," *Kultura* 9.

Dyoniziak, R. 1967. *Spoleczne Warunki Wydajnosci Pracy* (Social Conditions of Work Output), Warsaw: KiW.

Fisher, Wesley A. 1971. Letter, *Problems of Communism,* xx, 6.

Fromm, Eric. 1966. *The Fear of Freedom.* London: Routledge and Kegan Paul.

Gella, A. 1971. "Contemporary Sociology in Poland," *International Journal of Contemporary Sociology,* pp. 3–4.

————. 1971. "The Life and Death of the Polish Intelligentsia," *Slavic Review* 30, 1.

Gouldner, A. W. 1970. *The Coming Crisis of Western Sociology.* New York: Basic Books.

Hansen, J. E. 1967. "A Dialectical Critique of Empirism." *Catalyst,* 3, Summer.

Jain, Ajit and Alexander J. Matejko, eds. 1984. *Marx and Marxism.* New York: Praeger.

Katz, Z. 1971. "Sociology in the Soviet Union." *Problems of Communism* 20, 3.

Kolakowski, L. 1968. *Toward a Marxist Humanism: Essays on the Left Today.* New York: Grove Press.

Kolakowski, Leszek. 1978. *The Main Currents of Marxism.* London: Clarendon Press.

Kotarbinski, T. 1965. *Praxiology.* London: Pergamon Press.

Lane, David. 1971. *The End of Inequality? Stratification Under State Socialism.* London: Penguin Books.

A Leszek Kolakowski Reader. 1971. *Tri Quarterly,* 22,

Matejko, Alexander J. 1966. "Status Incongruence in the

Polish Intelligentsia." *Social Research* 33, 4.

—————. 1967. "The Organization and Stratification of Scientific Workers in Poland." *Sociology of Education* 40, 3.

—————. 1969a. "Planning and Tradition in Polish Higher Education." *Minerva* 7, 4.

—————. 1969b. "Some Sociological Problems of Socialist Factories." *Social Research* 36, 3.

—————. 1970a. "Newspaper Staff as a Social System." In *Media Sociology,* edited by J. Tunstall. London: Constable.

—————. 1970b. *Uslovia Tvorcheskogo Truda* (Conditions of Creative Work). Moscow: Izdatelstvo Mir.

—————. 1971. "From Peasant to Worker in Poland." *International Review of Sociology* 7, 3.

—————. 1973. "The Organizational Conditions of Scientific Inquiry." *Comparative Group Studies* 4, 1:89–126.

—————. 1974. *Social Change and Stratification in Eastern Europe: An Interpretive Analysis of Poland and Her Neighbors.* New York: Praeger.

—————. 1984. *Beyond Bureaucracy?* Cologne: Verlag für Gesellschaftsarchitekture.

—————. 1986. *Comparative Work Systems: Ideologies and Realities in Eastern Europe.* New York: Praeger.

Mills, J. S. 1948. *On Liberty.* London.

Murphy, R. F. 1971. *The Dialectics of Social Life.* New York: Basic Books.

Myrdal, G. 1944. *The American Dilemma.* New York: Harper.

Nettler, G. 1968. "Using Our Heads." *American Sociologist,* 3.

Osipov, G. W., ed. 1966. *Industry and Labour in the U.S.S.R.* London: Tavistock.

Ossowska, Maria. 1980. *Moral Norms: A Tentative Systematization.* Warsaw: PWN.

Parkin, Frank. 1979. *Marxism and Class Theory: A Bourgeois Critique.* New York: Columbia University Press.

Parsons, T. 1970. "The Intellectual." In *On Intellectuals,* edited by P. Rieff. Garden City, NY: Doubleday.

Podgorecki, A., and R. Schulze. 1969. "Sociotechnique." *Social Science Information* 7, 4.

"Procedures for Evaluating Instruction in a University Setting." *Folio,* Supplement, 1979, 8.

Szczepanski, J. 1970. *Polish Society.* New York: Random House.

Tuchman, Barbara W. 1984. *The March of Folly: From Troy to Vietnam.* New York.

Whyte, W. H. 1956. *The Organization Man.* Garden City, NY: Doubleday.

Wiatr, J., ed. 1971. *The State of Sociology in Eastern Europe Today.* Carbondale, IL: Southern Illinois University Press.

Wilensky, H. 1967. *The Organizational Intelligence.* New York: Basic Books.

7

OBSOLESCENCE OF BUREAUCRACY

The artificiality of organizational structures in modern mass societies, based on manipulation from the top and anomie at the bottom level of hierarchy, is a common fact in the capitalist West as well as in the communist East. This artificiality arises not only from the fact that the structures mentioned above are relatively new and uprooted; it is based mainly on the very superficial character of socialization practiced under bureaucracy. The latter prevails now not only under the state socialism which dominates in the communist countries, but also in the free-enterprise system of the West where, from 40 to 60 percent (depending on the country) of the GNP belongs to the public sector.

Bureaucracy might be defined here as an organizational condition under which the vested interests of the corporate body of organizational decision-makers prevail over and above the goals which a given structure is supposed to fulfill. This condition is difficult to achieve by a given organizational structure as long as it has to cope with uncertainties. Monopoly is the optimal state for bureaucracy and this is the main reason why the free-enterprise system is so popular among political oppositionists under the Soviet system; when, on the other hand, state interference is claimed by the Western critics as a remedy for concentration of power and wealth. In both cases the "reduction of certainty" enjoyed by the large market-controlling complex organizations is used as an argument in favor of bureaucracy.

231

Perrow claims that

> bureaucracy is a form of organization superior to all
> others we know or can hope to afford in the near
> and middle future; the chances of doing away with
> it or changing it are probably nonexistent in the
> West in this century. Thus, it is crucial to under-
> stand it and appreciate it. But it is also crucial to
> understand not only how it mobilizes social re-
> sources for desirable ends, but also how it inev-
> itably concentrates those forces in the hands of a
> few who are prone to use them for ends we do not
> approve to, for ends we are generally not aware of,
> and more frightening still, for ends we are led to
> accept because we are not in a position to conceive
> alternative ones" (1972, p. 7)

Of course, bureaucracy in a historical sense contributed
to the organizational development of mankind by exchanging
particularism for some kind of universalism. Particularism
and discrimination may be eliminated only by applying some
universalistic criteria. Selection of people according to
their competence, tenure, promotion based on merit, impersonality in dealing with fulfillment of organizational
goals, freedom from arbitrary authority—all are needed to
preserve the autonomy of a complex organization against
external pressures.

> One of the problems of organizations is that they
> are very leaky vessels. It is quite easy for a
> member of one of them to use some of his power
> and leverage for his own ends rather than for the
> ends of the organization. Organizations generate
> surpluses and leverage in our world, and those who
> have any power in them can use these for their own
> ends (Perrow 1972, pp. 17, 21).

The formal rules in bureaucracy provide at least some
guarantee of freedom for employees.

> The absence of written policy leaves him (the
> subordinate, A.M.) in a position where any decision
> he takes, however apparently trivial, may infringe
> upon an unstated policy and produce a repri-
> mand. . . . Rules are means of preserving group
> autonomy and freedom; to reduce the number of
> rules in an organization generally means to make it
> more impersonal, more inflexible, more standard-

ized. . . . The problem is not rules in general, but particular ones that need changing (Ibid., pp. 27, 30).

The unidimensional reductionism of human beings under bureaucracy originates from the systemic nature of the bureaucractic model based on the rationalistic intellectual tradition, highly appealing to administrators and technicians. There is some truth in the claim of R. Lilienfeld that systems theory has become the ideology of the administrative intellectual.

> The ideology of systems theory could be said to consist of having no ideology, in the popular sense of a specific political commitment. Like the dialectic, it provides a vocabulary that permits its predictiveness to celebrate and serve whatever social developments emerge over the horizon. It can be both conservative and revolutionary at the same time, perhaps in the same sense in which Marxian dialecticians are conservative with respect to their own societies and revolutionary with respect to others. . . . System theory as social doctrine may be regarded as a variant of organic or "organismic" approaches to society (Lilienfeld 1978, p. 263).

The image of bureaucracy as a more or less coherent system plays a very important sociopolitical role because it provides a myth of a supreme organizational being, an object of service and idolatry. The power accumulated in bureaucracies provides the reinforcement for this myth and makes it even more appealing. The present organizational complexity and the high-level technology on one side and utilitariansim, practicism, and the ideology crisis on the other side, make the myth particularly suitable.

> It is at such a time that the notion of society run by impartial benevolent technicians operating on the basis of actual logic and impersonal algorithmic methods could come to the fore as a new ideology (or nonideology), and in fact one that appears attractive to all advanced industrial societies regardless of their official eighteenth- or nineteenth-century needs (Lilienfeld 1978, p. 264).

This "nonideology" is well suited to the professional and semiprofessional cadres of the welfare-state agencies, the giant corporate enterprises, military institutions, and so forth. The system effectiveness provides a rationale for various groups of bureaucrats who badly need a scientific mystification in order to increase the justification of their actions directly to the public and to legitimize bureaucratic interventions that might otherwise be resisted (Moynihan 1973; Krause 1968). In this manner the bureaucratic elite imposes itself as the only problem-solver recognized and selected on account of its special capabilities.

The element of mystification is reinforced by the widespread utilization of experts, who are recognized as long as they play the role of the obedient servants of power (Barritz 1960). In the United States there has been a growth of the government by contract and grant; the ratio of federal employees per 1,000 population had diminished in the period 1956–76 from 14 to 13, but in 1973 almost 80,000 full-time government employees administered around $110 billion given as contracts and grants. According to R. Nader,

> fortified by personal relationships and contracts, the consulting industry services the needs of public and private institutions in specific and by now routine ways. Federal department officials achieve significant insulation from criticism of their behavior if they can cite a think-tank study. The imprimatur of consulting firms, sympathetic to and associated with the largest business interests in the land, conveys, to an inquiring congressional committee for example, that a department's action has the backing of an industrial or commercial establishment. Obviously, developing or recommending the types of government programs which enrich corporate interest, in turn, ingratiates the consulting firms with the business part of the triangle. A combination of the abdication of its responsibilities by the executive branch and the assertiveness of the firms themselves insinuates them solidly into the governmental process (Guttman and Wilner 1976, pp. xi–xii).

The "nonideology" of bureaucrats allows them to neglect the broader social interests and concerns under the disguise of "impartiality" and "rationality." In bureaucracies unity of command and centralization of decision making are based on a very simplified and one-sided understanding of the nature of power as free from moral responsibility, oriented towards manipulation, reduced mostly to coercion, sanctified by the priority of institutional good over the humanitarian concerns. The anonymous bureaucratic authority remains irresponsible when it is dispersed between various levels of the hierarchy and therefore diluted. Within the task specialization the utmost importance of sociomoral bonds becomes neglected even when they energize individuals, allow them to find the common understanding, provide stability and predictability, and assure some minimum of mental health. Standardization of role performance dilutes human responsibility, weakens the internal cohesion and identity of individuals and groups as natural elementary parts of social systems, and creates the illusion of "order," "rationality," and "coordination," in which the sociomoral and cultural factors are omitted.

According to Hummel, bureaucracy is an entirely new way of organizing social life. "It succeeds society, just as society has succeeded community" (1982, p. vii). Cases replace people. Functions replace actions and social relations. Means replace ends as ultimate norms. Operational codes replace social norms. Effectiveness replaces personality. Motive replaces ideas. Motivation replaces legitimation. Conditioning replaces socialization. Team replaces ego. Teamwork replaces mastery. Hierarchy replaces superego. System replaces integrated personality. Stimulus-response manipulating replaces social norms as a control mechanism. IQ satisfaction replaces ego satisfaction. Command replaces dialogue. Analogous reasoning replaces causal reasoning. The need of systems are put before the needs of people. Managers and experts replace politicians. Functionaries replace citizens. Administration replaces politics. Psychological power replaces ideological power. Corporations, public or private, replace, or become superior to, the nation or the state. Management replaces leadership (Ibid., p. 220).

The question remains open whether it is really worth it to make all these replacements.

All that is living is replaced by mechanism. But the end of mechanism is entropy, not the negentropy of biological life. Bureaucracy becomes an instrument without compare because it is able to remove the human spirit that is the obstacle to power. In doing so it also removes the only valid human purpose for the exercise of power—the affirmation of the human form of life. From its very beginning, bureaucracy has claimed it must destroy man to save him. . . . The logic of bureaucratization as the concrete institution of

Western rationalization as a historical process finally end in absurdity . . . (Ibid., p. 222).

THE "BENEVOLENT" BUREAUCRACIES

Complex bureaucratic organizations, as long as they gain a comfortable and secure position in society, are very often quite willing to ease the pressure on their own employees. It is common to offer permanent employees good salaries, comfortable working conditions, and various attractive fringe benefits. Bureaucracies compete among themselves for the quality of working life and for the loyalty of their employees. This is done sometimes even at the expense of the clients, who are treated as objects of manipulation and are much less able, in comparison with employees, to exercise an effective pressure on the decision centers in the corporation.

Bureaucracies pay great attention to esprit de corps but this is done in an isolationist manner. The "crystal palace" of a big corporation or of a state apparatus may be comfortable to the insiders but totally lukewarm to outsiders. "The fact that the individual is serving some group which is greater than himself blinds him to the fact that his group is only a part of the whole" (Boulding 1953). In bureaucracies this tendency is reinforced by the vested interests of the administrative elite, which become easily divorced from social interests. "The bureaucratic landscape is dotted with agencies which no longer serve any useful purpose and which may even frustrate the attainment of society's purposes. Yet such agencies can often cling to life with a formidable tenacity when confronted by possible extinction" (Berkley 1971, p. 147).

Vested institutional interests lead to a high level of defensiveness or even aggresiveness. Members of a given complex organization protect one another against any external scrutiny; external efforts to introduce some controls are sabotaged successfully by all levels of the bureaucratic hierarchy; coverups are a common occurrence of bureaucratic life. At the same time there are intense rivalries and animosities inside bureaucracies behind the facade of the solidarity versus the outside world.

Bureaucrats within their own ranks are divided according to organizational boundaries, unit loyalties, suppressed ambitions and personal animosities. The pseudorationalistic character of bureaucracies prevents them quite effectively from achieving any deeper internal solidarity as well as an adequate efficiency. "Resources are wasted, energies are sacrificed, and efforts are sabotaged. Thus, because of the isolation which it fosters, and because this isolation tends to build up internal pressures, the overtly cohesive organization is not only not all that cohesive but it is also not all that efficient" (Berkley 1971, p. 149).

The relative comfort of being employed by a bureaucracy is highly appreciated by many status- and security-seekers at the expense of a genuine work spirit inside of the organization, which itself enjoys a secure position and therefore is not required to bother about its own survival. This is one of the main reasons for an evident gap between "core" workers who are able to define effectively their relative privileged position (trade unions and professional or semiprofessional associations help them in this respect) and "peripheral" workers who remain in a marginal situation even if their numbers are constantly increasing. The "leisured" employment of *core* workers, who enjoy good working conditions, remuneration bargained collectively with the employer, promotion opportunities, security of employment, and so forth, is envied by the *marginal* workers, who have much worse working conditions, represent at most a very limited bargaining power, do not have the same opportunities for promotion, and are restricted to very insecure and low-paying jobs.

The unequal distribution of business power in the market is the main source of the gap between core workers and peripheral workers. The scope of unionization is of secondary importance in this respect. The progressing concentration of business power leads to the control of the market, which limits competition and at the same time, encourages the development of a privileged sector.

The overriding importance of business as a human activity is ideologically a product of the Protestant ethic. In comparison with business, leisure concerns were treated as frivolous and therefore not deserving any genuine esteem (even when the growth of culture depended mainly on them). In modern times, the Protestant ethic has lost its significance, not so much due to a decline in religious feelings, but mainly due to the development of a consumer society in which people pay attention primarily to their own material well-being.

Modern bureaucracies, under both free-market and command economies, still maintain some tradition of a quasi-religious seriousness and in this respect they do not fit the priorities of many modern people who pay more and more attention to leisure as the only available field of a genuine self-expression. This gap has to be overcome by artificial manipulations. The genuine goals of such complex organizations as big business corporations, mass political parties, and even several bureaucratized religious bodies, become more and more distant from the concerns of common people. In order to remain in control and to reach their goals (profit, power, growth, and so forth), big organizations increasingly depend on large-scale manipulation, such as advertising propaganda, public relations, lobbies, and so forth.

> Society expects firms to operate in ways that show social responsiveness and social responsibility to the broader social system. . . . The trend of each subsequent model of organizational behavior is toward more open human organizations. Generally there is also movement toward a wider distribution of power, more intrinsic motivation, a more positive attitude toward people, and a better balance of concern for both employee and organizational needs. Discipline has become more a matter of self-discipline instead of being imposed from the outside. The managerial role has advanced from one of strict authority to leadership and team support (Davis 1981, pp. 509, 513).

Modern organizations, in order to preserve their attractiveness, have to reconcile themselves with leisure as a new sociocultural priority. However, the crux of the problem is in the move to a more reliable seriousness that would be really appealing to people. The current progress in the social organization of work is a promising phenomenon in this respect but the quality-of-working-life movement will remain at the level of manipulation as long as the basic assumption of managerial thinking remain unquestioned.

The rationality of organizational decision-makers is not necessarily the same as the rationality of their subordinates or even more the rationality of organizational clients. It is clearly evident that people in higher organizational positions show much more commitment and job satisfaction than people down the hierarchy (Matejko 1979). The profit-orientation of business organizations quite often happens to be in conflict with the welfare-orientation of people who buy their products or rent their services.

With more and more leisure in these societies which have achieved socioeconomic progress, the ideology based on work and duty (Anthony 1977) becomes substituted by an ideology based on having fun and achieving some self-actualization. This is the reality that has to be accepted by the executive ranks in complex organizations.

THE BUREAUCRATIC MANAGEMENT

As Karl Mannheim made clear many years ago, in the bureaucratic organizations the *substantial* rationality, for example, "the capacity to act intelligently in a given situation on the basis of one's own insight into the intercorrelations of events," often becomes suppressed by the *functional* rationality derived by a given organization from its own logic and its own vested interests.

The traditional management epitomizes this functional rationality based on some general principles. Any task activity has its specific rationality adequate to the nature of tasks. The rationality of production is different from the rationality of education or from the rationality of winning wars. However, on the basis of a *praxiological* thinking it is possible to establish certain general rules of an effective action which may achieve maximum effect by minimum cost. For example, Tadeusz Kotarbinski (1965) proposes the following criteria of a successful action:

- Efficiency in fulfilling the expected goals: "The usefulness of a given action with respect to a given objective is nothing more than the property of making possible or facilitating the attainment of that objective owing to the action" (Kotarbinski 1965, p. 76).
- Precision: "The less the product differs from its standard in the given respect, the more precisely is the task performed in that respect" (Ibid., p. 78).
- Purity of product: "The greater the purity of a product, the fewer its negative properties, running counter to the main objective or to the secondary objectives" (Ibid., p. 79).
- Economy of action.
- Simplicity of action.
- Degree of skill (in terms of approximation of movements performed to movements intended, as well as in terms of sureness).
- Rationality of action (behaving according to the recommendation of the knowledge which is at the disposal).

There is now a very strong tendency in the management circles all around the world to assume that its monopolistic power should be unquestionable just because it is allegedly based on principles of a universal validity. However, the differences in external environment challenge the universal applicability of general managerial devices (Olberg 1963; Gonzales and McMillan 1961; Farmer and Richman 1964; Nowotny 1964; Chowdhry and Pal 1966, pp. 195–204).

Therefore what seems to be "general" on the North American ground does not fit into the local conditions of Brazil. It is quite obvious that, for example, the social legitimacy of employees' participation in decision making differs substantially depending on the local tradition; it seems that North American workers tend to consider participation as more legitimate than workers in several other capitalist countries (Harbison and Burgess 1954; Whyte 1950).

The comparison of Japanese and U.S. workers makes clear how much more importance has been given in Japan to meeting the expectations of significant others, accepting formal rules, continuing of employment, following personal advices of supervisors, and consulting views with coworkers (Whitehill and Takezawa 1968; Fürstenberg 1972). In some of the Japanese enterprises there are evident efforts to apply the creative teamwork principle on a wide scale. In the Sony Corporation, the production has been broken down into targets scaled for teams of no more than 20 people each. Operators in each team select their own leader. The team is managed chiefly through meetings of its members. Teams are linked with each other. "The top team was formed simultaneously with the teams at lower levels, and these teams at the top and bottom led to the formation of intermediary teams, like a chain reaction" (Kobayashi 1970, p. 14).

It is possible to say that in most of the developed countries there is now a growing tendency among workers to expect from the management more than just orders and money (stick and carrot). There is an manifest egalitarian impulse among the masses. "Indeed, the struggle for equality, arising out of the relationships between social classes in a capitalist society, may have been reinforced by the more directly political conflicts which now take place in various spheres over question of authority and participation in decision making" (Bottomore 1971, p. 406).

The steering of any workplace consists to a large extent in making use of power. "A has power over B to the extent that he can get B to do something that otherwise B would not do" (Dahl 1957). Power consists in an ability to change the probability that a person will respond in a certain way to a certain stimulus. "The more disagreement and conflict which exist between the wishes of each actor and the behavior of others, the greater is the motivation of each to find ways of changing the others" (Kahn and Boulding 1964).

The need for power at workplaces depends on the strength of disruptive forces which may endanger the unity, integration, and position of the particular system. Power of an authority within the particular system has to be sufficiently strong to overcome the centrifugal tendencies coming from without or within the particular system.

> Power is essential to the life of the organization; it prevents the emergence of conflicts which would subvert organizational effectiveness. . . . Human organizations are inherently conflict-ridden. Organizations consist of people performing interdependent tasks. Out of that interdependence arises a need for predictability and dependability on the parts of the individual performers; the intrusion of normal variability into their organizational behavior would render the organization ineffective or even uncooperative" (Ibid., pp. 4, 7).

In all three principal phases of the decision-making process: (a) finding occasions for making a decision, (b) establishing possible courses of action, and (c) choosing among courses of action (Cyert and March 1963), there is a constant bargaining process among members of a potential coalition (Simon 1960). Constraints related to that bargaining determine goals of the organization.

Quite often when two formalized systems are dealing with each other they neglect to estimate in a realistic way their factual ability to control power. For example, in collective bargaining between management and trade union an important fact is often overlooked that the real power of labor may be located much more in the informal structure of labor relations than in the formal structure of them. A lot of power may be activated by informal leaders. "The attitudes which are generated in the workplace by the interaction between managerial control systems and the control systems by which workers protect themselves from their possible consequences are outside the control of the unions" (Lupton 1966, p. 50).

In many situations it is possible, and very advisable of for the sake of an improved employees' morale, to exercise at workplaces the referent (personal) power instead of the coercive power. However, the basic need seems to be the general increase of the amount of social energy disposed by a particular system. The lack of an appropriate volume of social energy seems to be even more disastrous for the bureaucratic system than an unequal distribution of this power.

Having at its disposal resources of vital importance to all subordinates, management is in a position to manipulate them effectively. The reference here is not only to material resources, even if their importance should never be underestimated. There are also other resources related to the human need of safety, belonging, appreciation, self-esteem, and self-fulfillment. The appearance of those needs makes effective the application of the employees' participation and most of the human-relation techniques. It is up to management to manipulate the human passions and aspirations on one side, and the social forces of custom, social consciousness, and normative order, on the other side, having in mind the smooth functioning of the whole workplace. "The more participation accorded an individual, the more he would perceive that he was valued by those who accorded him this participation. . . . To the extent that the workers considered the participation accorded them as legitimate, it increased their understanding and acceptance of management," said J. R. P. French, Jr., following laboratory and field studies of power (Kahn and Boulding 1964, p. 42).

Power relationships are quite often based on some kind of *quasiequilibrium,* when the managing people follow a "dulgency pattern," instead of formally accepting all basic social factors of a given situation. We have here in mind all kinds of tactics developed by the decision-makers in order to preserve power without giving formal recognition to social forces which are constituent parts of the actual social setting. Keeping under police control the intellectuals in such a society which has intellectuals in high esteem, buying or blackmailing union leaders in such a factory in which management-labor bargaining is traditionally under the union control, corrupting informal leaders in order to make them harmless—all such tactics are used in order just to preserve a quasiequilibrium. Some kind of informal practices, buttressed by a strongly entrenched custom of bypassing the formal rules, is closely related to that kind of quasiequilibrium. There are cases, especially common in the Soviet bloc, in which the power holders and the subservients, the controlling and the controlled, all are involved in some kind of mutual blackmailing which evolves a lot of dissatisfaction, but on the other hand prevents potential innovators from striving for a new formal establishment (Richman 1965). Everyone has some vested interests in not revealing informal practices developed by him or her in order to satisfy their needs otherwise not acceptable at the level of a formal structure. Everybody is afraid that others know about his or her informal practices and that he or she may any time be accused for following them.

The effectiveness of the management depends very much upon finding solutions that would assure some kind of satisfactory equilibrium between the objective constraints of the situation (goals versus practical possibility of fulfilling them), nature of tools under disposal (technological constraints) and the preferences of people. Matching all those factors to one another, one may obtain various possible authority configurations determined by the environmental conditions of power execution (Woodward 1980).

The bureaucratic management in most cases so far seeks to preserve its monopoly of control, but the authoritarian rule is contradictory to the rising democratic expectations of workers. The distribution of rewards becomes the focal point of strain. The job security of workers is in conflict with the emphasis on rising productivity. The egalitarianism in the sociocultural background of modern workers clashes with the rigid absolutism of the traditional management, and even with its new manipulistic version (the human relations approach). The growing economic and communicational integration of the Western economy stimulates workers to overcome the existing regional inequalities in wages and working conditions (the demonstration effect).

It is especially the lower level of supervisory staff which quite often feels most threatened by loss of authority. However, higher levels of management, as well as even the trade-union elites, are also hesitant to undermine their own privileged position by allowing a job reform.

THE SIDE-EFFECTS OF DEPERSONALIZATION

Depersonalization of the office was a great organizational achievement in the historical beginnings of the bureaucratic form when it took over from the arrangements totally immersed in the tribal, familial, and privatized frameworks. It was once necessary to make a clear difference between the private and the institutional spheres, especially as long as the division of labor remained underdeveloped. The problem is that bureaucracy does not fulfill any more satisfactorily its historical function and must empty its place for the higher forms of work organization, more adequate to the new sophisticated level of socioeconomic development; the bureaucratic forms have survived and become a suitable organizational weapon for power and the success of those who gain from them. One of the very important reasons that this above-mentioned perpetration could take place is the ideological neutrality of bureaucracy as a machine disposable to anybody who is powerful enough to take it over and sophisticated enough to use it for his own benefit. In this machine, the ultimate values are pushed aside;

therefore it is easy to switch from one ideological program to another without effecting much change in the machine. Even the change of personnel may be achieved very smoothly by the application of appropriate selections and training devices.

Hummel makes a good point by claiming that modern organizations cannot function without recurrent manipulations of and attacks on the identity of their members, and this leads to the multiplication of informal structures that inevitably are the breeding ground for practices and values incompatible with organizational goals (1982, p. 259). The conflict between bureaucracy and humanity becomes evident at the macro-level as well as at the micro-level. The micro-networks created by bureaucrats in their relationships to superiors, subordinates, coworkers, and clients differ widely in their pro- or anti-human quality. The practical question is how to promote effectively the prohuman trend within existing bureaucracies.

Bureaucracy functions on the basis of routines frozen into permanently repeated patterns and this leads to the suppression of the *we-relationships* appealing to the uniqueness of mutual loyalties among those people who recognize each other. The growth of bureaucracy endangers the true essence of society. "Human beings so lose consciousness of their potential and their past as creators that they treat their social institutions as if they had a life of their own above and beyond control" (Hummel 1982, p. 41).

Bureaucratic personnel are supposed to be rewarded for merit, but this is interpreted mainly as disposability and institutional loyalty. The well-being of the bureaucratic organization itself is the ultimate institutional goal an the latent function of self-preservation and self-aggrandizement dominates over the manifest goals formulated and reformulated for the sake of good public relations. Under such circumstances the employees who really deserve merit are those who contribute to the good of the bureaucracy and not those who are committed to other goals of a professional, social, or moral nature. The gradual elimination of those who do not share the total bureaucratic commitment, are not willing to serve the hierarchy, and accept the stereotype of an "organization man" is the common social process in the "triumphant" bureaucracies (Whyte 1957).

Depersonalization has several side-effects which are disastrous for bureaucracies in the long run. In this dehumanized world of bureaucracy, human well-being has to be constantly neglected, work motivation does not crystalize, loyalties are superficial and ephemeral, responsibility to the external world becomes subordinated to the vested interests of the institution and its disposers. The growth of formalization thwarts the natural development of informal relationships: Organization becomes distorted, uncontrollable and dominated by private coalitions harmful to the institution. Cliques play a major role even if they do not appear on any organizational blueprint. Privatization flourishes unhampered within the formalized organizational environment, which is supposed to eliminate personalization.

The basic assumptions in the bureaucratic model often become counterproductive, not necessarily because they are wrong when taken individually but because their peculiar combination reinforces the gap between the organizational model and the sociomoral reality, as well as exposing the artificial character of this model. This is not the natural human environment, open to spontaneity, creativity, and dispute, but a machine suitable for the skillful manipulation by those who are willing and able to take full advantage of the fact that there is enough of a gap and inconsistency between various assumptions. The bureaucratic weapon estranges itself easily from the control by a society weakened in its moral unity, open to divergent interpretations, and confused by its own complexity. In the past, the rulers exercised a strong hand over the still weakly developed bureaucracies: Now the overdeveloped bureaucracies dominate over the socially and spiritually weakened societies emptied of their moral fiber and traditional roots. The control of bureaucracies from outside has become sporadic, superficial, highly inadequate, dispirited, with no adequate feedback. Those who are closest to the centers of bureaucratic power have all the advantages available to them and can easily do what they wish.

Bureaucracy separates human beings from each other. Relationships existing among them cease to be personal, emotional, and social and begin to be impersonal, "rational," and machine-like. The needs of the system dominate so much over human needs that the new culture of bureaucracy has to be highly conflictual. On the ground of bureaucracy, antagonistic bargaining becomes a common phenomenon, which is costly and, in addition, disintegrates the society. Collision between bureaucratic and social life pervades everyday life. By prohibiting any bottom-up determination of purpose, as well as any design from below of appropriately meaningful action, bureaucracy promotes the sense of purposelessness, and "leaves many inhabitants of that era and its structures in dark backwaters of confusion, irrationality, and myth when their attitudes and actions are contrasted against the rationalist light" (Hummel 1982, p. 85).

Bureaucracy denies its functionaries an independent judgment because "what the functionary is the organization intends to design exclusively from above" (Hummel 1982, p. 103). Individual moral conscience has no place in bureaucracy. Inner standards must be left at home before entering the office. Ego becomes fragmented and the superego remains separated from the rest of the psyche; the id is fully harnessed in the service of the bureaucratic organization. Bureaucracy tears from people their conscience. It fragments their ego. It satisfies and punishes them at their lowest level by titillating the id's craving for power or by threatening psychic identity (Ibid., pp. 106, 107).

In the modern multidimensional world the bureaucratic endeavor to reduce everything to unidimensionality becomes more and more difficult because of the growing complexity of problems faced by bureaucracies, the growing educational level of people, the lack of imagination among bureaucrats, neglect of the intelligence function, and competition between various bureaucracies.

According to Marcuse, "The more rational, productive, technical, and total the repressive administration of society becomes, the more imaginable the means and ways by which the administered individuals might break their servitude and seize their own liberation" (Marcuse 1964, pp. 6–7). He treats an effective suppression of liberation needs among common place people as the distinguishing feature of advanced industrial society. The pessimistic image of a bureaucratized society offered by Marcuse is far from social reality because his image of freedom is unreal. He claims that "self-determination will be real to the extent to which the masses have been dissolved into individuals liberated from all propaganda, indoctrination, and manipulation, capable of knowing and comprehending the facts and of evaluating the alternatives" (Marcuse 1964, p. 252). Liberation from unidimensionality does not necessarily mean achievement of a mythologized absolute freedom from any social influences, which are avoidable, but definitely means the resistance of people against the manipulation of them into the role of passive objects of the bureaucratic authority everywhere—under capitalism as well as under any kind of socialism.

THE INSTITUTIONALIZED "SERIOUSNESS"

Big business is not a laughing matter.

In the pantheon of the young business executives, there are goods of success, diligence, alertness, punctuality, timing and memo writing. But alas, there is none for humor. . . . Heightened seriousness among young people in general since the 1960s seems to be one reason for this clear attitude. But at least part of the blame lies with the business schools" (*Time* 1981: vol. 119, no. 9:45).

It is the role of "corporate etiquette" to keep people in order within the rules applicable to all levels of management.

Business represented by top management is strictly conventional with a hard-core determination to maintain the standards of customary amenities. . . . There is an unwritten corporate etiquette to which the average successful executive adheres most of the time. There are rules of business behavior as there are rules of social conduct. These rules help make business relations easier, pleasanter, and certainly more profitable" (Alihan 1970, p. 2).

Any etiquette has the tendency to ossify and serves mainly the preservation of the status quo instead of opening up new horizons. The matter of being gentle to each other has a universal validity; on the other hand, people who know how to be gentle to each other within their own circle quite often neglect to apply the same measure outside the circle of a privileged few. With the growth of leisure concerns of big business (country clubs, business parties, travel for business, and pleasure at the company expense), the etiquette has been extended to several new fields reaching much beyond work and money-making. Public relations concern influences now very strongly the image of people who are supposed to represent business interests. On the other hand, this image is to a large extent the product of manipulation by advertising experts. The leaders of business themselves become shaped by their own consultants and lose freedoms enjoyed before by the "robber barons" as well as by other early entrepreneurs. The growing business of image-shaping has become omnipotent and influences, among others, the field of leisure. Even the most powerful people are under the dictate of this business. The higher the position occupied by people in government or in business, the more they have to obey the requirements of propaganda.

The internal life of a bureaucracy has been based on assumptions which practically have excluded the leisure orientation. Even joking behavior and friendship ties serve a serious purpose related to profit-making, promotion, external struggle for more power, temporary diminishment of insecurity feelings, creation of valuable connections, and so forth. Leisure as practiced by the professional bureaucrat is always purposeful and does not allow for genuine relaxation. The exercise of bureaucratic power is a fulltime occupation to which all other concerns are subordinated. It is not the matter of vanity but mainly the matter of seriousness with which the vocation is treated by people committed to it. Among the young generation there are some significant changes in this respect, due to new values and life orientations dominating in the college life, as well as to the more and more obvious limits of the bureaucratic career. In societies dominated by big organizations, and primarily by the state, the entrepreneurial spirit does not have much chance on the mass scale, and many people entering the business ranks become disillusioned with the bureaucratic content of their jobs, as well as with the limited chances to go ahead.

The seriousness of business becomes more and more identified with the bureaucratic practice which in its true content does not differ much between the private corporation and the governmental agency or even between enterprises located in various fields. The rules and problems of organizational behavior may differ, but their bureaucratic essence remains more or less the same under various local circumstances. Managerial skills gained in business administration college courses have a universal validity because of the fact that different business organizations have so much in common with others and managers can move without much difficulty from one business to another (Davis 1981).

There is a question of whether the seriousness of business behavior, particularly at the managerial level, is really justified by objective considerations. At least a part of this seriousness is related to public relations motives as a justification for the high status and social-material benefits of managers. The cult of managers, and especially of executives, as heroes of modern society is a very important part of the commercialized model of a consumer society as well as of a socialist command economy (Matejko 1971). This cult contributes to the indoctrination of the masses into the free business creed as well as into the collectivistic doctrine.

The leisure orientation may possibly have a very considerable disruptive economic effect as long as this orientation goes beyond material consumption and diverts people from their market commitments. It is very significant that the dessemination of noncommercial values among North American youth during the 1960s had undermined very considerably the traditionally strong position of big business in the society and had stimulated several countercultures negatively oriented to the business world.

The power of big business in society depends significantly on its ability to impose its own seriousness on the rest of society. People who lose interest in constantly buying something new, and those who do not worship the financial success as the best way of making personal life meaningful, are not a suitable socioeconomic ground for big business. It is the problem, not only of the material basis of potential clients or employees, but even more the problem of a sociomoral climate in which big business has to exist. Therefore, a very considerable effort constantly is made in order to socialize people to the values, preferences, and behavior patterns suitable for big business. As long as ordinary people take seriously what is done and offered by business, a social order in which the corporations may pursue their goals in the traditional manner is relatively secure.

The denial of primary validity to business in general, and big business in particular, becomes almost unavoidable when leisure preferences take priority over work and duty preferences. People who take fun and relaxation as their first priority and who at the same time do not identify themselves with the acquisition of material goods and services, do not promise much as clients or even as loyal and fully devoted employees. In this respect the whole Western world was considerably changed in the last few decades and the far-reaching consequences of this change are fully recognized by only a few social scientists. One of them is Daniel Bell (1976).

CONFLICTS OF INTERESTS WITHIN BUREAUCRACIES

Should we take for granted that in a highly developed economy the compliance of organizational members arises almost automatically from the organic solidarity dictated by the far-reaching division of labor? The interests of various categories of employees are supposedly so interdependent in the functional sense that this in itself sufficiently disciplines everybody (Tausky 1970).

The daily experience of industrial relations shows clearly that it does not work this way. The conflict of interests between various pressure groups prevents the hierarchical organizations from achieving a high level of efficiency (Herbst 1976). The identification of an organization's members with the institutional goals is relatively high at high levels of skills, education, and power (executives show the highest level of participation), but at the lower levels there is a lot of frustration. Local loyalty with a work team, division, or occupation very often happens to be in conflict with the broader loyalties. Social distances which follow the progressing division of labor provide a basis for class tensions. The moral importance of work becomes marginal in the experience of many people due, among other causes, to their growing estrangement and distance from the vital decisions within the framework of complex organizations. Working conditions may be bearable and the remuneration satisfactory, but this does not make people happy, and moreover it does not allow them to find any deeper meaning in work.

There is now a considerable amount of evidence that hierarchical organizations based on inequality of knowledge, rewards, authority, power, and privilege are far from being the most efficient. On the other hand, the attempts to democratize the structure of complex organizations by introducing some elements of a representative industrial democracy very often remain on an elitist level and do not inspire grass-root participation (Evan 1972: 4, pp. 75–90).

In order to understand the insistence with which the hierarchical organizations manage to survive, several aspects of these organizations should be considered. First of all, a conservative bias of complex organizations as collective bodies integrated primarily by the internal interdependence produced by the subdivision of work, should be looked into (Blau 1973: 4, pp. 23–46). Order and discipline seem necessary for any organization with specific goals and scarce resources. However, it seems reasonable to assume that the participative organization is not necessarily in disagreement with them. "Perhaps the major goal for participative organization should not be that of promoting productivity, but that of moderating the discipline which seems necessary for effective industrial organization" (Franke 1973: 5, pp. 107–20).

The functionalistic explanation of a conservative bias shared by complex organizations seems unsatisfactory; power relations should be brought into the picture. It is possible to say that the hierarchical nature of complex organizations may be in the vested interest of some social forces against others. For example, in the state-owned enterprises, managers and professional staff may have a vested interest in the defense of their management prerogatives against the participatory endeavors of trade unions, political pressure groups, higher echelons of bureaucracy, and the rank and file.

The socialpsychological perspective bears attention. Namely, it seems possible to claim that the differences of perspective between role occupants in complex organizations probably have something to do with the type of the organizational model. The difference between the *perseverative* events and the *permutative* events, formulated by Kotarbinski (1965) has led me to the distinction between the task orientation and the status orientation (Matejko 1970, pp. 329–54). When applying this distinction to the role occupants in complex organizations it is possible to claim that these role occupants may be primarily distinguished by their preoccupation either with tasks, or with statuses.

ACHIEVERS AND MEDIOCRITIES

There is an obvious advantage in making a distinction between various types of role occupants within social systems. For example, Lester W. Milbrath, on the basis of an empirical study, maps relationships between people and government in terms of such roles as protesters, communicators, party activists, and patriots. These roles show "somewhat distinctive relationships to the pattern of expectations and satisfactions that people had with what they took out of the government" (Milbrath 1973). Applying a similar approach to the issue of a task-orientation in complex organizations it would probably be empirically possible to make distinctions between "achievers," who are willing and able to deal directly with primary tasks of a given organization, and "mediocrities," or those who are far behind the "achievers."

Protection of the inept, and protection of the group from the inept, are pervasive features of all societies (Goode 1967). "The inept create a 'floor,' the lowest permissible level of competence. To fire them is to raise that level, so that these who are now comfortably above it might be threatened. To some degree, the mediocre 'need' the really inept" (Goode 1967, p. 11). On the other hand, ignorance may be in the nature of certain institutional procedures (Whyte 1956). If, for some reasons, mediocrities dominate the scene in a given complex organization, the latter will not be effectively protected from the inept. First of all, it is atypical for nonprofit groups and institutions to dispose of people just because their performance is not quite satisfactory. Secondly, some vested interests may develop which would be oriented toward preservation of the mediocrity of performance or even of sheer ineptness. "People are only partially committed to the criterion of achievement as the basis for reward, and also accept other opposing norms" (Goode 1967, p. 8). The rhetoric of achievement is widely demonstrated in public, but much less practiced in reality.

The discrepancy between the external pressures and the internal potential of a given complex organization may be considerably reduced by offering a special place in the institutional goals to the protection of the inept. The rigors of external and internal competition may be avoided by carving out a monopolistic position for the organization; by providing special protection for the inept; by making the removal of the mediocre and the inept extremely difficult; by confusing the criteria of performance; by limiting the competition to some preselected individuals; by barring the gateways to training, and so forth. All these measures support ineptitude, or at least, mediocrity, and create difficulties for real "achievers" in promoting their cause.

One must distinguish here between the weakness justified by objective or subjective circumstances, and the mediocrity or ineptitude raised to the position of a social power due to the conditions which prevail in a given institutional setting. It is quite obvious that individual members in the task groups differ in their performance, but at the same time, they depend upon on another and therefore must cooperate. It seems necessary to agree with Goode that the protection of the less able is a necessity in the sense mentioned above. However, the immobilization and frustration of the more able within the system which protects or even promotes the less able is an equally important problem. Goode claims that "the modern system is more productive because its social structures utilize the inept more efficiently, rather than because it gives greater opportunity and reward to the more able" (Goode 1967, p. 17). It seems justified to claim that the modern bureaucratic system, especially in the nonprofit sector, promotes mediocrity and is to a large extent run by mediocrities to the detriment of the urgent social needs. The scope of possible initiatives is being narrowed.

For the purpose of sociological analysis, complex organizations may be approached as bargaining systems in which various individuals and groups have more or less opportunity to "get one's way" by controlling scarce resources, handling nonroutine situations (uncertainty), and applying power (Abell 1973, pp. 6–7). It is a common phenomenon in complex organizations that various social actors compete with one another for scarce resources, control, power and privilege. Coalition between bargaining actors is a common phenomenon if there is at least a minimum of common interest among them; if they are able to find a common language; if they are aware of the communality of interests (consensus), and if they share common will and ability to act in a collective manner.

The differences in the expert power of negotiators often make equal participation in negotiations quite impossible (Drenth 1973). Within complex organizations "loyalists" often dominate the "innovators" in their organizational expert knowledge; the latter are too busy dealing with their specific tasks and do not know enough about the intricacies of the organizational functioning. On the contrary, loyalists invest all their effort into learning how to control the organization.

The ability and willingness to contribute to a complex organization may be used here as the basic dimension of "mediocrity." Role occupants interested only in means should be distinguished from role occupants interested in influencing the policies and strategies, or from those interested in the fulfillment of organizational goals. In this respect, there are various levels of ability and willingness to participate in a given complex organization (Bergh 1973, p. 37).

Coalitions of "mediocrities" develop a strategy of preventing task-oriented people from functioning effectively. They monopolize information (this factor alone already leads to inequities in power distribution), discourage any entrepreneurship coming from beyond their own control, divert the attention from primary tasks to issues of a purely procedural nature.

The preoccupation of the "mediocrities" with the hierarchy has several reasons. Bureaucrats are paid largely in proportion to the number of people controlled by them, to the discretionary power of money spending, and the secrecy of information available to them. These three factors contribute to the dissemination of "mediocrity." The control of a large number of people very often prevents the supervisor his own professional growth. The money spending business is time-consuming. The secrecy of information limits the creative exchange of thoughts with other people.

THE ROOTS OF MEDIOCRITY IN BUREAUCRACIES

Bureaucracy is, in its design, a perfect system; this perfection, however, could also be considered its greatest weakness. The tendency to eliminate anything and all that does not follow the established model is erroneous. The bureaucratic organizations cannot operate in a vacuum, completely separate from the constantly changing internal and external conditions. On the contrary, adaptation through active participation in the environment is a must for bureaucracy. Social conditions form this environment and it is hardly possible to keep a bureaucratic system free from outside influence of the changing society. Thus a universal model of bureaucracy which relies on hierarchical order and the people affected by it, is under a strong influence of the local social, political, and cultural factors. The ideal system, as devised by Max Weber, is a useful abstract, but should only be considered as a purely methodological tool. Historical changes which take place in social reality make obsolete any rigid models.

However, certain general properties of bureaucracy survive and these allow us to recognize the system, even though there may be great differences in detail. Bureaucracy is always and everywhere an *impersonal machine*, based on clearly defined functions, where power is executed in accordance with the system's legal-administrative order. Generated by the impersonality of such an organization, a conflict between personal interests and ambitions and the public interest is almost inevitable.

Bureaucracy arranges a language barrier around itself. "One-directionality and acausality are the two major characteristics not only of computer language but of bureaucratic language in general, of which computer language is an advanced case" (Hummel 1982, p. 153). Agenda-setting within bureaucracies tends to favor those with wealth, power, expertise, time, and information. Bureaucracy also subverts politics within and outside itself. This is done by the denial that rules, structures, and bureaucracy itself are political, as well as by the denial that power is being exercised when bureaucracy acts (Ibid., p. 187).

The self-destructive impulses within modern bureaucracies are particularly evident in the field of leadership.

Bureaucracy, initially an exemplary pulpit for leadership on preexisting problems, becomes in the long run a leadership trap. If in the polity the solution is the replacement of leaders, this opportunity is no longer open in the bureaucratic age: managers may come and go but the sanity or insanity-ability to respond to the world of any particular bureaucracy remains preconstructed and unchanged forever" (Hummel 1982, p. 215).

The growing interdependence in *Gesellschaft* of people and functions exercised by them leads in the developed industrial societies to either democratization or oligarchization (Bergh 1973: 5, p. 37). Both tendencies are in dialectical relationship with one another. In order to survive and succeed, democratic leaders as well as authoritarian bosses must depend on the loyalistic support of the executors of their will. Quite often it is even difficult to guess who runs whom. "The persons or groups that control the monopolies become dependent upon their dependents for the administration of monopolized chances" (Bergh 1973: 5, p. 31).

The training of middle and even higher management is quite often inadequate—not only because of the eventual local shortage of skilled personnel, but more so because of the bureaucratic "blessing" which people gain when upgraded to managerial positions in hierarchical organizations. The power enjoyed by them is above any learning. Wisdom becomes a purely instrumental virtue, a commodity bought in the market. On-the-job training becomes a form of tax evasion and serves some purely window-dressing purposes. Nobody bothers about the fact that the worse trained the executive group "the worse will be the process of decision-making and the higher will be the pressure to eliminate self-management and move to technocratia" (Adizes 1973, p. 31).

While nonbureaucratic systems often appeal to aspects of personal nature (dependency of the followers on the leader, collective spirit in self-governing communities), bureaucracy seems to overlook these aspects. It was therefore necessary that scientific "discoveries" be made in order to return some rank to the humanistic thinking and acting of leaders brought up on bureaucracy. This is what happened in the United States in the human relations movement in the 1930s; this is what happens now in the Soviet bloc countries with their ever-increasing tendency towards less brutal, but often much more sophisticated manipulation of the subordinates by their superiors.

THE CONSPIRACY OF MEDIOCRITIES

Identification of the bureaucratic order with impersonality leads to a serious decrease in organizational potential when manifold human abilities are curbed to fit a pre-established mold. Order, of course, is always useful and necessary. Must it, however, lead to a general anesthesia? Cannot the demands of order be in agreement with the demands of humanitarianism? Such questions are very common, for example, among the intelligentsia in the Soviet bloc and they unavoidably lead to the widening gap between, on the one hand, the ruling elite who treat the existing bureaucratic model as the bulwark of their power, and on the other hand, the large number of people who are looking for innovations.

In extreme cases it could happen, as it happened in the Soviet Union in the 1930s, that blind obedience and complete devotion to the ruling individual and the clique surrounding him could become the most important principle. There is another expression of the same process, and that is the *conspiracy of mediocrities;* it takes place where, since more ambitious and enterprising individuals are eliminated in the process of selection and promotion, mediocre people dominate. Mediocrities then develop a common purpose, which is to defend their possessions against constantly threatening invasion of better human element. For this very reason state bureaucracies of many underdeveloped countries cannot rise from their intellectual slump (Andreski 1969).

The most common result of the process of separation of interests is, however, the disregard of the customers of a given bureaucratic institution. Many examples of this can be found in the totalitarian state socialism, but they may also be found where private capital dominates. The bureaucratized enterprises have public interest as their motto and a well-publicized reason for existence; they have, however, more and more often only their own well-being in mind. There is no reason for them to be concerned with the welfare of the shareholders if the management of the bureaucratized enterprise is much stronger than the disorganized mass of those who own the shares.

The alienation of hierarchical organizations from the environmental constraints is simultaneous with the reshuffle of priorities. Functioning of the hierarchy and its survival becomes the primary goal and the original goals become only a window-dressing arrangement. There are several internal and external factors which contribute to such developments. One of them is the organizational hierarchy in itself which is so important in the daily existence of the people working for a given complex organization that it soon occupies most of their attention.

In order to preserve its internal balance, the hierarchical organization depends on the loyalty of its functionaries; and the fact that such complex organization is oriented toward longitudinal survival as a social institution has importance here. The "loyalists" win in the long run against the task-oriented innovators because the stability of hierarchical organization depends on them. Risky endeavors become gradually eliminated; everything within the organization becomes standardized in order to limit the uncertainty. However, this progressing standardization leads at the same time to the dominance of mediocrity. The cause of innovators and organizational nonconformists becomes hopelessly subordinated to the cause of mediocrities who provide the bulwark of the status quo. In the long run the final outcome is easy to predict: complex organizations run by mediocrities become mediocre in themselves; there is a growing cleavage between them and the changing environment.

It can be said that, the greater the estrangement of the institution from the realistic needs of the society, the more noticeable the symptoms mentioned above. At the same time, a backward process takes place: selection happens according to loyalty and not productivity; mediocrities conspire; there is a disregard of customers. The individual and group interests of those who are taking part in the process of estrangement become crystallized; a specific manner of development of such a complex organization is established. The more complicated the structure of a complex organization, the more important are the roles played by the two factors mentioned above, and, at the same time, the greater the social loss caused by the separation of the complex organization from public welfare.

MEDIOCRITY IN VARIOUS TYPES OF BUREAUCRACIES

The price of bureaucracy to society is in fact quite high, not only because of proverbial incapacity of the former, but also due to the fact that bureaucracy remains aloof where social needs are concerned; needs which, in principle, bureaucracy is supposed to serve. As a result of this process, greater importance is given to loyalty toward the complex organization than to professional qualifications and merit, when hiring or promoting employees.

In economic institutions, formation of big-scale corporations leads to the standardization of hiring and promotion criteria. Loyalty and conformism are treated as desirable qualities in the candidates. The conspiracy of mediocrity emerges as soon as the element of initiative in managing positions vanishes. Conspiracy of mediocrity thrives when the whole issue of rentability becomes confused by artificial prices, administrative overhead, manipulation of budgets, and so on. Where big enterprises are concerned, the government, the customer, and even more so the public, have little to say. These enterprises influence the market, manipulate governments as well as their own shareholders, and do as they please with their profits.

In political institutions of an authoritative type, selection of people based on their loyalty to the institution leads to the separation of the ruling elite from the masses. The gulf between the top few and the rest widens with the development of mass culture as well as with the "revolution of growing expectations." This separation takes place even in democratic political institutions in the West, where needs and exigencies of the collectivistic type in advanced societies become almost inevitably opposed to the democratic mechanism. Democracy functions from election to election, without much thought to long-range social needs.

The conspiracy of mediocrity in political institutions is characterized by the change in the management from leadership to manipulation. While leaders steer their communities and are responsible for them, manipulators' only goal is to stay in power as long as possible, often with detriment to the people. Political play is more important than real social needs; social and economic programs serve the interests of political cliques who try to get as many advantages for themselves as they possibly can—at the expense of the public. Execution of power becomes an end in itself.

In educational and cultural institutions alienation is caused by more importance being given to ritual than to the genuine interest shown by their members. These establishments favor candidates with opportunistic inclination, while candidates with creative spirit are eliminated, for they are considered potential trouble-makers. Desire to search, inclination to start polemics, wish to find self-actualization in work, disqualify the potential candidate, rather than help him or her in his or her career (Whyte 1957).

The conspiracy of mediocrity in the institutions mentioned above is directed against any kind of novelty which might endanger the happy existence of the present managerial elite, or which might expose their inadequacy. One of the best indications of the separation of establishments from society is their loss of influence on the young generation. The less the young respect a given institution and its program, the less secure is this institution's future.

THE RULE OF MEDIOCRITIES
AND ITS CONSEQUENCES

The rule of mediocrities is based on their informal conspiracy which, in turn, is based on a specific social control. This strategy is easily distinguishable from the formal, impersonal control of bureaucracy; from the very personal control of the closed societies; or from the control practiced by traditional authority or a charismatic leader.

The tough controls are performed by cliques of mediocrities in institutions in which they thrive, where self-interest, cleverly disguised as public concern, is their only goal (Adizes 1973, p. 25). This is socially very expensive; the control is well disguised, while preying on the welfare of the people becomes the highest principle. A clique of this kind uses a public institution as a screen for their own interests, without the slightest regard for the good of the institution itself. Accordingly, key positions are soon filled; the whole institution is reorganized; people and supplies are moved from place to place; plans and programs are constantly changed. With its aggressive-defensive tactics, the clique soon has its tentacles through the whole organization, corrupting interpersonal relations, leading to unrelenting battles among the different cliques over the distribution of spoils and the division of spheres of domain. With great loss to the institution, cliques monopolize essential supplies; eliminate people who really care; demoralize personnel, and paralyze all legal procedures or attempts to change the status quo.

The activities of cliques similar to those described above are noticeable in the developing countries. Scarce advantages, such as attractive jobs, promotions, generous fringe benefits, well-paid travels abroad, and so forth, are distributed according to the clique interests. This leads to a high level of waste and, in addition, the state apparatus becomes involved in a permanent internal struggle.

The deviation introduced to the Third World bureaucracies by the cliques puts in doubt not only the Marxist concept of the "dictatorship of the proletariat," but also seriously undermines the Weberian ideal type of bureaucracy. The supposedly perfect model of bureaucracy does not take into consideration the existence of the conspiracy of mediocrities. Neither does it consider in any way the question of alienation. Changes to the theoretical model of bureaucracy would have to be so extensive that the significance of the whole model may become questionable. The ideal model of bureaucracy as devised by Max Weber is only partially reflected in social reality.

THE SELF-DEFEATING IMPULSE OF BUREAUCRACY

The bureaucratic model becomes more and more self-defeating in present times because it is highly inadequate to meet the challenges of the modern world. It does not fit into the rapid change. It does not mobilize higher motivation and human willingness to cooperate. It does not pay attention to the needs and anguishes of modern people. It is not able to considerably improve its efficiency. It does not improve human relations. It does not give any hope for the solving of the crucial socioeconomic and political problems of our times.

Perrow does not believe that bureaucracy will be replaced by "highly decentralized, problem-solving, profession-loaded organizations concerned with a responsible approach to society's multiplying social problems" (Perrow 1972, p. 175). The Weberian model, according to him, will still be with us because rationalization and routinization are the only reliable solutions. "Most organizations are, and will continue to be, moderately routine in terms of the tasks of the most of the salaries and hourly work force" (Perrow 1972, p. 175). It appears that Perrow confuses in this respect two things which do not necessarily have to contradict one another. One is a type of organization which offers the best opportunity to fulfill work tasks on the basis of rationalization and routinization, and the other is to offer working people enough opportunity to influence decisions which are of vital importance to them.

The artificiality of organizational structures in the modern mass societies, based on manipulation from the top and anomie at the bottom level of hierarchy, is a common fact in the capitalist West as well as in the communist East. This artificiality arises not only from the fact the above-mentioned structures are relatively new and uprooted. It is based mainly on the very superficial character of socialization practiced under bureaucracy; the latter prevails now not only only under state socialism dominating in the communist countries but also in the free-enterprise world of the West where in developed countries from 40 to 60 percent of the GNP belongs to the public sector.

Bureaucracy has become an organizational structure under which the vested interests of the corporate-body-based organizational decision-makers prevail over and above the goals which a given structure is supposed to fulfill. Such a misappropriation of institutional forms by the vested interest groups is particularly probable when the power elite does not have to cope anymore with some major uncertainties. Monopoly is the optimal state for power-hungry bureaucrats and therefore people who oppose them look for some competitive arrangements that would provide an effective challenge to the growing number of bureaucrats. This is the main reason why the free-enterprise system is so popular among political oppositionists under the Soviet system when on the other hand the state interference is widely claimed in the West as a remedy for the power and wealth concentration in business corporations. In both cases the "reduction of certainty" is treated as a defense against omnipotent bureaucracies.

Bureaucracies flourish in a condition of relative isolation and domination over countervailing forces. The unorganized clientele unable to exercise any control and pressure; lack of other organizational forces offering the same or even better services at a lower rate; the passive human environment unable to react against abuses practiced by bureaucracy; an inert but efficient challenge offered by new perspectives; the concentration of full power within one's own ranks and the rejection of any input by outsiders; professionals and experts kept at a distance; the effective prevention of personnel being exposed to any novelties; established mutual loyalties among bureaucrats pressing them to dominate over the forces of dissension; the recruitment of devoted candidates free from any broad external commitments; the ability to apply unidimensional procedures and approaches to current tasks—all these factors allow the "well" developed bureaucracies to function on the basis of a semiclosed system.

It is an open question as to how much bureaucratization is able to harm modern organizations by depleting their storage of energy, slowing down their organizational growth, undermining organizational endurance and survival, and diminishing the organizational control of the surrounding environment. Obviously, bureaucracies are strongly oriented toward survival and the satisfaction of the supreme disposer. But they place less emphasis on the long-term maximization of organizational returns; they reduce their own functionaries to mediocrities (Matejko 1979), creating a widespread anomie; force people to take a defensive attitude splitting human relations according to organizational lines; spread impersonality and anonymity; impose the procedural approach to all problems; idolize the institution over and above the human good; enforce rigidity; and substitute sincere commitment for goal-fulfillment by the pretentious manipulation of facts, materials, and human beings.

Uniformity of practices within the bureaucratic organizations is the major source of ossification and conservatism. Following mainly "the survival model" (Etzioni 1964), bureaucracies show a great hesitancy to accept any novelties which would upset the well-established order. The vested interests of bureaucratic functionaries located at various hierarchical levels prevent new ideas (and the people behind them) from being introduced successfully into the organizational reality. In bureaucracies there is no place for opinion differences, questioning, opposition, and the right of dissent. They are not designed to accept disagreement and debate as a source of progress and creativity. On the contrary, there is a strong tendency to localize, "pacify," and eventually eliminate any sources of potential disagreement. In the selection of personnel special attention is paid to the rejection of possible troublemakers.

The bureaucratic personnel is supposed to be rewarded for merit but the latter is usually identified with disposability and institutional loyalty. The well-being of the bureaucratic organization itself is the ultimate institutional goal; the latent function of self-preservation and self-aggrandizement dominates over the manifest goals formulated and reformulated for the sake of good public relations. Under such circumstances the employees who really gain merit are those who contribute to the good of the bureaucracy and not those who are committed to other goals of a professional, social, or moral nature. Nonconformists who do not share the total bureaucratic commitment, and are not willing to serve the hierarchy and accept the stereotype of an "organization man" (Whyte 1957), are carefully avoided in bureaucracies (Matejko 1979).

Bureaucracies are full of internal tensions which prevent them from achieving a permanent equilibrium and high productivity. Vested institutional interests lead to a high level of defensiveness or even aggressiveness; members of a given complex organization defend one another against any external scrutiny; external efforts to introduce some controls are sabotaged successfully by all levels of the bureaucratic hierarchy; coverups are a common occurrence of bureaucratic life. There are intense rivalries and animosities inside bureaucracies behind the facade of solidarity vis-à-vis the outside world. Bureaucrats within their own ranks are divided according to organizational boundaries, unit loyalties, suppressed ambitions, and personal animosities. The rigidly formalized character of bureaucracies prevents them quite effectively from achieving any deeper internal solidarity as well as an adequate efficiency.

> Resources are wasted, energies are sacrificed, and efforts are sabotaged. Thus, because of the isolation which it fosters, and because this isolation tends to build up internal pressures, the overtly cohesive organization is not only not all that cohe-

sive but it is also not all that efficient (Berkley 1971, p. 149).

In the world of bureaucracy human well-being is neglected, work motivation does not crystallize, loyalties are superficial and ephemeral, responsibility to the external world becomes subordinated to the vested interests of the institution and its disposers. The growth of formalization thwarts the natural development of informal relationships: organization becomes rigid, uncontrollable, and dominated by private coalitions. Cliques play a major role even if they do not appear on any organizational blueprint. Privatization flourishes unhampered within the environment which is supposed to eliminate completely any personalization.

Bureaucracy rests on command in the allocation of scarce resources and therefore should be treated as political and in its true nature opposed to the allocation based on customs or exchange contracts (Easton 1965; Heilbroner 1980). The distinction between friend and foe, Us and the Other (Schmitt 1963) is particularly valid for bureaucracy. Bureaucracy controls the scarce resources and in this capacity is vulnerable to external and internal dangers. At the same time bureaucracy itself artificially manipulates scarcity for its own benefit and becomes an active force within its own surrounding. This power of bureaucracy depends on the ability to countervail and rival sociopolitical forces as well as to achieve internal cohesiveness.

Bureaucracy is based traditionally on the authoritarian premises because its historical origins were in the nation-state building, army discipline, and the absolutistic dominance of souverains who delegated some parts of their power to the administrative staff who served them. The gradual growth of pluralism and the democratic aspirations have led to the growing resistance against the authoritarian traditions. On the other hand, the welfare state which has fulfilled the mass aspirations toward more social security and equality, by its fast growth has multiplied and extended the bureaucratic forms. In the public sector so far nothing has proved able to substitute these forms successfully. Also in the private sector, with the rise of big corporations, bureaucracy has flourished.

There is an obvious internal contradiction in the present-day bureaucracies. They are authoritarian in their true nature because the vested interests of the bureaucratic power-holders dictate that they impose their rule over their subordinates as well as over the clients. As long as the crucial decisions are of an arbitrary nature, the bureaucrats are secure in their relative privileges.

Under Soviet communism the bureaucratic system has achieved its highest development because any external interference and public control have been practically eliminated. Of course, the power struggle remains between these various bureaucratic bodies which try to challenge each other. However, it is the battle within one's own family and it does not necessarily endanger the status quo, as long as the nonbureaucratic bodies have little chance to enter the scene. The creation of free trade-unions in Poland in 1980 has been a new factor of great importance in the long run.

In the West, the situation is much more complicated because the unpopularity of bureaucracy has the chance to be articulated, and various pressure groups question from time to time the bureaucratic status quo. The advocates of consumers' interests have managed to impose on big corporations several restraints and expensive corrections. Voters, by changing their political preferences, exercise an effective pressure toward some reshuffles of the bureaucratic setup. Thus, in the United Kingdom under the Conservative government of Margaret Thatcher, the number of civil servants has been curtailed. However, in most of the cases the bureaucratic status still remains strong enough to survive the changes. For example, governmental changes in the United States so far have not led to any considerable reduction of public bureaucracies. The same is valid for Sweden and Canada. In all three cases it was too difficult (and politically dangerous) for the new occupants of top governmental offices to curtail bureaucracy.

One of the main obstacles in the introduction of reforms is the fact that bureaucracies constitute a conglomeration of various interrelated power groups which are constantly fighting, but all are vitally interested in the preservation of the existing order. Anything that may seriously endanger this order appears to them as suspectful and risky; therefore various interest groups join coalitions oriented against the reform. For example, in Sweden probably the majority of the population is very critical about the prevailing bureaucracy and would like to reduce the extremely heavy tax burden. On the other hand, the institutional status quo remains strong, thanks to the fact that the administrative reforms would undermine the present privileges and securities of so many very influential groups that nobody among the ruling politicians dares to limit the number of public-sector employees, undermine the well-established position of various powerful agencies, and so forth.

The fact is that the nonbureaucratic organizational

forms remain underdeveloped and it is an open question what would be able to substitute bureaucracy. The advocates of small- and middle-sized private business have a very limited appeal. It is in the nature of the private enterpreneurship that it takes a large-size bureaucratic form whenever it deals with big business tasks. The economic growth in the market economy leads unavoidably to the establishment of large corporations and the elimination of small business as less powerful. The weakness of being small remains a handicap in the competitive struggle. The cooperative movement, and particularly the consumer cooperatives, easily lose their social potential with the growth in size and the limited interest of people in spending their spare time for the sake of various social responsibilities. At the higher level of material well-being people have more interesting things to do than to attend the cooperative meetings, fulfill various voluntary obligations, shop only in cooperative stores, and so forth.

THE PROGRESSING OBSOLESCENCE

The bureaucratic model of organization based on the hierarchical division of power (a lot at the top, nothing at the bottom), the far-reaching subordination of subordinates to the supervisors, and the allegedly impersonal character of human relations, proves to become in the constantly growing number of cases just very inefficient and maladapted to the modern human condition. There is a need to overcome the narrow specificity of approach to people as clients or employees. The public interest in controlling bureaucracies from the social welfare perspective becomes widespread. There is a common opinion that secrecy and lack of information about the functioning of bureaucracy are widely utilized by bureaucrats just to hide their inefficiency. The same is with the vital issue of protecting the individual and group rights against the bureaucratic functionaries. The harmful effects of bureaucracy and its progressing maladaptation to modern society make probable that it will wither away (Bennis and Slater 1968).

Bureaucracies are able to flourish in the condition of relative isolation and domination over countervailing forces. The unorganized clientele unable to exercise any control and pressure; lack of other organizational forces able to compete effectively by offering the same or even better services at a lower rate; the passive environment unable to react against abuses practiced by bureaucracy; an effective resistance to the challenge offered by new perspectives; the concentration of full power within one's own ranks and the rejection of any input by outsiders; professionals kept at a distance; the effective prevention of personnel being exposed to any novelties; mutual loyalties among bureaucrats used to dominate over the forces of dissension; the continuous recruitment of loyalistic candidates free from any broad external commitments; the ability to apply unidimensional procedures and approaches to current tasks—all these factors allow bureaucracies to function on the basis of a semiclosed system, therefore remaining relatively autonomous.

However, in the modern world there are more and more trends which undermine these factors. Clients organize themselves and exercise pressures more or less effectively, for example, R. Nader and his consumer movement. The vigorous entrepreneurial spirit creates various enterprises which prove to be more successful than the ossified bureaucracies, for example, the private agencies competing with the governmental postal services in North America. With the growing surplus of collective consciousness in the sophisticated development societies (Bahro 1979) the external social environment of bureaucracies is becoming more and more sensitive to the misdeeds of bureaucracies. It is very significant that the public condemnation of bureaucracies is expressed more and more by people who used to be their obedient servants, from the CIA and KGB agents, through various civil servants—even to Roman Catholic priests. Organizational conformism is widely denounced in the popular literature and the stereotype of an "organizational man" is clearly negative.

Bureaucracies, whether they wish to or not, have to open themselves to new horizons, hire consultants, pay attention to strangers, depending upon professional personnel with strong external attachments, and introduce some innovations. However, a large part of these endeavors are just window dressing. Professional consultants are hired but their reports remain untouched in files; innovations are widely publicized for the sake of public relations and afterward they are discontinued. The conservative resistance against any deeper reforms is one of the characteristics of bureaucracies; the deep root of it is the inherent feeling of insecurity among the bureaucratic functionaries who owe everything to their institution and are helpless without its sponsorship. With the growing role of professionals in bureaucracies this feeling of insecurity is being substituted by the feeling of misplacement and alienation among people who entered bureaucracies with the trust in their own education background, and ambition to achieve in their lives something valid professionally, and the disinclination to be conformistic. Therefore, bureaucracies are exposed to growing internal tensions, especially in the public bureaucracies when the tenure of a civil servant position and unionization defend employees quite effectively against the interorganizational pressures.

It is an open question as to how much bureaucratization is able to harm complex organizations by depleting their storage of energy, slowing down their organizational growth, undermining organizational endurance and survival, and diminishing the organizational control of the surrounding environment. Obviously, bureaucracies are strongly oriented toward survival and the satisfaction of the supreme disposer but place less emphasis on the long-term maximization of organizational returns. "The organization shall not incapacitate its environment as a source of inputs and a receiver of outputs, since doing so would reduce its own effectiveness or even its power to survive. Maximization to that seemingly self-destructive point is by no means uncommon . . ." (Katz and Kahn 1978, p. 251). Bureaucracies deplete their environments by reducing their functionaries to mediocrities (Matejko 1979), creating a widespread anomie, forcing people to take a defensive attitude, splitting human relations according to organizational lines, spreading impersonality and anonymity, imposing the procedural approach to all problems, idolizing the institution over and above the human good, enforcing rigidity, and substituting sincere commitment for goal fulfillment by the pretentious manipulation of facts, materials and human beings.

In modern economy it is increasingly less important that results justify the input. Nevertheless, huge capital invested in modern machinery, complicated business operations and high qualifications of personnel, must be productively utilized since otherwise society suffers great losses if such an investment does not bring returns. Bureaucracy has inherent conservative tendencies since its very being can be reduced to the preservation and consolidation of its own legal-formal order and *not* to achieving objectives outside. Such objectives are as a rule manipulated by various groups representing different interests and exercising pressures within the bureaucracy. Under a bureaucratic order mediocre individuals are in collusion; it is to their advantage to oppose innovations which are beyond their own capabilities and which might unmask their shortcomings. The collusion among those mediocre elements safeguards to a certain extent the durability of bureaucratic order but it takes place above all at the cost of flexibility and adaptability to change according to new conditions and a corresponding change in goals and methods of achieving them. If bureaucracy perfects itself it does so primarily in the sense of strengthening its inner hierarchy and not in the sense of becoming more effective in relation to the outside.

It is in the nature of bureaucracy that it naturally drives in its endeavors beyond an optimum and stimulates countervailing forces. The process of task specialization entirely neglects the utmost importance of sociomoral bonds which energize individuals, allow them to find the common understanding, provide stability and predictability, and assure some minimum of mental health. Standardization of role performance fractionates human responsibility, endangers the internal cohesion and identity of individuals and groups as natural elementary parts of social systems, and creates the illusion of "order," "rationality," and "coordination," in which the social factors are omitted.

In bureaucracies unity of command and centralization of decision-making are based on a very simplified and one-sided understanding of the nature of power—power free from moral responsibility, oriented toward manipulation, reduced mostly to coercion, sanctified by the priority of institutional good over the good of human communities. The whole concept of community as the source of such power is foreign to bureaucracy in which its supreme disposer is reduced to something anonymous and therefore free from any ultimate responsibility. The dilution of responsibility between various steps in the bureaucratic hierarchy makes the latter factor particularly harmful to the human community.

Uniformity of practices with the bureaucratic organizations is the major source of ossification and conservatism. Following mainly "the survival model," bureaucracies show a great hesitancy to accept any novelties which would upset the well-established order. The vested interests of bureaucratic functionaries located at various hierarchical levels prevent new ideas and the people behind them from being introduced successfully into the organizational reality. Bureaucracies are more willing to accept counterfeit innovations rather than genuine innovations because the former are much easier to digest; especially if the pseudoinnovators and the entrenched bureaucrats share some common interests.

No duplication of functions is allowed in bureaucracies, but this principle is combined with the elimination of opinion differences, questioning, opposition, and right of dissent. Bureaucracies are not designed to accept dissent and disagreement as a source of progress and creativity. There is a strong tendency to localize, "pacify," and eventually eliminate any sources of potential disagreement. In the selection of personnel special attention is paid to the rejection of possible troublemakers who may contaminate the supposedly prevailing spirit of peace and agreement. The antidialectical nature of bureaucracies is one of the major sources of their self-defeat.

The adaptation of modern bureaucratic organizations to growing demands and expectations is not the problem of a more skillful manipulation only. In organization theory there is now a growing understanding that in order to face effectively modern challenges it is necessary to reconcile the traditional *rational* approach and the *natural-system* approach, as well as the *open-system* approach (Scott 1981, pp. 19–25).

The natural-system approach allows one to focus attention on various power and interest groups which influence a given complex organization. All these groups also represent certain subcultures, which have to be recognized as factors of more or less consequence for the functioning of an organization. Groups look for power and influence; they have a major influence on the work and leisure orientation of their members.

The growth of group life related to the functioning of bureaucratic organizations has to be appreciated positively or negatively in terms of its impact on organization, motivation, management style, and so forth. This is particularly evident in the societies still influenced by their traditional culture. The mechanistic transfer of organizational models and managerial patterns from developed countries to developing countries usually leads to several highly negative side-effects. The socialization potential of such models and patterns is quite often very low; there is not much chance to stimulate genuine organizational commitments; sociopsychological equilibrium of local people becomes upset; work and leisure remain in a permanent conflict; the foreign leisure patterns endanger the well-being of nations invaded by the army of fun-hungry tourists coming from the developed countries (Turner and Ash 1975).

In order to face new challenges of a sociocultural nature, and mainly the challenge of a mass leisure orientation, the modern bureaucratic organizations have to become much more open to acculturation. It has to be taken for granted that no contemporary complex organizations, how much sophisticated they may be, can be analyzed without consideration of the impact upon them of local social structures and cultures.

The qualitative growth of complex organizations as socioeconomic systems may be measured by their "maturity" in bringing all three approaches mentioned above (rational, natural, open system) under one denominator. Leisure demands represent in this respect a major challenge and therefore their changing nature needs to be considered. The work ideology has fluctuated historically (Anthony 1977) but only recently it has been successfully challenged by the growing leisure ideology. The dialectics of work and leisure within the complex organizations reflects several much more universal trends.

ALTERNATIVES TO BUREAUCRACY

There is a growing need for new forms of work organization geared to changing task exigencies. Of course, there is always a danger that without the objective, nonarbitrary application of calculable norms the situation may lead to the unequal treatment of individuals and their cases, favoritism and preference. However, with the progressing diversification of tasks, changing ratio of staff to line personnel, the improvement of communication up the line, transformation of authority relationships, decentralization and general relaxation of rules have become a necessity that makes the bureaucratic pyramid obsolete. Time becomes too precious to waste on procedural consideration. The span of time from discovery of a new technology to its practical application is constantly decreasing (Dorf 1974, p. 14). When the routine and repetitive tasks diminish in importance, there is more need for new organizational forms based on an easy cross-communication, high level of job discretion, teamwork, intrinsic motivation, management by objectives, and so forth. The mounting need for innovation

> places priority on men and women who can think for themselves and frowns on those who slavishly seek to imitate their peers and superiors. It requires organizations to blink at or even welcome human eccentricities when such features are part of a human being's package of potentialities. It forces organization to emphasize internal cooperation and discourage competitiveness. For innovation in the complex technology of today requires teamwork (Berkley 1971, pp. 69–70).

Particularly in the West there are now several trends that undermine the unequivocal acceptance of bureaucracy as the only organizational solution. What will move faster—the self-defeating trend of bureaucracy or the thriving of the administrative revolution (Berkley 1971)? The "calculable rules" on which the bureaucratic mechanisms depend lose in importance in modern societies that are manipulative in themselves because of their rational, technoeconomic basis. Dilettantism has ceased to be a major danger under conditions of a universal education and professionalism. Legality is already relatively well assured in developed democratic societies which show, in general, a much higher level of external and internal stability than in traditional agrarian societies (Lenski and Lenski 1982). Formalization could be a progressive trend in the preindustrial societies which suffered from too much intimacy; however, at the high stages of socioeconomical development it becomes a nuisance. Neutrality stops being an asset in modern times when bureaucracies have become the dominant form of work organization. In a dynamic society there is no room for the institutional structures based on longevity of their personnel, promotion of delay and inflexibility.

REFERENCES

Abell, P. 1973. "Organizations as Bargaining Systems." In *Participation and Self-Management*. First International Sociological Conference on Participation and Self-Management. Zagreb, Yugoslavia.

Abrahamsson, Bengt. 1977. *Bureaucracy or Participation*. Beverly Hills, CA: Sage.

Adizes, J. 1973. "On Conflict Resolution and an Organizational Definition of Self-Management," *Participation and Self-Management*. First International Conference on Participation and Self-Management, 5:17–34. Zagreb, Yugoslavia.

Albrow, Martin. 1970. *Bureaucracy*. London: Macmillan.

Alihan, M. 1970. *Corporate Etiquette*. New York: New American Library.

Andreski, S. 1969. *The African Predicament*. New York: Atherton Press.

Anthony, P. D. 1977. *The Ideology of Work*. London: Tavistock Publications.

Argyle, M., et al. 1958. "Supervisory Methods Related to Production, Absenteeism and Labor Turnover. *Human Relations* 11:23–40.

Argyle, Michael. 1974. *The Social Psychology of Work*. Harmondsworth, England: Penguin Books.

Argyris, Chris. 1964. *Integrating the Individual and the*

Organization. New York: Wiley.

Bachman, et al. 1968. "Bases of Supervisory Power." In *Control in Organizations,* edited by A. Tannenbaum. New York: McGraw-Hill.

Bahro, R. 1979. *The Alternatives.* London: New Left Books.

Barritz, L. 1960. *The Servants of Power.* Middleton, CT: Wesleyan University Press.

Bell, Daniel. 1976. *The Cultural Contradictions of Capitalism.* New York: Basic Books.

Bennis, W. G. 1969. *Organization Development: Its Nature, Origins and Prospects.* Reading, MA: Addison-Wesley.

Bennis, W. G., K. D. Benne, and A. Chin, eds. 1964. *The Planning of Change.* New York: Holt, Rinehart & Winston.

Bennis, W. G., and P. E. Slater. 1968. *The Temporary Society.* New York: Harper and Row.

Benveniste, Guy. 1977. *Bureaucracy.* San Francisco: Boyd and Frazer.

Bergh, Godfried van Benthem van den. 1973. "Some Remarks on Power, in *Participation and Self-Management* 5:35–38. Zagreb, Yugoslavia.

Berkley, G. E. 1971. *The Administrative Revolution.* Englewood Cliffs, NJ: Prentice-Hall.

Blau, Peter M. 1968. *Bureaucracy in Modern Society.* New York: Random House.

————. 1970. "A Formal Theory of Differentiation in Organization." *American Sociological Review* 35, 2.

————. 1973. "Interdependence and Hierarchy in Organizations." *Participation and Self-Management* 4:28–46. Zagreb, Yugoslavia.

Bottomore, T. B. 1971. "The Class Structure in Western Europe." In Margaret Scotford Archer and Salvadore Giner, eds., *Contemporary Europe: Class Status and Power.* London: Weidenfeld and Nicholson.

Boulding, K. E. 1953. *The Organizational Revolution.* New York: Harper and Row.

Britan, Gerald M. 1981. *Bureaucracy and Innovation.* Beverly Hills, CA: Sage.

Brown, J. A. C. 1963. *Techniques of Persuasion.* London: Penguin Books.

Burns, T., and G. M. Stalker. 1961. *The Management of Innovation.* London: Tavistock.

Champion, Dean J. 1975. *The Sociology of Organizations.* New York: McGraw-Hill.

Cherns, A. 1979. *Using the Social Sciences.* London: Routledge and Kegan Paul.

Child, J. 1973. "Predicting and Understanding Organization Structure." *Administrative Science Quarterly* 18:168–85.

Chowdhry, K., and A. K. Pal. 1966. "Production, Planning and Organizational Morale." In Alberta H. Rubenstein and Chadwick J. Haberstrok, eds., *Some Theories of Organization,* pp. 195–204. Homewood, IL: Irwin.

Crozier, Michel. 1964. *The Bureaucratic Phenomenon.* Chicago: University of Chicago Press.

Cyert, Richard M., and James G. March. 1963. *A Behavioral Theory of the Firm.* Englewood Cliffs, NJ: Prentice-Hall.

Dahl, R. A. 1957. "The Concept of Power." *Behavioral Science,* 2.

——————. 1970. *After the Revolution?* Yale University Press.

Davis, Keith. 1981. *Human Behavior at Work.* New York: McGraw-Hill.

Dean, D. G., and D. M. Valdes. 1965. *Sociology in Use.* New York: Macmillan.

Dorf, R. C. 1974. *Technology, Society and Man.* San Francisco: Boyd and Frazer.

Downs, Anthony. 1967. *Inside Bureaucracy.* Boston: Little, Brown.

Drenth, P. J. 1973. "The Works' Council in the Netherlands." In *Participation and Self-Management* 5:71. Zagreb, Yugoslavia.

Durkheim, Emile. 1947. *Division of Labor in Society.* Glencoe, IL: Free Press.

Easton, D. 1965. *A System Analysis of Political Life.* New York: Wiley.

Eldridge, J. E. T., and A. D. Crombie. 1974. *A Sociology of Organizations.* London: Allen and Unwin.

Etzioni, Amitai. 1964. *Modern Organizations.* Englewood Cliffs, NJ: Prentice-Hall.

——————. 1975. *A Comparative Analysis of Complex Organizations.* New York: Free Press.

Evan, William E. 1972. "Hierarchy, Alienation and Organizational Effectiveness in Participation and Self-Management." *Participation and Self-Management* 4:75–90. Zagreb, Yugoslavia.

Farmer, Richard, and Barry Richman. 1964. "A Model for Research in Comparative Management." *California Management Review.* Winter.

Fiedler, F. E. 1967. *A Theory of Leadership Effectiveness.* New York: McGraw-Hill.

Flanders, A. 1964. *The Fawley Productivity Agreements.*

London: Faber and Faber.

Franke, Richard H. 1973. "Critical Factors in the Postwar Economy Growth of Nations." In *Participation and Self-Management* 5:107–20. Zagreb, Yugoslavia.

French, J. R. P., Jr., and B. H. Raven. 1960. "The Bases of Social Power." In *Group Dynamics: Research and Theory,* edited by D. Cartwright and A. Zander. New York: Row, Peterson.

Fürstenberg, Friedrich. 1972. *Japanische Unternehmenungsführung.* Zürich: Verlag Moderne Industrie.

Georgopoulos, Basil, and Arnold Tannenbaum. 1957. "A Study of Organizational Effectiveness." *American Sociological Review* 22:534–40.

Gonzalez, Richard F., and Claude McMillan, Jr. 1961. "The Universality of American Management Philosophy." *Journal of the Academy of Management* 4, 1, April.

Goode, W. J. 1967. "The Protection of the Inept. *American Sociological Review* 32, 1:5–19.

Gross, Bertram M. 1964. *The Managing of Organizations.* Glencoe, IL: Free Press.

————. 1966. *The State of the Nation.* London: Tavistock.

Guttman, Daniel, and Barry Wilner. 1976. *The Shadow Government: The Government's Multi-Billion Dollar Giveaway of its Decison-Making Powers to Private Management Consultants, "Experts," and Think Tanks,* (with an introduction by Ralph Nader). New York: Pantheon.

Hage, J., and M. Aiken. 1970. *Social Change in Complex Organizations.* New York: Random House.

Handelman, D., and E. Leyton. 1978. *Bureaucracy and World View.* St. John's: Memorial University of Newfoundland.

Harbison, F., and E. Burgess. 1954. "Modern Management in Western Europe." *American Journal of Sociology* 60:1.

Heilbroner, R. L. 1980. *The Making of Economic Society.* Englewood Cliffs, NJ: Prentice-Hall.

Herbst, P. G. 1976. *Alternatives to Hierarchies.* Leiden: M. Nijhoff.

Hespe, G. W. A., and A. Little. 1971. "Some Aspects of Employee Participation." In *Psychology at Work,* edited by P. Warr. Harmondsworth (U.K): Penguin.

Hofstede, G. 1972. "Budget Control and the Autonomy of Organizational Units." In *Participation and Self-Management* 2:109–13. Zagreb, Yugoslavia.

Holter, H. 1965. "Attitudes Towards Employee Participation in Company Decision-making Processes. *Human Relations,* 18.

Horvat, B., et al. 1975. *Self-Governing Socialism.* 2 vol. New York: International Arts and Science Press.

Hummel, Ralph P. 1982. *The Bureaucratic Experience.* New York: St. Martin's.

"Innovations at Kingston Plant at Alcan." 1969. *McGill Industrial Relations Review.* Fall.

International Encyclopedia of Social Sciences. 1968. New York: Free Press.

Jacoby, Henry. 1979. *The Bureaucratization of the World.* University of California Press.

Jaques, E. 1961. *Equitable Payment.* London: Heinemann (republished in 1967 in Pelican Books).

—————. 1977. *A General Theory of Bureaucracy.* London: Heinemann.

Jenkins, David. 1974. *Job Power.* Harmondsworth, England: Penguin.

—————. 1975. "Beyond Job Enrichment: Workplace Democracy in Europe." *Working Papers for a New Society.* Winter.

Job Reform in Sweden. 1975. Stockholm: Swedish Employers' Confederation.

Joint Consultation in British Industry. 1952. London: HMSO.

Kahn, R. B., and E. Boulding, eds. 1964. *Power and Conflict in Organizations.* London: Tavistock.

Katz, Daniel, and Robert L. Kahn. 1978. *The Social Psychology of Organizations.* New York: Wiley.

Kavcic, B. 1973. "Some Trends in the Development of Self-Government." In *Participation and Self-Management* 6:159–78. Zagreb, Yugoslavia.

Kavcic, B., V. Rus, and A. Tannenbaum. 1971. "Control, Participation and Effectiveness in Four Yugoslav Industrial Organizations. *Administrative Science Quarterly* 16, 1.

Kobayashi, Shigeru. 1970. The Creative Organization—A Japanese Experiment, *Personnel,* 47, 6.

Kolaja, Jiri. 1965. *Workers' Councils: The Yugoslav Experience.* London: Tavistock.

Kotarbinski, T. 1965. *Praxiology.* New York: Pergamon Press.

Krause, E. A. 1968. Functions of Bureaucratic Ideology: "Citizens Participation," *Social Problems* 16, 2:129–43.

Lenski, G., and J. Lenski. 1982. *Human Societies.* New York: McGraw-Hill.

Likert, R. 1967. *The Human Organization.* New York: McGraw-Hill.

Lilienfeld, R. 1978. *The Rise of Systems Theory: An Ideological Analysis.* New York: Wiley.

Lippitt, R., J. Watson, and B. Westley. 1958. *Planned Change*. New York: Harcourt and Brace.

Lipset, S. M. 1970. "Trade Unions and Social Structure." In *Comparative Perspectives on Formal Organizations*, edited by H. D. Landsberger. Boston: Little, Brown.

Lupton, T. 1966. *Management and the Social Sciences*. London: Hutchinson.

Machiavelli, N. 1946. *The Prince*. New York: Hendricks House.

Mackenzie, W. J. M. 1967. *Politics and Social Science*. Harmondsworth (U.K.): Penguin Books.

Mann, F. C., and F. W. Neff. 1961. *Managing Major Change in Organizations*. Ann Arbor: Foundation for Research on Human Behavior.

Mannheim, Karl. 1961. *Man and Society in the Age of Reconstruction*. New York: Harcourt, Brace Jovanovich.

Matejko, Alexander J. 1970. Task versus Status. "The Contradictions of Modernization," *International Review of Sociology* VI, 1–3:329–54.

———. 1979. "From the Crisis of Bureaucracy to the Challenge of Participation." In *Management and Complex Organizations in Comparative Perspective*, edited by Raj P. Mohan. Westwood, CT: Greenwood.

March, J. G., and H. A. Simon. 1958. *Organizations*. New York: Wiley.

Marcuse, H. 1964. *One-Dimensional Man*. Boston: Beacon.

Martin, Roderick. 1977. *The Sociology of Power*. London: Routledge and Kegan Pual.

Marx, F. Morstein. 1957. *The Administrative State: An Introduction to Bureaucracy*. Chicago: University of Chicago Press.

McClelland and D. C. Winter. 1969. *Motivating Economic Achievement*. New York: Basic Books.

Menzel, J. M. ed. 1963. *The Chinese Civil Service Career Open to Talent?* Boston: D. C. Heath.

Merton, R. 1936. "The Unanticipated Consequences of Purposive Social Actions." *American Sociological Review* 3, 1:894–904.

Meskill, J., ed. 1963. *Wang An-shih, Practical Reformer?* Boston: D. C. Heath.

Meyer, M. W. 1979. *Change in Public Bureaucracies*. Cambridge: Cambridge University Press.

Milbrath, L. W. 1963. *The Washington Lobbyists*. Chicago: Rand McNally.

———. 1973. "Modes of Participation in the Polity." In *Participation and Self-Management* 5:163–78.

Moynihan, D. P. 1970. *Maximum Feasible Misunderstand-*

ing: *Community Action in the War on Poverty.* New York: Free Press.

Nadvorny, M. J. 1955. *Scientific Management and the Unions, 1900–1932.* Cambridge: Harvard University Press.

National Quality of Work Center. 1975. *The Quality of Work Program: The First Eighteen Months.* Ann Arbor: Institute for Social Research.

Nowotny, Otto H. 1964. "American versus European Management Philosophy." *Harvard Business Review.* March-April.

Obradovic, J. 1970. "Participation and Work Attitudes in Yugoslavia. *Industrial Relations* 9, 2.

—————. 1975. "Workers' Participation. Who Participates?" *Industrial Relations.* February.

Olberg, Winston. 1963. "Cross-Cultural Perspectives on Management Principles." *Journal of the Academy of Management* 6, 2.

Olsen, M. E. 1968. *The Process of Social Organization.* New York: Holt, Rinehart & Winston.

Ouchi, W. G. 1981. *Theory Z.* New York: Avon Books.

Parsons, T. 1970. "Social Systems." In *The Sociology of Organizations,* edited by O. Grusky and G. A. Miller. New York: Free Press.

Perrow, Charles. 1972. *Complex Organizations.* Glenview, IL: Scott, Foresman.

Peters, B. Guy. 1978. *The Politics of Bureaucracy: A Comparative Perspective.* London: Longman.

Podgorecki, Adam. 1975. *Practical Social Sciences.* London: Routledge and Kegan Paul.

Poggi, Gianfranco. 1978. *The Development of the Modern State.* London: Hutchinson.

Poole, M. 1975. *Workers' Participation in Industry.* London: Routledge and Kegan Paul.

Porter, L. M., and E. E. Lawler. 1968. *Managerial Attitudes and Performance.* Homewood, IL: Irwin.

Porter, L. M., and R. M. Steers. 1973. "Organizational, Work and Personal Factors in Employee Turnover and Absenteeism." *Psychological Bulletin* 80.

Prasad, S. Benjamin, and Anat R. Negandhi, eds. 1968. *Managerialism for Economic Development. Essays on India.* The Hague: Martinus Nijoff.

Presthus, Robert. 1978. *The Organizational Society.* New York: St. Martin's.

Ramirez, Bruno. 1973. "Industrial Conflict and Industrial Relations in Italy: New Perspective." *Relations Industrielles* 28, 3:617–26.

Reif, W. C., and P. P. Schoderbek. 1971. "Job Enlargement: Antidote to Apathy." In *Personnel Management,* edited by D. E. McFarland. Harmondsworh (U.K.): Penguin.

Rhenman, E. 1968. *Industrial Democracy and Industrial Management.* London: Tavistock.

——————. 1970. *Co-operation and Conflict in Organizations.* New York: Wiley.

Richman, B. M. 1965. *Soviet Management.* Englewood Cliffs, NJ: Prentice-Hall.

Ritzer, George. 1977. *Working: Conflict and Change.* Englewood Cliffs, NJ: Prentice-Hall.

Roberts, B. C. 1956. *Trade Union Government and Administration.* Bell.

Roethlisberger, F. J., and W. J. Dickson. 1939. *Management and the Worker.* Cambridge: Harvard University Press.

Roosevelt, F. 1970. "Market Socialism: A Humane Economy?" *Review of Radical Political Economics* 2, 1.

Schein, E. H. 1965. *Organizational Psychology.* Englewood Cliffs, NJ: Prentice-Hall.

Schmitt, C. 1963. *Der Begriff des politischen.* Berlin.

Schumacher, E. F. 1973. *Small is Beautiful.* New York: Harper Torchbooks.

Schurmann, F. 1966. *Ideology and Organization in Communist China.* Berkeley and Los Angeles: University of California Press.

Scott, W. R. 1981. *Organizations.* Englewood Cliffs, NJ: Prentice-Hall.

Seitz, S. T. 1979. *Bureaucracy, Policy and the Public.* St. Louis: Mosby.

Shils, E. A. 1956. *The Torment of Secrecy.* Chicago: Free Press.

Silverman, David. 1970. *The Theory of Organizations.* London: Heinemann.

Simon, Herbert. 1960. *The New Science of Management Decision.* New York: Harper.

Sutermeister, R. E., ed. 1976. *People and Productivity.* New York: McGraw-Hill.

Tannenbaum, Arnold, ed. 1968. *Control in Organization.* New York: McGraw-Hill.

——————, ed. 1974. *Hierarchy in Organizations.* San Francisco: Jossey Bass.

Tausky, C. 1970. *Work Organizations.* Itasca, IL: F. E. Peacock.

Thoenes, Piet. 1966. *The Elite in the Welfare State.* New York: McGraw-Hill.

Thompson, J. D., ed. 1971. *Approaches to Organizational Design.* Pittsburgh: University of Pittsburgh Press.

Touraine, Alain. 1969. *La Societé Post-industrielle: Naissance d'une Societé*. Paris.

Turner, L., and J. Ash. 1975. *The Golden Hordes*. London: Constable.

Udy, S. H., Jr. 1959. *Organization of Work: A Comparative Analysis of Production Among Non-industrial Peoples*. New Haven: Hraf Press.

Vroom, V. H. 1976. "Leadership." In *Handbook of Industrial and Organizational Psychology*, edited by M. D. Dunnette. Chicago: Rand McNally.

Warwick, Dennis. 1974. *Bureaucracy*. London: Longman.

Weiss, C. H., and A. H. Barton. 1980. *Making Bureaucracies Work*. Beverly Hills, CA: Sage.

Whitehill, A. M., Jr. and S. Takezawa. 1968. *The Other Worker*. Honolulu: East-West Center Press.

Whyte, W. M., Jr. 1950. "Framework for the Analysis of Industrial Relations: Two Views." *Industrial and Labor Relations Review* 3, 3.

—————. 1957. *The Organization Man*. Garden City, NY: Doubleday.

Woodward, Joan. 1980. *Industrial Organization. Theory and Practice*. London: Oxford University Press.

8

THE DISCONTENTS
OF MASS SOCIETY

PARADOXES OF GROWTH

The process of historical change is full of paradoxes. The ruling classes evolve from the promoters of progress into the defenders of status quo. Formal organizations, by promoting their effectiveness, become alienated from their original goals. Accumulation of goods and privileges converts people into slaves of their own power. Freedom becomes a self-defeating desire. Conversion of people in commodities leads to a "mass society" in which no one any longer controls the machinery. Widespread planning concludes in a wide-ranging chaos of competing private interests. Myths become realities and social realities become mythologized for the sake of political manipulation. The question which should be asked is how much real democracy exists in the various kinds of democratic institutions.

The founding fathers of the Protestant revolution did not intend to contribute to the development of capitalism, just as Marx or even Lenin probably did not intend the Stalinist version of totalitarianism. Revolutions quite often lead to something entirely different than was intended (Brinton 1965). Any utopia becomes a reactionary enterprise if its authors try to impose their dreams upon people against the public will. The danger of disorder and common deprivation has to be avoided even at a high cost. There is something utopian in a dream about such an equality which would allow some kind of order and efficiency to dominate over chaos and ineptitude (Audrey 1970).

What the future will look like depends upon us. There is an obvious dialectical contradiction between our *active* role in shaping the future and practical inability to predict the final outcome of our own efforts. How to find a satisfactory synthesis?

Taking the position of a prophet one may pretend to *know* the future and formulate authoritarian judgments about the past, present and future. Another alternative, much more attractive, is to take the stand of a *jester*, in the sense used by Leszek Kolakowski:

> The jester's attitude is an endless attempt to reflect on the various arguments for contradictory ideas, an attitude dialectical by its very nature—simply to overcome what is because it is: a jester does not jeer out of sheer contrariness; he jeers because he mistrusts the stabilized world. In a world where allegedly everything has already happened, the jester's contribution is an always active imagination which thrives on the resistance it must overcome (Leszek 1971, p. 7).

There is a need to make a distinction in societies between on the one hand the *historical* social order as a product of a long-term socialization processes and the culture-creating activities, and on the other hand the *manipulatory* social order based on the more or less conscious and purposeful conditioning of the masses to behave in a way expected and promoted by those in power. Of course, both these models of social order coexist with one another and the social reality is the product of spontaneous as well as manipulatory processes. However, depending upon which factor prevails in a given social order, historical or manipulatory, there are different problems to be faced.

Social systems are traditionally of a conventional character, namely they are based on mutual understandings and agreements sufficiently petrified to appear as relatively stable. Conventions allow people to communicate and cooperate meaningfully and also to formulate judgments effectively and make decisions on the basis of a minimum mutual acceptance. Dependence on conventions goes together with the tendency to close the system and to make it independent of external factors.[1]

The modern developed market society is also of a con-

ventional nature and has a strong tendency to close itself
to the external world, allocating its own resources mainly to
the internal manipulation of consumption, power, and
values. Thus, the conventional nature of social bonds is
alienated from the historical context (the denial of continuity), becomes a matter of convenience, and appeals only to
its own supposed rationality, practicality, and utility.[2] In
this way the Western "rational" societies, whether they want
to or not, gradually isolate themselves from the rest of the
world which does not accept the same rules of reasoning.

In Western thinking it is taken for granted that everything can be reduced to rational proportions, that nonra-
tionality must decrease progressively and finally disappear.
However, the nonrational factor underlies societies and this
is what myth is all about. Societies exist by virtue of
history, and they try to pretend it does not exist, they do
not measure themselves by it.

The role of history is to furnish us a framework with
which we can superimpose the present onto the past so that
we may predict a future (Levy-Strauss 1979, p. 29). In
historical social orders, continuity is crucial and quite often
for the sake of it the innovative endeavors are sacrificed.[3]

In the existential game of an artificial society those
leading and those led depend on one another and in order
to survive must accept certain rules of mutual adaptation;
but this relationship is void of any deeper feeling of mutual
trust and appreciation. On the contrary, those led by
compliments and reassurances which reinforce their own
self-image, are constantly endangered by the insecurity of
their own existence; at the same time they treat assurance
of the manipulators as a pep talk and are aware of the
interests which are behind. Those leading may have a
deeply rooted distaste for the objects of their manipulation
who have to be complimented or even cheated in order to
keep the establishment intact. The nature of the game is
who finally will outwit whom, or push the partner into a
corner, enforcing his or her own interest by an effective
submission of the remaining interests.

The development of this game is conditioned and reinforced by the progressive decline of traditional social bonds
and authorities, as well as the dominance of big complex
organizations (state, political parties, schools, corporations,
unions, and so forth) in the modernizing societies based on
money economy, market exchange of goods and commodities.
Changes in the social organization of modernizing societies
make necessary the adequate transformations of policies and
manipulations; on the other hand, the latter have some
impact on the organizational transformations by reinforcing

some of them and discouraging others.[4]

The culture of mass society is devoid of anything that unites people beyond their material interests. The gradual decline of religious beliefs plays here also an important role. In the period 1900–1980 the nonreligious and atheists have grown in the world from 0.2 percent to 21 percent at the cost mainly of Chinese folk religion (a decline from almost 24 percent to a little over 4 percent), Eastern Orthodox (a decline from 7.5 percent to 3 percent), tribal and shamanist (a decline from 7 percent to 2 percent), and so forth. The Roman Catholic share has grown a little (from 17 percent to 18.5 percent) and Christians in general have preserved their one-third share of the world population. The Muslim and Hindu shares have grown (the first from 12 percent to almost 17 percent, and the second from a little over 12 percent to 13 percent). The percentage of Protestants has declined from a little over 9 to 8 (Barrett 1983).

The ethos of present-day Westerners is shaped by mass media, easily available educational facilities, promises given by competing politicians, growing exposure to the experience outside locality, and large-scale import of foreign goods, but also by the worries which arise from the permanently high level of unemployment (especially among the young people), individual and collective debts, rising cost of living, shortage of reasonably priced housing, industrial strife, conflict between the metropolis and the peripheries, diminishing importance of religion in personal life, the generation gap, and so forth.

The liberal character of education and of a considerable part of the mass media contributes to the high level of life expectations that become frustrated by limits constantly met by the common people in the daily life: authoritarian work relations, financial inability to satisfy growing personal needs, traditionalistic character of existing social and cultural institutions, persistence of political patterns that do not meet the challenge of new reality. All this leads to the growing discrepancy between what people expect from life (which may not be realistic enough) and what they obtain. This imposes a great strain on society as a whole.

Many social institutions are in a growing crisis: costs of education, health services, public administration, and other rapidly developing services are constantly growing at the expense of the taxpayers, but the average wage or salary earner does not necessarily gain proportionately. Chronic unemployment puts into question the value of at least some educational inputs, especially if there is a gap between what kind of labor power the economy needs and that which is the educational product of the school system.

The progressing sophistication of the modern health services allows people to live who would die earlier without aid; at the same time the returns from inputs into the health services are very much diminishing. In order to improve these returns it would be necessary to change the daily life and eating habits of the population (preventive medicine), which would mean acting against the vested interests of the most powerful and influential pressure groups. The education of a responsible and thoughtful consumer is very much neglected in many modern societies, and preventive medicine is treated as something marginal.

In the field of public administration there has been a very substantial growth of bureaucracy (for example, in the United Kingdom during the period 1900–1970, the total governmental expenditure grew eleven-fold but the GNP only three-fold (Sleeman 1973, p. 106), but it has not been followed by an adequate improvement of services such as social planning, elimination of poverty pockets, better standards, more peaceful social relations, and so forth. On the contrary, growth of the nonprofit sector has been closely followed by the establishment of several new groups of particularistic interests, looseness of the performance criteria, low motivation of people who work in this sector, and dissatisfaction of their clients. In the United States the role of the state has grown and even under Republican administrations the civil service remains a powerful factor. The disassembly of the government, and a really free market are a far cry even under the Reagan presidency.[5]

The preoccupation of people and institutions with economic security leads to the rules and regulations which persist because someone's income is higher than it would be if the regulations did not exist. All economies are sets of rules and regulations—there is no such thing as the unregulated economy.

> Without government regulations there are no property rights, and without property rights there is no free market. . . . The real question and the real debate revolves not around the virtues of the regulated versus the unregulated economy, but around the question what constitutes a good set of regulations (Thurow 1981, pp. 129, 131).

PROBLEMS OF THE MASS SOCIETY

In the mass society, complex organizations replace communities, competition for scarce resources replaces cooperation,[6] mass media replace localized social bonds as well as moral and cultural commitments of a personalized nature.

> Like mass organizations, mass arenas are managed from the center rather than structured through social relations. . . . All members of mass society are equally valued as voters, buyers, and spectators. Numerical superiority therefore tends to be the decisive criterion of success. . . . Mass equalitarianism emphasizes the similarities of individuals rather than the uniqueness of persons (Kornhauser 1968, vol. 10, p. 59).

Complex institutions based on bureaucratic principles became organizational weapons in modern societies.

Organization is supposed to function as an extension of human natural capacities as well as a device to coordinate the efforts exercised by the individuals and groups who are supposed to cooperate with each other. However, any organization becomes almost automatically a playground for various vested interests, aspirations, and concerns. They introduce an important correction to the existing conditions which either may harm the goal-achievement of a given organization or help quite substantially to implement the goals. From a sociotechnical perspective, it is very important to perceive organizations simultaneously as "rational" machines as well as "natural" collectivities (Matejko, 1984). The first perception gives priority to the optimal coordination of various functions and structures in the terms of efficiency. The second perception gives priority to the satisfaction of all stakeholders involved in a given organization: members, leaders, clients, sponsors, and so on.

An artificial order enters many fields, and even leisure patterns become influenced by progressing standardization. The "common man" purchases a stimulation which introduces into his or her monotonous life some attractive hazards. "The great mass of people who participate in institutional gambling like football pools and bingo are in the lower paid, low-skilled or repetitive occupations" (Glasser 1970, p. 140).[7]

Mass consumption patterns shape the mentality of the labor class, its position versus professionals, and the "higher circles," as well as exercise a meaningful influence on the relationship between developed and developing countries.

During the 1970s there were some observable changes in the pattern of consumer spending in the U.S. population, due mainly to unemployment and inflation. The richest quintile of households have maintained their comfortable position (only 20 percent spent in the household budget on food, energy, household supplies, personal care, alcohol and tobacco) when in the poorest quintile this basic expenditure has grown to 79 percent (energy has grown from 14 percent to 25 percent); the average for all households has grown from 31 percent to 34 percent. According to the 1980/81 data, with the growth of household income there is a fast growth in the amount of food eaten away from home; the share of this food expenditure has grown from around one-fifth to one-third since the 1960s (Robey and Russell 1983).

The consumer changes have much to do with some structural transformations. During the 1970s the share of households with more than one earner has grown from a half to three-fifths, mainly due to the growing employment of women. "The rise of two-earner households has spurred markets for luxury items and other discretionary spending, while households with lower incomes are worse off today than they were a decade ago because they must spend more for the basic" (Ibid., p. 20). For example, persons aged 65 and older spend almost half of the income on basics (food, energy, and the like) in comparison with less than one-third among people aged 25 to 34.

Within mass society there are some obvious strains on the labor market, in the field of higher education, politics, application of the scientific approach to social policy, relative position of middle strata in the social hierarchy, freedom of dissent within the existing social institutions, and so forth.

One of the difficult problems in mass societies is related to the "surplus" people; for example, old people become estranged from the society. This is the result of several factors; first of all, if successive generations internalize different sets of values then common language is lacking between parents and their children, and even more, between grandparents and grandchildren. Without at least some common values, which may be provided only by an intergenerational common culture, there is a small probability that an effective communication will exist between generations.

Second, in the modern Western civilization the social role of old people is quite limited. There is no need for their contribution.

In some respects the elderly could be said to be kept at arm's length from the social structure.

Many of their problems, though by no means all, arise as the consequence of formal actions on the part of mass society that confirm their separate retired status. Political actions are taken to introduce social security legislation, permit cheap travel on public transport, and build special types of housing. Public services, private corporations, and large firms adopt fixed ages of retirement. The public increasingly identifies "the old," "pensioners," or "the retired" as a special category in society. Many of the elderly themselves tend to resist such identification and reveal their uneasiness about it" (Shanas 1968, p. 425).

Third, as long as the isolation of old people is in progress, there is for them less and less hope of maintaining some meaningful social relationships with others.

Role loss leads to role ambiguity in old age. . . . There is a general devaluation of the aged. . . . Older people share the invidious beliefs about the aged. . . . To exempt themselves from these invidious social judgments, the aged retain youthful self-images. . . . Viable friendships do not spontaneously develop between age groups, but are confined almost exclusively within them. . . . Under these conditions, the social world of old people contracts. Their estrangement from previous roles and memberships deprives them of central group supports as well as responsibility, power, privilege, resources, and prestige. These deprivations are a distinctive discontinuity in life which they have little incentive to accept and for which they are not systematically prepared or socialized (Rosow 1967, pp. 30–35).[8]

The criticism of a mass society from the elitist viewpoint (Ortega, Tocqueville) as well as from the antitotalitarian positions (Mannheim, Neumann, Arendt, Brzezinski) misses to a large extent the positive aspects of liberating human resources from ascriptive bonds.

While in the Western developed mass societies there is a general decrease of primary relations because of "the attenuation of the *links* between primary relations and the major functional areas of society" (Kornhauser 1968, vol. 10, p. 62), in many other modernizing societies the primary relations gain an entirely new role. As long as the secondary relations do not function effectively, and as long as the supply of old age benefits is much inadequate, the primary bonds are the only security. Kinship, friendship, and common descent provide mutual support. The "folk community" imposed upon the formally depersonalized socio-economic system represents an antisystem which is in constant conflict with the formal structure; both of them are unable to develop to a full extent because they contradict one another.

On the other hand each has some vested interests in preserving the existing shaky order: the "folk community" takes advantage of all shortcomings of the formal structure (bribary, promotion on informal criteria, distribution of resources according to mutual benefits and not according to merit, and so on); the formal structure is unable to function without being supplemented by a whole network of informal channels. Traditional authorities lose their moral appeal, except the authority of temporary informal alliances, which allows people to achieve a relative security within the set of interwoven formal and informal relations.

The search for community becomes limited to the search for a few friends upon whom it would be possible to rely. However, these friendship ties are also spurious because they are not strong enough to survive under the impact of complex organizations. Whenever the latter achieve some measure of effectiveness, as in the case of secret police, the army, or the disciplined political party of an elitist nature, mutual personal loyalties no longer count. Disloyalty becomes a common phenomenon because in a mass society there are not effective informal sanctions. The change in the formal organization becomes a substitute for a change in substance. The manipulation of structural units becomes an end in itself.

There has been a long historical tradition of manipulating people through work (Anthony 1977) but now, leisure, too, has become an object of manipulation on a scale never appearing before in history. This is not a matter of the ruling class conspiracy, as suggested primarily by Marxists, but first of all of the systemic necessity.[9] In *mass society* people have been reduced to the standardized role objects of manipulation by mass media, complex organizations and centers of power (Kornhauser 1968, p. 59). Monotonous lives and boring jobs lead many members of mass societies, especially in the lower pay brackets, to an intensive search for attractive hazards and narcotics: gambling, hazardous sports, excessive consumption of spirits, heavy smoking, and so on.

A substantial weakening of primary bonds in the mass society and a relatively high rate of social mobility (or at least the aspiration to move up on the social ladder), both introduce the factor of *mass anxiety,* which stimulates mass consumption but at the same time leads to mass neuroticism. The progress of material well-being does not necessarily contribute to a higher level of satisfaction; on the contrary, people who have more very often show a much higher level of aspirations which are at least partly unfulfilled and therefore, breed dissatisfaction.[10]

THE IMPACT OF MASS SOCIETY ON LEISURE

The rapid development of modern mass media and the deep penetration of private life by them has opened room to the mass manipulation of leisure by big organizations. In the market it is becoming more and more difficult for small organizations to preserve their independence; larger and more *powerful* organizations squeeze their weaker rivals out of the market.[11]

In the Western world the model of an "organizational society" (Presthus 1978) and the social control based on "the business of inventing and flourishing treacherous parodies of freedom, joy and fulfillment" (Roszak 1969, p. 15) have led to a negative reaction, particularly among the young generation, against the society "in which those who govern justify themselves by appealing to technical experts, who, in turn, justify themselves by appeal to scientific forms of knowledge. And beyond the authority of science, there is no appeal" (Ibid., p. 8).

People now have more free time than before and what they do with it becomes of crucial importance not only for them as individuals but also for society. In the model of an organizational society there is a very strong emphasis on the manipulation of free time through mass media in order to extend the volume of consumption and conformism.[12]

Industrial democracies under the pressure of growing expectations related to improved standards of education, the relative well-being, and the growing articulation of special interests (various pressure groups), have to pay more attention to public demands. The sociopolitical and economic balance of modern society becomes more and more vulnerable to mass anxiety. The growth of inflation has undermined the trust of consumers in the rationality and morality of a system under which thriftiness does not pay and wastefulness pays. The growth of unemployment, particularly among the young, has undermined the trust in the developmental potential of the system. At the same time there are no attractive alternatives, especially because communism is a disappointment. People around the world migrate now more than before and change their allegiances in the search of better conditions but the chances to find a "leisure paradise" are diminishing instead of growing.[13]

In developed mass societies people have regained time, which was taken away from them during the Industrial Revolution. However, it is uncertain how much leisure people really gain during their free time activities, in the sense of a disinterested relaxation that would be liberated from daily routine and would be spiritually enriching (Dumazedier 1974, pp. 75–76). So far, spare time is experienced by many people as a vacuum and they look to fill the void (Friedmann 1970). This awareness of emptiness as well as the urge to gain more money for more spending, pushes one-quarter of the workers in developed countries to moonlight (Dumazedier 1974, p. 23).[14]

It is the vested interest of modern complex organizations to promote a work commitment among employees. They praise the virtues of a "serious" worker who is loyal to his or her employer, enjoys his or her work and is willing to commit time and effort for the benefits of the company. At the same time, in order to gain clients and sympathizers, the big organizations have to accommodate themselves to the growing leisure orientation of the general population. This leads to some contradictions; on the one hand, big organizations expect their own employees to behave in a traditional manner, but on the other hand, they encourage the general public to pursue a far-reaching consumerism.

Big organizations are forced to promote their own "seriousness" against the leisure-oriented countercultures, which are in many respects much more responsive to the problems and worries of modern people facing inflation, the danger of unemployment, estrangement from their own human environment, and meaninglessness of life. The manipulatory nature of means available to these organizations is in itself a limiting factor.[15]

From the perspective widely shared by many modern people, including the members and employees of big organizations, leisure should be something spontaneous in order to fulfill its important sociopsychological functions. According to Dumazedier, man achieves a state of leisure only when he liberates himself from the strains of daily boredom, and escapes the routine (1974, p. 76). People try also to achieve some maturity, self-awareness and a better understanding of the relationship between themselves, nature, other people, and the universe. In all developed countries, the growth of countercultures has cast a doubt on the conformistic and manipulative character of the styles of leisure which are widely promoted by mass advertising.[16]

The climate of seriousness around complex organizations is a heritage of the past that does not necessarily fit into modern realities; pretension and falsification of reality both become almost necessities. There is a growing effort to manipulate the motivation of employees, but already the widely manifested "seriousness" of these efforts is self-defeating. Games played by various organizational units against each other, as well as the pomposity of the grandiose projects promoted without a genuine concern for the final outcome, strengthen the achievement motivation of their promoters but in the long run they are damaging.[17] There is not much chance that complex organizations will be able to incorporate successfully the concept of public welfare into their own meaning of "seriousness."

Within the market society, the competitive game played by business organizations puts aside the common welfare, giving priority to particularistic interests. Within the socialist economy, the vested interests of bureaucratic bodies dominate over the interests of the population, which is denied the articulation of their specific priorities. Under both democratic systems and communism, the rise of common well-being is followed by more articulated mass demands related to the whole scope of new needs which could not crystallize under the modest material conditions.

PLURALISM UNDER SCRUTINY

The pluralist perspective of the modern democratic societies, widely accepted among liberals as well as among conservatives, is based on questionable assumptions. Do the existing sociopolitical systems possess adequate means of redress, representation, and responsiveness of leadership? Does the competition among various elites really allow maintenance of a counterbalance among them?

> The theorist perceives the plural political society as a guarantor of widened participation and representation, increased diffusion of power, and minimization of coercion; both the reality of contemporary democratic society and the dynamics of a pluralist political system significantly fail to exhibit an achievement of the ends for large sectors of the population" (Halebsky 1976, p. 184).

The corporate structure of the "establishment" based on mutual connections and interdependencies between big business, government, unions, various pressure groups, politicians, and the military allows absorption and smoothing out of tensions but at the same time makes broader public control highly ineffective. The growth of moral conscience in society leads to the progressing recognition of several needs and demands that not long ago were available only to the elite.[18]

With a growing number of people "in the middle," their life orientation plays a greater role in the developed mass societies, but this does not necessarily mean more individualism. The upward shift of incomes has given governments much more opportunity to extend taxation; the share of the public sector has grown enormously.[19] The dependence on the public sector has become a fact of life under "guided" capitalism and the question is how, in the long run, this may be reconciled with the traditional spirit of individualism and free enterprise.

The growth of corporate private and public power puts into question the practical ability of the powerless "outsiders," (even if the latter constitute the great majority of the population) to exercise a significant pressure, especially when these "outsiders" are objects of a highly sophisticated mass manipulation. Competition among the powerful corporate bodies does not necessarily constrain their power as long as this competition remains within the framework of certain standards beneficial to all competitors and therefore maintained by them voluntarily and dutifully.[20]

Power is diffused even in the highly centralized systems, as for example in the Soviet socialist state. The totalitarian explanatory model of society (Friedrich and Brzezinski 1966) simplifies the complicated state of affairs, whether socialist or capitalist, by underrating the pressure exercised by various groups of vested interests.

The reality of the highly authoritarian societies seems to be better explainable in terms of mutual interdependence of those who lead and those who are led. Polyarchy is the natural state of affairs in social structures which grow in their complexity under the impact of technological progress, the rise of population and territorial extension. Sources of influence necessarily become redistributed with the general growth of resources and their dispersion. Many diverse groups seek power at the local level and compete one against another. With the progressing division of labor, various occupational categories crystallize their own vested interests and provide impetus to the establishment of groups and institutions which do their best to make the higher centers of power responsive to their demands.

Those undeniable facts of life show that at least some

decentralization of power is a reality. However, the process of conceptualization of this pluralistic social reality is not only an intellectual exercise but also a political fact. The pluralist model may be prevented from appearing in public by the denial to certain social categories and groups the possibility to articulate their interests. Some interest groups dominate over others and their respective chances of articulation remain highly unequal. For example, in the United States, "in the areas of defense spending, farm programs, tariffs, trade provisions, transport and highways, fields, road and housing construction, land use, and mass media and communication, policy becomes almost the distinct province or enclave of specific interests. The broader public, including some of those most directly affected by decision-making in these areas, frequently has little access or control over them in practice" (Halebsky 1976, p. 195). However, the pluralistic trends are also evident and seem to now be much stronger than ever before in the history of mankind.

THE NATURE OF MASS MANIPULATION

The theatrum mundi of mass societies is dominated by the factor of manipulation, and the "conspiratory" function of various elites is only one aspect of it. The elimination of an elite without changing the rules of the game must necessarily lead to the repetition of the same pattern under a new leadership. Manipulation enters the place emptied by traditional religious doctrines and ideologies that have lost touch with reality. The moral bonds among people deteriorate, leaving the individual to himself and opening room to narcissism. Industrialism and urbanization both have contributed to the growing horizontal and vertical mobility of people without necessarily more genuine freedom.

In the democratic mass societies, the people enjoy the legal opportunity to organize themselves in defense of their freedoms as citizens, consumers, producers, members of various ethnic or religious groups, and so on. On the other hand, the manipulation of collective consciousness under the conditions of a relative freedom happens to be quite often much more penetrating than when civil freedoms are lacking. The commercialized mass society appeals to the material needs of the individual, his or her ambition and self-respect. The success of socialization for good or bad so far has been much higher under democratic capitalism than in the totalitarian mass societies founded mainly on brutal force.

The Marxist analysis of modern mass Western society usually provides a vulgarized conspirational interpretation of it. In a modern theatrum mundi all actors are involved and the manipulators become slaves of their own manipulations. The seriousness with which people act on the market prevents them from outdistancing themselves from their own deeds.

Divisions and struggles between various decision-making elites of modern mass societies are deadly serious and do not cease even under the condition of external threat. The penetration of human minds by the collective consciousness, typical of a mass society, is far-reaching. In the traditional societies based on a strict social hierarchy and cultural differentiation, there was naturally much less mutual class interpenetration. The modern popular culture in the West as well as in the East is so dominant that in the cultural sense people belonging to various strata become more and more alike in many respects. The situation in modern times is in this respect much different from the early stages of industrialization.

In the modern "intimate society" (Sennett 1978, p. 220) based on the narcissistic obsession of individuals, self-gratification, suspension of independent judgment, erosion of public life, the mystification of collective identities in order to make people amenable to manipulation, the human freedom and the self-development become limited due to the external restrictions and falsifications of reality. "A society with a very low level of interaction between its members, dominated by ideas of the individual, and unstable personality, is likely to give birth through fantasy to enormously destructive collective personalities" (Ibid., p. 238).

The decline of deeper social bonds among members of modern societies prevents them from fulfilling the role of "public men," who are expected to act from the position of their moral responsibility. This, together with the development of modern cities, industrialization, commercialization, and democratization has been creating for a long time, a process of transformation that finally has led to an imbalanced personal life and empty public life (Ibid., p. 16).

The criticism of "intimate society" raised by Sennett makes a great deal of sense as long as the negative aspects of it are considered, mainly the fact that the "privatization" of public affairs and commercialized manipulation both act to the detriment of individual and society. What can be done in order to re-establish "the public man" as a valid alternative? Sennett is vague in this respect and he does not go beyond suggestions that people should defend their individual and collective interests. "The extent to which people can learn to pursue aggressively their interest in society is the extent to which they learn to act impersonally" (Ibid., p. 340). He would like to see in modern urban conditions "the forum in which it becomes meaningful to join with other persons without the compulsion to know them as persons" (Ibid., p. 340).

Tasks of public nature may bring together people vitally interested in them and provide a suitable platform for deeper sociomoral bonds in which the sense of duty would become reinforced. Under the reign of complex bureaucratic organizations, there is not much room for the spontaneous crystallization of "public interests" which would function as the agents of socialization. Sennett misses this point almost completely and in addition he does not seem to be aware of the process of reification and its impact on narcissism. The commercial endeavor to stimulate needs among the customers explains why narcissism has become a mass phenomenon.

The reinvigoration of social bonds and of the "public man" who would take active interest in the promotion of common good, happens usually as a function of necessity.[21] In addition there is also the problem of a moral revolt of people against a system which does not satisfy their deeper needs, offends their self-esteem, undermines their dignity.

Commercialization of human feeling goes together with the development of modern services. In order to enhance the status of the customer, as in the case of the flight attendants, or to deflate this status, as in the case of the bill collectors, service people commit themselves to the artificial games of emotions. This "emotional labor" involves a considerable psychological and moral cost carried by the "emotion makers" and potentially harmful to them. The "false self" is promoted as a commercial product, which benefits the service company but harms the worker.

> When the product—the thing to be engineered, mass-produced, and subjected to speed-up and slowdown—is a smile, a mood, a feeling, or a relationship, it comes to belong more to the organization and less to the self. And so in the country that most publicly celebrates the individual, more people privately wonder, without tracing the question to its deepest social root. What do I really feel? (Hochschild 1983, p. 198).

Mass society, being based on manipulation and the reduction of human beings to standardized objects maneuvered according to the vested interests of the manipulators, profoundly limits individual freedom. This is especially evident in mass societies where the civil rights of citizens are not tolerated by rulers. However, even in the democratic mass societies, in practice individual freedoms and opportunities for self-growth are endangered by the manipulation of consciousness from the top.

Sennett is right in emphasizing the sinister role in this respect of narcissism which

> is now motivated in social relations by a culture deprived of belief in the public and ruled by intimate feeling as a measure of the meaning of reality. . . . The result of the narcissistic version of reality is that the expressive powers of adults are reduced. . . . Boundaries are erased between the person's actions in the institution and the judgments the institution makes of his innate abilities, character strengths, and the like. . . . Action at a distance from the self is rendered difficult for the person to believe in. . . . The focus upon the innate qualities of the self is on potentials for action rather than specific actions accomplished (Sennett 1978, pp. 326–27).

THE DANGER OF MISINFORMATION

A considerable danger for society is involved in the powerful complex organizations masking their real intentions and their own internal conflicts in order to present the grandiose facade of bureaucratic feudalism.

> Outsiders will then conceive of the organization as a whole rather than as an array of diverse and even conflicting interests. . . . Good workers are increasingly defined in terms of their ability not to cause trouble; good work is "hassle free" for those above them, who in turn resolve the majority of problems before they reach their superiors. . . . Bureaucratic propaganda and its related justificatory accounts divert attention toward an "enemy out there," rather than the "enemy within" (Altheide and Johnson 1980, pp. 235–36.).

Truth becomes the object of organizational manipulation in order to promote the vested interests of a given complex organization. The real organizational performance cannot be adequately encompassed within the parameters purposefully selected by the organization and imposed on the ignorant public. Who really knows that the TV rating is doubtful methodologically, that accounts of inefficiency are doctored in order to hide obvious failures, that soul-counting in evangelical crusades is obviously unreliable, that news reports are a vehicle for self-serving organizational accounts, that welfare records do not necessarily coincide with the public service accorded to welfare recipients, and so on? Who is powerful and honest enough in society to prevent misinformation from continuing? As long as the reports "have a purpose, a career, and a meaning in their own right" (Ibid., p. 237) and the qualitative difference between appearance and reality remains confused, there is a real danger that the society remains ignorant about some vary basic dimensions of its own existence and future.

Modern complex organizations have not only a vital interest in creating their good image but in addition they have the power to do it deliberately and effectively. The public suspects distortion of truth and revolts against experts, but rich and influential organizations have the power and money to manipulate an image of reality that suits them. As long as the public is fed with information manipulated by organizational promoters and has essentially no other sources easily available, there is no choice but to accept the information provided, character of this information, and the editing process that has shaped it. The merits of the case are usually unknown to the public, and there is no alternative but to choose one of the vested interest groups and to accept its expertise. The appearance of fairness counts under such circumstances as a propagandistic weapon and is skillfully manipulated by the public relations men in order to benefit their sponsor.

One of the problems here is that science becomes an extension of bureaucratic propaganda and scientists in various fields become servants of power without even being conscious of it. Scientists may be helpful to complex organizations by providing them with the foundations of an efficient propaganda that "inhibits citizens from seeing that their own reifications of cultural myths are the major impediments to social change, including governmental performance" (Altheide and Johnson 1980, p. 41). On the other hand, science equates in the public image with the promotion of a rational approach and this may happen at the expense of truth and real effectiveness. Even evangelical counseling, as a practical and formally rational task, may easily become contaminated by its bureaucratic forms and the moral content of evangelism may be blurred. On the other hand, in order to make evangelical crusades a mass success, it is almost impossible to avoid the efforts of a rational nature that would allow upgrading of these crusades according to the principles of organizational effectiveness and *rentability.*

The public relations function of bureaucratic propaganda is almost unavoidable in a modern world dominated by complex organizations. However, the full awareness of dangers related to this propaganda—among others, in the field of leisure—is also badly needed. The moral aspects of any activity oriented toward the distortion of truth are quite obvious and should be appreciated by everybody. According to Altheide and Johnson, "The most creative work in organizations, including new bureaucracies, has been directed to improving appearances and rhetoric rather than substance; indeed, the appearance and front work have become the 'real substance,' what really counts for all practical purposes" (1980, p. 237).[22]

The "seriousness" of modern complex organizations becomes questionable when image-making considerations of a propagandistic nature gain full priority. This is particularly evident in the leisure-oriented business advertising. On the other hand, the present-day mass obsession with leisure may be justified at least to some extent by the defensiveness of people against organizational manipulation. The lack of trust in relation to big organizations leads many people to mental withdrawal from organizational "seriousness," and later to the heavy reliance on leisure as an essence of private life.

THE SOCIAL IMPACT OF MASS ADVERTISING

The social impact of technological progress is very often not fully understood by contemporaries.[23] As McLuhan says,

> The "message" of any medium or technology is the change of scale or pace or pattern that it introduces into human affairs. . . . It is the medium that shapes and controls the scale and form of human association and action. The content or uses of such media are as diverse as they are ineffectual in shaping the form of human association and action (1974).

"Nobody yet knows the languages inherent in the new technological culture. We are all technological idiots in terms of new situations" (1969).

Complex organizations in the manipulation of societies are using television as one of the major weapons and therefore it is useful to understand the nature of persuasion daily bombarding people through the screens located in family rooms all around the world, except the poorest regions, where in any event people have little control of their own destiny. To what extent may human minds and emotions be shaped through TV messages? Taking into consideration that the TV business itself constitutes a network of powerful organizations, and cooperates closely with other centers of organizational power, the impact of TV on human life needs to be carefully scrutinized.

In all developed countries TV-watching now occupies much time, and especially among those less educated, less affluent, old, very young and unemployed. Passive home entertainment still dominates even in the affluent societies, and TV has the major role in it.[24] Complex organizations have a vested interest in maintaining and even strengthening the above-mentioned state of affairs in the field of entertainment. It exposes the TV-watchers to the established channels of a one-sided communication, and on the other hand, weakens the social bonds and prevents the establishment of countervailing forces.

Modern organizational society consists of individuals devoid of strong primary bonds and totally dependent on secondary bonds effectively controlled by the centers of organizational power. This is particularly evident in the societies run by big state bureaucracies; for the latter state-controlled mass media, and among them primarily TV, become a major mechanism in keeping the consciousness of citizens under control.

TV-watching declines with a better education level and higher income. In the period 1965–75, average TV-watching per week has grown in the United States from 11 hours to 15 hours, more among women than among men. However, the percentage of those people who watch TV three hours and more daily has declined during the second half of the 1970s. According to the survey data, in the period 1975–78, the proportion of the population watching TV three or more hours per day fell from 52 percent to 46 percent, and the proportion of those watching per day no more than one hour grew from 21 percent to 27 percent.

Television-watching, if practiced excessively, has certain disadvantages related to the fact that the "medium is the message" (McLuhan 1974). It gives watchers the experience of being immediately present and living the experience of others, without gaining a really deep knowledge, without the understanding of the nature of things.

"Television gives to things the reality of being immediately present but denies their openness to inspection and scrutiny" (Emery and Emery 1975, p. 45). Familiarity is not the same as understanding. A real knowledge about things can not be provided by TV; it can only come through an active and personal involvement with the subject (Ibid., p. 107).

TV-viewing is goal-seeking but purposeless; its end is in its immediate consumption (Ibid., p. 70). While television rewards, it cannot motivate. It is true that people involve and even identify themselves with the television more than with other mass media. They seek in the television a relief from their own problems and become emotionally involved (Arons 1960). However, the affects aroused by the television modify only the relative intention of viewing itself (Emery and Emery 1975, p. 93).

The media of television evoke the basic assumption of dependency because they are essentially an emotional and irrational activity. It is like hypnotism; pleasant and rewarding as long as the escape from responsibility and control continues to be rewarding (Ibid., pp. 105–6). According to McLuhan, viewers do not count much because they are in a state of narcissistic narcosis. "Television is the non-stop leader who provides nourishment and protection" (Ibid.).

Television addicts are vulnerable to a growing distance between themselves and others, to the crisis of responsibility and to withdrawal. They become perfect parts of the mass society based on fragmented services and on the manipulative imposition upon people of unrealistic dreams. Affluence of television-watching becomes a substitute for the sense of community and plays the role of a self-deception (Pawley 1973; Bradbury 1953; Spinrad 1972). In this sense, television-watching, taken together with other mass media, is the vehicle of manipulation according to vested interests of the dominant pressure groups. These interests are quite often in disagreement with one another, if not in an open conflict, and this leads to the disharmonious programing of the television watchers' minds.[25]

Modern large organizations take full advantage of television advertising. Almost all households in the developed societies have television sets. There is a growing exposure of children as well as of old people to the television. In their formative years children spend around two-fifths of their spare time watching television, mostly shows and advertising. Middle-class stereotypes promoted by big organizations (for their own benefit) are imposed on children and shape an unrealistic image of the world which is heavily focused on leisure (Adler et al., 1980; Noble

1975; Brown 1975; Schramm and Parker 1961). People are misled into believing what is presented on the television such as: jobs shown on the television screen are in reality shared by relatively few people; life in general is much harder and more frustrating than is judged by television watching; expectations based on knowledge obtained through mass media may be highly misleading and frustrating.

The big organizations themselves become heavily dependent on television and this influences their functioning: advertising strategies have to be adapted to television conditions; managers who look well on the television screen gain advantage over others who do not share the same personal asset. On the other hand, television advertising based on superficial impressions of an emotional nature develops quite often at the expense of other concerns such as safety, quality products, good and inexpensive service, and so on.

THE DECLINE OF AUTHORITY

The present-day revolution of growing expectations in the mass societies is the ultimate consequence of the fact that under the impact of liberalism and the economic necessities of industrializing societies, the previously disenfranchised and generally neglected lower social classes managed to enter the historical scene since the nineteenth century. These classes in the process of their gradual upgrading mostly abandoned social bonds and institutions of a traditional nature, which at least partly, and in several cases even predominantly, functioned as control mechanisms for the benefit of upper classes. The economic, political, and social upgrading of the lower classes was followed by their gradual estrangement from the previous milieu, its social organization and culture. The traditional collective identity and solidarity were substantially weakened and dependence on external manipulatory forces has been unavoidable (Sennett 1978).

The next upper level of social stratification, the middle class, or at least its lower brackets, has become the reference group for the upgraded poor in respect to the material aspirations, leisure, and morals. However, even in the richest societies status and well-being have the tendency to grow faster than the ability and willingness of the establishment to meet the demands of the status-seekers; more and more lower class people strive to leave the traditional communities and find themselves among the middle-class suburbanites.

Under the impact of mass education (whatever its real quality), mass advertising and the egalitarian spirit of democracies, the number of people who look for social upgrading is constantly growing and they look for a place in the higher brackets of social hierarchy. On the other hand, the limits of growth met by developed countries, mainly the shortage of new jobs lead to unfulfilled desires and to the general feeling of insecurity. The establishment, in order to preserve the internal political and social equilibrium, is willing to assign several benefits for the masses within the framework of the welfare state. But inflation and unemployment undermine general welfare and make the achievement of the upgraded masses quite illusory. This appears dramatically in the case of the youth, who, after completing heavily subsidized educational programs enter the labor market. More and more job-seekers chase the few jobs available on the market, especially when the public sector does not grow so fast as it used to in the 1950s and the 1960s.

The decline of authority and prestige of the intermediary socializing institutions goes together with the expediency replacing tradition (Talmon 1952), rationalism replacing religion, and manipulation replacing trust relationships. Individuals want to be on their own instead of depending upon collective bodies. Freedom is identified with disengagement and the role of organizational structures is in reality not to socialize but to manipulate. In this way the social field has become emptied of any limits to the big play of vested interests which overshadows anything else and substitutes the "real man" by the whole variety of clichés like "mankind," "class," "nation," "common will," "public interest," and so on. Human dignity and well-being become abstract notions reduced to public relations by big organizations that bombard the masses with advertising and propaganda (Sennett 1978).

The idea of *equality* has played a major role in the conscious or subconscious destruction of deeper social bonds, which are not necessarily related to the constantly changing configurations of vested interests, but also rooted in moral commitments of a general nature. Under capitalism, equality has been very functional in upgrading all members of society to the status of consumers eager to have everything anytime. Under state socialism, equality strengthens the state power by making all people clients of the governmental institutions and this enlarging the control. In the developing countries the authoritarian regimes on the left as well as on the right use the cliché of equality in order to destroy the tribal and local affiliations which constantly endanger the centralized power. Under totalitarianism, the concept of general will taken over from Rousseau justifies the absolute rule exercised by the establishment which pretends to embody historical necessity.

Under all the above-mentioned circumstances, the idea of equality becomes widely misused for the benefit of manipulation under the pretense that equality is identical with public interest. It is taken for granted that inequality equals injustice—this assumption is at least questionable. The modern crisis of the welfare state, and especially the growing mass opposition to high taxation, sooner or later has to lead to a much more critical approach to the whole idea of social equality. Basically, there is nothing wrong with people remaining unequal as long as there is a guarantee that the inequality will not lead to exploitation (see the example of Sweden).

The reality of modern mass societies under capitalism as well as under socialism is far from equality anyway. Manipulators and manipulated do not have equal power. The strong vested interest groups enjoy several advantages over the general public: They are better informed, have means and adequate channels to act swiftly, control large areas of strategic importance, have will and power to act, are able to establish coalitions. The common people are very often misinformed, fragmented, do not dispose of adequate resources to countervail organized actions, become easily discouraged and even scared, have to depend mainly on themselves.

In the competition between the corporate interests and the unorganized crowd of common people the latter almost unavoidable become losers. Formally, the democratic system should remain open to all contending pressures. In reality, "without planned and intensive efforts, and these are usually lacking the functioning of a pluralist order will in practice establish areas of privilege. . . . Power is likely to beget power; and administrative procedure becomes the handmaiden of the most persistently organized entities in specific areas" (Halebsky 1976, p. 200). Virtually the whole system responds only to organized entities, and their relative power is a decisive factor; the powerless and the dispossessed lack opportunity and even self-confidence to play any significant role within the system.

It is almost impossible to achieve equality under conditions of scarcity and manipulation. The powerful utilize the idea of equality for keeping masses under control and usually contribute to scarcity instead of alleviating it. Progress of well-being is not the natural result of equality and it is enough to look closer into the history of social thought in order to understand how much intellectual confusion is involved here (Andreski 1975).

How to achieve better economic results through more efficient use of existing resources is a major problem in all developed economies. This is particularly evident in the area of energy, with economies dependent on increasingly expensive, dwindling oil supplies. Also important is the effective utilization of available industrial equipment. Take the following example: 75 percent of metal working parts manufactured are produced in developed countries in lots consisting of less than 50 pieces. From the period of time in which an average workpiece stays in the batch-type metal cutting production shop 1.5 percent is spent on actual cut, 3.5 percent is spent in loading, gaging, unloading on a machine, and 95 percent of time is spent of moving and waiting. The average machine spends half of its time waiting for parts. The average machine tool in a batch-type is actually cutting metal about 15 percent of the time (National . . . 1975, pp. 324–25, 344).

The bureaucratization and the centralization of decision-making in the modern Western societies leads, among other things, to tension between the center and the peripheries.

> As the state regulates, invests and provides services, it stimulates demands which begin to overtax its capabilities. The benefits and costs of its multifarious activities are distributed differentially among classes and among regions. Having stimulated expectations, central governments become at the same time the focus of demands and the target of grievances (Esman 1977, p. 373).

Revival of the *ethnic conflict* in industrialized societies may be explained to a substantial extent by the above-mentioned clash of interests between the center and the periphery. In the societies which are segmented according to ethnic, religious, cultural or ideological lines, communal pluralism may be the best solution (McRae 1974; Esman 1977, p. 14). However, in many cases this solution may be achieved only by the the long process of gradual, mutual accommodation among the various groups that are constituent parts of the society. The modern mass media very often enhance regional, ethnic, and class perception of grievances looking for the sensational aspect of them. Ambitious young people and local politicians find in these grievances a very attractive promotional capital.

Taking into consideration the diminishing legitimacy of several traditional Western institutions (church, government, school, military, police, political parties, and so on), it becomes understandable why the political organizers of the periphery (ethnic, cultural, racial, economic, and so on) are able to gain mass appeal in the deprived segments of the population (National Front in the United Kingdom and France, extremists in Northern Ireland, nationalists in Quebec, extreme leftists in Latin America). They propose to substitute the remote central institutions with local structures directly controlled by the people and much more responsive to mass needs. Under the conditions of relative peace and security such centripetal tendencies are usually tolerated in the democratic West. In the undemocratic sociopolitical system these movements usually are persecuted by the governments.

THE CRISIS OF THE WESTERN WELFARE STATE

The ability of government intervention to build a better society is uncertain; the level of involvement is high, but with the widely varying demands of different social claimants the position of public sector is a difficult one. Government is a major provider of middle-class jobs and services focused on middle-class needs and priorities.

> With inflation there is a demand to cut back on government expenditures. But any cutback will increase the economic pressure on the poor (fewer income transfer payments) and the middle class (fewer good jobs). With slow growth there are demands to further cut taxes on the rich to encourage savings and investment. But any cutback will necessitate increased taxes for the middle class (Thurow 1981, p. 158).

Various groups demand a larger fraction of the whole pie and the government has to respond to all their conflicting demands.

It is not easy to cut on transfer payments to the needy; in the United States half of the income of the elderly comes from these payments. The inequality of earnings between the bottom quintile and the top quintile of earners has grown considerably since the late 1940s but the income position of the poor has improved. Highly educated women are heavily dependent on government expenditure in their jobs. Minority people are better paid in the public sector

than in the private sector. "Government raises the earnings of women and minorities above what they would be if
only the private economy were to exist" (Thurow 1981, p.
165).

Under the pressure of growing demands for greater
equality of income distribution in society, it will be more
and more difficult for the government to satisfy the major
contending partners. The distribution of family income as
well as of wage and salary earnings has remained around
the same during the whole period since the Second World
War. However, the mean earnings of the fully employed
white males are about three times as high as those of the
rest of the labor force, and in addition they are much more
equal. The relative earning status of women versus men
has deteriorated. "The lack of employment opportunities is
not a temporary, short-run aspect of the U.S. economy. It
is permanent and endemic" (Ibid., p. 205).

There are no easy and painless solutions to the conflicts of economic interests promoted and defended by
various groups of the American population. On the other
hand, it is not possible to satisfactorily solve the existing
problems without making decisions which may be unpleasant
for some privileged groups. In the society based on mass
manipulation, people gradually learn how to organize themselves into pressure groups and promote their own cause.
For the elite it is no longer possible to depend on the
naiveté and defenselessness of large groups of people
traditionally handicapped.

The growing internal contradictions of the Western
democratic societies need some solutions. One of them is
the social-democratic model. In all countries in which social
democrats managed to exercise much influence (Sweden,
West Germany, Great Britain, Austria, and so on) the
public sector has grown considerably even if the economy
has remained basically private. The public spendings
(excluding investment) as the share of GDP have grown in
the period 1960–76 in the Western countries governed by
social democrats; for example, in Sweden from 16 to 26
percent, in the United Kingdom from 16 to 23 percent, in
West Germany from 14 to 21 percent. By comparison, in
France they increased from 13 to 14 percent and in Japan
from 9 to 11 percent. It is significant that even in the
United States they have grown quite considerably, from 18
to 22 percent (Some Data . . . 1978, p. 39).

It is still an open question if (and to what extent) the
socialist welfare state of a social-democratic nature is able
to solve the growing internal contradictions of a modern
developed society. The Swedish case may be particularly

significant in this respect and therefore it deserves a particular attention. The major achievement of social democrats in the West has been in social welfare, wherever they have held power long enough to introduce some basic reforms. In Sweden they have been in power for over 50 years, controlling around half of the seats in parliament. However, they do not promote nationalization, because they find it more effective to tax private business and well-to-do individuals. In the United Kingdom, public expenditure has grown in the period 1938–70 from 30 percent to 50 percent of GNP, but the expenditure on social services has grown even more, from 11 percent to 24 percent.

However, this growing attention given by governments to the general well-being of the population is not peculiar to socialists. The cost of social insurance in West Germany was one-fifth of the GNP in the late 1960s before social democrats came to power (Krejci 1976, p. 36). In the most developed capitalist country of the world, the U.S. federal budget doubled during the relatively short period 1974–79 and social security expenditure grew almost eight times from 1965 until 1979 (*Time*, May 15, 1978, p. 39).

The revolution of rising entitlements includes, among other things, the mass demands of social security in the broad sense of this term. "We now move to state-managed societies. And these emerge because of the increase in the large-scale social demands (health, education, welfare, social services) which have become entitlements for the population" (Bell 1976, p. 24). The state expenditure is roughly more than half of the GNP in the social-democratic countries but it is near a half also in several developed capitalist countries, for example, in Canada.

Several pressures exercised on the modern democratic state by various groups are so effective that the ruling elites prefer to extend the deficit rather than cut the state expenditure. In the United States "the runaway spending is producing a stumbling nanny-state that tries to help powerful special interests but in fact hurts the whole nation by ravaging it with inflation" (*Time*, May 15, 1978, p. 39). The U.S. federal deficit has grown much since the early 1970s. Other developed countries have also a high deficit and their balance of payments has been negative for years.

This trend is almost unavoidable and will persist under any political system as long as the basic realms of modern society remain in antagonistic relationship to one another. Bell claims that

three realms—the economy, the policy, and the culture—are ruled by contrary axial principles: for the economy, efficiency; for the polity, equality; and for the culture, self-realization (or self-gratification). The resulting disjunctions have framed the tensions and conflicts of Western society in the past 150 years (Bell 1976, p. xii).

Social democracy so far has proved unable to reverse this trend, making people more secure, but at the same time even more dependent on the welfare state. Wage and salary workers account for more than 90 percent of all gainfully employed persons in the developed Western countries, and the big complex organizations, such as state agencies, private corporations and trade unions run the society under the push exercised by various formal or informal lobbies. The commercialization of all mutual relations and the continuous collective bargaining for entitlements both dominate the social and cultural climate of modern societies.

CONCLUSIONS

The shortage of basic natural resources and the urgent need for reshaping the current international order in the spirit of genuine cooperation between the developing and the developed countries (Tinbergen 1976) contributes to the new social awareness in the developed democratic countries. The socialist model of a new society appears as insufficient to achieve a balance between various contradictory factors. The hedonistic social culture becomes historically obsolete and moral principles on which the whole socioeconomic order is based are in the urgent need of reevaluation. The welfare state of a conservative, liberal, or even socialist nature has proved to be unable to deal effectively with the crisis of the democratic developed society. This crisis has much to do with the fast growth of services in the modern society and with the reallocation of human resources.

In the industrial democracies, even the welfare state (and the heavy taxation on which it is based) has not led to a genuine equalization of incomes and wealth. "Most anti-poverty policies eventually help the rich and middle-income groups more than they help the poor. . . . It is much easier to make the income distribution worse than to improve it" (Adelman and Robinson 1978, p. 1919). The case of the United Kingdom may be particularly interesting in this respect due to the fact that under the socialist rule a considerable effort was made to lower the level of socioeconomic inequality.

The radical orientation, of the leftist or the rightist persuasion, may potentially have a mass appeal among the disillusioned and disoriented people, especially because their knowledge of social and economic problems remains superficial and one-sided. Never before, on such a large scale, were the young kept for such a long time in a state of prolonged adolescence, characterized by a subordinate and dependent position; at the same time youth is glorified and offered various privileges denied to the older generation (grants, excellent facilities, and so on) (Lipset 1971).

This ambiguous situation of the youth leads to mass frustration and discontent, especially when the school does not provide a clear and convincing life orientation and when the young people do not learn to improve themselves in a systematic manner. Blaming society becomes an obvious answer to all the problems experienced in daily life. Simplified doctrines are more attractive than the more sophisticated and diversified intellectual approaches. Personal frustration and immaturity, and not necessarily deep social involvement, lead some young people to professional careers in the social field and thus the heavily biased patterns of understanding reality are perpetrated from one generation to another.

The manipulatory nature of mass society (Kornhauser 1968) in the long run defeats the purpose of this society when the socioeconomic problems become aggravated. The manipulators are defeated by their own weapon when they are no longer able to offer satisfactory solutions. New social technology has to replace, sooner or later, the prevailing manipulatory techniques, which are losing their appeal among the masses. The analytical substantiation of the whole business of governing people becomes of crucial importance, and therefore the concern for sociotechnics has a future. It is also very important to treat mass participation in various fields seriously, and to approach it not as a purely political device but as a humanitarian problem.

In the present-day developed society there is great need, among social scientists as well as politicians, to understand not only the urgent global problems taken separately (the expert approach) but also the interrelation of these problems in the whole society. This understanding exists among Marxists, but unfortunately it is based on the very simplified and historically outdated assumptions. The negative aspects of state socialism, as it is implemented in some parts of the world, are either totally neglected by the western Marxists or at least minimalized by them (Jain and Matejko 1984). It is just naïveté to assume that state socialism offers a ready answer to the major social problems

of the modern Western society, with its individualistic tradition, commitment to freedom and democracy, interest in
private well-being (opposite to the well-being of the state,
as in the Soviet Union), leisure orientation and the free
play between various pressure groups.

Modern societies need a large-scale reconstruction of
human bonds which would provide people with a moral and
cultural content free, as much as possible, from narcissism,
vested interests, commercialism, and manipulation. There is
a place for altruism and the genuine concern of people for
each other. There is also a growing understanding that
narcissism prevents human beings from growing and matur-
ing. Unfortunately, most of the modern complex organizations which dominate the modern *theatrum mundi* are unable
or unwilling to allow the above-mentioned social reconstruction to happen. There are many interests invested in
the status quo. Many influential people treat as a danger
to themselves any new type of social bonds which would
oppose the values and goals of mass society. There is a
hope that greater awareness will appear in modern societies
of the inevitability of reconstruction. It is in the vital
longitudinal interest of all major social institutions to
promote the nonmanipulatory perspective.

The future of mass societies will be very much influenced by the almost unavoidable confrontation between the
"manipulatory" model of human relations and the "moralistic"
model. In political life we have more and more groups and
coalitions that go much beyond the traditional party
machines or even directly confront them. In religious life
the existing churches face growing difficulties in satisfying
the faithful members who organize themselves into various
caucuses. In economic life, the organized consumers exercise growing pressure and do not want simply to follow
blindly the messages imposed upon them by the advertising
business. In labor, the new forms of industrial democracy
(autonomous work groups, and so on) and the quality-of-
working-life movement gradually change the traditional
power structure based on the triangle of management-trade
union-government.

With growing sophistication, the masses stop being
servile and obedient; the process of individualization is
unavoidable under the conditions of growing pluralization.
In this respect the pessimism of the mass-society theorists
is not justified: reduction to mediocrity has happened in
some fields but not in all; the cultural upgrading of people
through education, art, and exposure to sophisticated mass
media has been stronger than the above-mentioned theorists
expected. To a growing extent the concept of individual

freedom in society is understood not in narcissistic terms, but as a moral obligation to be open-minded and committed to the public welfare.

With the growing dependence of social systems on their external environment, the isolationistic system strategy becomes impractical. Of major importance is the question how to admit the critical inputs, and at the same time preserve the system autonomy. In contradistinction to the arbitrary difference between "scientific" and "practical," the praxiological approach (Kotarbinski 1965) brings everything to the common denominator of *purposefulness*.

Sociotechnics is one of the practical sciences, as "aggregates of general propositions, stating how the states of affairs recommended by the accepted evaluations can be realized by making use of established factual "regularities" (Podgorecki 1975, p. 22).

The task to *elucidate reality* is methodologically different from an analysis how to change this reality, taking account of value judgments, orienting action to the fulfillment of specific goals, taking into consideration the limits of possible change and the unanticipated consequences of purposive action. There is a whole spectrum of practical problems[26] which necessitate not only fact-finding activities but also diagnostic, evaluative, and prognostic concerns. Another set of questions is related to strategy of a purposeful and efficient feeding of change agencies with inputs which may improve the general performance of these agencies. There is a whole complicated problem of how to transform the outputs of scientific research into the inputs of the change agencies. "To connect theory and practice means, among other things, to conceptualize and formalize the necessary regularities and corollaries between them" (Podgorecki 1975, p. 6).

The purposefulness of practical actions may be substantially enhanced, thanks to the substitution of verified knowledge for idiosyncratic evaluations, and this is exactly what the rationality factor within Western civilization is about. This rationality is much more easily achieved in the nonsocial field than in *human relations,* where personal inclinations and values play a major role. However, in both cases a certain course of purposive procedure is expected to be followed. It includes a diagnosis[27] (based on research, comparison of evaluations, conclusion, explanation, postulative suggestions, and hypotheses),[28] justification, project building, realization of the project, control and judgment of results (Podgorecki 1975, p. 27).[29]

One of the basic sociotechnical problems of modern times is how to improve the performance level of those institutions of the nonprofit sector that are particularly vulnerable to the "rule of the conspiring mediocrities" (Matejko 1984).

For example, in the United States the knowledge level of secondary education students in the last 25 years has declined instead of improving, even if the teachers are now better paid, schools are better equipped and in general the cost of secondary education is much higher. This deterioration of performance is due, among others, to the fact that schools of education put more emphasis on manipulatory abilities of the future teachers than on their mastery of specific subjects. The present-day U.S. teachers are now more inclined than their earlier colleagues just to play it safe, instead of teaching their students something substantial, and therefore much more demanding. The same has happened in several other countries.

Pressure exercised by various interest groups may be very harmful to the quantity and quality of services offered to the society by its various institutions, and the nonprofit sector is more vulnerable to this pressure than the profit sector. The rapid growth of nonprofit services in the Western societies so far has not been adequately analyzed in terms of its sociotechnical consequences.

NOTES

1. Bureaucracy is one of such conventional arrangements. It is typical for bureaucracies to select carefully all external input and to react very negatively to anything which may upset their internal equilibrium.

2. It is assumed that people, being fully free, make the best possible choice by arranging their mutual relationships in a given manner. Everything that does not fit into this scheme is automatically rejected as irrational, impractical, useless, not up-to-date (reactionary).

3. On the other hand, the modern manipulatory social orders are of an artificial nature and their sociotechnics do not generally appeal to deeper human motives, historically well rooted and reinforced by the whole network of traditional interrelationships. It seems easier to impose on the masses a manipulatory order than to socialize them into it.

4. This mutual relationship between the structural aspects and the manipulatory aspects of modern societies has several far-reaching consequences. First of all, modernization based exclusively on material values identifies efficiency with standardization, and reduces to commodities all items of interhuman exchange at the broadest (and at the same time lowest) common denominator. Secondly, the

exchange relationships take place in moral limbo because they have lost any close relationships to the social culture. In order to open room to the most effective and rewarding material traffic, various moral links among people have become destroyed and a high level of homogeneity has been achieved. However, this is a homogeneity based on mind-less uniformity and conformism and *not* on common cultural and moral values.

5. U.S. society faces major challenges from outside as well as from inside and the current answer to them remains unsatisfactory. Since the Second World War, industrial productivity rose 1 percent per year in the United States, in comparison with around 5 percent in Japan and in West Germany. Many categories of the U.S. population that had remained shy until not long ago have now become out-spoken: the super-rich meet presently much more resistance in the promotion of their own goals and interests.

6. In the zero-sum game, in order for somebody to gain, somebody else has to lose and, of course, in the democratic developed society fewer people are willing to be losers. For example, the increase of the price of energy is much more painful for the poor than for the rich, and the latter are opposed to the free-market option in the energy policy. "The problem is not finding economics that will lower incomes, but being able to impose them" (Thurow 1981, p. 42). "Each potential solution to the inflation problem lowers someone's income by a large amount; each increases someone's economic insecurity" (Ibid., p. 75).

7. In the years 1936–66, the consumption of spirits has grown in Great Britain 100 percent and the consumption of beer 34 percent, while the growth of population was only 14 percent (Glasser 1970, p. 123).

8. Is it a valid generalization that the only environ-ment which remains for old people is that of their own age peers? The study done by I. Rosow on older middle-class and working-class residents of Cleveland apartment build-ings shows that "friendships are formed between persons of similar status, notably of age, but also of sex, marital status, social class, beliefs, and life-styles" (Rosow 1967, p. 295) and that "the old are likely to become isolated in an indifferent environment of younger people" (Ibid., p. 324). "Because industrial society is formally committed to the objectives of greater prosperity, higher productivity, and accelerated technological change, it tends to give prece-dence to the value of youth, innovation, and achievement and therefore to develop means rather of accommodating than integrating the elderly" (Shanas 1968, p. 426). However, the cross-national survey of living conditions and

behavior of elderly people in Denmark, Britain, and the United States provides a convincing evidence that

> persons aged 65 and over are more strongly integrated into industrial society than is often assumed either by the general public or by sociological theorists. . . . By their general health or, more specifically, the personal and household functions they perform, in the services they receive from their families, and in the frequency of their contacts with children and other relatives, most old people are fairly securely knitted into the social structure. Physical activity is largely self-sustaining. Integration with the family and the local community is maintained by the immediate network of personal, or "privatised," relationships, based on reciprocity, common interests, inculcated loyalties, and affection (Townsend 1957, p. 425).

Also, the study by B. N. Adams of kinship relations in one middle-sized American city shows that "relations between young adults and their kin are dominated by involvement with their parents. The parents are objects of extremely frequent contact" (Adams 1968, p. 164).

9. The well-being and the equilibrium of developed societies is based on the one-sided progress of their economies within the capitalist market system and within the state socialist system (Matejko 1983). Leisure is treated as an object of manipulation aimed at keeping the masses within the existing rules of the power game. Under the market economy, the leisure motivation of people is constantly stimulated by mass media, in order to channel adequately the buying behavior of consumers and to arrange the necessary inputs. Under state socialism, people are skillfully conditioned to use their leisure in the way beneficial to the omnipotent state. In both cases, leisure ceases to fulfill its traditional hedonistic and liberating functions; it becomes a battleground between individuals who are trying to gain their own satisfaction at the expense of others. The more people are free to choose their leisure the more they will spoil it for each other (Emery and Emery 1975, p. 176). The total devotion to having fun, regardless of the social and individual cost, promotes mediocrity, stimulates neuroticism, and diverts attention from serious activities.

10. "Rising national productivity entails an individual need for income to secure certain satisfactions unattainable with lower income. Admittedly, rising national productivity will also add unequivocally to availabilities of other kinds,

specifically of material goods. But this increase in material goods will be accompanied by frustration of rising demands for satisfactions dependent on relative position. It may be that frustration has offset the extra commodities. . . . Relative position affects what we get, as well as what we feel" (Hirsch 1976, pp. 113–14).

11. It is true that leisure organized by authorities such as churches, unions, corporations, and so forth, has diminished in its scope and importance with the growing personal well-being in developed societies. On the other hand, the centralized manipulation of leisure has also grown very substantially in order to fulfill the interests of producers, distributors, civil servants, and politicians. The spectator sport is widely supported by governments, business, and mass media because of its crucial role in entertaining the masses. Even in the Soviet Union during the period from the middle 1920s to the end of the 1950s, the time devoted by urban workers to study has remained quasiconstant, while the time spent on spectator sports has quadrupled (Strumilin 1964). In democratic societies the scope of political interest and involvement remains at a modest level but money spent by people on leisure constantly grows.

12. There is a question of whether it would be possible to abandon the model of a mass society and to liberate people from the far-reaching manipulation without eliminating at the same time the economic advantages of a free-market system. The far-reaching concentration of economic power in the Western world (Heilbroner and Thurow 1975, pp. 194–211) on the one side, and the shortage of natural resources, on the other side (Tinbergen 1976), both impose restrictions upon people regarding their consumption.

13. The pressure of needs moves many people from one place to another. Several people look for advantages in other regions and countries. A selective drain of the skilled labor force may be damaging when such people leave who would be able to contribute to the well-being of their own country. The cost of educating and training people is borne by their native countries, yet the benefits of their skills are enjoyed by the country to which they emigrate. On the other hand, remittances sent back by expatriates constitute a major source of income in several countries. In 1976, in Greece, Morocco, Pakistan, Turkey, and Yugoslavia these remittances totaled from one-third to a half of export earnings.

14. U.S. workers choose improved income over status, and the French data show that two-thirds of blue-collar workers prefer an increase in wages over a reduction in

working hours (Dumazedier 1974, p. 19). Even without a
financial incentive, people do not imagine their life without
gainful employment. In the United States, 61 percent
among the middle class and 34 percent among the working
class would continue in the same type of work even if it
were not financially necessary.

15. Some large organizations try more or less successfully to incorporate leisure activities into their own framework. In Japan, generous entertainment funds available to
management personnel are treated as an important part of
remuneration. Companies all around the world sponsor
leisure facilities for their employees. In socialist countries,
holiday hostels are available to employees at a reduced rate
as a supplement to their meagre incomes (Matejko 1983).
However, when freedom of choice is an issue of importance,
the above-mentioned projects meet only a limited success.
For example, the young generation of Japanese becomes less
company-bound than older generations and leisured fringe
benefits lose their attractiveness. Subsidized entertainment
facilities all around the developed countries are of no great
attraction for the young generation. Many people prefer to
pay more for leisure facilities but to be entirely free. It is
significant that in socialist Poland private tourism has
grown in the 1970s much faster than subsidized state-
sponsored collective tourism.

16. These countercultures differ in depth and in general orientation but their common message is quite clear.
They are oriented against submissiveness, passivity, and
conformism. They challenge the wisdom of being like
others, following blindly the changing fashion, and accepting ready answers programmed into people by mass media.

17. Fortunately, there is a growing understanding that
the gap between the organizational facade and the realities
of life within organizations (especially large organizations)
has become too great and too expensive for society to
maintain. There is more and more room for some "leisured"
forms of organization such as autonomous work groups,
meditation sessions, outdoor activities, fine arts projects,
and so forth. All of these forms function as channels
through which the realities of a leisure-oriented modern
society become introduced into complex organizations,
thereby reducing their pretended "seriousness" and human-
izing this organizational content. There is now enough
empirical evidence to suggest that too much external seriousness may be damaging for productivity and that leisure-oriented people are not necessarily unproductive.
Creativity and entrepreneurship may be enhanced by making complex organizations more "leisured" than has occurred

thus far.

18. This is the reason why in the present-day mass societies in the West, as well as in the Soviet bloc, the moral opposition to the "big game" played by the local establishments (in which a great part of societies is involved directly or indirectly), takes generally the character of a countercultural movement, which denounces the dominating coalitions of recognized pressure groups (Roszak 1969; Zinoviev 1979). The countercultures are usually too weak to endanger the status quo; however, by questioning the moral emptiness of the establishment, they undermine quite effectively, in the long run, the future commitment of people, particularly the young, to the existing manipulatory order. The public becomes critical and disillusioned but the prevailing vested-interest groups still exercise power. This is exactly what is happening now in the Western world as well as in the Soviet bloc.

19. In the United States from the end of the 1920s up to the beginning of the 1970s, income tax as a percentage of total consumption has grown from 1 to 13, and all governmental purchases as percentage of GNP have grown from 8 to 21 (Heilbroner 1975, p. 165). The rise of federal expenditures is mainly related to military expenditures (they grew by a half during the 1970s in the United States but doubled in the Soviet Union) and welfare-state commitments, as well as the growth of bureaucracy; taken together they make the difference between the present and the past.

20. For example, it happens very often in the economic market that price levels are kept at certain levels, highly profitable for all entrepreneurs but detrimental to their clients. This is evident in housing, drugs, and automobiles in North America.

21. In situations such as war, crisis, or another great stress, people become active at the individual as well as collective level. In the West, as well as in the Soviet bloc, the conditions of a mass society established by the status-quo forces are questioned and even challenged by various ad hoc groups as long as there is evidence of a structural strain: the involvement of the United States in an unpopular war, the deterioration of real incomes in several Western countries, food shortages in Poland, opportunities to leave the Soviet Union by Jews, and so on.

22. In order to defend the public against manipulatory impression-management it is necessary to encourage a critical and cautious approach to organizational information, formulated in the following basic questions: What is the possible extent of information distortion? How complete are

the reports? Which are the basic services of information and how reliable are they? Who may have some vested interests in distorting the information? How much the organizational reality may become an object of informational distortion?

23. We are now spending more and more money and effort on research and development. Thanks to better knowledge, we are able to control several spheres of our life much better than ever before in history. For example, our whole approach to life has changed, thanks to the fact that, contrary to the situation in medieval times, we are able to eliminate plagues which before mass inoculation took more casualties in the armies than enemy actions; in the middle of the fourteenth century, plague killed a third of Europe's population (McNeil 1976). However, by depending to a growing extent on technology in our daily life, we expose ourselves to dangers which we are still not fully aware of.

24. Comparative data for 1965 and 1975 show a growth of leisure time, especially among the young and those close to retirement. Most people show satisfaction with their nonwork activities, as well as with their friendships. Those better off seem to relax more often in their daily life (Social Indicators III 1981).

25. Of course, it would not be reasonable to treat TV as an evil in itself. Its cultural and leisure value depends very much on selective and well-intented utilization of TV. Survey data have shown that TV-watching does not necessarily displace other media, despite the large amount of time devoted to it by the majority of watchers. For example, in Canada a high involvement of people in entertainment activities is clearly associated with high involvement in creative activities. Data show "a consistent positive association between time spent on media-related leisure and time spent with arts and crafts. . . . Constraints on resources, such as low family income, do not reverse this effect, although they do moderate it somewhat" (Schliewen 1977, p. 99).

26. The practice is based on valuational propositions which express an active relationship between the actors of change and the reality treated by them as the object of their manipulations. The language of acting differs from the language of studying, not only because the intentions are dissimilar but also because in the process of acting, the necessity of constant reevaluation is quite often much more pronounced, being related to the original intention much more than to cognition per se. The utilitarian aspect of valuation quite often, but not necessarily, appears jointly with the purely moral and personal aspect; this is the main

source of several problems. Practical actions are to a large extent the projections of the individual and group idiosyncrasies; on the other hand, personal involvement is the guarantee that practical actions will be performed more or less effectively.

27. The diagnosis is a "formulation of a hypothesis for the changing of actual states of affairs, established by complete description and evaluation of empirical situations" (Podgorecki 1975, p. 28). It plays the major role in all applied social sciences, primarily in sociotechnics.

28. The hypothesis has to be probable, in the sense that the given cause or set of causes is apt to bring about the postulated state of affairs (Podgorecki 1975, p. 49).

29. The great variety of social factors and situations makes it necessary to consider the whole spectrum of alternatives (scenarios) in order to avoid the failure arising from an unrealistic approach. A diagnosis of such a nature includes several steps. Only one of them is presented here: a general characterization of major trends towards manipulation and the social cost involved.

REFERENCES

Adams, Bert. 1968. *Kinship in an Urban Setting.* Chicago: Markham.

Adelman, Irma, and Sherman Robinson. 1978. *Income Distribution Policies in Developing Countries: A Case Study of Korea.* New York: Oxford University Press.

Adler, R. P., et al. 1968. *The Effects on Television Advertising on Children.* Lexington, MA: Lexington.

Altheide, David L., and John M. Johnson. 1980. *Bureaucratic Propaganda.* Boston: Allyn and Bacon.

Andreski, Stanislav. 1968. *The African Predicament: A Study of Pathology of Modernization.* New York: Atherton Press.

————. 1969. *Parasitism and Subversion: The Case of Latin America.* New York: Schocken.

————. 1975. *Reflections on Inequality.* London: Croom Helm.

Anthony, P. D. 1977. *The Ideology of Work.* London: Tavistock.

Audrey, Robert. 1970. *The Social Contract.* New York: Atheneum.

Barrett, David. 1983. *World Christian Encyclopedia.* New York: Oxford University Press.

Bell, Daniel. 1976. *The Cultural Contradictions of Capitalism.* New York: Basic Books.

—————. 1977. "Teletext and Technology: New Networks of Knowledge and Information in Post-Industrial Society." *Encounter* June:9–29.

Bradbury, R. 1953. *Farenheit 451*. New York: Ballantine.

Brinton, Crane. 1965. *The Anatomy of Revolution*. New York: Vintage.

Brown, J. R. 1975. *Children and Television*. Beverly Hills, CA: Sage.

Cherns, Albert. 1979. *Using the Social Sciences*. London: Routledge and Kegan Paul.

Dumazedier, J. 1974. *Sociology of Leisure*. New York: Elsevier.

Emery, R., and M. Emery. 1975. *The Choice of Futures*. Canberra: National University of Australia.

Esman, Milton J., ed. 1977. *Ethnic Conflict in the Western World*. Ithaca: Cornell University Press.

Hochschild, Arlie Russel. 1983. *The Managed Heart: Commercialization of Human Feeling*. Berkeley and Los Angeles: University of California Press.

Jain, Ajit, and A. Matejko, eds. 1984. *Marx and Marxism*. New York: Praeger.

Finsterbusch, Kurt. 1980. *Understanding Social Impacts. Assessing the Effects of Public Projects*. Beverly Hills, CA: Sage.

Friedmann, G. 1970. *La Puissance et la Sagesse*. Paris: Gallimard.

Friedrich, Carl J., and Zbigniew Brzezinski. 1966. *Totalitarian Dictatorship and Democracy*. 2d ed. New York: Praeger.

Glasser, R. 1970. *Leisure: Penalty or Price?* New York: Macmillan.

Halebsky, Sandor. 1976. *Mass Society and Political Conflict: Towards a Reconstruction of Theory*. Cambridge: Cambridge University Press.

Heilbroner, R. 1975. *The Making of Economic Society*. Englewood Cliffs, NJ: Prentice-Hall.

Heilbroner, R., and Lester C. Thurow. 1975. *The Economic Problem*. Englewood Cliffs, NJ: Prentice-Hall.

Hirsch, F. 1976. *Social Limits to Growth*. Cambridge: Harvard University Press.

Kornhauser, Arthur. 1968. "Mass Society." In *International Encyclopedia of Social Sciences*. New York: Free Press.

Krejci, J. 1976. *Social Structure in Divided Germany*. London: Croom Helm.

Leszek Kolakowski Reader. *Triquarterly,* 1971, no. 22.

Levy-Strauss, Claude. 1979. "The Rebirth of Ideology." *Atlas* 26, 8:28–30.

Lipset, Seymour M. 1970. *Revolution and Counter-Revolution, Changes and Persistence in Social Structures.* Garden City, NY: Doubleday.

————. 1971. *Rebellion in the University.* Boston: Little, Brown.

Matejko, Alexander. 1972. "Can Social Systems Mature?" *Sociologia Internationalis* 11, 1–2.

————. 1974. *Social Change and Stratification in Eastern Europe.* New York: Praeger.

————. 1975. "The Dialectical Approach to Social Reality." *Sociologia Internationalis* 13, 1–2:5–27.

————. 1976. "The Qualitative Growth of Social Systems: Criteria for its Evaluation." In *Sociotechnics,* edited by Albert Cherns. London: Malaby Press.

————. 1979. "From the Crisis of Bureaucracy to the Challenge of Participation." In *Management and Complex Organizations in Comparative Perspective,* edited by Raj P. Mohan. Westport, CT: Greenwood.

————. 1980. "The Structural Criteria of Social System Maturity." In *Soziale Beziehungsgefechte,* edited by H. Niemeyer, pp. 57–76. Berlin: Duncker and Humbolt.

————. 1983. *From State Socialism to Democracy? The Polish Case.* Edmonton: University of Alberta Bookstore.

————. 1984. *Organization or Manipulation?* Edmonton: University of Alberta Bookstore.

McLuhan, M. 1974. *Understanding Media.* London: Routledge and Kegan Paul.

———— (with H. Parker). 1969. *Counterblast.* New York: Harcourt Brace.

McNeil, W. 1976. *Plagues and Peoples.* Garden City, NY: Anchor Books, Doubleday.

McRae, Kenneth, ed. 1974. *Consociational Democracy: Political Accommodation in Segmented Societies.* Toronto: McClelland and Stewart.

Morse, Nancy, and Robert S. Weiss. 1955. "The Function and Meaning of Work and the Job." *American Sociological Review* 20, 2:191–98.

National Productivity and Quality of Working Life. 1975. Hearings before the Committee on Government Operations. United States Senate. Washington, DC: Government Printing Office.

Noble, G. 1975. *Children in Front of the Small Screen.* Beverly Hills, CA: Sage.

Pawley, M. 1973. *The Private Future.* London: Thames and Hudson.

Podgorecki, A. 1975. *Practical Social Sciences.* London: Routledge and Kegan Paul.

Presthus, R. 1978. *The Organizational Society*. New York: Vintage.

Robey, B., and C. Russell. 1983. "How Consumers Spend." *American Demographics* 5, 10:17–21.

Rosow, I. 1967. *Social Integration of the Aged*. New York: Free Press.

Roszak, Theodore. 1969. *The Making of a Counter-Culture*. Garden City, NY: Doubleday.

Schliewen, R. E. 1977. *A Leisure Study—Canada*. Ottawa: Comstat Consulting Services (published for Arts and Culture Branch, Department of the Secretary of State, Government of Canada).

Schramm, W., J. Lyle, and E. P. Parker. 1961. *Television in the Lives of Children*. Palo Alto: Stanford University Press.

Sennett, Richard. 1978. *The Fall of Public Man: On the Social Psychology of Capitalism*. New York: Vintage.

Shanas, E., et al. 1968. *Old People in Three Industrial Societies*. New York: Atherton.

Sleeman, J. F. 1973. *The Welfare State: Its Aims, Benefits, and Costs*. London: Allen and Unwin.

Social Indicators III. 1981. Washington, DC: Department of Commerce.

Social Trends, No. 8. 1977. London: Her Majesty's Stationary Office.

Social Trends, No. 9. 1979. Edited by E. J. Thompson and J. Peretz. London: Her Majesty's Stationary Office.

Some Data About Sweden. Stockholm: Skandinaviska Enskilda Banken (published every second year).

Spinrad, N. 1972. *Bug Jack Barron*. New York: Panther.

Strumilin, S. G. 1964. *On Problems of Labor Economics*. Vol. 3. Moscow.

Talmon, J. L. 1952. *The Origins of Totalitarian Democracy*. New York: Praeger.

Thurow, L. C. 1976. *Generating Inequality*. New York: Macmillan.

————. 1981. *The Zero-Sum Society*. New York: Penguin.

Tinbergen, Jan. 1976. *RIO: Reshaping the International Order*. London: Sutton.

Townsend, P. 1957. *Family Life of Old People*. London: Routledge and Kegan Paul.

Woodsworth, David E. 1977. *Social Security and National Policy: Sweden, Yugoslavia, Japan*. Montreal: McGill-Queen's University Press.

Zinoviev, Alexander. 1979. *The Yawning Heights*. New York: Random House.

9

TOWARDS "MATURE" SYSTEMS?

CONTRADICTIONS WITHIN SOCIAL
REALITY AND THEIR INTERPRETATION

The basic problems of interpretative sociology are still far
from being solved (Schutz 1972; Lazarsfeld 1972). Modern
positivism distorts these problems (Oberschall 1972; Nisbet
1967) pretending that only science is knowledge. A critical
approach in the social sciences has become diluted under
the impact of such an empirical approach which simplifies
the nature of reality. Is it true that modern social scientists make ponderous restatements of the obvious and that
their smoke screen of jargon covers only trivialities
(Andreski 1972)?

There are vital questions on how "objective" the insights of the social sciences are (Babbie 1983, pp. 16–23),
or how such insights may change the social reality by
becoming additions to it. Of even more importance is the
issue of *interpretation*. Our facts are always preselected.
As Gardiner has said, "what we expect is closely tied to
what we find understandable in the light of our own experience as rational purposive agents" (Gardiner 1968, p. 432).
We do not have the alternative to recreate the image of the
reality on the basis of available data. We jump from a
particular to a *general* without always being aware how
much risk is involved (Babbie 1983). We talk about the
"possible" but this is not necessarily the "happening."

The logic of *explanation* necessitates much more than
just knowledge of facts. First of all, these "facts" have to
be meaningfully interrelated (Bottomore 1968, p. 46).

Secondly, the historical background must be exposed. Thirdly, social reality must be treated more in terms of its dynamics than its statics. Finally, the conflictual nature of social change has to be exposed.

It is in the old tradition of Vico and Hegel, as well as in the more recent tradition of Simmel, Rickert, Dilthey, Crose, and Collingwood, to treat social behavior in its historical uniqueness, and not as "mere pieces of observable behavior, reducible to (or explicable in terms of) purely physical items" (Gardiner 1968, p. 430). It is necessary to understand the nature of social phenomena in their environmental and historical context, as a contradiction between the "rational" and the "practical," between what people want to achieve in order to find self-fulfillment and the situational constraints that tell them what is achievable (Collingswood 1956).

Sociology, from our standpoint, is a scientific discipline dealing with the structure and dialectical dynamics of various social systems. The dilemma which these systems have to face in their functioning should be treated as the focal problems of sociology. Sociological analysis should cover all basic problems of making use of social energy including "the importation of energy from the environment, the through-put or transformation of the imported energy into some product form which is characteristic of the system, the exporting of that product into the environment, and the re-energizing of the system from sources in the environment" (Katz and Kahn 1966, p. 28).

Models of the social structure as "an assemblage of independent bricks" (Murdock), a working mechanism (Radcliffe-Brown), a set of rules (Nadel), a set of corporate groups (Weber, Fortes), a relational set inherent in the process of transformations (Levy-Strauss)—all of them entail the notion of *persistence*. "None of these theorists has as yet dealt at all adequately with the time dimension in social affairs" (Leach 1968, p. 487).

In making the distinction, after Firth (1961, p. 35), between the *static* (patterns of stable elements) and the *dynamic* (patterns of change) models, it seems necessary to develop adequate methodological approaches to these two alternatives. Udy is wrong in saying that "it is misleading to treat patterns of stable interrelations as if they were basically different from patterns of change" (Udy 1968, p. 493).

By imposing some kind of an order upon the chaos of the external world, and by subduing nature to their own will, people create values for themselves, but at the same time they mobilize energies which act against the product of their creation. These energies are in the environment as well as in man himself. Enthropy spoils products. Internal weakness, shame, doubt, inconsistency and illness undermine the will of man. It is a drama of human existence that in order to survive and to achieve self-fulfillment, men have to shape events, but in doing so they expose themselves to counterpressures, external and internal contradictions, thus wasting energy and effort. The profane becomes supplemented by the sacred, and praxis becomes anchored in myths.

In social life we constantly witness the striving between two opposite drives: *the drive to an order and stability,* which assumes concomitantly a considerable integration of a given set of elements, and *the drive to innovation,* which assumes concomitantly the autonomy of individual actors and their actions, as well as weakens the integration of a system. On one hand, a clear-cut tendency appears to support the cohesion of a system and to convert its participants into obedient, controlled, and reliable organizational members. On the other hand, among the participants there is a need for nonconformism, especially when they are objects of countervailing expectations (related to the multiple social membership), or when they want to be creative.

THE MODEL OF A SOCIAL SYSTEM

In the study of organizations there exists a serious methodological difficulty in establishing common features which may serve as a basis of study. The model of system, however, provides such a basis. In general terms a system is: (1) something consisting of a set (finite or infinite) of entities, (2) among which a set of relations is specified, so that (3) deductions are possible from some relations to other or from the relations among the entities to the behavior or the history of the system (International Encyclopedia . . . 1968, p. 243). Depending upon which viewpoint we approach, organizations, different entities and relations will be specified and different deductions will become possible. From the sociological viewpoint, organizations interest us as social systems. This means *autonomic complexes of social roles* whose occupants (individuals or groups) cooperate in fulfilling certain goals which solve certain functional problems. "For any system of reference, functional problems are those concerning the conditions of the maintenance and/or development of the interchanges with environing systems, both inputs from them and outputs to them" (Ibid., p. 460). By being a part of the action, *social systems,* according to Parsons (1977), are closely connected to organisms, cultural systems, and personalities. Segmental and functional components of the social system are bound together on the principle of solidarity and pluralism. The higher level of that solidarity (organic solidarity as opposed to mechanical solidarity) is based on the division of labor, authority, leadership, and sociocultural superstructure.

The social system may be distinguished from other systems on the basis of substantial problems which waited to be solved. The *dialectic contradiction* between the necessity of achieving some levels of integration and the need to provide sufficient room for the flexibility of the actors, constitutes the core of the *social system*. In contrast to it, the *technological system* "involves the utilization of empirical knowledge, structured by the perceptual feedback through the cultural system, for the design and production of commodities having utility for human social function" (International Encyclopedia 1968, p. 466). Both systems are closely interconnected.

> The technological system sets certain requirements of its social system and the effectiveness of the total production system will depend upon the adequacy with which the social system is able to cope with these requirements. . . . The leadership of an enterprise must be willing to break down an old integrity or create profound discontinuity if such steps are required to take advantage of changes in technology and markets (Emery and Trist 1969, pp. 284, 292).

There are also meaningful relationships between the social system and the *economic system* which deal with the contradiction between interest in achieving maximum gains and the necessity of saving scarce resources, and the *administrative system* which deals with the contradiction between effective management (disposability) and the rank-and-file initiative (entrepreneurship). The effectiveness of actions depends on the possibility of harmonizing various systems and their principles of problem-solving.

Dimensions of social systems provide a convenient opportunity for interpreting several problems of organizations. Such media of interchange as code (language), power, influence, commitment, affect, and ideology may be more or less effectively utilized by the particular organizations. The concept of *system steering* coincides very well with the problems of management. Distribution of power within the system and its impact on the system performance may help to interpret the relationship between various styles of management and organizational efficiency. Inputs, throughputs, and outputs provide a basis for explaining the boundary exchanges of various organizations. However, one should also be aware of the limitations of systems analysis. System is merely an abstraction and it would not be reasonable to identify with real objects. What will be designated as a system is an arbitrary decision of the researcher. Secondly, the concept of equilibrium is also artificial in the sense that the achievement of balance of one set of elements does not preclude the balance of other elements of the same system. Thirdly, boundary exchanges are quite difficult to ascertain in many cases. Systems differ in their differentiation, interdependence, and openness, but it is difficult to establish reliable criteria of how much they differ.

In analyzing a system, it is necessary to distinguish various *functions*. According to D. Emmet, the notion of function is applicable when the object of the study is considered to form a system which is a unitary whole so ordered as a differentiated complex that it is possible to speak of part-whole relationships; and the parts are elements which can be shown to contribute to the fulfillment of the purpose for which the whole has been set up, or if it has not been purposefully set up, to maintaining it in a persisting or enduring state (Emmet 1968, p. 46). Functions may be manifest or latent, constructive or destructive for the systems integration (on manifest and latent functions, see Demerath and Peterson 1967, pp. 10–76).

It is possible to apply to organizations the concept of *basic functional needs and system requisites,* which have to be satisfied in order to permit the system (organization in this case) to exist and develop. Parsons (1977) talks about goal attainment, adaptation, integration and latency. Others, for example, D. F. Aberle, talk about provision of an adequate membership, role differentiation and role assignment, communication, shared cognitive orientations, shared and articulated sets of goals, the normative regulation of means, the regulation of affective expression, socialization, and the effective control of disruptive forms of behavior (Demerath and Peterson 1967, p. 317). This does not mean, however, that the system requisites do not contradict one another. According to Sjoberg,

All social systems are, at one time or another, plagued by contradictory functional requirements (or imperatives) and these are associated with the

> formation of mutually antagonistic structural arrangements that function to meet these requirements. Implied in this is the notion that some of these mutually contradictory structures may actually be essential to the operation or maintenance of the system (Demerath and Peterson 1967, p. 340).

It seems methodologically fruitful to approach the social phenomena in terms of systems theory, supplemented by the cybernetical approach. We are looking, in social life, for patterned activities of individuals or groups which may be treated as more or less stable sets of interdependent social roles. Following Katz and Kahn, "our theoretical model for the understanding of organizations is that of an energetic input-output system in which the energetic return from the output reactivates the system. Social organizations are fragrantly open systems in that the input of energies and the conversion of output into further energetic input consist of transactions between the organization and its environment" (Katz and Kahn 1966, pp. 16–17).

Like other systems, social systems may be treated as bases for "activity through which the import-conversion-export processes are carried out. A process is a transformation or a series of transformations brought about in the throughput of a system, as a result of which the throughput is changed in position, shape, size, function, or some other respect" (Miller and Rice 1967, p. 5).

We look at social systems as the parts of larger systems constellations, which are founded on vivid intersystem transactions across the boundaries of separate systems.

> Any open system, in order to live, has to engage in intergroup transactions. The members of any group are thus inevitably in a dilemma; on the one hand safety lies in the preservation of its own boundary at all costs and the avoidance of transactions across it; on the other hand survival depends on the conduct of transactions with the environment at the risk of destruction (Ibid., pp. 23–24).

Theories of social systems deal mostly with the structural properties of systems, and much less with their dynamics.[1] To study any systems change, and even more so systems growth, it seems of primary importance to establish some reliable criteria of progress. Any theory which neglects such criteria has to neglect at the same time the possibility of progress. That is exactly what happens, for example with the theory of Pareto.[2] The basic difficulty with the criteria of progress lies in their evaluative nature. The idea of progress is of a normative character and everybody feels compelled to judge social phenomena as "progressive" or "reactionary," according to his or her own ideological assumptions.

It is possible to find a criterion which would be free of a normative bias? The answer to this question is of crucial importance to the future of sociology as a science and for its utility in predicting the future. I would like here to focus attention on one particular possibility of overcoming difficulties as mentioned above: to switch from the problem of "progress" to the problem of growth toward maturity.

The basic question which should be answered is: What is the specific nature of a social system? Like any system,[3] a social system (a) consists of elements interrelated tightly to one another, (b) functions according to the established rules, and (c) strives to achieve some goals which are related to its own survival as well as to its position within the larger systems constellation (external environment) (Matejko 1968a).

Social systems deal with human energy, and their primary purpose is to use that energy to reconcile the particularistic needs of subsystems (individuals or groups) with the more universalistic needs of subsystems, this means constellations of systems which include, among others, a given system. By converting the contributions (intakes) of its members, whom we will call *actors* (after Parsons 1977), into some kind of output which would have for other systems an *exchange value,* it is possible for a given system to obtain some gratifications and to distribute them among its actors and subsystems.

Sociology, from our standpoint, is a scientific discipline dealing with the structure and dynamics of various social systems. The sociological analysis should cover all basic problems of making use of the social energy including "the importation of energy from the environment, the throughput or transformation of the imported energy into some product form which is a characteristic of the system, the exporting of that product into the environment, and the re-energizing of the system from sources in the environment" (Katz and Kahn 1966, p. 28).

Maturity of a social system is indicated by its ability to resolve the following dilemmas,[4] which stand in opposition to each other:

- in the relationship between the system and its supersystem: maximum symbiosis and cooperation between

them and minimum external interference into internal affairs of the system.

- in the internal sphere of the system: maximum integration of its subparts (in terms of coordination, cohesion, and socialization), and minimum internal ossification, which diminishes the adaptive abilities of the system.
- in the relationship between the system and the subsystems: maximum polycentrism permitting the subsystems to develop their internal abilities, and minimum disorder coming from satisfactory central control.
- in the dynamics of the systems: maximum development, which establishes for the system a satisfactory position within the particular social setting, and minimum instability, which assures the effective functioning of the system.
- in the management of system's affairs: maximum effectiveness in the coordination of member's activities and in the stimulation of them (in order to gain their full contribution to the well-being of the system), and a minimum concentration of power in a few hands only, which would seriously limit the initiative of the rank-and-file, on the other.

In order to survive, the system has to establish a certain stable internal order, which will enable the clear mutual identification of its participants, the delineation of its boundaries, the predictability of actions developed in the framework of a system, and the amalgamation of all participants around the commonly recognized values, patterns, and norms of social behavior. The functional coordination of all actions, achieved simultaneously with the cohesion of the internal structure of interhuman relations, and also with a widespread acceptance by participants of the group ideology (high degree of socialization)—these three factors indicate the achieved level of integration actively supported by all those social powers which profit from the order and the conservative stability.

The kind and the degree of integration appropriate in a given set of social factors depend on the system. Rigidity, conservatism, callousness, blind obedience to one another, and the far-reaching ossification of the total system may cost the system more than the benefits expected from the high integration. Quite often the inner-oriented system considerably weakens contacts with surroundings, and thereby diminishes its adaptability to the changing external situation. What is more convenient depends on the nature of a system: to pay the costs of maladaptation, because of a lack of elasticity, or to experience all the possible risks related to a large margin of freedom given to its own sub-parts.

The problem of *systems equilibrium* has created many controversies. According to F. Machlup, it is possible to view equilibrium as "a constellation of selected interrelated variables so adjusted to one another that no inherent tendency to change prevails in the model which they constitute. . . . Equilibrium may be also defined as a mutual compatibility of selected interrelated variables of particular magnitudes" (Demerath and Peterson 1967, p. 447). In social systems equilibrium is achieved by voluntary actions of partners vitally interested in balancing their powers.

> The difference between organisms and societies rests . . . in the degree of freedom of their parts, and the degree of effectiveness of their recombinations to new coherent patterns of activity. This in turn may rest on specific properties of their members: their capacity for readjustment to new configurations, with renewed complementarity and sustained or renewed communication" (Buckley 1968, pp. 398–99).

Self-regulation becomes extremely difficult in all complicated systems which do not base their existence on tradition and routine. The regulative effects vary—according to S. F. Nadel—"inversely with the separation of social roles, with the specialization of offices and tasks, and, implicitly, with the size of groups (since only small groups can function adequately without considerable internal differentiation)" (Buckley 1968, p. 404). Industrial activity introduces—according to G. Vickers—an increasing amount of disturbance which makes new regulations necessary even if, at the same time, they become more difficult (Buckley 1968, pp. 460–73). The regulator must be able to receive information about how things are going in relation to how they should be going to maintain (governors of behavior–A.M.); and it must be able to send signals to initiate behavior which will affect the course of events in the interest of (equilibrium) E. And between these two functions of "information in" and "information out" we must posit, according to G. Vickers, the all-important function of selecting what to do out of limited numbers of behaviors which are possible in the circumstances (Buckley 1968, p. 462).

Some kind of *ultrastability,* this means the capacity to persist through the change of structure and behavior, must be achieved by the system—according to M. L. Canwal-lander—in order to survive (Buckley 1968, pp. 437–40).

> Any social organization that is to change through learning and innovation, that is, to be ultrastable, must contain certain very specific feedback mechanisms, a variety of information, some kinds of input, channel, storage, and decision-making facilities. This may be stated in the form of an axiomatic proposition: that complexity of purposeful behavior is the function of the complexity of the communication components or parts of the system. More specifically, every open system behaving purposefully does so by virtue of a flow of factual and operational information through receptors, channels, selectors, feedback loops, and effectors. Every open system whose purposeful behavior is predictive, and this is essential to ultrastability, must also have mechanisms for the selective storage and recall of information; it must have a memory. . . . The communication net must contain or acquire information that makes learning and innovating behavior possible. . . . In order to innovate, the system must be able to analyze information, that is, it must separate it into constituent parts (Ibid., p 438).

THE DEVELOPMENT OF SYSTEMS

Social systems evolve on the basis of mutual association and interdependence among people who strive to adapt themselves to the environment and need one another in this respect. Some measure of identity and autonomy is needed in order to distinguish social systems from one another. On the other hand, some measure of conformism is necessary to maintain within systems the social mechanisms which will ensure the survival and the continuity of human bonds. Social systems differ in their reproductive capacity, ability to store and transmit information (symbol systems), reliance upon learning, dependence on other systems, internal controls, and so forth. The basic components of societies as sociocultural systems are: population, culture, material products, and social structure (Lenski and Lenski 1978, p. 35).

Every system has a core of strategic features (invariant) which is often difficult to locate, but can provide for the system its social identity.[5] Any activity which may eventually change the system by crossing its boundaries, has its impact on the above-mentioned features. When the impact is strong enough, it leads to the changes *of* the system instead *in* the system. The maturity of the system may be measured, among others, in its ability to allow for many internal changes without destroying the invariant.

A difficult question, relevant to social systems, is the amount of *deviance and conflict* the systems are able to tolerate. According to R. Net,

> Since the creative strength of a society must be sought in the capacity of individuals to evaluate, extend, correct, and ultimately to alter existing definitions and understandings (a process which is, in effect, deviation), the problem of ordering a society becomes one of utilizing the vital element—deviation—in social-organizational context. . . . Persons in the role of conformer fail to revitalize society and sustain a healthy social organization. Under conformer dominance, institutions lose their vitality, neglecting needs of individuals, or satisfying them only in token fashion (Buckley 1968, p. 412).

The disruptive tendencies have to be kept within certain limits, so that the system would be able to function fully. It is the fundamental principle for establishing some built-in mechanisms to keep various system elements under an effective control within the framework of a formal as well as an informal organization. For example, within the trade unions, leadership has to deal effectively with informal leaders who gain popularity among the rank-and-file by either incorporating them into the union establishment or by getting rid of them (for example, by undermining the source of their popularity).

The internal maladjustment of a system comes mostly from the disproportional development of system elements. For example, in societies which emphasize educational progress without providing adequate jobs and other facilities for graduates, the disproportions of growth are unavoidable. In some cases the alternatives are so limited that they predetermine the human behavior. For example, in most developing countries people who have acquired a baccalaureate degree work mainly for the government or public institutions. This means, of course, that the intentions and capabilities of the government overwhelmingly determine not only the future demand for trained manpower, but also the institutional framework within which this manpower will be employed.

The development of social systems depends on the progressing distinction between roles (as well as distinctive behavioral expectations attached to them) and the occupants of these roles. Repositories of useful knowledge become impersonal at the higher levels of system complication. Social surplus, the part of the total product of a system that is left over after the basic requirements needed to maintain the people at the appropriate level of living, become also controlled and allocated by the depersonalized powers. The idea that men can transform society has become widespread on the basis of the conversion of problems and conditions from the ancient theological contexts of good and evil to the rationalist contexts of analytical understanding and control. The consequences of a progressing institutionalization of social life become so costly that they must be counted and controlled. It is no longer justified to claim that evil causes evil in society. Anything that is at odds with dominant social values and expectations becomes an object of rational concern—even if it will be taken for granted that full consensus is just impossible within a highly differentiated society.

There is a tendency to treat social systems as malleable and to reject the concept of human nature as a biological constant among all men. The traditional solutions to recurring problems are being put into doubt. Artificial systems of rewards and punishments are being conceptualized in order to manipulate human beings. With the growing magnitude of available information it is possible to plan the innovation (and to stimulate it in response to environmental and intrasocietal influences) much more effectively than ever before. This has become a purposeful and deliberate action of various agencies that specialize in such an activity. Most of innovations can give rise to a wide series of others (a multiplier effect), and therefore the rate of innovation is constantly growing.

Is it possible to talk about "maturity" of social systems in a way similar to individuals? In the process of individual development several stages may be distinguished and the relative maturity of the individual is ascertained by investigating how able one is in problem-solving at a given stage of growth (Bühler 1935; Dabrowski and Piechowski 1977). According to Piaget (1956) and afterwards Kohlberg and others (Goslin 1969), in the problem-solving process at the higher stages of individual maturation the "higher" motives start to play a greater role than the purely practical and social considerations. The successful coping with problems by the individual is based not only on luck but also on a realistic diagnosis of conditions, acquisition of knowledge and experience, formulation of obtainable personal goals, positive approach to partners, self-dependence, and so on.

According to J. M. Miller (1971, 1972, 1978), the growth of systems in general strives in the direction of more differentiation of subsystems, more decentralization of decision-making, more interdependence of subsystems, more elaborate adjustment process, sharper subsystem boundaries, increased differential sensitivity to inputs, and more elaborate and patterned outputs. This growth is not necessarily equal—at least in the case of social systems—to the readiness of a given system to cope with the problems of growth. For example, the progressing occupational differentation of the modern society opens the contradiction between common well-being and the vested interests of various professional categories organized into the pressure groups (Ritzer 1977). Another example is the cleavage between the objective need to decentralize several economic activities (Herbst 1976) and the vested interests of groups vitally interested in preservation of the status quo. In a social system, the progressing interdependence of subsystems, mentioned by J. G. Miller as one of the dimensions of system growth, is frequently handicapped by the particularism of people who constitute various subsystems and who give priority to group interests over the common well-being (Matejko 1974).

Not only individuals but also social systems learn from each other and are able to modify their own behavior on the basis of the past experience. The reinforcement administered by leaders is not necessarily the only way for the social system to modify its collective functioning. The members of many social systems acquire better understanding of what happens around them through cognitive processes and initiate the adequate modifications within the systems. Social systems, like the individual, can move from one developmental stage to another following the maturational process sponsored and promoted by a group of innovators (modernizers).

Leaving aside the whole, highly debatable issue of the historical education of societies, there is the possibility of approaching the issue of system "maturity" from the perspective of general systems theory. Social systems can be considered at various levels of their socioeconomic development (in a broad historical sense), but the emphasis here will be in search of several possible criteria of "maturity" related to various subsystems.

"MATURITY" OF SYSTEMS

Social systems "mature" not only by learning how to make a better use of information and of matter-energy available to them but also by becoming more self-aware, cooperative, industrious, and dynamic. The individual qualities of human beings who constitute the membership of social systems unavoidably influence these systems, and vice versa. The high rate of change in the modern world makes the process of collective learning particularly important. In order to control their own destiny, it is basic for societies to dispose of the much more comprehensive storage of information than before, and at the same time to preserve the system continuity from generation to generation.

The consensus formation activity plays a major role in any democratic social system that depends on the common will of its members in order to survive and develop. The "mature" democratic system is based not only on the formal participation of its members in the decision-making process but also on the overlapping interest groups that can match one another in preventing the monopolization of power by any one of them. The socionormative integration of social systems becomes more and more urgent, and at the same time difficult under modern conditions. The far-reaching division of labor, urbanization, reification of human re-lations (market orientation) and the rising demands of people—all these factors make people within their social systems more materially dependent on one another but at the same time less morally integrated. In several social fields, primarily in the field of collective work, there are attempts to reorganize the modern social systems in order to humanize them (Emery and Thorsrud 1976; Matejko 1973b, 1976).

In psychology such phenomena as self-actualization, self-realization, realization of potential, and growth mo-tivation, are often discussed. By overcoming their own limitations, human individuals are able to progress in their psychological maturity. For example, Erikson looks upon this growth from the point of view of the conflicts which people have to solve in order to achieve a higher level of self-control (Erikson 1959, p. 51). According to Dabrow-ski, "personality develops through the loosening of its cohesiveness—an indispensable condition of human exis-tence. . . . The development of the personality occurs through a disruption of the existing, initially integrated structure, a period of disintegration, and finally a re-newed, or secondary integration" (Dabrowski 1964, pp. 2–3).

The dialectical growth of human personality as a model of a psychological analysis should inspire some theoretical searching for analogous models of social systems growth. It seems self-evident that the human nature expresses itself, among others, in social systems. What seem especially attractive for this purpose is the assumption that disorganization represents a creative potential.

The above-mentioned potential involved in dialectical contradictions exists not only in personalities but also in social systems. The whole concept of open and closed systems, so popular in modern social sciences, exhibits some similarities to the distinction Dabrowski makes between "psychopaths" and "psychoneurotics." What Dabrowski says about psychopaths may be applied to closed systems:

> The more cohesive the structure of primary integration, the less the possibility of development; the greater the strength of automatic functioning, stereotype, and habitual activity, the lower the level of mental health. The psychopath is only slightly, if at all, capable of development; he is deaf and blind to stimuli except those pertaining to his impulse-ridden structure, to which intelligence is subordinated (1964, pp. 121–22).

In contrast to psychopaths, among psychoneurotics features of an open system are common:

> The psychoneurotic's personality is plastic and variable since he is in a dynamic state of awareness of the subtleties of both his internal and his external environment. He is, therefore, a personality capable of disintegration and has the ability for distinct and often rapid development. . . . Unlike the psychopath, who inflicts suffering on other people and causes external conflicts, the psychoneurotic suffers and struggles with conflicts in relation to himself (Dabrowski 1964, pp. 74–75).

Would it be possible to distinguish, in a manner analogous to psychology, between "psychopathic" and "psychoneurotic" social systems? In the first case the guiding principle of a system is to defend its core values "invariant" against anything new, external, foreign, unknown, and therefore strange. In the second case the guiding principle of a system is to utilize all internal and external resources in order to achieve a new equilibrium which requires a considerable remodeling of the invariant at the same time.[6]

In order to make practical conclusions out of such an approach it would be necessary to look for an artificial manipulation of social systems, sociotherapy based on the verified social knowledge. Thus, when talking about maturity of social systems it appears necessary to accept the viewpoint of *social engineering*. The hope for growing maturity of social systems is based on the potential success of sociotechnics as an applied or practical social science informing "the practitioner on how to find effective means to realize intended social goals when a given set of values is accepted and a given body of tested propositions describing human behavior is accessible" (Podgorecki and Schulze 1969, pp. 142–43).

CRITERIA OF SYSTEM MATURITY

A system may be defined as mature when it has the ability to resolve effectively several dilemmas that any system has to deal with. In the *outside* sphere this is the question of a cooperative and peaceful relationship with external powers but preserving by the system its freedom from interference (autonomy). In the *internal* sphere this is the issue of finding some acceptable compromise between the necessity to integrate all subparts of the system (coordination, cohesion, and socialization), and the need to avoid ossification that may substantially lower the adaptive potential of the system. In this respect, one of the major contradictions deals with the polarization between polycentrism and monocentrism. In the sphere of system management there is a dilemma of unified leadership (motivation plus coordination) versus the participation of the rank-and-file in the decision-making process. Both functions of stimulation and coordination have to be reconciled one with the other and preoccupation with the system effectiveness should not exclude the possibility of local initiatives.

The following criteria are proposed as potentially useful in judging how mature are social systems under consideration:

1. The ability to activate, when necessary, a high social energy potential in order to face the critical tasks: By "social energy" is meant the willingness and skill of the system members to cooperate in the problem-solving process and in task implementation. The well-qualified contribution of each member is something which ought to be counted on within a mature system.

2. Easy elimination of all redundant factors in the process of critical tasks planning and implementation: Everything which is not needed contributes to additional difficulty and to a higher cost of task-fulfillment. For example, in the preparation of a stage performance, any additional actor above the necessary number may detract from the quality of the play (Matejko 1972b). In bureaucratic organizations the growing number of clerks very often becomes dysfunctional.

3. Availability of a stable invariant that allows the system to continue its existence and preserve its identity without necessarily making the system very rigid, ossified, and unadaptable to the changing circumstances. External and internal strains are the permanent aspects of any living system and they do not necessarily harm the system as long as the invariant remains intact.

4. Relationships among subsystems and components are more mature when they are harmonious, based on mutual trust and cooperation, subordinate to the idea of common welfare. With the growing number of system components, differences among them in size and power become more extreme, and this may lead to conflicts. In the modern social systems, a backlog of support and compliance typical for the traditional types of social ties is missing. An individualistic spirit and market competition both stimulate bargaining between the system components and reduce its cohesion. A mature social system is able and willing to tolerate some deviance and even dissidence in order to learn how to achieve higher levels of integration. In any social system, the heritage of stability and prosperity helps to achieve the steady state and self-assurance even in a crisis.

5. The external relationships of a social system are particularly suitable for the maturity analysis. Competition among various social systems brings out their strength in full relief. Intrasystemic conflicts impose upon these systems the necessity of utilizing to the full extent their internal resources and introducing several organizational improvements which contribute to the higher level of maturity. Development of the system has to be adequate to the changing internal and external conditions but at the same time its identity and some basic equilibrium have to be preserved. The greater a threat or stress upon a system, the more strength has to be mobilized in order to preserve the steady state in relation to the environment. The number and the amount of input demands of the system have to match the available resources. The mature social system remains flexible in its adjustment to the environment and in

its control of the steady state.

There is a large variety of criteria which may be useful in evaluating the maturity of social systems. Every element of the system has its own characteristics. The boundary-crossing transactions may be more or less effectively regulated. The delineation of systems boundaries may be done with precision. The procedures of conflict location and conflict resolution may achieve various levels of efficiency. In order to appreciate fully the wide theoretical horizons of evaluating systems in terms of their maturity, sociology needs much more of what is called the "systems thinking" (Emery 1969).

From the standpoint of systems maturity, it seems of primary importance to interpret in sociological terms the whole problem of change from a closed system to an open system. How does it happen? Why are some systems more eager to resign from their closed state than others? Which system elements are of crucial strategic importance in the process of change? Which social factors prevent systems from making progress toward their maturity? Which structural properties of systems play an important role in the whole process of growth?

Questions of such a general nature have to be transformed into questions of a much more specific nature to elicit meaningful answers. There is much to be done in this respect but the task seems to be an exciting one.

MATURITY OF SUBSYSTEMS

Not only the social system as a whole but also its various subsystems can be evaluated with regard to their relative maturity. The following approach is indebted to the classification of subsystems developed by J. G. Miller (1971, pp. 302-98).

Reproducer

The ability of a system to give rise to other similar social systems allows it to continue certain historical trends and to achieve some long-term objectives. The successful adaptation to changing circumstances necessitates a flexible transformation from one system to another; post-Franco Spain can be a positive example of this case. The Hutterite colonies, which split after achieving certain maximal size, may be another example. The awareness of the system when it should evolve into some new forms, and its ability to implement it, is a very important quality.

Boundary

A clear delineation between the system and its external world protects the former from the excessive pressures and stresses. It is up to the system to keep this delineation intact without damaging the contact with external world. Excessive preoccupation with the control of boundaries or with the extension of them is harmful to the system and may be treated as the sign of its immaturity.

The social system fully aware of its own limits and potentialities will focus the collective effort on making the best within the framework of existing boundaries instead of trying to solve its own internal problems by invading the territories belonging to other systems.

The boundary-filtering process tells much about the maturity of systems. Enforcement of the excessive boundary barriers as well as, on the opposite side, lack of an adequate regulation of the flows across the boundary, may provide evidence that the system is immature.

Usually more information is transmitted within a system (particularly a larger system) than across its boundary. A mature social system will stimulate the flow of energy and information inside and outside in order to benefit from both of them; it will also strive to optimize the relationship between this flow and the goal-achievement activity.

Ingestor

Bringing matter-energy (human and material) from the environment to the social system is needed for its survival as well as for its development. A mature system is able not only to obtain the necessary inputs but also to digest them. For example, some developing countries hire foreign specialists but do not always know how to utilize them adequately. The imported human resources have to be socialized into the system in order to become fully useful and reliable. Long-range planning is needed within social systems in order to anticipate future needs.

Distributor

Inputs coming from outside have to be allocated adequately within the system. The circulation of goods and services among various components of a social system has to be smooth in order to assure effective functioning of the latter. The maturity of social system in this respect is not only a technoeconomic problem but also a sociotechnical problem; namely, how the rationality of distribution (and circulation) of goods and services goes together with the vested interests of people who are directly or indirectly involved.

The centralized economies, primarily the Soviet one, suffer because of the great difficulty in reconciling the interests of groups and individuals, located down the hierarchy, with the interests represented by the central decision-makers only. There is a great waste of matter-energy (entropy) between the input and output points of a distributor when the social system does not provide satisfactory solution to the conflict of vested interests.

Converter

Inputs into the social system usually have to be changed in their form and content in order to fit into the existing needs within the system. The efficiency of conversion depends, among others, on the harmony between the formal organization and the social organization of production. In the mature social system management is able and willing to pay attention to the human aspects of collective work, offering an adequate stimulation, coordinating the efforts of people in a manner acceptable to them and reconciling the principle of leadership with the principle of participation (Matejko 1973c). Also in the mature system energy and resources are available for longitudinal social needs.

Producer

Reproduction, manufacture, and repair of system elements have to be assured. People in the mature social system are willing and able to secure its continuity by providing adequate socialization to members, manufacturing products to satisfy social needs, and making timely required repairs. Negligence in the preparation of new cadres, lack of care of their health and welfare, poor education of citizens, and so on, may be harmful to the society to no lesser degree than the negligence in the field of the economy. More mature social systems are characterized by the more attention paid to the whole spectrum of social and economic needs.

Matter-energy Storage

The security and the effective functioning of the system both depend, among others, upon the availability of deposits (capital savings). Social systems not paying attention to this necessity suffer defeat or poverty. Existence of the deposits and their economic utilization may be treated as the possible measures of system maturity. For example, families differ in the maturity of their approach to savings and investments.

Extruder

Transmission of matter-energy out of the social system in the forms of products, services, or wastes is still another factor in system equilibrium. Waste within the system is harmful to the system, functioning of the system may be endangered by an inadequate waste extrusion. On the other hand, the export of utilities to other systems is usually beneficial. Social systems mature by developing their active relationship to the world outside.

Motor

Social systems, in order to develop their potential to the full extent, need some stimulants as well as an effective utilization of the energy resources. In history, societies have been able to achieve much by following great ideas: moral order in Greece and ancient Israel, a generalized legal order as a hallmark of modernity (Parsons 1977, p. 13), and monotheism, and so on. On the other side, the advances of technology have allowed people to explore the potential of societies.

> Technological advance has been responsible for the growth in numbers of the human population, and the average size of societies and communities, the creation of new kinds of symbol systems (for example, written languages, musical tonation), the growth of vocabularies, the development of new kinds of ideologies, the increased production of material goods, the growing complexity of social structures (for instance, increased division of labor among individuals, among communities and associations, and even among societies), and other related developments" (Lenski and Lenski 1978, p. 68).

Maturity of a social system goes together with its high mobilization toward goal achievement in the subjective as well as the objective sense. Members of the system are motivated to act for the benefit of it; their individual and collective well-being is harmoniously reconciled with the common good. The system offers its members all that is needed to implement effectively the collective tasks. Kibbutzim and several religious communes, for instance, Hutterites and several monasteries, provide the best examples of such a maturity.

Supporter

Maintenance of the proper relationships among components of the social system, so that they do not interfere with one another, is the task implemented by the supporter subsystem. J. G. Miller limits this to spatial relationships, but in the social system the legal and moral order also play a very important role in this respect.

The ability of a social system to create and maintain such an order is the sign of maturity. Great civilizations in their dynamics depend on their own basic ideas about the backbone of what they are striving for. These ideas substantiate the social order that supports the specific social hierarchies and the adequate institutions. As long as this support lasts, the civilization is able to continue. The attainment of dynamic equilibrium between a given social system and the processes acting upon it is the sign of maturity.

External Information Input Transducer

Data coming from outside have to become decoded and adequately prepared for utilization by the social system. There is a problem of doing it without damaging the internal balance of the system. Responsible and socially motivated behavior of people and agencies active in the field is of great importance for the well-being of the system. For example, in Finland, there is an understanding among the mass media not to publish anything that would give the Soviet Union an occasion to endanger the very delicate political balance of the country. This solution seems to be more mature than government-administered censorship.

Internal Information Transducer

Lack of an adequate information exchange among various parts of the system limits extensively its potential, leads to various misunderstandings and tensions, contributes to the passivity of people, and offers room to the distorted views. In addition, the information circulation may be limited only to certain privileged persons, groups, and agencies with exclusion of other contributors. The trend toward impoverishment and elitism of the information circulation may be treated as an evidence of immaturity. The mature approach to information within the system is based on the encouragement of a well-informed, critical, and active citizenship and not on manipulatory gimmicks.

Channel and Net of Information

The information network should penetrate the whole social system to be efficient. The mature system pays special attention to it in order to avoid such a situation in which some parts of the system remain outside the information exchange. The view that it is functional to keep most of the population uninformed, as well as to limit the channels of information between the center of a system and its peripheries, appears to be irreconcilable with the view that systems should strive to become mature.

The informal network of communication is quite often no less important than the formal network, especially in creative work (Matejko 1973c). It is up to the mature social system to establish a harmonious relationship between both networks so that they can support each other. Very often people who belong to different groups have difficulties in communicating to one another and this becomes a problem. Another problem is the filtering of information at various levels of the hierarchy and the distortion of its content dictated by the vested interests of people who are placed at different levels. The mature social system should be able to deal effectively with those problems.

Decoder of the Information

Clarification and interpretation of information for use by people who are members of a given social system are very important functions. It makes much difference whether these vital functions are performed in the flavor of indoctrination, propaganda, and selling techniques (manipulation) or in the flavor of educating the responsible public. The mature system will appreciate the dignity of common man and will be free of the cynical manipulation of him typical for a mass society.

Mutual understanding and trust among members of the social system need to be substantiated by a common culture.

Therefore, the mature system is vitally interested in the promotion of such a culture which would express its basic needs, goals, and values. It is very difficult to maintain the unity of the society when the common cultural roots are missing.

Associator

The bits of information have to be associated with one another, made meaningful for the system and for its members. The massive learning process gained in importance with the progressing complexity of social systems, and the awareness of this fact is the evidence of system maturity. Complex systems depend very much on the great and regular inputs of a new comprehension of things. The common-sense approach is not enough in these cases; feedback process has to be effective and free from errors. In immature systems there is a drift to low performance; the learning processes are slow; and there is confusion and negligence arising from the conflict of various vested interests. Challenge and active response to the environment are characteristics not only for the development of civilizations (Toynbee) but also for the development and maturity of social systems in general.

Memory

An adequate storage of information within the system is necessary to prepare programs of action. The continuity of a system depends largely on the extent of storage. The mature system not only has adequate storage but in addition knows how to utilize it beneficially. In modern times the problem lies not so much in the inadequacy of information but rather in the oversupply of it and the need of selectivity. With the growing difficulties in the complex social systems with information retrieval and application, more and more attention has to be paid to the organization of system memory. Negligence in this respect shows the immaturity of a social system.

Decider

Steering of the system on the basis of information obtained from its subparts and from the outside is a problem of legitimacy, power, competence, and foresight. The maturity is particularly important and at the same time difficult to achieve in this field. Various aspects of steering have to be reconciled in order to achieve the steady state.

In the mature systems, the deciders look not for force but mainly for persuasion in order to elicit compliance. The power of deciders to punish others is limited and their authority has a moral basis. The acquiescence of the system members plays a decisive role and for this reason they are encouraged to participate actively in decision-making processes. The pluralistic nature of a mature system originates not only from the power-sharing setup but also to a large extent from the economic arrangement based on the whole variety of competing agents. All economic systems which reduce the majority of people to a subservient and passive role through manipulation have to be treated from this perspective as immature.

In order to achieve consensus and participation in decision-making among all members of the system, members must have enough in common with one another, be able and willing to make some valuable contribution to the common well-being, and willingly accept some discipline (Escriva 1979). The design of mature systems has to take into consideration several possible contradictions: sufficient consensus but not too much conformism; commitment, but not too much restriction; unity but also diversity; leadership, but not an authoritarian dominance; collectivism going together with the individualistic values; discipline and control, but at the same time freedom of the rank-and-file initiative.

Decisions within a social system are taken under various internal and external constraints; the awareness of these constraints, the rational choice and the maximal benefit, show that the system is mature enough to face its challenges. Considerations of risk are particularly serious in the mature systems in which prudence prevails over goal-seeking and ambition.

With the growing size and complexity of social systems, the decision-making process becomes more difficult and more vulnerable to errors; therefore, a mature solution may be to decentralize the decision-making process as much as to bring it closer to the specific needs and realities. However, there are always some fundamental choices to be made that have a general validity for the whole system.

Encoder

The mature system is able and willing to translate its internal (private) code into the external (public) code of communication with other systems. This is the problem of openness against closeness in relationship with the external world.   As the individuals who take the attitude which prevents them from finding common language with others, so the social systems may become intransigent, intolerant, self-oriented.

Authoritarian rule within a system may contribute heavily to the intransigence and self-centeredness of the latter.   The rulers, in order to justify, at least to some extent, the tough regime, tend to be intransigent in external relations.   Moreover, the internal power struggle within the system may prevent the adequate functioning of the encoder mechanism.

Output Transducer

The transmission of information from the system to the outside world may take a variety of forms.   In the social systems the middlemen are widely used in order to facilitate the external contacts.   The mature system will keep channels open to the outside world in order to prevent any isolation which in the long run may harm very much the system and its members.

THE MATURE BOUNDARIES

Every social system has boundaries specifying the realm of autonomous control executed on people and things, as well as transactions between them.   In order to create effective barriers against external influences, which may potentially endanger the total subordination of the system to the external social forces, "social systems develop their own mechanism for blocking out certain types of alien influence and for transforming what is received according to a series of code categories.   Though the coding concept can apply to the selective absorption and transformation of all types of input into a system, it is characteristically employed for the processing of information" (Katz and Kahn 1966, p. 60).

The functioning of any system necessitates a constant exchange of services and gratifications among all its constituent parts.   As P. M. Blau points out, social exchange is limited "to actions that are contingent on rewarding reactions from others and that cease when these expected reactions are not forthcoming" (Blau 1964, p. 6).   In other words, the internal communication within the system assumes some mutual benefits for the partners, or deprivation of potential benefits.   The cohesion (integration) of a system is based on an assumed rational character of the solidarity among all its members. "All social roles, including those which involve the exercise of power must, in the long run, be governed by norms mutually acceptable to all parties" (Cohen 1968, p. 168).

Systems, in order to achieve integration, develop several manipulations oriented toward equilibrium. The whole situation is, however, quite fluid and success is neither full nor permanent. It is again related to the imperfect nature of social systems, as well as to the variety and the dynamic nature of social environment. The regular and unhampered exchange within the social system, as well as outside, should be taken as one of the most important criteria of systems maturity. There are several aspects of this exchange.

Systems effectively arrange their relationship to the outside world by: controlling the traffic through the boundary, establishing explicit criteria of accepting or rejecting the cross-boundary communication, separating the belongings of a given system from the belongings of other systems, and maintaining some visible symbols. By tracing demarcation lines it becomes possible to establish the self-identity of a particular system in relation to the external world. "Without such special provisions, organizational members at the boundaries would become susceptible to outside influence. The incursion of environmental influence would be uncontrolled and would vitiate the intra-system influences" (Ibid., p. 61).

In conclusion, boundaries are of vital importance for the system's identity and relationship with other systems. However, one should not assume that all these functions are fully reasonable and useful. In quite a few cases some exaggerated emphasis on the rigid delimitation of boundaries and on the strict control of all boundary crossings may lead to several dysfunctions. For example, a particular system may separate itself too much from other systems and resign (to its own disadvantage) from several useful external inputs. There may be also an opposite case, when a system does not bother enough about its own boundaries and controls related to them. In many cases of cooperation among various systems, this problem of optimal boundary delimitation has not been solved properly. For example, a supersystem may recognize some vital boundary prerequisites of subordinated systems. Therefore, it seems justified to talk about maturity of systems also in the terms of their rational approach to the problem of boundaries. In order to examine this question one has to consider first of all several basic sociological aspects of the system boundary.

The social space delimited by systems boundaries contains not only people defined as system members, but also several other social elements needed for the existence, development, and transformation of a given system: social-cultural concepts on which the activities of a system are based, the means of actions, structures into which various actions are organized, and methods of coordinating these actions, and so on. All these elements are interrelated and any transaction which crosses a system's boundary may lead to a whole variety of direct (manifest) and indirect (latent) functions of an intrinsic, as well as extrinsic character.[7]

What interests us here is the variety of problems related to the crossing of the system boundary by people as performers of some specific social roles. We would like to look for the implications to the maturity of the system which arise from this boundary crossing. Depending on the nature of the transaction as well as on the way of handling it, it will be possible to estimate appropriately the functional value of such a transaction.

Systems differ widely in their ability of self-regulation within a framework of certain autonomy. According to E. J. Miller and A. K. Rice,

> What distinguishes a system from an aggregate of activities and preserves its boundary is the existence of regulation. Regulation relates activities to throughput, ordering them in such a way as to ensure that the process is accomplished and that the different import-conversion-export processes of the system as a whole are related to the environment (Miller and Rice 1967, p. 8).

In order to avoid any kind of a chaotic boundary crossing, as well as to keep the system members within the areas of activity prescribed for them, a social system has to apply some regulatory mechanisms which deal with all these things. The function of management consists primarily in stimulating and coordinating activities of all members. However, the coordination of the system with other systems within the same system network is also important.

One of the main predicaments related to the management function is the dilemma of dealing effectively with the human factor. Management often is inclined to neglect that factor. If we regard the organization "as a tool designed primarily for task performance" then, of course, the human factor has to be approached as having much significance, and "human needs—for satisfaction or for defense against anxiety—should be regarded as constraints on task performance" (Smelser 1965, p. 11).

Among various dimensions of technology, the dimension of *uncertainty* puts the greatest strain on the human factor. This strain become especially acute in creative jobs. By being able to reconcile the creativity of individuals with organizational cohesiveness, social systems show their ability to progress toward maturity. The conflict between individual freedom of contribution and the prerequisite of organizational uniformity of actions provides a constant challenge.

There are many possible ways of classifying boundary crossings from the standpoint of the position of a system within the broader framework of relationships. It seems necessary to distinguish firstly the regular boundary crossings related to the normal functioning of a system within the prescribed parameters of an exchange of goods and services with other systems. A planned economy functioning exactly according to the assumptions may serve as an example.

The "ideal model" of a regular and uninterrupted boundary crossing may be useful as a pattern, but in reality we deal mostly with imperfect models. The exigencies of social life are so manifold and mobile that there is a constant necessity to reorder the whole business of boundary-crossing for the sake of system's efficiency or even its survival. "Imperfect" models are, in terms of social efficiency, more perfect than "ideal" models, because the former offer more room for constant change and improvement. In order to preserve the pretended "ideal" pattern of boundary-crossing against changing circumstances it is necessary to develop an artificial manipulation, which, however, leads sooner or later to rigidity and maladaptation. Therefore, the maturity of systems should be measured not in the terms of how regular and stable the traffic of boundary-crossing is, but of their functionality.

The ability of the system to cope with irregular boundary crossings seems to be basic for maturity. All attempts to eliminate irregularity entirely are not only futile but also provide evidence of some rigidity. Irregularity has to be accepted as something natural, to which the system has to adapt itself in order to achieve social maturity.

Irregularity happens most often in the spheres located between various forms of organization, where there is less control. Any social system, like "any enterprise requires three forms of organization—the first, to control task performance; the second, to ensure the commitment of its members to enterprise objectives; and the third, to regulate relations between task and sentient systems" (Miller and Rice 1967, p. 13).[8] There is constant communication among all three forms of organization themselves as well as between them and the outside world. Within this communication, loopholes are possible.

All boundary crossings have to be related meaningfully to import-conversion-export processes on which depend both the existence and the development of systems. From this standpoint, it seems advisable to distinguish between the *functional* (contributing, integrational) crossings and *dysfunctional* (not contributing, disintegrational) crossings. The operating, maintenance, and regulatory activities of a system necessitate much of boundary-crossing between various sections of a given system, as well as between the system as a whole and the external agencies of other systems. The effectiveness of all these crossings has to be evaluated from three basic standpoints: (a) from the standpoint of local framework of a particular crossing (for instance, the effectiveness of economic activities in terms of their costs), (b) from the standpoint of the whole system's well-being, and (c) from the standpoint of a meaning which a particular crossing may have for the outside world. All three of them provide a suitable basis for formulating some important criteria of system maturity.

PROBLEMS OF CHANGE AND CONFLICT

One of the basic internal dilemmas of systems deals directly with the problem of change. For any system "safety lies in the preservation of its own boundary and the avoidance of transactions across it; on the other hand, survival depends upon the conduct of transactions with the environment and the risk of destruction" (Miller and Rice 1967, p. 24).

The social order may be maintained by coercion, by appealing to common interests, or by strengthening the values shared by the people. Relying on coercion, inducement, or commitment in their pursuit of some satisfactory level of integration, all social systems have to develop the appropriate methods of achieving not only the coherence but also some consensus.[9] One should not be mislead by the appearance of conflict. In fact, it is because all sections of a particular larger system share something in common that the conflict is possible. "It is because all sections of industrial societies share certain common values—the desire for higher incomes to acquire an increasingly wide range of goods and services—that there is so much conflict over the distribution of rewards" (Cohen 1968, p. 145).

Systems show their maturity by locating the trouble spots and dealing with them effectively. Internal relations within social systems may be classified according to certain basic combinations of four factors: actors, actor' motivation, object of striving, and the direction of striving. Even this very simple classification reveals several types of clashes between the actions of actors, such as: interference (conscious or erratic), fight, disturbance, and extinction.

It is always an arbitrary decision what will be called a *conflict*. We propose, following the suggestion of P. S. Cohen to treat conflicts only in those cases when actors consciously hinder one another in achieving their goals by performing appropriate actions of a disturbing character.

The delimitation of boundaries, within which various actors are allowed to pursue their goals without any hindrance, is basic for the concept of *order* (Collins and Guetzkow 1964).

> Social conflict exists where the goals of one group are pursued in such a way as to ensure that the goals of another group cannot be realized. Struggle occurs when an action is taken to remove the source of conflict by reducing the power of another party, or by eliminating another party from the conflict situation (Cohen 1968, pp. 184–85).

The sources of conflict have to be looked for in a particular configuration of resources, goals, and strivings of partners, and not so much within the sphere of human attitudes. Therefore, in order to achieve the conflict resolution it is more important to change the balance of forces than to bring partners to a kind of peaceful coexistence. "Structured conflict, when it involves a fairly equal balance of forces, actually obstructs change which might otherwise occur" (Ibid., p. 184).

Conflicts experienced by individuals have usually their institutional background. Being enmeshed in a network of institutionalized social ties, becoming exposed to the conflicting demands of various institutions, people are affected by pressures arising from incompatibilities within the institutional structure. Quite often they are not aware of the fact that their individually unfortunate experience has a deeply rooted structural background. The malintegration of the institutional complex, as well as the maladaptation of human beings to the institutional environment, lead to several tensions. Social systems by improving their institutional integration can progress substantially toward the higher level of maturity.

However, in the social reality there are quite many systems which are far from being equilibrated. In the long run, all social systems are exposed to changes. Therefore, the regularities of *transformation* are more meaningful than the regularities of a structural-functional *interdependence* of parts.

Talking about conflict as a social phenomenon in the system framework it is necessary to look at its function: eufunctional or dysfunctional, depending on how the conflict influences system throughput. There are conflicts in any case of discoordination of a system's crucial parts. For example, when the supplier of energy puts into the system more than the system really needs, or if the vested interests of any system's element prevail over the interests of the whole system.

Taking the viewpoint presented above, it is possible to locate all conflicts within the network of interconnections between various systems' elements. The subsystems may differ in their orientations. The various individuals and groups occupying posts within the framework of a system may clash in their vested interests. Most of the conflicts can be interpreted in the terms of: (a) lack of unity among the system's parts, and (b) chaotic boundary-crossing. On the other hand, conflicts contribute substantially to the rejection of an existing boundary delineation. As P. S. Cohen points out, "conflict itself involves a relatively low degree of normative definition of role performance between the conflicting parties" (Cohen 1968, p. 147).

The dialectical approach to the social structure and to the performance of systems should emphasize the potential of conflict as the source of eventual improvement. According to Kahn,

> Group conflict has positive social functions, just as individual conflicts contribute to individual development. What is inherently evil in conflict is its resolution through violence and destruction, for violence corrupts its users. Without conflict, however, there would be a few problems, little stimulation and little incentive for constructive effort (Kahn and Boulding 1964).

One has also to agree with B. M. Gross when he says that

> conflict among and within systems is probably the greatest source of continuing change. Internal

conflicts are inescapable even in the "normal" personality. They are created by the multiplicity of competing or even contradictory human interests, social roles and group attachments. Similar conflicts develop among and within the subsystems of all systems. The common interests and goals that keep a system together are always imbedded in a network of divergent and competing interests and goals. Conflict usually becomes more dramatic in the intersystem relations of rivalry, competition and combat. Extreme forms of conflict, of course, may readily undermine or destroy the system. However, some degree of conflict—both internal and external—is an essential stimulus to system adaptability and creativity (Gross 1966).

It seems also appropriate to add what R. N. Sandford says, that "the hardening of the role structure which is an organization's best defense against the inroads of individual irrationality gives equal protection against failure and against success" (Kahn and Boulding 1964, p. 100).

The social system open to creativity, and in this sense mature, is characterized by successful integration into the system of several conflicts which may have a value as stimulating creativity. Therefore, the elimination of contradictions and the achievement of some kind of system stability should by no means be treated as the only effective way of establishing a working system. D. Lockwood emphasizes that

When we talk of the stability or instability of a social system, we mean more than anything else the success or failure of the normative order in regulating conflicts of interests. Therefore, in an adequate view of social dynamics it is necessary to conceptualize not only the normative structuring of motives but also the structuring of interests in the substratum. . . . It is necessary to know about the forces generated by norm and substratum if we wish to understand why patterns of behavior persist or change. . . . If we wish to understand the balance of forces working for stability or change we must look not only to the normative order, but also and principally to the factual organization of production and the powers, interests, conflicts and grouping consequent on it (Lockwood 1967, pp. 285–86).

The functions of conflicts within the system depend very much on their relationship to the configuration of that system presented by its social structure. In order to control the conflicts it is necessary to build into the system some safety devices. As K. E. Boulding says, "there is some boundary, on the far side of which the system becomes pathological. A conflict system, then, exhibits control if it has an apparatus somewhere in the system and pulls it away from the boundary. This is an example of a familiar mechanism known as a cybernetic, or homeostatic, mechanism" (Kahn and Boulding 1964, p. 143).

At a time of fast growth and social change the internal stratification within a given system may become entirely upset by the fact that people acquaint themselves with new circumstances, acquire some new qualification, and begin to strive for some new social positions. Under the impact of new experiences, the stratification lines and the boundary-crossings determined by them become unstable; this happens, for example, with traditionally rigid gender barriers in developing countries. Progress in employment leads to demands for the removal of these barriers. Women play an increasingly important role in many sectors of the modern economy.

From the perspective of maturity, the accelerated exchange between social strata requires the consideration not only of the advantages of abolishing traditional social arrangements but also its costs. Take an example: young people wander off to the cities. Unable to grow roots in the new environment, primarily because of employment shortages, they remain suspended between two different worlds (Mangin 1970). Social mobility within the given system is one of the basic factors of exchange. It would be extremely fruitful to establish criteria of such a mobility which helps the system to mature without disrupting its cohesiveness.

In order to achieve some substantial change, the newly emerging social powers must be able to cross freely not only the economic and social boundaries, but also the cultural and moral boundaries. For example, in Europe the progress of economic activities had been hampered for centuries by the traditional legal, social, and cultural obstacles. However, "during the last six centuries of European history there has been a basic change in the structure of differential evaluation of occupational roles" (Barber and Barber 1965, p. 2). The move from the traditional status-oriented society to the new task-orientation may be eased by ideologies which promote task-related human virtues.

Appreciating fully the importance of social mobility for the growth of a social system toward its maturity one should not, however, exaggerate its extent as well as its positive contribution. There is a convincing historical evidence that in most cases social mobility remained limited to certain social strata, and even when it was broader it followed certain established patterns of cultural and social inheritance (Ibid., p. 6).

THE MEASUREMENT OF ORGANIZATIONAL MATURITY

There has been already a considerable experience in studying the organizational effectiveness (Price 1968), but in order to make it more efficient it seems necessary to introduce some additional criteria of system maturity. For example, the concept of an "organic organization"[10] allows one to gain a broad comparative perspective by showing that there may be a more mature organizational pattern with which to make a comparison.

The problem areas have to be located in order to measure the maturity of a given social system in its most strategic dimensions. For example, in examining the maturity of a local governmental branch in Alberta in 1971, the following problem areas were selected for measurement: goal clarity and fulfillment, performance, coordination, standards, authority support, the resource supply (task-oriented resources, in distinction to the coherence-oriented resources), information supply, leadership, structuring of activities, cooperation within the branch, cooperation with external agencies, integration, organizational efficiency, and recognition of customers' needs and expectations (Matejko—an unpublished research report). The system maturity was measured on the basis of a test administered to all people working in a given governmental branch. In each problem area the praxiological criteria were utilized in order to formulate the adequate test items (Kotarbinski 1965).

The "steady state" of the U.S. general hospitals as complex social systems was studied in the early 1960s,[11] taking into consideration the following problem areas: organizational and members' goal attainment; availability and allocation of organizational resources; organizational coordination; social integration; intra-organizational strain; and organizational adaptation (Georgopoulos and Matejko 1967). By measuring the relative success with which the hospital handles its problems in these key areas, it is possible to determine how mature a given hospital is as a complex social system. The traditional rule of a well-integrated organizational elite consisting of trustees, doctors, and administrators has been challenged by the new claims originating inside hospitals as well as outside them. This challenge points to the necessity of some structural reforms in the specific hospitals. Depending on their recognition of the new situation, urgency of needs and ability to face the challenge, the hospitals appear as mature social systems. The much fuller participation in the affairs of the hospital organization and the better performance of nonmedical personnel becomes a necessity. The acceptance of it by the hospital establishment says much about its systemic maturity. The traditional alliance of doctors and administrators has to incorporate some new claimants whose collective strength is the product of hospital modernization. The internalization of organizational goals is high among the hospital personnel, but in order to utilize it fully it would be necessary to create the formal channels of management participation for all occupational groups included in the hospital (Georgopoulos 1972, pp. 45–46).

During the 1960s in Poland, the author, together with several other collaborators, studied the relative maturity of professional work teams: 14 teams in science (nuclear physics, biochemistry, mathematics, medicine, technology, and so on); 20 teams in applied research (electronics, housing, meteorology, commerce, and the like); four editorial teams in creative journalism; and a team of architects (Matejko 1973c). The in-depth interviews were done with all members of any given team as well as with the management personnel. All possible data on the team and its performance were also collected from the files and reports (the methodology was influenced to some extent by the study done by D. C. Pelz and F. M. Andrews)(Pelz and Andrews 1966).

All data collected from the interviews and files were later utilized for a comparative analysis of system maturity in the following problem areas:

- collective aims, and their interdependence with the individual aims;
- membership of a team in terms of their skills, motives, and willingness to cooperate;
- means available to a team and their adequacy;
- the status structure of a team (prestige, social distances, and so on);
- division of work within a team in terms of specialization, coordination and control;
- social climate within a team (morale of people, initiative,

commitment);
* work culture within a team (patterns, values, and norms);
* stimulation of members within a team (perspectives of promotion, material and moral rewards, and so on);
* placement of a team within its environment (acceptance, relationship with the higher authorities, popularity);
* the social, cultural, and moral integration of the team as a human group;
* standards of performance and behavior applied to the team and their fulfillment;
* conflicts and their resolution within the team;
* leadership and management of a team in terms of inspiration and coordination.

The maturity of a team was evaluated for each of the above-mentioned problem areas, and on this basis the maturity profiles of various teams were compared. This measurement based on the qualitative evaluations in the long run may be particularly useful for the experimentation in industrial democracy promoted not so much by external experts as by the people directly involved in work.

With the growing importance of public projects and services in modern or modernizing societies there is also more and more need for evaluation and evaluative research. The social-system approach may be utilized for the development of evaluative studies which would allow to ascertain whether the given programs or procedures are really achieving some desired results. There are too many vested interests which bias evaluative reports and prevent one from obtaining a real picture of what is achieved. To the program administrator "to question the underlying assumptions of the objectives (which he has already defined—A.M.) is both difficult and painful. To subdivide these objectives further in terms of intermediate steps toward some ultimate objectives often appears to the program administrator as an attempt to limit and destroy his program" (Suchman 1967, pp. 22–23).

In many cases the goals of systems treated as objects of evaluation are not even clear enough to identify them. Besides, there are such issues as: location of problems with which the activity must cope (for example, a heavy political bias in the case of dealing with some local issues), description and standardization of the activity, measurement of the degree of change that takes place, determination of whether the observed change is due to the given system's activity or to some other cause, and indication of the durability of the effects (Ibid., p. 31).

Defining evaluation as the determination (based on opinions, records, subjective or objective data) of the results (desirable or undesirable; transient or permanent; immediate or delayed) attained by activities (a program, or part of a program, a drug or a therapy, an ongoing or one-shot approach) designed to accomplish valued goals or objectives (ultimate, intermediate, or immediate, effort or performance, long- or short-range) (Ibid., p. 31-32) one comes to the conclusion that the measuring of goal attainment is just only one of several aspects in the whole process of systems evaluation. A main issue is always the conflict of values within a given system. Any system consists of several groups which exercise their pressures and promote their own viewpoints. System's goals are the outcome of all those pressures and expectations. Depending which group is currently in the dominant position within the particular system, its orientation prevails.

On the other hand, the evaluator imposes upon the system reality his or her own values and judgments. They may be, and quite often they are, in conflict with those represented by people in power as leaders, managers, experts, clients or sponsors. There is nothing basically wrong with disagreement of viewpoints—as long as it does not prevent the evaluator to cooperate with "organization men" and to provide them a chance of self-improvement. It is the main service of the evaluator to help in answering questions related to the proper formulation of system objectives, location of people and issues which are targets of a particular activity, timing of expected achievements, and ascertaining their desired magnitude and methods of achieving the expected goals, and so forth.

It is important not to confuse in evaluation various levels of system objectives. From the long-range perspective on performance, a particular system may look different than from the short perspective. One of the main difficulties in system evaluation is the contradiction between rewards offered by certain actions and long-run rewards which may be lost in the case of looking only for current gains. For example, R. Likert (1967, p. 11) brought the issue of managers who preferred the authoritarian style over the democratic style of managing people just because their time perspective was too short. It is always a big issue in evaluation to ask how much the immediate goals and the intermediate goals do contribute to the achievement of ultimate goals.

It is necessary to check carefully the validity of all assumptions related to underlying values and causal relationships in order to avoid some obvious errors. The objectives of action may be either too much idealized or based on inadequate empirical proof. The input of energy may be erroneously treated as more important than the actual performance. Achievement may actually be good but not high enough to meet some specific social needs. Clients of a particular program of activities may be wrongly selected. Alternative methods and paths of actions may be considered as not paying enough attention to clients. Comparative efficiency ratings may be wrongly estimated. Planning of the program and the fulfillment of a particular plan may be inadequate.

Suchman is right in saying that "the evaluative project must include an analysis of the intervening process between the program and result. In evaluative as opposed to non-evaluative research, however, the manipulability of these intervening variables rather than their explanatory power is more likely to influence their selection" (Suchman 1967, p. 87). An evaluative research design should not exclude intervening variables, when in pure research such a manipulation becomes a necessity. "Acceptance of an open-system, naturalistic, multi-causal model as opposed to the closed-system, mechanistic, single-cause model has tremendous implication for the formulation of evaluative research projects" (Ibid., p. 84).

The evaluative research projects must be based on some normative assumptions which would allow a clear distinction between "good" and "bad" performance. The suggestion here is that these normative assumptions should be related to the growth of a system toward its functional and structural maturity. The first thing to do is establish criteria of maturity specifically for every systems element.[11] Afterwards it would be necessary to look into the interdependence of various elements; how they fit into each other, what is their mutual adequacy, and so on. Anticipation (program)—actors—goals—energy and information supply—means—structures—steering mechanism—feedback, all have to be treated as a chain which consists of parts bound together.

To evaluate the maturity of the whole system, it seems necessary to study carefully the many possible combinations of elements. Take for example the first possible combination of anticipation as related to any of the remaining seven elements. We would call this combination mature if there were no serious contradictions among the parts of it. The actors have to be logically related to the program of action. The energy and information supply have to be planned carefully. The same is valid for the means of action. The various structures have to be combined with each other to provide the best social basis for programmed action. The steering mechanism has to be able to fulfill the program. The feedback has to assure the necessary corrections of the program during the whole duration of its execution, and so on.

FUNCTIONALISM AND THE PROBLEM OF CONFLICT

Until now, the approach to the whole question of social organization has been dominated by functionalists. However, there is a growing awareness of the fact that functionalism has serious methodological shortcomings, and that alternative approaches should be investigated.

Functionalism is based on the assumption that the system does exist and that it is able to resist more or less successfully the pressures exercised upon it. "A primary indicator of the applicability of a functional model is the persistence of a social pattern despite forces that tend to destroy the pattern. . . . The usefulness of models of functional systems in particular depends on the extent to which the phenomena investigated by social scientists exhibit equilibrating or self-maintaining processes" (Cancian 1968, p. 41).

The exposure of social objects to external and internal tensions is almost neglected within the structural-functional approach. "The typical functionalist approach to the concept of integration is to equate it with lack of conflict" (Cancian 1968, p. 36). Consistency among social patterns, absence of conflicting normative expectations, adequacy of motives to expectations—all these things are meant as *integration*. However, "it seems very unlikely that any society or large social system is perfectly integrated, regardless which definition is used" (Ibid., p. 36).

The functionalistic approach to social systems in general, and to the workplaces in particular, implies that integration—for example, interdependence and compatibility between the parts of a system—is the natural and normal state of a system. In modern civilization, characterized by rapid changes and growing contradictions, the above-mentioned approach evidently becomes unsatisfactory. A dialectical approach, as P. L. van den Berghe (1967) says, "which treats change as axiomatic and stability as problematical," seems to be necessary. We agree with van den Berghe that "functionalism is slanted in that it underrates conflict and disequilibrium, and assumes too much continuity, gradualness and conformity in the process of change. . . . To account for endogenous change through conflict and contradiction, the dialectic must be introduced to complement functionalism" (Ibid., pp. 297–99, 305).

The approach to the social structure and to the performance of systems should emphasize the potentiality of conflict as the source of eventual improvement. The social system may be potentially open for creativity, and achieve in this sense maturity; this may be reached by a successful integration into the system of several conflicts; tensions and contradictions are valuable as long as they stimulate creativity. Therefore, the elimination of contradictions and achievement of system stability should by no means be treated as the exclusive way of establishing an *effective* system.

The functions of conflicts within the system depend very much upon their relationship to its social structure. In order to control conflicts, it is necessary to build into the system some safety devices. As K. E. Boulding says, "there is some boundary, on the far side of which the system becomes pathological" (Demerath and Peterson 1967, p. 143).

The institutionalization of conflict within the framework of a particular system may be more or less successful. Anyway, this institutionalization saves much in terms of human and economic resources. For example, look what happened with strikes in the United States since the World War II just because they became institutionalized (Kornhauser 1954, p. 12). The institutionalization of conflicts within social systems gives rise to their social utility. J. L. Horowitz points out that "there are, to draw an analogy from game theory, conflicts programmed for continuation of the game (such as parliamentary debates), and there are those programmed to end the game through a change of the roles as such (such as coup d'états)" (Demerath and Peterson 1967, p. 275). The ratio of first-hand conflicts to second-hand conflicts may provide a good basis for rating the maturity of system in the field of conflict resolution.

There is the cultural conception of a system (structure), based on values and commitments of people oriented toward these values, as well as the interactionist or morphological conception of a system based on patterns of mutual contacts among people, groups, and institutions. Both do not take into consideration the internal balance of conflicting structures, pressures, and commitments.

Instead of asking what must be done to maintain the system on the adequate level (the issue of functional requisites), we should ask how to locate and eventually to reconcile the opposing tendencies within the system (and outside of it) that influence its identity and location within the broader social framework (Levy 1968, p. 23). The continued existence of systems seems to be less important than their changing role within the framework of inter-crossing pressures. Eustructures and dystructures, as well as eufunctions and dysfunctions—all of them may change from one to the other depending on circumstances. "No condition or aspect of a condition is inherently eu-functional or dysfunctional. The same condition that is eufunctional from one point of view may be dysfunctional from another" (Levy 1968, p. 25).

THE DIALECTICAL APPROACH

From the dialectical perspective, social life is first of all a process of *becoming,* and not just as *being.* The human psyche is an active element and not simply a passive re-ceptor of an external world. Thought and activity pene-trate one another. We impose our own order upon reality which in its true nature is chaotic and multidimensional. "The mind selects only certain characteristics of phenomena as significant; it finds cultural meaning in only a segment of reality; it falsifies the world at the very least, by omission. Culture, then, turns upon the mind and perpet-uates the illusion" (Murphy 1971, p. 239). Furthermore, Murphy says that "the estrangement between Subject and Object derives from the Subject's failure to understand that the locus of reality lies in the mind" (Ibid., p. 93).

From this position, objects in the world are not naturally discrete and separate. It is a great simplification to treat them as entities linked together or manipulated according to a certain scheme.

> The world of phenomena is continuous, and the human mind, aided and abetted by language, breaks it up into discrete objects. . . . We believe in a universe of separate and independent things that become somehow related to each other, but we could just as profitably, perhaps more so, look upon reality as continuous and study the means by which it becomes fragmented" (Ibid., p. 208).

"Social life is visibly chaotic. Its basic characteristic is flow and flux; its concrete ingredients are people num-bering into millions and hundreds of millions; the substance of our observations is events, each of them unique, just as each human is unique" (Ibid., p. 39).

Social reality in its true nature is dynamic, and in order to anlayze any social object it is necessary first of all to treat it in its relation to a given configuration of sources of energy that are socially significant. People and their institutions are sources of dynamics together with nature. It is necessary to become aware of how powerful these dynamics are, how they condition a given object externally as well as internally, how they are related to one another (conflict or cooperation), which directions they follow, which are the outcomes of their mutual coinfluence, and how the whole situation changes because of the transformations in the energy balance existing behind a given object.

Social reality should not be reduced to any one particular level of analysis, but has to be approached on a whole variety of levels considered simultaneously. The internal harmony of objects is just one of the many possible states of affairs.

In the sociological explanation it is necessary to apply the strategy of a *multidimensional approach* which would allow us to understand what happens with a given object by relating various levels to one another (Podgorecki and Los 1981). Positivistic reductionism to the so-called "empirical facts" leads to simplification and distortion of social reality whenever no counterfacts are taken into consideration. Social objects should be interpreted in relation to the whole variety of "realities" that may, and in most cases do, contradict one another.

Social actions, by interfering in a given state of events, mobilize *counteractions* oriented toward the potential annihilation of goals, and eventually the agents of the actions. Actions and counteractions (reaction) have to be considered together as internally split units of social activity. Any proposal has to be analyzed together with its counterproposal: unity together with disunity, coherence together with looseness, social bond together with social anomie, love together with hate, commitment together with disengagement, and so on. Everywhere there are goal-directed activities which effectively and simultaneously negate each other. "The opposed elements do not negate each other in a simple mutual cancellation process but as an essential part of their existence. They pass into each other, and in going beyond their limitations they realize their possibilities" (Murphy 1971, p. 205).

Within any social process there is a dialectical sequence (Sartre 1960, 1963). "Its essence, its core, is the principle of unity and struggle of opposites. . . . Movement does not undermine the logical principle of contradiction but is the unity of opposites that we discover in investigating its concrete forms. The source of all movement and change is the struggle of internal opposites proper to every thing and every phenomenon. In this sense any thing and any phenomenon is contradictory as containing internal opposites" (Schaff 1960, p. 250).

Each object involved in the dialectical process has to be treated together with its inverse, as something which generates its own contradiction (antithesis). "Every positive statement that is made infers another contradictory one, and it is only through understanding this oppositional quality of all our categories that we can see the larger framework in which they are lodged" (Murphy 1971, p. 238). There is no such state as stable equilibrium, but one may discover something like a "moving equilibrium" (Pareto), analyzing regularities within the process. "There are three aspects of every thought which is logically true or real: the abstract or rational form, which says that something is; the dialectical negation, which says what something is not; and the speculative-concrete comprehension: A is also that which is not. A is non-A. These three aspects do not constitute three parts of logic, but are moments of everything that is logically real or true" (Hegel 1959, p. 82). "Time and force are more real than substance of things, and the essence of reality is the process of transformation of perceived reality. Things are not to be understood as fixed entities but are in a continual state of transition into other forms of themselves. The structure of reality is a structure of oppositions, of elements that contradict each other and limit each other's possibilities. Out of this clash of antagonistic tendencies, new forms arise that incorporate the opposing elements, albeit in altered form and with their contradictions now resolved" (Murphy 1971, p. 95). "Underlying the oppositions of the sensate, phenomenal world, there lies another, deeper reality, which is the process through which the contradictions are contained within a unity—a transcending of their mutual negation through synthesis, which is a negation of negation" (Ibid., p. 95). It is necessary to understand this undercover of phenomena in order to learn about the nature of social phenomena.

The gap between the normative order and the social order has to be taken for granted. "Values may be incongruent with actions, but they are never irrelevant to them" (Ibid., p. 218). Activity and consciousness taken together create the need for norms but the process of imposing these norms upon the reality is a matter of manipulation (more or less effective).

Hegel counterposed the rationality of the social in-

stitutionalization embodied by him in the state, to the
anarchic nature of individual desires and strivings. He did
not believe, as Rousseau did, that the fusion of individual
wills should be treated as the basis of social order. Only
the process of institutionalization may generate a true
consensus. "The Hegelian concept of dialectical change can
be, and has been, reformulated as a description of processes whereby social organisms create their own environment and are in turn influenced by it" (Lichtenheim 1968,
p. 343).

> The relationship between mind, or the totality of
> the psychic life and society is not unilaterally
> causal, but is one of interplay and conflict. In
> this oppositional setting, neither mind nor society
> emerges wholly victorious, for each is a product of
> the struggle and neither is completely reducible to
> the other. Social life is not a mechanism, or even
> an organism, but a dialectic (Murphy 1971, p. 85).

Social reality consists of a whole variety of structures
which may be distinguished in an analytical way. These
structures change and have to be reconciled with one
another adequately to changing circumstances. The system
has to preserve its identity. "Structure is not fixity and
harmony but an abstraction of movement" (Ibid., p. 238).

In dealing with culture it is necessary to distinguish
first of all "between behavior and expectations of behavior,
between action and ideas about action. . . . Culture is a
product, the synthesis of mind and action" (Ibid., p. 240).

There is an obvious contradiction between dialectics and
positivism. "Positivism destroys time to assert a common-
sense reality; dialectical reasoning destroys common-sense
reality to assert time" (Ibid., 96). Leszek Kolakowski, a
well-known Polish philosopher who abandoned Marxism,
rejects the positivistic version of rationalism, but offers his
own version based on the preference given to the best-
grounded answers to a question, rejection of judgments
which contradict our previous experience, and the general
suggestion that it is always better to know more rather
than less. Kolakowski prefers to "sharpen his awareness
of contradictory elements than attempt to reconcile
them. . . . Such rationalism is not a doctrine but an
attitude, a way of keeping one's mind to the possible
pluralism of the world and the possible relativity of
values," says George L. Kline (Leszek . . . 1971;
pp. 18–19).

Kolakowski rejects entirely the antidialectical absolute

justification of actions. If something is permitted or enjoined it does not necessarily mean that it is good. The disharmony between values and obligations seems natural to Kolakowski. It is necessary to accept "a world with holes." "Anxiety will always accompany our attempts to find the best way to live. This anxiety has no value by itself but it is a necessary weapon in combatting our innate conformism and laziness" (Leszek . . . 1971, p. 179). It is the vision of "a world with holes which we close by our free movements, only to open new ones" (Ibid., p. 182).

A similar reasoning Kolakowski applies to the issue of *knowledge*. He doubts if it is possible to say that the motives for someone's acceptance or rejection of a given judgment have significance for the question of the cognitive value of that judgment. Especially in all humanistic phenomena there is not a reliable way of eliminating the plurality of alternative solutions, except by appealing to a *consensus omnium*. "Intellectuals, as a social group distinguished by its special situation, do not hold as epistemologically provileged, but only a cognitively privileged, position" (Ibid. p.233).

James E. Hansen summarizes in the following way the basic points which dialectics bring against positivism.

> The dialectician argues that it is extremely misleading, if not actually regressive, to claim that "objects" exist in a particular way apart from either man's theory or activity. The so-called "objects of nature" with which science deals are without a doubt external to man's consciousness of them, but the particular characterization ("identity") by which man knows them—and it is only because man knows them that they loom important—is a function of man in an historically determinate situation. It is a commonplace that there exists a natural world; no one except a wild-eyed constitutive idealist would deny this. But it is thought, by the empiricists among others, that the meaning of that world either remains constant or is immanent in the "facts." This is so because it is claimed that we "see" things as they "really are."
>
> Like phenomenologists who "constitute" *meanings* while not denying the existence of a referendum external to consciousness, the dialectician argues that it is man in the world that is to be considered to be a primary importance in meaning determination; the dialectician wants to avoid the fetishism of facts and objects which man has *created to serve*

his interests. He wants to avoid the transference of epistemological meaning into the world of ontlogical necessity. To effect such a transformation is to be subject to the most alienated type of fetishistic reification an "objectivistic" society can dictate. The situation of praxis renders the meaning-laden objects of scientific inquiry meaningful in man's world. Man determines what he will investigate, why and how he will investigate it; without man there would be no science. The objects or "brute facts" of empiricist science do not dictate to man either the methods or conclusions of his praxis. We human beings predicate the "meaning" of the world, although it certainly is not argued that we in any way "create" the range of possible subject matter of inquiry (Hansen 1967, pp. 6–7)

THE DIALECTICAL CRITICISM OF STRUCTURAL FUNCTIONALISM

The structural-functional model of sociological analysis has reduced the multidimensional social reality to such an extent that it has led to serious distortions and omissions. "Time stops in structural-functional analysis because the underlying ways in which we view *our* data are fixed and timeless" (Murphy 1971, p. 60). In the scientific analysis there is always some move from variation to homogeneity and from flux to stability, which are dictated by the need to abstract and to reify phemomena. However, in the case of the structural-functional model there is much more involved. "At the root of the most modern social theory are twin theorems: action generates structures and norms, and structures and norms stabilize action and convert it into expectation" (Ibid., pp. 34–35).

The validity of functional prerequisites is highly doubtful from a dialectical viewpoint. The latent pattern maintenance may be disastrous for a system which has to transform itself in order to survive. Such an integration which involves a high level of conformism, prevents any innovation to develop and to be socially accepted. It seems socially more important to act toward goal achievement than count on success. What happens after the goals have been achieved? Some degree of maladaptation is safer and more culturally rewarding than full adaptation. What is the utility of functional prerequisites if their fulfillment does more harm than good to the dynamic potential of systems?

STEPS OF ANALYSIS

(A comparison of two approaches)

1. Define the unit of phenomena to be studied.	1. Define the powers whose opposing pressures maintain the unit within a given state.
2. Discover the setting (that is, those factors determining the limits within which the ranges of variations of the unit concerned take place).	2. Formulate the polar alternatives within which the unit actually and potentially oscillates under the given set of pressures.
3. Discover what general conditions must be met (that is, functional requisites) if the unit is to persist in its setting without change (that is, alteration of structures) on the level under consideration.	3. Discover all major external and internal contradictions which the unit has to deal with effectively in order to continue its identity. Take into consideration the mutual interdependence of various levels and structures which exercise their concerted pressure.
4. Discover which structures must be present in the system, as a minimum, if action in terms of the system is to result in the persistence of the unit in its setting without any change on the level under consideration (that is, the structural requisites).	4. Discover the regularities within the process of change experienced by the unit in its dealing with the variety of pressures and situations. Look for transformations of the unit as products of its coping with external and internal constraints.

The normative order has been treated by structural functionalists in an almost absolutistic way. It is worth mentioning that even long ago theorists made some subtle distinctions between social norms in terms of their relative power of coercion. For example, Leon Petrazycki made clear that depending on the interpretation of norms they may be either moral or legal or both depending on their own imperative (norms which command certain behavior without authorizing a reciprocal claim) or imperative-attributive nature. (The latter are not only unilaterally binding but also give to others a right to claim the fulfillment of the norm) (Petrazycki 1955).

THE MATTER OF CONFORMISM

It is true that "even under completely private conditions the individual is likely to surrender, at least in part, to the pressures of a group making an obvious wrong judgment," and that the laboratory experiments on conformism, "clearly demonstrate the degree to which groups may control individual behavior and perception" (Zajonc 1968, p. 259).

In the conformity process opposing forces are involved. The individual is more or less interested in pleasing others. The "significant others" are willing and able to influence the individual. In the final outcome, the individual mostly yields to the significant others, especially if some important gratifications are at stake. How willing the individual is to yield depends on his or her certainty or confidence, commitment to his or her point of view, dependency, need for social approval, submission to the authority, need for affiliation and achievement, availability of supporters, the amount of divergence between the individual and significant others, attractiveness of the group, and exposure to public situations.

HISTORY AND DIALECTICS

From the dialectical point of view, all analyzed social phenomena have to be first of all located within the historical framework, and treated in themselves as sources of eventual transformations, together with other historical forces.

Friedrichs sees the sociologist's central task in setting forth "dialectical process empirically in concrete historical situations" (Friedrichs 1972, p. 269). He is strongly against the identification of sociology with the logic of the natural sciences. However, at the same time he seems to miss the distinction between *knowing* and *acting*. Korsch (1930, 1938) as well as Lukács (1971) (also Piccone 1969; Meszaros 1971) treat society as a historical process of establishing new realities influenced by the doctrinaire image. It is natural for dialecticians, and particularly for

Marxist dialecticians, to focus on historical phenomena, when on the other hand structural-functionalists tend to avoid the broader historical framework.

The internal dynamics of whole societies have been explained within the framework of Marxist theory in terms of a dialectical contradiction between the infrastructure (which consists of economic forces and economic relations) and the superstructure (which consists of institutions and ideologies). From this perspective, it is constant drive toward achieving a satisfactory harmony between both structures which constitutes a core mechanism of social change. Seeking to explain social change in terms of the inner processes of social systems as such, Marxist theory provides a good platform for studying the interplay of various social forces with respect to their contribution to social change.

For Marxist revisionists the traditional Marxist historical approach is far from being satisfactory. Leszek Kolakowski says that "it is necessary to surpass history by an act of faith if one wants to accord it a meaning. . . . History is not intelligible as a meaningful structure unless an extra-historical essence which embodies itself in its temporal course is accepted as a matter of principle" (Leszek 1971. p. 115). "Since the Enlightment, philosophers have elevated their faith almost to a science. It is time to place the alleged science at the level of faith" (Ibid., p. 116).

The case of Luther discussed by Kolakowski in his essay on "The Philosophical Role of the Reformation" may be treated as an example of a historico-dialectical analysis. The Reformation challenge has for Kolakowski two basic lines: the mystical and the existential.

> In the former case, man, in trying to discover and identify himself in opposition to the world, finds nothing but corruption and evil, contained in his very existential status, in his very separateness; he thus abandons individual existence and believes that in the act of self-destruction in favor of an absolute, he will find his way back to the root of being from which his sickly individual existence has unfortunately grown. In the latter case, on the other hand, deprived subjectivity discovers itself as being absolutely irreducible; that is, not reducible to anything in the world of things or the world of ideas: if it discovers God, it attempts to establish an intimate dialogue with him which no one from outside can either hear or understand or judge; if it does not discover him, it is compelled to conveive

itself as a sterile absolute, coming from nowhere and going nowhere, and empty being for itself, pure negativity, a *passion inutile* (Ibid., pp. 137–38).

This is why, according to Kolakowski, "Luther's appeal entrusted to later times the discovery of subjectivity—the embryo of modern philosophical culture" (Leszek . . . , p. 138). On the other hand, this kind of subjectivity, if taken absolutely, in the final outcome "inevitable dismisses philosophy as metaphysical speculation, as system-building" (Ibid., p. 138). Luther and his disciples had contempt for any philosophy.

The Reformation provided to be more barren philosophically than the Roman church and, if it was capable of the continued production of intellectual stimuli in the field of philosophy, this was only because of those who consciously broke out of its rigors, appealing to its own original source of inspiration and attempting to restore the vigor to its initial slogans. . . . The Protestant belief in the fundamental corruption of human nature and thus in the powerlessness of reason in the face of ultimate metaphysical questions had, in the natural course of things, a paralyzing effect on philosophical undertakings (Ibid., pp. 122–23).

By questioning Rome's monopoly of dogma, and by establishing centers independent of Rome which challenged its philosophical authority, the Reformation created the ground for new philosophical developments, even if it was against the true intentions of its founders.

What the Reformation accomplished for philosophy, it accomplished in spite of itself, by way of men who not only grew up in the social situation it created, but—and it is these we have in mind—were also positively inspired by its values. It can be said that philosophy repaid the Reformation handsomely for its negative stance by co-creating its results from the raw material the Reformation supplied (Ibid., p. 124).

CONCLUSIONS

One of the basic internal dilemmas of systems deals directly with the problems of change. For any system "safety lies in the preservation of its own boundary and the avoidance of transactions across it; on the other hand, survival depends upon the conduct of transactions with the environment and the risk of destruction" (Miller and Rice 1967, p. 24). T. Parsons (1977) has pointed out five pairs of dilemmas which have to be faced by any system: affectivity versus affective neutrality, specificity versus diffuseness, universalism versus particularism, achievement versus ascription, and self-orientation versus community-orientation. In order to preserve its identity, the system has to find proper solutions for all these dilemmas, Its success in this respect gives evidence of some "maturity."

In the process of achieving consensus, the issue of dealing with dissensus is of crucial importance. The margin of an acceptable deviance differs in different social configurations. How to achieve a unity in diversity is a question of major significance because "dissensual patterns of belief are often more explicit and systematic than are the consensual patterns which affirm the existing central institutional system" (Shils 1968, p. 262). In order to promote the maturity of social systems it is necessary to acknowledge the dialectical nature of processes into which these systems are involved when coping with internal and external environment. The conflictual nature of systems growth and transformation is still inadequately treated by sociologists and experts in complex organizations. Methodology here proposed may be helpful as an inspiration.

NOTES

1. Talcott Parsons applies to social systems the concept of four main processes of structural change: differentiation, adaptive upgrading, inclusion, and value generalization. In *Societies: Evolutionary and Comparative Perspectives* (Prentice Hall, 1966) and in *The System of Modern Societies* (Prentice Hall, 1971), Parsons assumes directionality of the social development, at least as regards the Western civilization. In his ahistorical analysis, he looks for factors that contribute to the completion of a system of modern societies. Parsons (1977) devotes most of his attention to exposition of various structural components and their relative contribution to systems integration.

2. It ought to be called a theory of antihistory, for Pareto militates both against the historicism of his age, and the philosophy of progress. There is some justice in the saying that he "has succeeded all too well in his attempt to abolish history." James H. Meisel, editor. *Pareto and*

Mosca, p. 30 (Introduction). (Englewood Cliffs, NJ: Prentice-Hall).

3. According to A. Rapoport, "The most fundamental feature which distinguishes a system from other aggregates or from an arbitrarily circumscribed portion of the world is the possibility of describing it in purely structural terms. . . . A system, roughly speaking, is a bundle of relations. For this reason a general systems theory . . . ought to single out purely relational isomorphisms that are abstracted from content." Anatol Rapoport, "General Systems Theory," in *International Encyclopedia of the Social Sciences*, pp. 453, 454. (New York: Free Press, 1968).

4. For the dialectical approach to social phenomena, see Louis Schneider, "Dialectic in Sociology," *American Sociological Review* (August 1967), pp. 667–78.

5. See an interesting Russian theoretical study which deals with this issue: W. Blauberg and E. G. Judin, "Sistemnyj Podchod w Socyalnych Issledowanijach" (Systems Approach in Social Research), *Woprosy Filosofii* (1967) 9. See also A. Matejko, "A Cybernetic Model of the Social System," *Kommunikation* (Germany), 6, 4 (1970), and A. Matejko, *Socjologiypracy. System spoleczany zakladu pracy* (Sociology of Work: Social System of Workplace) (Warsaw: PWE, 1968).

6. T. Kotarbinski makes a distinction between *permutative* and *perseverative* events. The first apply to the contributions to the existing set of values. The second apply at most only to reallocation of existing values. Tadeusz Kotarbinski, *Praxiology*. (Oxford: Pergamon Press 1965), pp. 23–24. On this basis I made a distinction between task-oriented and status-oriented societies. See Alexander J. Matejko, "Task versus Status: The Contradictions of Modernization," *International Review of Sociology* 6, 3 (1970), pp. 329–54.

7. "Intrinsic function refers to the immediate and direct outcome of a system or subsystem in terms of its major product. It should be distinguished from extrinsic functions, which are the system outcomes as they affect other systems or subsystems to which the structure in questions is related" (D. Katz, R. L. Kahn, *The Social Psychology of Organizations*, p. 62. (New York: Wiley 1966).

8. Miller and Rice write about sentient systems or groups, referring to those systems or groups which demand and receive loyalty from their members. In this way they denote groups with which human individuals identify themselves as distinct from task groups.

9. "Cohesiveness of a unit is likely to be high when

the divisions within it intersect, and low when the divisions are overlapping or congruent with one another. But . . . even if there are cross-cutting ties within a group or collectivity, some ties may be so much stronger than any others as to withstand the effect which these others may have on them; for example, class loyalties are often not weakened by local loyalties, while national loyalties are seldom weakened by those of class" (P. S. Cohen, *Modern Social Theory*, p, 134. (London: Heinemann).

10. The organic organization is characterized by decentralization of decision-making; an emphasis on mutual dependence and cooperation based on trust, confidence, and high technical and professional competence; a constant pressure to enlarge tasks and interrelate them so that the concern for the whole is emphasized; the decentralization of responsibility for, the use of, information, rewards and penalties; the responsibility of participants at all levels for development and maintaining loyalty and commitment at as high level as possible; and an emphasis on status through contribution to the whole and through intergroup and interindividual cooperation (*International Encyclopedia of Social Sciences*, 1968, New York: Free Press).

11. I did it in my article, "The University as a Sociotechnical System." See also my article "Die Genossenschaft als Soziales System," *Zeitschrift für das gesamte Genossenschaftswesen* (1971), No. 23.

REFERENCES

Andreski, Stanislav. 1972. *Social Sciences as Sorcery*. London: Deutsch.

Babbie, Earl. 1983. *The Practice of Social Research*. Belmont, NY: Wadsworth.

Barber, B., and E. G. Barber, editors. 1965. *European Social Class: Stability and Change*. New York: Macmillan.

Berghe, van den, P. L. 1967. "Dialectic and Functionalism: Toward a Synthesis." In *System, Change and Conflict*, edited by N. J. Demerth and R. A. Peterson. New York: Free Press.

Berrien, Kenneth F. 1968. *General and Social Systems*. New Brunswick, NJ: Rutgers University Press.

Blau, Peter M. 1964. *Exchange and Power in Social Life*. New York: Wiley.

Bottomore, T. B. 1968. "Marxist Sociology." *International Encyclopedia of Social Sciences*. New York: Free Press.

Buckley, W. 1966. *Sociology and Modern Systems Theory.* Englewood Cliffs, NJ: Prentice-Hall.

——————, editor. 1968a. *Modern Systems Research for the Behavioral Scientist.* Chicago: Aldine.

——————. 1968b. "Society as a Complex Adaptive System." W. Buckley, editor. In *Modern Systems Research for the Behavioral Scientist.* Chicago: Aldine.

Bühler, Ch. 1935. *From Birth to Maturity.* London: Kegan Paul.

Caro, Francis G., editor. 1971. *Readings in Evaluation Research.* New York: Russell Sage Foundation.

Cancian, F. M. 1968. "Varieties of Functional Analysis," *International Encyclopedia of Social Sciences.* New York: Free Press.

Clark, Peter. 1972. *Organizational Design.* London: Tavistock.

Cohen, P. D. 1968. *Modern Social Theory.* London: Heinemann.

Collings, B. E., and H. Guetzkow. 1964. *Social Psychology of Group Processes for Decision Making.* New York: Wiley.

Collingwood, Robert G. 1956. *The Idea of History.* Oxford University Press.

Dabrowski, Kazimierz. 1964. *Positive Disintegration.* Boston: Little, Brown.

——————. 1967. *Personality-shaping Through Positive Disintegration.* Boston: Little, Brown.

Dabrowski, Kazimierz, and Michael M. Piechowski. 1967. *Theory of Levels of Emotional Development.* Oceanside, CA: Dabor Science Publishing.

Demerath, N. J., and R. A. Peterson, editors. 1967. *System, Change and Conflict.* New York: Free Press.

Emery, F., editor. 1969. *System Thinking.* Harmondsworth, England: Penguin Books.

——————, and F. L. Trist. 1969. "Socio-technical Systems." In *System Thinking,* edited by F. E. Emery. Harmondsworth, England: Penguin Books.

Emery, F., and E. Thorsrud. 1976. *Democracy at Work.* Amsterdam: Nijhoff.

Emmer, D. 1958. *Function, Purpose, and Power.* London: Macmillan.

Erikson, E. 1959. *Identity and the Life Cycle.* New York: International Universities Press.

Escriva, Josemaria de Belaguet. 1979. *The Way.* New York: Scepter.

Feyerabend, Paul K. 1965. "Problems of Empiricism." In *Beyond the Edge of Certainty,* edited by Robert G. Colodny. Englewood Cliffs, NJ: Prentice-Hall.

Findlay, John N. 1962. *Hegel: A Re-examination.* London: Collier.

Firth, Raymond W. 1961. *Elements of Social Organization.* Boston: Beacon Press.

Friedrichs, Robert W. 1972. "Dialectical Sociology: Toward a Resolution of the Current 'Crisis' in Western Sociology." *British Journal of Sociology* September.

Gardiner, P. 1968. "The Philosophy of History." *International Encyclopedia of Social Sciences.* New York: Free Press.

Georgopoulos, B. S., editor. 1972. *Organization Research and Health Institutions.* Ann Arbor, MI: Institute for Social Research.

Georgopoulos, Basil S., and Alexander Matejko. 1967. "The American General Hospital as a Social System." *Health Services Research* No. 1, pp. 76–112.

Goslin, D. A., editor. 1969. *Handbook of Socialization Theory and Research.* Chicago: Rand and McNally.

Gross, B. M. 1966. "The State of the Nation." In *Social Indicators,* edited by R. A. Bauer. New York.

Hansen, James E. 1967. "A Dialectical Critique of Empiricism." *Catalyst* No. 3, Summer.

Hegel, G. W. F. 1959. *Encyclopedia of Philosophy.* New York: Philosophical Library.

————. 1961. *The Phenomenology of Mind.* London: Macmillan.

————. 1942. *The Philosophy of Right.* Oxford: Clarendon.

————. 1956. *The Philosophy of History.* New York: Dover.

Herbst, P. G. 1976. *Alternatives to Hierarchies.* Amsterdam: M. Nijhoff.

The International Encyclopedia of Social Sciences. 1968. New York: Free Press.

Leszek Kolakowski Reader. 1961. *TriQuarterly* No. 22, Fall.

Kahn, R. L., and E. Boulding, editors. 1964. *Power and Conflict in Organizations.* London: Tavistock.

Katz, Daniel, and Robert L. Kahn. 1966. *The Social Psychology of Organization.* New York: Wiley (2d ed. 1978).

Kohlberg, L. 1969. "Stage and Sequence: The Cognitive-Developmental Approach to Socialization." In D. A. Goslin, editor, *Handbook of Socialization Theory and Research.* Chicago: Rand McNally.

Kornhauser, A., et al. 1954. *Industrial Conflict.* New York.

Korsch, Karl. 1930. *Marxismus and Philosophie.* Leipzig:

Hirschfeld.

————. 1938. *Karl Marx.* London: Chapman.

Kosok, Michael. 1966. "The Formalization of Hegel's Dialectical Logic." *International Philosophical Quarterly* 6, No. 4.

Kotarbinski, T. 1965. *Praxiology.* New York: Pergamon Press.

Lazarsfeld, Paul. 1972. "Critical Theory and Dialectics." In *Qualitative Analysis: Historical and Critical Essays,* edited by P. Lazarsfeld. Rockleigh, NJ: Allyn and Bacon.

Leach, Edmund R. 1968. "Social Structure: The History of the Concept." *International Encyclopedia of Social Sciences.* New York: Free Press.

Learned, A. T., and A. T. Sproat. 1966. *Organization Theory and Policy.* Homewood: Irwin.

Levy, Marion J., Jr. 1968. "Structural-Functional Analysis." *International Encyclopedia of Social Sciences.* New York: Free Press.

Lenski, G., and J. Lenski. 1978. *Human Societies.* New York: McGraw-Hill (latest ed. 1982).

Lichtenheim, George. 1968. "George Wilhelm Frederick Hegel." *International Encyclopedia of Social Sciences.* New York: Free Press.

Likert, R. 1967. *The Human Organization.* New York: Wiley.

Lockwood, D. 1967. "Some Remarks on 'The Social System.'" In *System, Change and Conflict,* edited by N. J. Demerth and R. A. Peterson. New York: Free Press.

Lukacs, George. 1971. *History and Class Consciousness.* London: Merlin Press.

Mangin, W., ed. 1970. *Peasants in Cities.* Boston: Houghton Mifflin.

Marcuse, Herbert. 1960. *Reason and Revolution: Hegel and the Rise of Social Theory.* Boston: Beacon Press.

Matejko, Alexander J. 1968a. *Sociologia Pracy: System Spoleczny Zakladu Pracy* (Sociology of Work: Social System of a Workplace). Warsaw: Panstwowe Wydawnictwo Ekonomiczne.

————. 1968b. "The University as a Sociotechnical System." *Kommunikation* 4, 2.

————. 1970. "A Cybernetic Model of the Social System." *Kommunikation* 6, 4.

————. 1972a. "The Sociological Meaning of Organization." *Prakseologia* Nos. 39/40.

————. 1972b. "The Theatre of J. Grotowski." *International Review of Sociology* 8, 2–3: pp. 57–73.

—————. 1973a. "Can Social Systems Mature?" *Sociologia Internationalis* 11, 1–2: pp. 37–82.

—————. 1973b. "Industrial Democracy: A Socio-technical Approach." *Our Generation* 9, 1: pp. 24–41.

—————. 1973c. "Institutional Conditions of Scientific Inquiry." *Small Group Behavior,* 4, 1: pp. 89–126.

—————. 1974. "The Sociological Nature of Complex Organizations." *Sociologia Internationalis* 12, 1–2: pp. 105–46.

—————. 1975a. "Diagnosis of Conflict in Sport." *Revista Internacional de Sociologia* Nos. 15–16: pp. 63–87.

—————. 1975b. "The Dialectical Approach to Social Reality." *Sociologia Internationalis* 13, 1–2: pp. 5–27.

—————. 1975c. *The Social Technology of Applied Research.* Meerut, India: Sadhna Prakashan.

—————. 1976a. *Overcoming Alienation in Work.* Meerut, India: Sadhna Prakashan.

—————. 1976b. "The Qualitative Growth of Social Systems." In *Sociotechnics,* edited by A. B. Cherns. London: Malaby Press.

McGill, V. T., et al. 1948. "The Unity of Opposites: A Dialectical Principle." *Science and Society* 12, 4.

Meszaros, J., editor. 1971. *Aspects of History and Class Consciousness.* London: Routledge and Kegan Paul.

Miller, E. J., and A. K. Rice. *1967. Systems of Organization.* London: Tavistock.

Miller, J. G. 1971. "The Nature of Living Systems." *Behavioral Science* 16: pp. 277–301.

—————. 1972. "Living Systems: The Organization." *Behavioral Science* 17, 1: pp. 1–182.

—————. 1978. *Living Systems.* New York: McGraw-Hill.

Murphy, Robert F. 1971. *The Dialectics of Social Life.* New York: Basic Books.

Nisbet, Robert A. 1967. *The Sociological Tradition.* New York: Basic Books.

Oberschall, Anthony. 1972. *The Establishment of Empirical Sociology.* New York: Harper and Row.

Olsen, M. E. 1968. *The Process of Social Organization.* New York: Holt, Rinehart and Wilson.

Parsons, T. 1977. *The Evolution of Societies.* Englewood Cliffs, NJ: Prentice-Hall.

Pelz, D. C., and F. M. Andrews. 1966. *Scientists in Organizations.* New York: Wiley.

Petrazycki, Leon. 1955. *Law and Morality.* Cambridge, MA: Harvard University Press.

Piaget, J. 1956. *The Origins of Intelligence in Children.*

New York: International Universities Press.

Piccone, Paul. 1969. "Lukacs' History and Class Consciousness Half a Century Later." *Telos,* No. 4.

Podgorecki, A. 1966. *Zasady Sociotechniki* (The Principles of Sociotechnique). Warsaw: Wiedza Powszechna.

————, editor. 1970. *Socjotechnika* (Sociotechnique). Warsaw: Ksiazka i Wiedza.

————, and R. Schulze. 1969. "Sociotechnique." *Social Science Information* 7, 4.

Price, J. L. 1968. *Organizational Effectivness.* Homewood, IL: Irwin.

Ritzer, G. 1977. *Working.* Englewood Cliffs, NJ: Prentice-Hall.

Sartre, Jean-Paul. 1966. *Critique de la Raison Dialectique.* Paris: Gallimard.

————. 1963. *Search for a Method.* New York: Knopf.

Schaff, Adam. 1960. "Marxist Dialectics and the Principle of Contradiction." *Journal of Philosophy* 57, No. 7.

Schneider, E. 1970. *Industrial Sociology.* New York: McGraw-Hill.

Schutz, Alfred. 1972. *The Phenomenology of the Social World.* London: Heinemann.

Shils, Edward. 1968. "Consensus." *International Encyclopedia of Social Sciences.* New York: Free Press.

Smelser, N. J., editor. 1965. *Readings on Economic Sociology.* Englewood Cliffs, NJ: Prentice-Hall.

Stace, Walter T. 1955. *The Philosophy of Hegel.* New York: Dover.

Suchman, Edward A. 1967. *Evaluative Research: Principles and Practice in Public Service and Social Action Programs.* New York: Russell Sage Foundation.

Udy, Stanley H., Jr. 1968. "Social Structural Analysis." *International Encyclopedia of Social Sciences.* New York: Free Press.

Zajonc, Robert B. 1968. "Conformity." *International Encyclopedia of Social Sciences.* New York: Free Press.

Zieleniewski, Jan. 1967. *Organizacja Zespolow ludzkich* (Organization of Human Teams). Warsaw: PWN.

INDEX

INDEX

absenteeism, 128, 156, 160, 163, 165, 171

achievers, mediocrities and, 251–53

advertising, social impact of, 298–301

anomie, 105, 231, 260, 261

appearances code, 68

assembly line, 152, 174

Aston (Birmingham, England) study, 56–57

authoritarian cooperation, participatory versus, 101–4

authority, dilution of, in mass society, 102–3, 301–5

autonomous work groups (AWG), 104–35; adaptational problems facing, 130–31; collective maturity of, 113; conformity within, 114–15; decision making in, 111; effective functioning of, 121–24, 161–62; environmental considerations in, 113–14; formal structure of, 111; goals and tasks of, 115–16; group morale in, 127–29; interhuman relations in, 108–13; leadership of, 116–19; management participation in, 106, 118; power relationships within, 115; prerequisites for, 103–4; rules and norms in, 115; self-image of workers in, 133–35; size of, 116; small group research and, 111–21; socialization vehicles in, 129–31; sociotechnical directives for, 119–21; structuralization of, 108–9, 114–15; task performance in, 105–8, 110–11, 116, 133–35; team dimension of, 104, 105–8; work satisfaction in, 131–32

average, cult of, 191

boundary(ies), 348–52; management focus upon, 153; purpose of, 348–49; social space delimited by, 350

boundary-crossing, 327; aspects of, 348–52; functional versus dysfunctional, 352; ideal model of, 351; irregular, 351–52; problems related to, 350–54

boundary subsystem, 341

buffers, 166, 173

bureaucracy, 231–71; alternatives to, 48–52, 270–71; antidialectical nature of, 268–69; benevolent, 236–38; conflicts of interest within, 249–51; definition of, 231; de-

ABOUT THE AUTHOR

Alexander J. Matejko is Professor of Sociology at the University of Alberta. Until 1968, he worked at the University of Warsaw, teaching mostly industrial sociology, and later on he was for two years a Visiting Professor at the University of Zambia. During his academic career he acted as a visiting fellow at Saint Anthony's College, in Oxford, University of Leningrad, University of Moscow, University of North Carolina, Carleton University, University of Gothenburg, and the Centre National de la Recherche Scientifique in Paris.

Professor Matejko has written extensively on complex organizations, industrial sociology, East European problems, the Polish society, and comparative societies in general. In his book *Beyond Bureaucracy?*, published in 1984 (Cologne: Verlag für Gesellschaftsarchitektur) he has summarized his thesis on the gradual transfer from bureaucracy to the participatory management style, as fitting much better modern needs. Professor Matejko has been devoted to this thesis since his original organizational activity in the cooperative movement in the late 1940s. He is currently a vice president of the Research Committee 26 on Sociotechnics at the International Sociological Association and member of the Research Council of the same association.

The author received his Ph.D. in sociology from the University of Warsaw as well as the Docent degree. He did his research in Eastern Europe, Zambia, Western Europe, Sweden, and North America. He cooperates with several professional journals, writing articles, and book reviews published in Canada, the United States, India, France, Italy, and West Germany. Professor Matejko has also done consulting work in the alternative forms of organization and building trust relationships at workplaces.